ELT GUIDE

Sixth Edition

MW01529272

Managing Editor
Daniel Ward

Illustrations
Chris Duggan

Advertising
Shaun Collins

Desk Top Publishing
Sheldon Pink, Andrew Baird, Roger Preston

Publishers
John Gorner and Daniel Ward

Written and researched by
Alison Higgins, Matthew Connolly, Philip Neville, Richard Wood, Daniel Ward

International Contributors
David Cervi, KDC Consulting, Australia; Jon Felperin, Berkeley University, USA; Richard West, CELSE - Manchester University, UK.

Acknowledgements
The publishers would like to thank the following for their invaluable help
Christine Nuttall, John Wheeler, John Whitehead of the British Council and British Councils worldwide; Kate Naameh & Michelle Watson, International House; Charlotte Boyle, Trinity College; Cathy Connolly, East European Partnership; Concha Delgado-Cubero, English and Spanish Studies; Lynette Murphy O'Dwyer, UCLES; Chris Graham, English Worldwide; Simon Learmount, Saxoncourt; Oksana Higglesdon, ARELS; Jonathon Foley, L'Electrofil; Richard Harrison, English Education Services, Madrid; Stuart Rose, NZEIL; Jill Stajduhar, IATEFL; Duncan Baker, Lydbury English Centre; Jennifer House, Vancouver Community College; Hilary MacElwain & Mary Large, RELSA; Gregory Rosenstock, ATT; Andy Cowle, Keltic; Geraldine Egan, Irish Tourist Board; Dominic Gallagher, Dept. of Education, Dublin.

Cover Illustration by Richard Caldicott.

ISBN 0 951 4576 59

Published by EFL Ltd.,
9 Hope Street, Douglas, Isle of Man IM1 1AQ, British Isles.

Printed by Mannin Printing, 28-30 Spring Valley Industrial Estate, Braddan, IOM.

Get ahead in EFL Get the GAZETTE

Claim your free Gazette and get US$10 off the price if you subscribe for two years.

Whether you're new to the world of EFL, or are an experienced professional building a career, you need the *GAZETTE*.

The *GAZETTE* gives you news and views from around the world plus all the best jobs every month. From Bangkok to Bournemouth, from top teaching posts to the best in training, the *GAZETTE* brings it direct to your door.

Each issue is packed with useful information on how to make money, where the new opportunities are, how you can get in on the world of EFL.

If you would like your free copy, fill in the form below or write to:

GUIDE OFFER,
EFL GAZETTE,
10 WRIGHT'S LANE,
KENSINGTON,
LONDON W8 6TA.

And if you return two years' payment within one month of receiving your sample, you can deduct $10 from the cost of your two-year subscription.

New Subscription

Please register my subscription for 1 year/ 2 years.
I enclose my cheque/PO for the value of £_____, made payable to **The EFL Gazette**.
Or debit my Mastercard/Visa account with the sum of £_____

My card no is: ⬚⬚⬚⬚ ⬚⬚⬚⬚ ⬚⬚⬚⬚ ⬚⬚⬚⬚   Expiry date:_____
Name: Mr/Mrs/Miss/Ms_____
Address/Company S c h o o l_____
_____
_____
City_____
Postcode_____Country_____
Orders to: EFL Gazette, 10 Wrights Lane, London W8 6TA, UK

Currency	United Kingdom	Rest of Europe	All other Countries
British Sterling	£22.50	£26.00	£30.00
US Dollars		$50.00	$65.00
Australian Dollars			$90.00
Japanese Yen			Y9000.00
Method of Despatch	*Surface Mail*	*Air Mail*	*Air Mail*

Preface

How the ELT Guide will help you:

The Guide is for anyone considering or already involved in English Language Training; prospective teachers, teachers, training/personnel managers, publishers, consultants, etc., but different sections will naturally be more relevant to some groups than others.

●Prospective Teachers

Turn straight to **Section One - Becoming a Teacher -** for anyone considering EFL/ESL teaching as a career, or as a short-term means of working while you travel, this section maps out a route for you by providing clear advice and information on basic teaching courses and qualifications. Once you have read this, go to **Section Three - World English**, to find out what opportunities there are for you in the countries of your choice.

If you are relatively sure that EFL is the career for you, **Section Two** shows you how to go about getting a job and **Section Four** will help you to plan a long-term career strategy.

●Training/Personnel Managers, or Consultants

Start with **Section Five - English in Business**, which examines the commercial benefits of language training and English in particular. It is especially relevant for the training manager of a small to medium-sized company, who are considering investing in language training, but wants to make sure that the company gets value for money.

For local information and schools, consult your country's section of **World English.**

To get a real understanding of what you can expect from teachers, read through **Sections One and Four,** which will show you what teaching qualifications actually enable teachers to do. You can now produce a specification for any language training provider with authority.

●Teachers/EFL Professionals

If you do not have a qualification, go to **Section One.**
If you want to improve your career prospects, **Section Four** explains how further qualifications will help.

For ideas about teaching and associated jobs, turn to **Section Two.**

Section Five will give you an insight into the hugely important Business English market, which can provide some of the most exciting career options.

AND, if you are looking for a new job, anywhere in the world, **Section Three** has opportunities in over 100 countries.

In recognition of its international readership, the EFL Guide has been renamed the ELT Guide in this its sixth edition. The Guide emphasises the opportunities and programmes in Britain, but most information should be relevant to the profession worldwide. It is the ELT Guide's policy to be international in its outlook, so any suggestions/information from any source in any country would be appreciated.

CAMBRIDGE
EXAMINATIONS, CERTIFICATES & DIPLOMAS

• Language development for teachers	Teacher Training Courses		
	Teaching experience	• Language development • Language systems • Methodology	• Language systems • Methodology
Cambridge **E**xamination in **E**nglish for **L**anguage **T**eachers II (Cambridge Level 5)	*In-service*	**D**iploma for **O**verseas **T**eachers of **E**nglish	**D**iploma in the **T**eaching of **E**nglish as a **F**oreign **L**anguage to **A**dults
	Early in-service	**C**ertificate for **O**verseas **T**eachers of **E**nglish	
Cambridge **E**xamination in **E**nglish for **L**anguage **T**eachers I (Cambridge Level 3)	*Pre-service*		**C**ertificate in the **T**eaching of **E**nglish as a **F**oreign **L**anguage to **A**dults
Specifically designed for non-native speakers		Specifically designed for non-native speakers	Specifically designed for native speakers

The RSA/Cambridge TEFL Schemes are currently being reviewed and it is anticipated that the revised certificates and diplomas within an integrated and expanded framework of provision will be available from 1996/97. Full details of the timetable for the introduction of the revised schemes will be advised in Autumn 1995.

The most widely used assessment schemes for EFL teachers

University of Cambridge Local Examinations Syndicate

RSA EXAMINATIONS BOARD

Contents

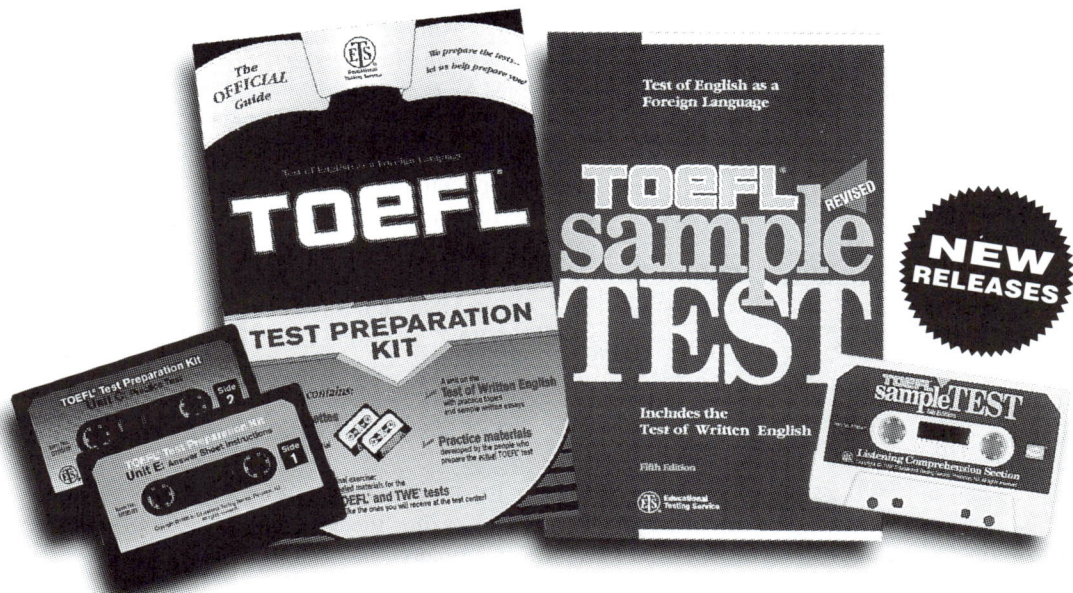

Introduction

English is a corner stone of the new global culture, argues Ben Ward, barrister, archaeologist and former editor of the EFL Gazette. Here he takes stock of the prospects for speakers and teachers of the English language.

Technology has made planet Earth a smaller place in the decades following the end of the last world war. Aircraft speed through the atmosphere carrying an ever more mobile population to new destinations and, hopefully, better opportunities. The rapid development of the global Internet has facilitated communication without the need to leave home or office. Computerised intercourse - once the preserve of American academia - is available to schools, colleges, businesses and individuals throughout the world. The now scientifically humble facsimile transmission has become widespread even in less materially developed regions.

But what use are these tools without an efficient common language to access, utilise and interpret all this information?

Throughout history, people speaking different languages have needed to understand each other: to trade, to conduct war and peace, to tell each other what they think. Latin is often quoted as the first true *lingua franca*, but even before the prevalence of Latin, Akkadian was the commercial and diplomatic language of the great civilisations of the ancient Near East, only to be replaced by the Greek *koine* ('common tongue') after the conquests of Alexander the Great.

The reasons for the evolution of English as the global language of our times have been covered by previous editorials in this publication and need not be repeated. Economic, social and political factors have combined to place English as the means of communication among the different peoples who make up the planet's population. Accusations of imperialism and cultural hegemony have been laid at the door of the English speaking world but these charges hold an equal validity when applied to Spanish, Portuguese or French. It is the vigour of the English language itself - its flexibility, its capacity for expression and its sensitivity to change - which has enabled it to prevail as the international language of business, science and culture.

A common language is a unifying force. An exchange of views can occur within it - even when people disagree with each other. Current debate in the United States is focused on the need to balance the right of its citizens to speak a native language against the divisions that may arise by not insisting that people speak one language. Bilingual programmes funded by federal and state monies are seen in some quarters as unproductive. In the new South Africa, the nurturing of English - in preference to Afrikaans - is regarded as a progressive and integrative step for a population speaking 11 native tongues.

To deny or discourage people from learning English is to deprive them of the opportunity to enrich themselves - both financially and culturally. For example, Kerala, a southern state in India, was among the country's poorest; the government decided to make English compulsory in the 1960s, and now Kerala is prosperous because it can conduct business on a global scale.

In the face of the overwhelming desire of the world's population to learn English, attempts by nations to prevent their citizens from using English terminology are counter-productive and cannot succeed. English does not need to be protected by academies or pressure groups. As Europe moves toward political and financial union, it is clear that English is being adopted by its institutions (whether officially or not) as the working language.

As the English language continues its inexorable march throughout the world an increasing sense of responsibility falls upon its proponents and its teachers. To speak English is to be in a privileged position: to teach it enhances that privilege. A vibrant and progressive industry has grown up around the teaching of the English language and this publication is a guide to the many opportunities that exist within it.

1995 sees a change in name for the Guide: ELT - English Language Teaching - avoids the confusion that sometimes arises between the use of EFL (English as a Foreign Language) and ESL (English as Second Language). The different terminologies used in ELT reflect the various professional structures that have been established within the industry. Although the obvious success of these institutions is to be applauded, there is a strong argument - in the interests of harmonisation and clarity - for a more unitary approach to the profession to be adopted. As the English speaking peoples use a diverse but mutually intelligible language, so might its practitioners in their field.

It is the vigour of the English language itself which has enabled it to prevail as the international language of business, science and culture.

To speak English is to be in a privileged position: to teach it enhances that privilege.

Becoming a Teacher

You can start teaching English if you are fresh out of college, seeking a new career, newly retired or even if you have no qualifications or experience. This section explains all the options, shows you what qualifications to get, where to get them and even guides you through your first class.

So, you want to teach English?

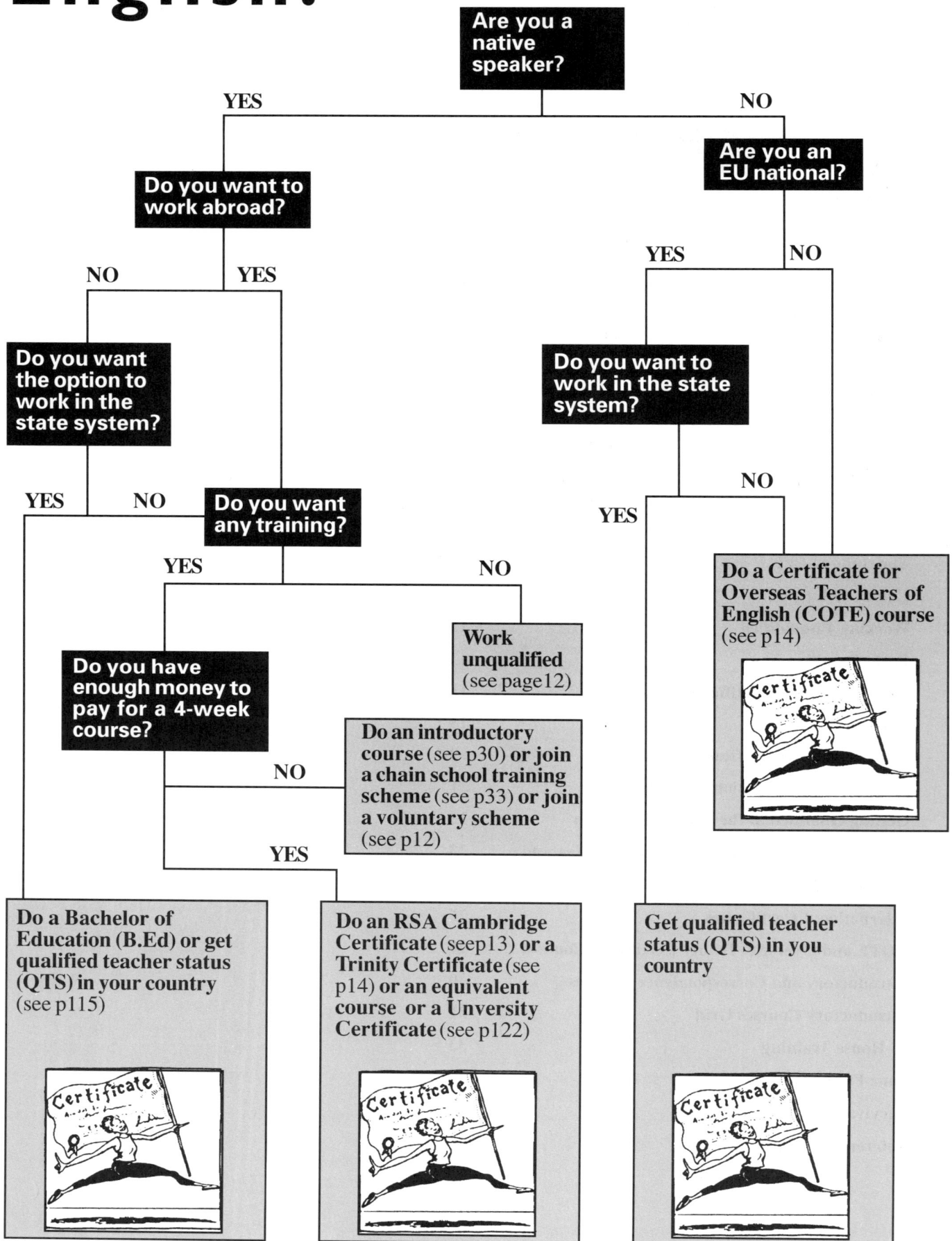

Are you a native speaker?

YES ─── **NO**

On the NO side:

Are you an EU national?

YES ─── **NO**

YES branch (native speaker)

Do you want to work abroad?

NO ─── **YES**

NO → Do you want the option to work in the state system?

YES ─── **NO**

YES (work abroad) → Do you want any training?

YES ─── **NO**

NO →

Work unqualified (see page 12)

YES → Do you have enough money to pay for a 4-week course?

NO →

Do an introductory course (see p30) **or join a chain school training scheme** (see p33) **or join a voluntary scheme** (see p12)

YES →

Do an RSA Cambridge Certificate (see p13) **or a Trinity Certificate** (see p14) **or an equivalent course or a Unversity Certificate** (see p122)

From "Do you want the option to work in the state system?" YES:

Do a Bachelor of Education (B.Ed) or get qualified teacher status (QTS) in your country (see p115)

EU national branch

Do you want to work in the state system?

YES ─── **NO**

NO →

Do a Certificate for Overseas Teachers of English (COTE) course (see p14)

YES →

Get qualified teacher status (QTS) in you country

Can I teach EFL?

Do I have to get a qualification?
No. There are some countries where you can teach English unqualified (see p12). Remember that schools will pay more and generally treat you better if you are qualified.

Is it better to look for a job once I reach my destination?
It is often easier to get a job if you are already in the country where you want to work. Check in the local English language newspaper for job adverts or approach individual schools (see p51-118). Note that some countries will only offer work permits to teachers who have been offered work before they enter the country.

I am already a teacher. Can I teach EFL?
If you want to teach in the state educational system, you must achieve QTS (Qualified Teacher Status). Unless you have a PGCE in EFL or ESL or hold another EFL qualification, a PGCE does not automatically qualify you to teach EFL.

What is an EFL qualification?
At present there are no standard international EFL qualifications. In the UK, recognized schools are only permitted to employ teachers with at least a certificate. These are widely recognized overseas and the courses last about a month. If you are unable to take one of these courses, there are plenty of alternatives, some of which will be regarded highly by employers.

Are there shorter courses in EFL?
There are various introductory courses in EFL which give you an EFL grounding even if not a formal qualification. They are worth considering if you do not want to commit yourself to a long time in EFL. They also tend to be cheaper. Some schools run their own courses for unqualified teachers that train you in the methods of that particular school which is worthwhile if you wish to work for that organisation (see p33). It may also be worth considering a course which combines distance learning with a short course.

Where can I train?
You can take TEFL courses throughout the world (see p22-29). The price generally reflects the economy - and/or the popularity - of the country or destination.

Do I have to have teaching experience to do an EFL course?
No, although many people do teach first before doing a course.

Do I need to be a graduate to get on a course?
Most courses demand some sort of further education qualification, not necessarily a degree. Non-graduates may be required to do an introductory course. Remember that some countries demand a degree before issuing work permits (see p54-117).

I want to go to university before I teach EFL. Where should I go?
In the USA there are various courses that train teachers of EFL at undergraduate level. There is not an undergraduate qualification in the UK for teaching EFL, although the modern languages degree at East Anglia University contains an RSA/Cambridge Certificate in TEFL as a module.

How can I pay for my course?
In the UK you cannot get a grant to do a teacher training course at a private institution, although there are further education colleges that offer subsidised courses, and, if you have been unemployed for more than six months, you may be eligible for free training. However, you may be eligible for a Career Development Loan, which is a government-backed scheme, whereby banks make unsecured loans at preferential rates to students - call 0800-585505 for details.

Am I too old for EFL?
Many teachers start after retiring from their traditional careers. Indeed if you have had a career in a specialist field such as banking, you may have the expertise to teach ESP (English for Special Purposes), teaching French stockbrokers useful English

terminology, for example (see p144). EFL could therefore be a part-time job during your retirement.

Can I be an EFL teacher if English isn't my mother tongue?
Yes, although most of these job opportunities will be within your own country unless you are completely fluent. See information on COTE courses (p29).

Can I train by post?
Some courses are offered partly by correspondence, partly with on-site training involving teaching practice. Courses which are totally correspondence courses are not always recognised by employers (see p30).

Will the place I train at find me a job?
Most establishments will give you advice on finding a job, and some may offer you employment especially if you have a good grade (see p33).

How much can I expect to earn?
This will vary greatly from country to country and school to school (see p67-117).

How do I know a school is reputable?
There are organisations that have been set up to monitor schools. It is often useful to contact the local British Council. If you are working in the UK or for British schools abroad, contact ILTB. Elsewhere, contact the local teaching union or relevant association (see p190-196 for addresses).

If I get a job abroad, will I get my airfare paid for?
This will depend on the employer. Many employers will pay at least a proportion of your fare, but some will not, or will only do so on completion of your contract.

What will my career prospects be if I go into EFL?
There are various further qualifications which can lead to specialist jobs related to EFL (see p121). There are also various spin-off careers such as publishing (see p61).

Working unqualified

As a native English speaker, you should be able to find work, at a school, through a local agency, or by giving lessons privately, virtually anywhere in the world. Some countries and specific programmes offer the best opportunities for the complete novice. Here's how to find work without EFL training.

There are possibilities if you have business experience and can speak the native language

In Eastern Europe there is a huge demand for teachers in both state and private schools.

Although the majority of EFL teachers are qualified and most language schools nowadays insist on formal qualifications and a minimum of experience there are still opportunities for unqualified native English speakers.

Equipping yourself with a basic teaching qualification before hitting the EFL road is advisable since qualified teachers tend to secure proper contracts, decent wages and better conditions all round. Nevertheless it is still possible to get teaching work without qualifications.

Western Europe

Many summer schools in the UK will consider graduates without an EFL certificate. A degree in modern languages or a Postgraduate Certificate of Education may be enough to persuade some. 'Receptiveness, and a willingness to learn, change and develop would compensate for the lack of a qualification', says one major teacher recruitment agent in the UK. Again, priority is given to qualified, experienced teachers so you have to be very determined.

The EFL market is becoming much more professional and teacher selection is more rigorous, especially in the well-established schools. Competition is tough, and without qualifications and experience you will have a hard time finding regular work. Yet there are possibilities if you have business experience and can speak the native language, particularly in France and Germany.

In Italy there are a number of language schools which train teachers themselves and do not require a formal qualification. Others have in-house training programmes, normally in the form of a truncated version of the RSA/Cambridge Certificate course, though many of these require the RSA/Cambridge Certificate as well.

In Southern Europe some language schools tend to be more flexible with regard to qualifications. Many schools in Spain, for example, are run by Spanish nationals who employ unqualified teachers to help state school students with their English exams. You will need to be relatively proficient in Spanish to get this kind of work. Some schools pay less if you are unqualified so try to get some kind of basic contract.

Eastern Europe

In Eastern Europe a new, dynamic market has emerged over the last five years and the opportunities for working unqualified are greater than in Western Europe. There is a huge demand for English language teachers in both state and private schools. Poland, the Czech Republic, the Baltic States and the Ukraine are all crying out for teachers, but do remember that local teachers are often impressively trained and qualified.

The Far East

Many countries in the Far East are willing to employ unqualified teachers, yet few will recruit from abroad. In Thailand, for instance, many schools recruit native English speakers on a temporary basis as they pass through the country on their travels. Wages are low, however, if you are unqualified. Until now Japan, Korea and Taiwan have provided work for unqualified teachers, particularly those with experience in business. Governments in these countries have tightened up on illegal workers and unqualified teachers may sometimes fall into this category.

Teaching work will not be that difficult to find, qualified or not, in Egypt, Morocco, Turkey and the larger Latin American countries as long as you are there and offering your services.

Government programmes

The governments of many countries worldwide run programmes which accept unqualified teachers. Japan's Exchange and Teaching Programme (JET) is one scheme. You can apply through any Japanese embassy and you do not need experience or a teaching qualification, though candidates should be native English speakers under 35 with a university degree. The JET scheme recruits around 500 teachers each year to work in Japanese secondary schools. The salary is good (UK£18,000) but the cost of living is high. Air fares are also paid. Recruitment begins in October for the following July.

There are government-run English teaching programmes in Central and Eastern Europe, and opportunities for unqualified teachers in the voluntary sector worldwide. Contact the Central Bureau of the East European Partnership, which is part of Voluntary Services Overseas.

Basic qualifications

If you want to be reasonably confident of securing of employment with a good salary and legal rights, a qualification in teaching EFL is invaluable. However, there is not one standard qualification, and some qualifications are more useful than others.

Although anyone can teach English once their proficiency in the language reaches a high level, and it is often said that those who have learned English themselves are better placed to teach it, native speakers have a natural advantage, and, indeed, a certain 'cachet' when it comes to looking for employment outside their own country. Therefore, this section is aimed mainly at Americans, Britons, Australians and the Irish.

Probably as a result of the recession, more and more people have been trying to find work in the 'boom' area of EFL. Most centres offering teacher training courses agree that demand is still rising, and, interestingly, report that the percentage of applications from more mature candidates with experience - such as engineers, bankers or mothers going back to work, as opposed to young graduates - has increased dramatically. The objective of nearly all of these people from different backgrounds is to find the quickest and cheapest route to a well-paid teaching job in the country of their choice.

Beginners' courses can vary from a few days to a few years with corresponding variances in coverage and cost, but most employers consider certificates resulting from courses lasting at least four weeks full-time to be the minimum qualification.

The important thing to remember is that most schools throughout the world only recognise certain qualifications depending on their status and location. Most American teachers will have completed an MA course (see p131), which will obviously cover considerably more than a four-week course, although it may not involve teaching practice, which is of fundamental importance to employers and is an important component of most certificate courses. The most commonly accepted qualifications in Europe are the RSA Cambridge and Trinity certificates or state Qualified Teacher Status (QTS), preferably with a TEFL component (although there are cutbacks on such courses). These are generally seen as a minimum qualification.

This does not necessarily mean that alternative courses are not very good. A qualification of some sort will certainly be considered preferable to no qualification at all. Make sure, though, that your course has a practical element.

At present there is no set policy in European countries towards other TEFL qualifications obtained in the United States, Canada, Ireland, New Zealand or Australia. This does not mean they are not recognised, but the policy of recruitment is to take each case as it comes. A teacher with such a qualification will be expected to have completed a course containing a balance of theory and practice. Remember that teaching practice is particularly valued - a course that only involved theory would not normally be considered adequate.

Larger organisations such as the British Council, ELS, International House and the Bell Educational Trust would normally require a diploma or QTS in TEFL. The RSA or Trinity certificate may be accepted, but only in certain centres, such as in the Middle East where there are relatively few locally qualified teachers. However, teachers already in a particular country should not be put off applying to such organisations if they only have the RSA or Trinity certificate, as recruitment often depends on local management. Unfortunately, local contracts may be less lucrative.

Non-EU nationals who hold an RSA or Trinity certificate or QTS should not assume this is an automatic means to getting a job teaching in Europe - they will still need to obtain a work permit.

The British Association of TEFL Qualifying Institutions was set up in 1991 to look at teacher qualifications across the European Union, and it is possible that certain aspects of teacher training will change as part of EU policy.

RSA/Cambridge Certificate
The RSA/Cambridge Certificate (also known as the RSA CTEFLA or the RSA Preparatory certificate) is a four-week intensive course. As it is so well established, it is the most widely recognised and respected minimum TEFL qualification internationally. Although the majority of their centres are in the UK, there are centres throughout the world which run RSA/Cambridge courses (see p24-26). For example, one of their newest centres is Georgetown University, Washington D.C. It can sometimes be cheaper to take the certificate course overseas than in the UK.

Most employers consider certificates resulting from courses lasting at least four weeks full-time to be the minimum qualification.

Most schools throughout the world only recognise certain qualifications depending on their status and location.

The course is aimed at training teachers to teach adults from beginners to Cambridge First Certificate (upper intermediate) level, and is highly practical. Lecture and seminar sessions dealing with language teaching techniques are followed up by observed teacher practice. The course is very intensive, and if you have no teaching experience, some sort of background reading is recommended before you embark on it (see p37). If you are not familiar with basic grammatical terms, find out about the tense system and common terminology first.

It has been suggested that the RSA/Cambridge Certificate is probably more suitable for trainees who have had some language training, as it emphasises methodology, but thousands of non-linguists successfully complete the course every year. Experienced teachers sometimes complain that the RSA Certificate expects you to conform too rigidly to their methods and ideals, but this is probably necessary if you are to learn such an enormous amount in such a short space of time. If you have a lot of teaching experience, you may find that you will have to 'unlearn' certain teaching habits.It certainly helps if you are outgoing, but sensitivity to students' difficulties is also appreciated.

Trinity Certificate in TESOL
Trinity College London run the Certificate in TESOL (Teaching English to Speakers of Other Languages), which has been running for over ten years. The number of validated centres offering this course has been growing rapidly in recent years, and, like the RSA, there are centres outside the UK and the qualification is now recognised worldwide.

The Trinity syllabus has a basic set of requirements that all its validated centres must meet. However, the course designer in each centre is free to submit his or her own course design to supplement these requirements. This means that individual centres may give a different weighting to certain elements. For example, one course may focus more on phonetics, another on discourse analysis. This degree of flexibility has proven popular with trainees and teacher trainers alike, but check that the focus of the course meets your requirements. Some students claim that the lack of emphasis on methodology during the course tends to favour people who have taught other subjects.

Most Trinity centres also offer pre-sessionals before the one-month or six-week intensive course begins, giving the trainee some basic grounding. Several institutions offer a correspondence module in addition to the 130 tuition hours. Most centres emphasise the importance of actually teaching foreign students. However, ensure that the course you choose offers sufficient teaching practice, as the criteria for the number of hours offered in this are unclear. The Trinity syllabus may include teaching practice at centres with young learners, and covers the use and design of materials for children.

Trinity trainees also do a student profile, with a detailed study of background and linguistic difficulties encountered by a particular student, and a plan for their progress, to make teachers aware of individual needs.

Trinity College is now hoping to increase its centres overseas. In addition to the Associate Diploma courses for non-native teachers in Singapore, Dubai and Uruguay, Trinity plans to offer TESOL certificate courses in Spain and Malaysia. The college has also developed a non-native teacher scheme to teach young learners, called CertTeyl (Certificate in Teaching English to Young Learners).

International certificates
There are a number of other certificate courses of roughly the same level as the RSA and Trinity, which are listed on pages 27-28. They may not be as well known on a global level, but they are often very well respected within their own geographical sphere.

University courses
In addition to their degree and diploma courses (see Section Four), there are also EFL cerificate courses run by universities (see p128). Make sure they contain teaching practice with foreign students, not just with other teachers.

COTE/DOTE
COTE (Certificate for Overseas Teachers of English) and DOTE (Diploma for Overseas Teachers of English, for more advanced English speakers) are non-native English speaker courses. The courses take regional conditions into account and use local classrooms for teacher training. COTE requires that teachers are roughly at the standard of Cambridge First Certificate. The course is popular in Spain, Turkey, Egypt and South America, and is being developed to suit Eastern Europe.

See page 29 (COTE) and page 125 (DOTE) for detailed information on these courses.

RSA/Cambridge Certificate (CTEFLA)

College	Course length	FT/ PT	Fees	Start dates	Entry requirements	Contact	Comments	Max no. of students
Anglia Polytechnic Univ, Cambridge	4 wks	FT	£820	July	University entrance level	Anne Dover		15
Anglo-Continental, Bournemouth	4 wks	FT	£880	Feb, May, Aug	'A' levels or equiv	Miss J Haine		10
Anglo School, London	4 wks	FT	£845	Throughout year	Univ. entrance level; Min age 20; Native speaker	John Adams		14
Basil Paterson, Edinburgh	4 wks 6 mths	FT PT	£875 + exam fee	Throughout year	University entrance level; Degree pref	Dianna Allan	Apply early	15
Bedford College of Higher Education	8 mths	PT	£695 + exam fee	Sep	University entrance level; Degree pref	Ken Wilford	£62 for unemployed	12
Bell Language School, Cambridge	4 wks 27 wks	FT PT	£895 + exam fee	Throughout year	University entrance level; Min age 20	Sue Sheerin	Intensive P/T=4hrs/wk	15
Bell Language School, Norwich	4 wks	FT	£895 + exam fee	Throughout year	University entrance level; Min age 20	Sarah Knights	Intensive	15
Bell Language School, Bath	10 wks	PT	£950 + exam fee	Mar	University entrance level; Min age 20	Howard Thomas		15
Bournemouth & Poole College of Further Ed	24 wks	PT	on appl	Sep	University entrance level or equiv	TEFL Coordinator	Apply early	12
Brasshouse Centre, Birmingham with Handsworth College	18 wks	PT	£800+ exam fee	Oct	As per UCLES	Deborah Cobbett		12
CILC, Cheltenham	5 wks	FT	£750	Jan, Feb, Apr, May, Oct, Nov	University entrance level or equiv, Interview	Gillian James	Apply early	14
Clarendon College, Nottingham	16 wks	PT	£300	Sep, Feb	Interview	Neil Pearson		12
Concorde Intl, Folkestone	4 wks	FT	£798 + exam fee	Throughout year	University entrance level; Relevant life exp; Min age 20	Ann Kennedy	Accom avail	12
Department of Modern Languages Glasgow	5 wks	FT	On appl	On appl	University entrance level; Interview; Min age 21	Pat Blockley		12
Devon School of English, Paignton	4 wks	FT	£860	Throughout year	University entrance level; Degree pref	Joan Hawthorne		12
Eastbourne College of Arts & Tech	1-2 terms	PT	£180	Sep, Apr	2 'A' levels	John Pomeroy	Write for leaflet	12
Eastbourne School of English	4 wks	FT	£840	Throughout year	Degree or equiv pref	Dorothy Rippon	Accom arranged; Apply early	£12
Edinburgh Language Foundation	5 wks	FT	£825	Jan, April, November	University entrance level	Anne Rowe		15

College	Course length	FT/ PT	Fees	Start dates	Entry requirements	Contact	Comments	Max no. of students
ELT Banbury, Oxford	4 wks	FT	£837	Throughout year	Good Higher Ed; Native speaker comp; Min age 20	Mike Sayer	Apply early	10
Filton College, Bristol	9 mths	PT	£700	Sep	University entrance level; Degree pref	Helen Bowen		12
Frances King School of English, London	4 wks	FT	£749	Throughout year	High standard of education	Nathalie Ivemy	Entry by interview	12
GEOS English Academy, Hove	4 wks	FT	£770 + exam fee	Throughout year	University entrance level; Native speaker comp; Min age 20	Academic Director	Accomm avail	15
GLOSCAT, Cheltenham	6 wks 1 yr	FT PT	On appl	Sep, Jan, Apr	On appl	Paul Burden	FT course incl a study week	12
Greenhill College, Harrow	6 mths	PT	£480	Nov, Jan	'A' level; Native speaker comp	Sheila Tracey	Eves Nov-Jun Days Jan-Jun	15
Hammersmith & West London College	1 mth 6 mths	FT PT	£550	Throughout year	University entrance level; Native speaker comp	CTEFLA Course Information Centre	Apply 2 months before start date	15
Harrow House, Dorset	4 wks	FT	£750	Throughout year	Min 2 'A' level; Native speaker comp; Min age 20	Gaynor Wells	Full board host family accomm avail	8
Hendon College, London	9 mths	PT	£620	Sep	As per UCLES	Dina Brook		12
Hilderstone College, Broadstairs	4 wks	FT	£795 + exam fee	Throughout year	Good education; Native speaker comp; Min age 20	Andy Caswell	Accomm avail	12
ICELS, Oxford Brookes University	1-2 terms	PT	On appl	Apr, Sep	Good education; Native speaker comp; Min age 20	Liz Sayigh		12
International House, Hastings	4 wks	FT	£787 + exam fee	Throughout year	Interview	Adrian Underhill	Accomm service	18
International House, Newcastle upon Tyne	4 wks	FT	£860	Throughout year	Good education; Native speaker comp; Min age 20	Sue Gaston		12
International House, London	4 wks 12 wks	FT PT	£805 +exam fee £945 + exam fee	Throughout year	Interview	TT Dept	Apply early	15
International Language Institute, Leeds	4 wks	FT	£825	Throughout year		Steven Procter	Accomm & job counselling	10
ITTC, Bournemouth	4 wks 8 mths	FT PT	£888	Monthly; Oct	University entrance level	Annette Halwood		18
Leeds Metropolitan University	4 wks	FT	£760	Throughout year	As per UCLES	Language Centre		18
Liverpool Community College	20 wks	PT	£500	Sep	3 'A' levels 3 GCSE or equiv	D Lane		-
London Study Centre	5 wks 15 wks	FT PT	£830	Throughout year	High Standard of English; Interview	Ken McNicholls		12

RSA/Cambridge Certificate (CTEFLA)

College	Course length	FT/ PT	Fees	Start dates	Entry requirements	Contact	Comments	Max no. of students
City of Manchester	20 wks	PT	£400 +exam fee	Sep, Mar	Degree or equiv	Admissions		16-18
Newnham Language Centre, Cambridge	4 wks	FT	£840	Jan, Feb, May, Jul, Aug, Oct	University entrance level or Degree; Good standard English	Michael Short	Pre-selection Interview	16
University of Northumbria at Newcastle	2 yrs	PT	£650 + exam fee	Oct	Degree; Teaching Qual or equiv	Dept Office Hist & Crit Studies	Flexible entry & exit points	15
Oxford School of English (Godmer House)	4 wks	FT	£950	Monthly	Pre-selection Interview	TT dept		14
Pilgrims, Canterbury	1 mth	FT	£989	Throughout year	Language awareness & people skills	Sam Preston	Intensive & thorough	12
Regent Language Training, London	4 wks	FT	£750 + exam fee	Monthly	University entrance level; Min age 20; Native speaker comp	Declan McNally	Central London location; Advice on jobs	12
St Giles College, Brighton	4 wks	FT	£840	Monthly	University entrance level; Min age 20	Sue Laker		15
St Giles College, London	4 wks	FT	£840	Monthly	Degree or University matriculation	TTC Administrat	Interview	15
Saxoncourt Teacher Training, London	4 wks	FT	£775	Throughout year	2 'A' levels or equiv, Native speaker	Russell Yates		12
Skola Teacher Training, Marble Arch	8 wks 4 wks	FT	£1250+ exam fee £830	July; Throughout year	Min University entry level + 2 yrs exp	Lyndel Sayle		15
SOAS, London	4 wks	FT	£840	July	Degree pref or equiv	Fiona English	University facilities	16
South Thames College	10 wks 20 wks	PT PT	£550 - £650	Throughout year	Degree or equiv	Monica Nicholls		18
Stevenson College, Edinburgh	4 wks 19 wks	FT PT	£750	Jul, Oct	Degree pref or equiv	David Gibson		12
Stanton School of English, London	4 wks	FT	£738	Monthly	2 'A' levels or equiv	David Garrett	Lang exp preferred	18
Stoke-on-Trent College	12-13 wks	PT	£700	Throughout year	Min 2 'A' levels	Central enquiries	Also full time course July	15
Thames Valley University, London	6 wks 16 wks	FT PT	£832	Feb, Jun	Degree or equiv; Min age 20	Sophia Davis		18
UCF Birmingham	1 yr	PT	£320	Sep	Exp in TEFL	Alison Dale		16
University of Glamorgan	4 wks 6 mths	FT PT	£850 + exam fee	Oct	Degree + TEFL exp pref	Maggy McNorton		12
University of Portsmouth	1 yr	PT	£510	Oct	2 'A' levels	Mrs V Carter		23
University of Hull	4 wks 20 wks	FT PT	£740 + exam fee	Jun Oct		Debra Marsh		12
Westminster College, London	5 wks	FT	£550	Mar, Apr, May, Jun,	'A' levels Degree or equiv			18
Wigston College of Further Education	9 mths	PT	£600 + exam fee	Sep	University entrance level	D E Harris	Apply early	14

Certificate Diary

Matthew Connolly wanted a change from his stressful life as an advertising sales executive for the national press. Teaching EFL in Italy proved to be a new and satisfying career.

This is not a course for the fainthearted. It requires complete dedication for a whole month.

Five years ago I was selling advertising space in London for a national quality newspaper. I was in the wrong job and felt I was only just on the right side of thirty. Several friends had left London to go teaching English abroad and I'd heard nothing but positive news from them. One friend who was teaching in Milan, Italy, dared me to quit my job, work out my notice and join her. Two months later I was in Milan flicking excitedly through the yellow pages for the language school section.

After a week of traipsing around and impromptu interviews, I was offered a job at one of the top language schools. They insisted I did the RSA at the end of the academic year but felt confident I would survive beforehand in the classroom, with five years' work experience behind me. It was in at the deep end.

By the time I started the RSA course several months later I'd gained little experience of teaching large classes but had become an expert at one-to-one lessons with vain Italian bank managers. This certainly hadn't prepared me, however, for the rigours of the one-month intensive RSA/Cambridge Certificate course run by Regent School, Milan.

This is not a course for the fainthearted. It requires complete dedication for the whole month, including evenings, weekends and even those silent nocturnal hours. It is exhausting, the workload is heavy and it is high pressure but if you have the stamina it turns you into a competent teacher.

There is a formula and quite simply you must follow it in order to pass.

The course contains many elements including classroom management, lesson preparation, effective use of teaching material and written assignments. You learn the presentation, practice and production approach - the hallmark of the modern communicative teaching method . You're also trained to develop a language learner's speaking, listening, reading and writing skills.

Every aspect of your performance in front of 15 to 20 bemused learners is scrutinised. Afterwards the lesson is dissected in lengthy postmortems. At least one tutor and several other trainees observed all my lessons. On one occasion both the course director and an external assessor suddenly appeared while I was wrestling with the present perfect continuous tense.

There was less time spent on the intricacies of English grammar on the course than I would have liked so if you're not sure of how to explain the difference between 'I went to Madrid' and 'I've been to Madrid', for example, I'd recommend you read one of the prescribed grammar books before the course.

The practical nature of the course intensifies as it proceeds. You will be required, by the final week, to give a one-hour lesson (as opposed to twenty minutes in the first week), putting into practice all the skills you have acquired, and submit a lesson-plan accounting for every minute in microscopic detail. You must also submit an extended written assignment. I wrote a review of a coursebook but there were numerous other options.

The course tutors are not looking for linguistic geniuses, or smart alecs who do it their own way. There is a formula and, quite simply, you must follow it in order to pass, regardless of your own ideas. In a third-week tutorial the course director told me, 'Think of it as like learning to drive. You learn the rules, do everything by the book, then once you've passed the test you can drive your own way, as long as you know how it's done'.

Although the RSA Certificate course was challenging, it was enormous fun. There was a real camaraderie between the trainees, despite the fact that we'd been forced to criticize each other constructively throughout. If you do have serious difficulties the tutor will give you extra help and point you in the right direction.

I'd really recommend slaving away on this course because the minimum pass grade is often not good enough for some of the more notable language schools nowadays. The school doors have opened relatively easily for me since getting the RSA Certificate. I returned to England two years ago and now teach at a language school in Central London, and I know I have the qualifications and experience to confidently apply to the best schools. (Apart from the British Council for which you generally need the RSA Diploma).

That's the great thing about TEFL. You are free to go wherever you like and the RSA/Cambridge Certificate has a 'that'll do nicely sir' effect on language schools in most countries.

Trinity College Certificate in TESOL

College	Course length	FT/PT	Fees	Start dates	Entry requirements	Contact	Comments	Max no. of student
Aberdeen College	6 mths	PT	£185	May, Sep, Feb	First Degree pref	Anne Bain		10
Abbey College, Malvern Wells	5 wks	FT	£1,298	Oct, Feb, Apr	Degree + Practising teacher	David Arrowsmith		12
Abon Language School, Bristol	6 mths	PT	TBA	Sep, Oct	Fluent in English	David Berrington Davies		-
Blackpool & Fylde College	10 mths	PT	£400 approx	Sep	Higher Ed qual or equiv experience	Tony Foster	1 eve p/w + 6 hrs home-study	18
Bracknell College, Wokingham	32 wks	PT	£536	Sep	'A' level or equiv	Colette Galloway	2 eves per week	14
Bradford & Ilkley Comm. College	4 wks 34 wks	FT PT	£500 (EC) £680 (Non EC)	Throughout year	University entrance level; 2 'A' levels	Nancy Hall	Large EFL dept	14
Cicero Lang Intl, Tunbridge Wells	4 wks	FT	£745 + exam fee	Throughout year	A level+Interview	Dr John Brown	Accom avail	10
Colchester Institute	8-10 wks	FT	£500 + exam fee	Sep, Mar	Degree or equiv	Simon Haines		10
Coventry Technical College	4 wks + 1yr PT	FT DL	£695	Throughout year	Good English; Min age 18	Christopher Fry	Incl Teaching practice + 1:1	12
Croydon Coombe Cliff Centre	4 wks 22 wks	FT PT	£495	Sep	Course Director's discretion	Course Director	Pre-course study pack	6
East Berkshire College, Langley	23 wks	PT	£495	Sep	2 'A' levels 3 'O' level or equiv	Mr C Hammonds		15
Edinburgh Tutorial College	4 wks 10 wks	FT PT	£785 £735	Throughout year	TBA	Mr Bob Bell		10
EFL Unit, Kingsway College, London	8 wks 22 wks	FT PT	£595	Jan, Jul	By interview	Felicity Henderson		18
European Training & Communications	6 wks 4 wks	FT	£694	Throughout year	Min 2 'A' levels, degree pref	Linda Harrison Patrick Kemp	Appr NVQ centre	14
Surrey Adult Ed, West Molesey	20 wks	PT	TBA	Sept	Trinity specified	Nick Lockstone	1 day per week	15
Surrey Adult Ed, Woking	4 wks	FT	£472 + Moderation fee	Mar, Jun, Jul, Nov	Interview	Ursula Over		16
Grimsby College	30 wks	PT	£250	Jan	Degree + teaching exp	School of FOCE		15
Grove House, Dartford	4 wks	FT	£735	Throughout year	Course Director's discretion	Heather Jeynes	Accom avail + help with jobs	12
Hart Villages, Odiham	9 mths	PT	£450	Sep	Degree or equiv	Course Director	Includes teaching-practice placements	16
Hopwood Hall, Rochdale	36 wks	PT	£690	Apr	2 'A' levels, English Proficiency, Min age 20	Philip R Day		16
inlingua, Cheltenham	5 wks	FT	£760 + moderation fee	Throughout year	University entrance level	Dagmar Lewis	Poss posts overseas on completion	10

Trinity College Certificate in TESOL

College	Course length	FT PT	Fees	Start dates	Entry requirements	Contact	Comments	Max no. of students
Language Link, London	4 wks	FT	on appl	Every 5 wks	'A' level English min	Robyn Bowman Zayade		10
London Study Centre	5 wks 15 wks	FT PT	£830	Throughout year	Interview; High standard of English	Kevin McNicholas		16
University of Luton	2 sems	FT PT	on appl	Oct	Good standard educ	Vicki Vidal	Part of modular BA degree	20
Oxford House College, London	4 wks 13 wks	FT PT	£690 + £750 + exam fee	Monthly	Degree pref Min age 20	Jan Brindle	Central London	12-16
Polyglot Lang. Services, London	4 wks 21 wks	FT PT	£695	Throughout year	University entrance level	The Administrator		8
Richmond Adult Comm College	33 wks	PT	£800	Sep	Degree or equiv	Barbara Beaumont	Day course; Apply early	12-16
St Brelade's College, Jersey	4 wks	FT	£700 + exam fee	April	Degree or appropriate training	Mr Brown		10
Sace-Woking & Chertsey	4 wks	FT	£472 +exam fee	Nov, Mar, Jun , Jul	Interview; Aptitude test	Ursula Over		12-16
Sandwell College, West Midlands	24 wks 36 wks	PT	£700	Oct, Feb	Good ed background; Qualification in English	Gill Gibbins		10
Scot-Ed Courses, Edinburgh	5 wks 12 wks	FT PT	£798	All year	University entrance level	Christine Young		1 1
Sheffield College, Stradbroke Centre	35 wks	PT	£650	Sep	Good ed background	Carole Tehrani		12
Sheffield Hallam University	4 wks 16 wks	FT DL	on appl	All year	Degree	Gill King	DL incl 4 wks FT	20
South East Essex College	1 yr	PT	on appl	Sep	First degree or equiv; Native speakers	Marketing	Informal interview	15
Sutton College of Liberal Arts	32 wks	PT	£500	Oct	'A' level	Sonja Compton		12
Thurrock College, Essex	16 wks	DL	on appl	Feb, Aug, Nov, Dec	Degree or teaching qual	Beryl Andrews	Incl 4 wks FT; Accom avail	14
Universal Language Training	4 wks 12 wks	FT PT	£796	Apr, Jun, Jul, Sep, Nov	Min age 20; Good ed background	Bodile Streeten		14
Waltham Forest College, London	5 wks	FT	£500	Sep	University entrance level	Course Tutor	Interview	12
University of Wales, Cardiff	4 wks 10 wks	FT	£850 (£1900 non-EU)	July October	First Degree	Secretary	Intensive and standard courses	12
University of Wolverhampton	40 wks	PT	£800	Sep	University entrance level	Tony Shannon-Little		16

Equivalent Qualifications in Ireland

How to get basic qualifications in Ireland.

In the past the qualification system in Ireland was rather loose. Although a large number of Irish teachers have always worked overseas, there has frequently been confusion over their qualifications, despite the country's long tradition of quality English language training.

To teach in Ireland, a degree is required, but until recently the regulations of the Advisory Council on English Language Schools (ACELS) have allowed recognised language schools to employ anyone with a TEFL qualification, including one of the huge variety of short course certificates. Many of these short courses are run within Irish colleges, but last less than 20 hours. The problem with them is that foreign students generally go to Ireland only in the summer months (although this too is changing towards all year courses), and outside this time trainee teachers simply do not have enough students to practise on.

Language schools in Ireland are now trying to find common ground to ensure there is more consistency in their qualification system.

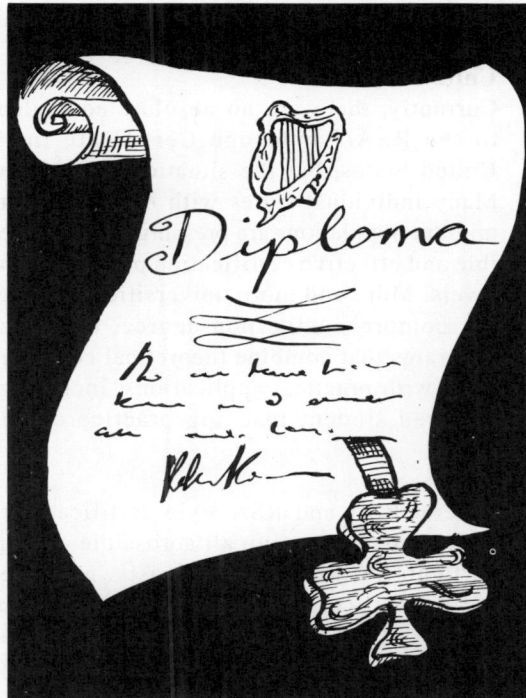

Language schools are now trying to ensure there is more consistency in their qualification system.

RELSA

The **Recognised English Language Schools Association** is the main association of EFL schools in Ireland, and in 1992 it introduced its own teacher training Certificate. The course lasts 70 hours and involves teaching practice, observation and a project. At present there are twelve schools licensed to run such courses. The RELSA Certificate is considered an acceptable qualification in some schools overseas, who were previously baffled by the diverse range of certificates Irish teachers presented them with. However, the RELSA course is still shorter and less well known than the RSA/Cambridge Certificate. See p27-28 for RELSA Certificate course details.

ATT

The **Association for Teacher Training** in TEFL is a relatively new association of nine schools concerned with standards of teacher training in Ireland. At the forefront of curriculum innovation, they run a Preliminary Certificate (40 hrs), an International Certificate (106 hrs), Refresher courses for both Native and Non-Native Teachers (40 hrs), as well as a Distance Learning course. The Preliminary Certificate is designed to persuade trainee teachers away from the less reputable short courses. The International Certificate is comparable to the RSA and Trinity College Certificates. Course fees range from 150 to 450 Irish punts. All the courses enjoy recognition by a substantial number of schools in Europe and overseas, and standards are assured and maintained by the ATT's own panel of moderators. See p27-28 for course details.

RSA/Cambridge and Trinity Certificates

The RSA/Cambridge and Trinity College Certificates are respected in Irish schools. RSA/Cambridge Certificate courses are available at two centres and the Trinity Certificate is offered at one centre (see p24-26).

State sector qualifications

The state EFL sector is fairly small in Ireland, although the Universities of Dublin and Cork do a teacher training course, the College Certificate in EFL, which runs in conjunction with the Higher Diploma in Education over two years. This is considered as an equivalent to the RSA/Cambridge Certificate.

The RELSA and ATT Certificates are considered acceptable qualifications overseas.

Getting Qualified in the USA and Canada

There are an ever-increasing number of EFL training programmes on offer at schools and universities in North America. As states push for more flexible programs, you are more likely to find a course tailor-made for you.

More universities are offering comprehensive non-degree certificate programs.

The minimum qualification to enter most programs is a BA or BS degree.

United States

Currently, there are no absolute equivalents to the RSA/Cambridge Certificate in the United States, but the situation is changing. Many individual states with burgeoning immigrant populations are pressing for more flexible and effective certification programs at all levels. More and more universities are offering comprehensive non-degree, certificate programs that combine theoretical considerations with practical applications, including a required student teaching practice component.

Several RSA and RSA-style certificate programs have sprung up all across the country, particularly on the West Coast where there are at least six. Meanwhile, it is still possible in some states - California is one - to obtain an adult credential or secondary authorization to teach ESL to adults. Finally, a large number of non-profit, community-based organizations offer effective, free training programs for volunteers willing to teach English.

The minimum qualification to enter most programs is a BA or BS degree. However, university BA programs in TESOL and many of the private, intensive teacher training schools or volunteer programs will accept trainees with a high school diploma. You do not need any previous teaching experience to enter one of these programs. However, it is a rare program today that does not encourage, if not require, practice teaching and classroom observation as part of the curriculum. The fact that Georgetown University, Washington, has begun running RSA/ Cambridge Certificate courses is a sign that English language teaching in the United States is changing.

In the past, English language teaching in the United States meant TESL (Teaching English as a Second Language). For decades, TESL took place mainly at the university level with academic students. Beginning in the 1970s and into the 1980s, the United States experienced a mass migration of non-English speaking immigrants with special needs, many of whom lacked basic literacy skills in their own language. As these individuals began to enter schools and the workplace, a strong need for eclectic methodology arose.

Today, with the encroaching 'global village', a new recognition of the importance of teaching English as a foreign language is gaining currency.

Most of the better jobs at state-run institutions in the United States are for TESL and generally require an MA degree. However, hundreds of English teaching positions do not require an advanced degree, particularly in private language schools where overseas experience and an RSA or similar certificate may be more valuable than a Masters.

Canada

In Canada the basic English as a Second Language teacher training qualification for instructing adult learners consists of an undergraduate degree, a recognised ESL teacher training course, and a standard of spoken and written English equivalent to that of an educated native speaker of English.

Canada has become well-known as a destination for teachers wishing to improve their skills. In the eastern provinces McGill University in Montreal, Quebec, and Toronto University in Ontario both offer an array of teacher training programs, including short summer courses designed for teachers without English as their mother tongue.

The proximity of the western coast to the Far East and its large immigrant community have made it popular as a teacher training destination. The International Teacher Training Institute at Vancouver Community College, British Columbia, specialise in short programs.

Prospective students must have passed a university course or hold a certificate.

Getting Qualified in Australia and New Zealand

The EFL sector is growing rapidly in Australasia, so short, intensive teacher training courses are becoming more popular.

Australia

EFL courses are mainly taught in accredited ELICOS (English Language Intensive Courses for Overseas Students) institutions. The National ELICOS Accreditation Scheme (NEAS) has set minimum standards for teacher qualifications within such institutions. These guidelines state that teachers must have at least:

EITHER a recognised pre-service teaching qualification (minimum three years) plus or including an appropriate TESOL qualification,

OR a recognised degree or diploma (minimum three years), plus at least 800 hours classroom teaching experience, plus an appropriate TESOL qualification.

To be deemed 'an appropriate teaching qualification', the course must have a content focus on English language learning and teaching, a practical component including at least 6 hours supervised and assessed practice teaching, and no less than 100 contact hours. The course must also be accredited by the appropriate accrediting body. For more details of the NEAS policy, contact: **NEAS, Locked Bag 2, Post Office, Pyrmont, NSW 2009.**

'Study tours' cater to a small but growing sector of the TEFL market. Many of the ELICOS colleges provide courses for groups of tourists, and teacher qualifications are unregulated for this sector. It may be possible for teachers to get work with as little as a certificate in TESOL in some institutions. However, most colleges require the equivalent to NEAS minimum qualifications.

A wide range of teacher training courses, from introductory level upwards, is available. In Sydney, the Australian TESOL Training Centre offers RSA Certificate and Diploma courses, as well as an introductory one-week course for those wishing to travel. The Australian Centre for Languages has an intensive 4-week certificate-level course, co-validated by the RSA, which can be taken part-time over fifteen weeks. The Institute of Languages, University of New South Wales, runs a pre-service Certificate in TESOL which is run over 20 weeks part time and a range of introductory courses for overseas students of non-English speaking backgrounds.

In Queensland, the University of Queensland's Centre for Language Teaching and Research offers courses from graduate certificate level upwards, some pre-service and some for practising teachers. The University of South Australia also offers a graduate certificate for trained teachers. In Western Australia, RSA Certificate courses are provided by the Milner International College of English, and in Victoria both certificate and diploma level courses are available through the International TESOL Training Centre.

The EFL sector in Australia appears to be entering a growth period, and this provides a more optimistic view for teachers wishing to get higher level teaching positions in ELICOS centres. Generally, employers would expect a coordinator or head teacher to have a qualification at RSA Diploma level or above, and there are many courses being offered at the level of graduate certificate or diploma and MA which would prepare teachers for a senior teaching position. See p146 for more details of postgraduate and MA courses on offer.

New Zealand

The export of education is easily the fastest growing industry in New Zealand. Due to the country's size and population of only 3.5 million people, the industry is naturally smaller than its neighbour's, but this growth in demand has probably led to the increased popularity of short, intensive teacher training courses. A certificate along with a degree is the accepted qualification for NZQA (New Zealand Qualification Authorities) accredited schools.

Languages International in Auckland was the first school to offer the RSA Cambridge CTEFLA, which is now also run by the Capital Language Academy in Wellington. The Trinity Certificate in TESOL course is available at Seafield School of English in Christchurch, while Dominion English Schools, based in Christchurch and Auckland, run special courses for teachers throughout the year, which are examined through Pitmans.

'Study tours' cater to a small but growing sector of the EFL market and teacher qualifications are unregulated.

The certificate along with a degree is the accepted qualification for NZQA accredited schools.

College	Course length	FT/ PT	Fees	Start dates	Entry requirements	Contact	Comments	Max no. of students
Academia Lacunza, San Sebastian	110 hrs	FT	on appl	Aug	As per UCLES	Head of TT		15
American University in Cairo	4 wks	FT	US$ 850	Throughout year	Native speaker English	Christine Zamer/ Magda Lawrence		10
Auckland Language Centre	4 wks	FT	NZ$2,75	Jan, Jun, Sep	Min age 20 'A' levels or degree	Nick Marsden Wayne Dyer		12
Australian Centre for Languages, New South Wales	4 wks 15 wks	FT PT	A$ 2080 A$ 2230	Throughout year	As per UCLES	Antoinette Rossiter		12
Australian TESOL Training Centre, New South Wales	4 wks 12 wks 1 wk	FT PT FT	A$ 1990 A$375	Throughout year	University entrance level; Min age 20	Gloria Smith		12
Bell Language School, Zurich	4 wks 5 wks 12 wks	FT PT PT	SFR3500 SFR3500 SFR3500	Aug Feb Mar, Sep		Keith Sprague		12
Bell Language School, Geneva	4 wks 5 wks 12 wks	FT PT PT	SFR3550 SFR3600 SFR3600	Aug Jan Sep, Feb	Min age 20 2 'A' levels or degree	Sean Power		12
British Council, Abu Dhabi	5 wks 15 wks	FT PT	DhS 7,000	TBA	Degree or equiv	Kevin Nolan		12
British Council, Cairo	5 wks	FT	£600	June	Pre-course task + interview	Charles Walker		12
British Council, Doha	10 wks	PT	on appl	Mar, Oct	Uni entrance; Min age 20	Michael Manser		12
British Council, Hong Kong	9 wks	PT	HK$ 17,000	May, Sep, Nov, Feb	Uni entrance level; Native speaker comp; Min age 20	Rebecca Ho	Incl intensive 1st week	25
British Council, Instanbul	TBA	FT PT	£800	Jun Oct	Min 'A' level or equiv	Dorothy Gwillim		18
British Council, Kuala Lumpur	5 wks 10 wks	FT PT	£890	Jan, Apr, Jul, Oct	University standard education	Patricia Thorley		15
British Council Madrid	150 hrs	PT	195,000 PST	Sep	Pract teachers EFL min level FC	Maria Trivino		20
British Council, Milan	4 wks 6 mths	FT PT	2.3m ITL	Jun, Sep, Oct Feb	Native speaker; Min age 20; 'A' level or equiv	Amanda Bourdillon	Help with accomm	15
British Council, Muscat	5-10-16 wks	FT PT	RO 575	Oct, Jan, Mar	University entrance level	Melanie Pender		10
British Council, Naples	4 wks	FT	2.5m ITL	June, Sep	As per UCLES 2 'A' Levels; Min age 21	F C de la Motte		10
British Council Qatar	10 wks	PT	QR 6,000	Mar	Min age 20; 2 'A' + 3 'O' levels pref	Michael Manser		-
British Council, Singapore	10 wks	PT	S$ 2575	Jan, Apr, July, Sep	'O' Level + screening	Vickie Tang		18

Overseas RSA/Cambridge Certificate (CTEFLA)

College	Course length	FT/ PT	Fees	Start dates	Entry requirements	Contact	Comments	Max no. of students
British Institute of Florence	4 wks 1 yr	FT PT	2.3m ITL 2.4m ITL	Jun, Jul	As per UCLES	Sarah Ellis	Some help with accom	9
British Language Centre, Madrid	4 wks 15 wks	FT PT	£625	Throughout year		Alastair Dickinson	Help with accom	18
British School of Milan	4 wks 15 wks	FT PT	2.1m ITL	Throughout year	Gd education; Native speaker English age 21	Janine Thomas	Pre-course interview (tel poss)	12
British School of Fruili-Venezia Giulia	5 wks	FT	2.1m ITL	Jun	Interview	Richard Baudains	Pre-course selection test	10
British School The Hague	12 wks	PT	fl 3400	Feb		Mrs M Kielnar		12
Cambridge School, Verona	4 wks 5 mths	FT PT	2.280m ITL	Oct	'A' levels or equiv	Anne Parry	Help with accomm	15
Cambridge School Lisbon	4 wks	FT	£750	Jul, Aug	As per UCLES	Jeffrey Kapke		12
Capital Language Academy, Wellington, NZ	4 wks	FT	NZ$ 2550	Jan, May, Oct	On appl	Fliss Hope		12
Centro Anglo Paraguayo, Paraguay	9 mths	FT& PT	US$600	Oct	CEELT 1Min English level	Lorraine Jackson		10
Columbia College Canada	2 mths	PT	$2,000CA	TBA	University degree	CTFLA Co-ordinator		12
Dominion English School, Auckland	1 mth	FT	A$2725	Jun, Aug	Good education Pre-course int & task	Andrew Williams		12
Elcra-Bell, Geneva	4-12 wks	FT PT	SFR 3550 SFR 3600	Jan, Feb, Aug, Sept	As per UCLES	Sean Power	Also in Zurich	12
English International, San Francisco	4 wks	FT	on appl	Monthly	Degree + knowledge of foreign language	Deanne Manwaring	Professional job guidance	12
Georgetown University, Washington DC	5 wks	FT	on appl	May, Jul, Aug	Degree + 2nd Language	F Mary Marggraf		18
ILA South Pacific, New Zealand	4½ wks	FT	NZ$ 2800	Feb, Mar, Oct	Degree; 2nd language; Min age 20	Susan McAllister		12
ILC Paris	4 wks	FT	9660 FFR	Throughout year	Uni entrance level; Native speaker comp	Bror Gliemann	Pre-selection task	15
International House, Barcelona	4 wks 4 mths	FT PT	133,000 PTS	July	Min age 20, good standard of education	Lilias Adam	Help with accom	18
International House, Budapest	Variable	FT PT	£670	Jan, Feb, May, Jul	Interview; Min age 21	Frances Hughes		18
International House, Lisbon	4 wks	FT	172,000 Esc	Throughout year	Degree pref	Kathryn Gordon		15
International House, Madrid	4 wks 12 wks	FT PT	130,000 PTS	May, Jun, Oct	Higher ed pref; Native speaker comp; Min age 20	Steven Haysham		12
International House, Palma de Mallorca	4 wks 5 mths	FT PT	on appl	July Feb	Degree or equiv; Min age 20	Jan Wright		12

College	Course length	FT/ PT	Fees	Start dates	Entry requirements	Contact	Comments	Max no of students
International House, Rome	110-120 hrs	FT PT	2.150m ITL	May, Jul Aug, Oct	Native speaker higher education	Director		12
International House, Sabadell	4 wks	FT	133000 PTS	July	Uni entrance level; Age 20+	Lilias Adam		18
International House, Valencia	4 wks 8 wks	FT PT	on appl	Apr, Jul	Degree preferred	Seamus Campbell		15
International House, Vienna	4 wks 10 wks	FT PT	on appl	Feb, Aug	Native speaker competence	Head of Training		12
International Language Academy, Christchurch NZ	4.5 wks	PT	$NZ 2,800	Oct, Nov, Jan, Feb	Degree; Second language	Susan McCallister		12
International Language Institute Nova Scotia Can	4 wks	FT	CND $1700	May, Jul, Aug	First Degree; Min age 20	Graig Riggs		18
International Language Institute, Cairo	4 wks	FT	£560	Throughout year	Native speakers; Degree preferred	Paul Mason	Accom on request	12
Instituto Chileno Chile	14 mths	PT	£500	Mar	Teaching exp FCE level	Anthony Adams		20
ITTC, Melbourne	4 wks 20 wks	FT PT	$1820	Throughout year	Interview; Tertiary qual; Min age 21	F Nuttall	Help with employment	18
Language Centre of Ireland, Dublin	4 wks 9 wks	FT PT	on appl	Jan, Jun, Jul, Sep, Oct	Pre-course interview	Tom Doyle		14
Language Institute, Athens	1 mth 3 mths	FT PT	On appl	Jan, May, Jun, Sep	Personal Interview	Course Tutor	Poss jobs on completion	15
Languages International, Auckland	4 wks	FT	NZ$ 2750	Jan, Apr, Jun, Nov	Degree; Interview	Graig Thaine		12
Language Resources Ltd, Japan	4 mths	PT	On appl	Apr, Oct	As per UCLES	Bill Stanford		16
La Trobe University, Victoria	4 wks	FT	A$1800	Throughout year	As per UCLES	Admissions Officer		20
Milner Intl Coll of Eng, Perth	4 wks	FT	A$1995	Throughout year	Tertiary entrance	Lorraine Duval	Accomm avail	12
RMIT Melbourne	4 wks 16 wks	FT PT	A$1800	Throughout year	Tertiary entrance; Min age 20	RSA Student Services		12
St Giles College, San Francisco	4 wks 3 mths	FT PT	on appl	Throughout year	Higher ed; Knowledge of foreign lang & exp pref	Conrad Heyns	Course was first CTEFLA in US	15
South Australian College, Adelaide	4 wks	FT	A$1900	Throughout year	Matriculation; Age 20 yrs min	South Australian College		18
University College Cork, Ireland	4 wks	FT	on appl	Feb	University entrance level	Goodith White		12
Volkshochochschul Zuerich	14 wks	PT	SFR3500	May, Oct	Pre-selection & interview	Margrit Stark		12
York House, Barcelona	1 mth	FT	130000 PTS	Jul, Sep	Min 20 yrs; 2 'A' levels or equiv	Montserrat Solé	Help with accomm	12

International Certificates

College	Course Title	Course length	Fees	FT/ PT	Start dates	Entry requirements	Contact	Comments	Max no of students
Australia									
University of Canberra	Grad Cert TESOL	5 mths	A$4,650	FT	Feb	6.5 FELIS or 550 TOEFL	Dr P A Denham		-
University of Queensland	Grad Cert	3 wks	A$1,750	FT	on appl	Degree or equiv	Dr Ron Holt		20
University of South Australia	Grad Cert TESOL	6 mths	A$5,500	FT PT	Jan July	4 yrs testiary	Anny Bye		
Chile									
Instituto Chileno-Britanico Santiago	Degree Course in TEFL	4 yrs		FT	Mar	Test & interview	Anthony Adams		20
Brazil									
International House, Goiania	ITTI Cert	1 mth		FT	Jul	Test & interview	Maria Brown	Intensive	15
Ireland									
Alpha College of English	TEFL	2 wks	£275	FT	All year	Advanced level of English	Patrick J. Shortt	For overseas teachers	10
Blue Feather School of Langs, Dublin	ATT Prelim Cert	2-3wks		FT PT	All year	Good standard of education	Gregory Rosenstock	Help with accomm	10
	ATT Intl Cert	106 hrs		FT PT	All year	Degree or equiv + 2 yrs exp	Gregory Rosenstock	Help with accomm	10
Centre of English Studies, Dublin	RELSA Prep Cert	4 wks 2 wks		FT PT	Jun, May	Degree or equiv; min age 20	Rosemary Quinn		15
Cork Language Centre	RELSA Prep Cert	2 wks 3 wks		FT PT	Mar, Jun Feb, Sep	Degree; Min age 20	Cathriona Coade	Job advice given	12
Dublin School of English	RELSA Prep Cert	70 hrs	IR£210	FT	All year	Degree or relevant exp	Brenda Whelan		21
Emerald Cultural Instiute, Dublin		3/4 wks	IR£250	PT	March	Degree or equiv	Eithne Kelly		15
English Language Education Centre, Co Kerry	RELSA Prep	2 wks 10 wks		FT PT	Apr Sep	Higher Ed; Min age 20; Good Eng	John Kennedy	Help with accomm	15
English Language Institute, Dublin	RELSA Prep Cert	2 wks	IR£250	FT	Mar, May, Sep	Degree pref	Louise Byrne		15
Galway Language Centre	TEFL Cert Course	4 wks	IR£225	PT	All year	Degree or equiv			12
International Study Centre, Dublin	RELSA Prep Cert	2 wks		FT	Througho year	Degree; Min age 21	Tim Connolly		12

College	Course Title	Course length	FT/PT	Start dates	Entry requirements	Contact	Comments	Max no. of students
Ireland								
Irish College of English, Dublin	ATT Prelim Cert	1 wk	FT PT	on appl	Uni entrance level; Min age 18	Francis Leavey	Summer work on completion	15
TEFL Training Inst, Dublin	ATT Prelim Cert	40 hrs	FT PT	All year	School level education	Angela Sweeney		10
	ATT Intl Cert	106 hrs	FT PT	Sep, Jan, Apr, Jul	Degree or equiv	Kevin McGinley	Incl teaching practice	12
University College Dublin	Cert TEFL	1 yr	PT	Aug	Degree or equiv; Native speakers only	Mary Ruane	Funding poss	18
University of Ulster	PGDip TEFL	9 mths	FT	Oct	Degree or Teaching Cert or equiv	Dr Pritchard	Incl 6 wks teaching in Hungary	18
Westlingua Language School, Galway	TEFL Teachers Training	70 hrs	FT	Jan, Apr, Jun	3rd level qual	Sandra Bunting		10
	RELSA Cert	70 hrs	PT	All year	3rd level qual	Sandra Bunting		10
Words Language Service, Dublin	ATT Prelim Cert	6 days 3 wks	FT PT	All year	University entrance level	Director	Career advice	10
	ATT Intl Cert	4 wks 18 wks	FT PT	Jun, Oct	Degree or equiv	Mary Butler	Career & accom help	8
Mexico								
Instituto Anglo-Mexicano de Cultura, Mexico	Initial Teacher Training Cert	3 mths	PT	All year		Paul Sellers		18
New Zealand								
Auckland College of Education	Cert TESOL	6 mths	PT	on appl	On appl	Roly Golding		-
Auckland Inst of Tech	Cert in Lang Teaching to Adults	1 yr/ 1 mth	on appl	on appl	No exp necessary	Clare Conway		20
Christchurch College of Education	Cert TESOL	varies	FT	on appl	On appl	Geoff Ormandy		-
Massey University Palmerston North	Cert Teaching of Second Language	1 yr 2yrs	FT PT	on appl	Teaching exp	Dept of Linguistic		
Victoria Univ. of Wellington	PG Dip in Teaching ESL	9 mths	FT	March	Degree + 2 years' exp	Helen Middleton		-
United States								
University of California, Riverside	Cert in TESOL	9 mths	FT PT	Jan, Feb, Mar, Jun, Aug	500-550 TOEFL score	Co-ordinator	$ 1725 pr qt	
Eastern Mennonite University, Harrisonburgh	Cert in TESOL	Four 3 wk	FT	May, Jun, Jul	Non native teachers	Ervie L Glick		
St Michael's College, Vermont	Inst in TESL	9 credits	FT	Jun	On appl	Dir of Studies		-
	Advanced Cert in TESL	18 credits	FT PT	Jan, Jun, Sep	On appl	Dir of Studies		-
School of Teaching EFL, Seatle	TESL/TEFL Cert	4 wks	FT	All yr	degree	Nancy Tulare		-
Transworld Teachers, San Francisco	TT Certificate	4 wks	FT PT	All year	On appl	Secretary		-

Overseas Trinity College Certificate in TESOL

College	Course length	FT/PT	Fees	Start dates	Contact	Comments
ECS, Abu Dhabi	4 wks	FT	7000 UAE Dirhams	Throughout year	Kate MacFarlane	Intensive; Incl Teaching Young Learner components
ECS, Dubai	4 wks / 22 wks	FT / PT	7000 UAE Dirhams	Throughout year	Charles Boyle	Intensive; Incl Teaching Young Learner components
Grafton Tuition, Dublin	4 wks / 6 mths	FT / PT	IR £625	Throughout year	Denis O'Donoghue	Help with accomm given; Careers advice; help with employment
Saxoncourt Teacher Training, Japan	TBA	TBA	TBA	TBA	Saxoncourt Teacher Training	First Trinity Cert run in Japan

RSA/Cambridge COTE

College	Course length	FT/PT	Fees	Start dates	Entry requirements	Contact	Comments	Max no. of students
American University in Cairo	14 wks	PT	on appl	Sep, Dec	Adult Educational experience	Magda Lawrence/ Christine Zaher		12
Bilkent University, Turkey	10 mths	FT	TBA	Sept	Teaching Qual or 300 hrs ELT	Simon Phipps	Practising EFL teachers	16
British Council, Lisbon	9 mths	PT	TBA	Oct	As per UCLES	Julie Tice		12
British Council, Mexico	1-2 yrs	PT DL	on appl	varied	Good English + 300 hrs exp			25
British Council, Thessaloniki	1 yr	PT	on appl	Oct	CPE + 300 hrs teaching exp	Camilla Ralls		16
Centro Anglo Paraguayo	9 mths	PT	US $600	Oct	Degree + 300 hrs teaching exp	Lorraine Jackson	Incl 1 mth intensive block	10
Eastern Mediterranean University, Turkey	1 yr	PT	on appl	Sep	Degree + 1 yr teaching exp	Edward Casassa	In-house & external candidates	20
ESADE, Barcelona	1 yr	PT	on appl	Oct	Degree + 300 hrs exp + CPE English	David Block		20
Instituto Anglo-Mexico	6 mths	PT	MP4,000	Oct	Degree + 300 hrs teaching exp	The Director	ITTC available Apr	14
Instituto Anglo-Mexicano de Cultura, Mexico	6 mths	PT	MP4,500	Oct	FCE English + 300 hrs teaching exp	Paul Sellers		20
Language Institute, Athens	3-5 mths	PT	on appl	Jan	Personal Interview	Clare O'Donoghue/ Jennifer Smith		15
International House, Goiania, Brazil	10 mths	PT	TBA	Aug	300 hrs teaching exp	Maria Brown		12
SPELT Pakistan	150 hrs	PT	PS 4000	Jun	Proficiency in English	Workshop co-ordinator		20

Introductory and correspondence courses

A good way to get an idea of what teaching EFL is all about without committing yourself to the time and expense of a full training course is to take an introductory or correspondence course.

Some UK centres offer introductory training courses linked to certificates that are also useful if you do not hold a degree.

Avoid companies that do not advertise a telephone number.

If you are unwilling or unable to commit yourself to the time and expense involved in the RSA/ Cambridge or Trinity College Certificates, but are keen to have some sort of training in EFL, there are a wide range of introductory courses on offer. Most of these courses are about one week long. As they are inevitably limited in what they can teach you in this time, they are not generally considered as sufficient to enable you to go straight in to the classroom, but they have provided plenty of teachers with their first jobs.

Many centres who offer such courses will help you find permanent jobs, even if their range of posts may be limited. Such courses are also useful if you are interested in vacation work. In the summer in the UK and Ireland there are hundreds of EFL jobs (see p55-6), and there are also plenty of vacancies in Australia and New Zealand in the Christmas period (their summer). Due to the demand for teachers during these periods, an introductory course certificate may be looked on as a good enough qualification.

It may also be worth doing an introductory course to see if you would be interested in moving on to a full training course. Some UK centres offer introductory training courses linked to certificates that are also useful if you do not hold a degree (usually required for the RSA Certificate) such as Marble Arch Teacher Training, which offers direct entry for successful students to their RSA/Cambridge course and Coventry Technical College does a one-week course, which counts as stage one of the Trinity College Certificate. Stage two must be done within a year. (See grid on following pages for details.)

Other courses inevitably vary in quality. Try to ensure that the courses have a balance between theory and practice and that you have practice with foreign students, not just peer groups, i.e. other trainee teachers. Some schools run classes in their own teaching method. For example, the Butler School of Languages offer the Butler Question Method. Teachers are trained in 'significant question techniques'. Butler School recruit from their course for their associate schools in Europe.

Distance learning/correspondence courses

Distance learning is becoming more and more popular, and courses are now available not only from EFL specialists, but distance training specialists, such as the National Extension College. Some of these are purely correspondence courses, others are a combination of self-study and a short intensive course, often a long weekend. If you are short of time or money, they may seem an attractive option, but choose the course carefully. Ask to speak to former students and avoid companies that do not advertise a telephone number and that operate from a PO Box or a business mailing address, rather than an actual school.

Courses that are totally by correspondence may seem very good value, but they are not recognised by some employers. Avoid them unless you already have teaching experience - learning to teach without having teaching practice is like learning to swim without going near water.

Despite these warnings, certain courses seem to be achieving their objective of providing worthwhile, convenient training at an affordable price, as has been shown by the The College of Preceptors' recent accreditation under Royal Charter of the distance learning courses administered by Eurolink in Sheffield and Language 2 Associates in London.

Another interesting development is the growth of courses that combine distance learning with a two-or three-day, intensive (often residential) course. These courses manage to cram an enormous number of training hours in to a short space of time, so you have to make sure that you have prepared very well. As with most courses, their quality is variable, but some programmes, such as those run by TEFL Training in Oxfordshire, are led by experienced teacher trainers, who certainly understand the business.

Taking in to account the time and money you have available, choose your course very carefully. Remember that the acid test of any vocational course is its success or failure in impressing prospective employers and securing a job for you.

Introductory Courses

College	Course Length	FT/PT	Fees	Starting Dates	Entry Requirements	Contact	Comments	Max no. of student
Aberdeen College	30 hrs	FT PT	£65	Sept, Jan, Jun	Native Speaker	Anne Bain		12
Abon Language School, Bristol	1 wk 10 wks	FT PT	£125	Throughout year		David Berrington Davies		10
Bedford CHE	11 wks	PT	£95	Jan, Apr	Degree pref	Ken Wilford	College Cert awarded	16
BEET Language Centre, Bournemouth	2 wks	FT	£575	June	Eng proficiency	Lindsay Ross	Interview	14
Brasshouse Centre, Birmingham	1 wk	FT	£110	Throughout year		Deborah Cobbett		15
University of Brighton	2 wks	PT	£205	Jan, Jun, Sep	Good Eng	Eric Tyrer		20
British Council, Singapore	5 wks	PT	S$581	Jan, Apr, Jul, Sep	Good Eng	Vickie Tang	To Pre-school Children/Adults Young Learners	18
CILC, Cheltenham	1 wk	FT	£195	Feb, May, Jul		Registration officer	Intensive & practical	15
Colchester Institute	1 wk 10 wks	FT PT	£90	Jan, Jun	None	Simon Haines		15
Coombe Cliff Centre, Croydon	4 wks 8 wks	PT	£40 £100	Oct, May	Interest in teaching EFL	Course Director		20
Devon School of English	1 wk	FT	£150	Throughout year	University entrance level	Joan Hawthorne		12
Dublin School of English	70 hrs	FT PT	IR£210	Throughout year	Degree or equiv	Breda Whelan		21
University of Essex	10 wks	FT	£1,185	Apr, Jun, Oct, Dec		Dilly Meyer		10
Frances King School of English	1 wk	FT	£149	Throughout year	Min age 18	Natalie Ivemy Sean Leahy	Suitable candidates CTEFLA	12
Godmer House School of English	1 wk	FT	£150	April, June	Degree pref	Course Director	Intensive	14
Goldsmith's College, London	1 yr	PT	on appl	Sept		Cont & Comm Education	Apply July latest	25
Greenhill College, Harrow	1 wk 5wks	FT	£150	Throughout year	A level, Native speaker	Sheila Tracy	Courses run on demand	16
Grove House, Dartford	1 wk 2 days + home	FT PT	£185 £165	Throughout year		Emma Higgins	Accomm avail	12
Harrow House, Swanage	1 wk	FT	£175	Throughout year		Gaynor Wells	Fully residential	8
Hilderstone College, Broadstairs	1 wk	FT	£185	Apr, Oct, Nov	Good education; Min age 20	Andy Caswell	Accomm avail	12

Introductory Courses

College	Course Length	FT/PT	Fees	Starting Dates	Entry Requirements	Contact	Comments	Max no. of students
inlingua, Cheltenham	2 wks	FT	£300	Apr, Jul, Aug	Degree or equiv	Dagmar Lewis	Poss posts abroad	10
Intl Language Institute, Leeds	1 wk	FT	On request	Throughout year		Steven Procter	Help with jobs & accom	10
International Training Network, Bournemouth	1 wk	FT PT	TBA	Throughout year	Good education; Min age 20	Mr D Pendle		12
The Language Project, Bristol	1 wk	FT	£120	Throughout year	None	The Language Project		10
Language Institute, Athens	2 mths	PT	£415	Feb, Sep	Interview	Clare O'Donoghue		15
Linguarama, Birmingham	1 wk	FT	Various	Throughout year	Degree	Manager/Director of Studies		-
University of Luton	1 wk ½ sem	FT PT	£95	Aug Oct	University entrance level	Vicky Vidal	Informal interview	20
Mancat Manchester	25 wks	PT	£195	Oct	Degree pref, interview	Judith Porter		20
Multi Lingua, Guildford	1 wk	FT	£215	Throughout year		Dr G Connolly		12
Pilgrims, Canterbury	1 wk	FT	£195	Throughout year	Interest in TEFL	Sam Preston	Practical & thorough	20
Polyglot Language Services, London	1 wk	FT	165	Feb, Jun		The Administrator		8
Saxoncourt, London	1 wk	FT	£135	May, June, Aug, Oct		Russell Yates	Also involved in recruitment	12
Skola Teacher Training, London	1 wk	FT	£175	Throughout year	Interview	Lyndel Sayle		15
Stevenson College, Edinburgh	4 wks	FT	£400	Aug, Sep	Degree or equiv	Sarah Woolard		12
University of Liverpool	6 wks 6 mths	FT PT	£950	Jan, Jul, Aug	1st Degree	Mike Scott	Equiv to RSA/Cam	12
Sandwell College	42 hrs	PT	£165	Throughout year	GCSE or equiv	Gill Gibbins		10
South Devon College	1 wk 10 wks	FT PT	£205	Sep, Jan, Mar		The Language Centre		12
Study Space, Thessalonica	2 wks 15 wks	FT PT	£250 £285	Feb, Oct	Level of English proficency	Christine Taylor		8
University of Sussex, Brighton	1 wk	FT	£95	Dec, Mar, Jun		Margaret Khidhayir		20
TEFL Training, London	w/end + selfstudy	FT DL	on appl	Throughout year		Randi Berild	Various locations in UK	18
Trythall English Centre	2 wks 10 wks	FT PT	£180 £120	July, Aug	Good basic education	John Trythall		12
Waltham Forest College	2 terms	PT	£500	Sep	Degree or equiv	Course Tutor		12

In-house training

Some organisations own chains of schools, and run their own short courses to prepare people to teach in them. Schools within the chain normally either run their own courses or recruit directly from courses run by their headquarters. If you do not have the time or money to study for a certificate, they may be a good route to your first teaching job.

Although there are universally accepted EFL teaching methods (see p13) a number of schools train their teachers in their own in-house method. This may be a disadvantage later if you want to find work outside that particular chain, but most are highly respected and a qualification from them should count in your favour. Here are some of the major chains:

BERLITZ (320+ schools worldwide)
This long-established chain has branches throughout the world and offers introductory courses in the Berlitz method. The courses are mainly for experienced or EFL-qualified teachers but they will consider people who have worked abroad, are language graduates or have skills in specialist fields, such as law or accountancy.

Courses last for one to two weeks and are only open to native English speakers. Berlitz have recently introduced CD-ROM facilities for use in their courses. If you work outside the UK, Berlitz may pay you a modest sum to see you through the course. Berlitz provide extra training courses for their teachers during working hours in skills such as Business English and English for Children, again using their own methods.

Contact **Berlitz International Inc.,** Research Park, 293 Wall Street, Princeton NJO8540 USA or **Berlitz School,** Wells House, 79 Wells Street, London WIA 3BZ. Written applications only.

GEOS
Geos Corporation provide teacher-training courses for native English speakers recruited as teachers for their schools in Japan.
Contact: **Geos Corporation,** PO Box 512, Ark Mori Building, 33rd Floor, 1-12-32 Akasaka, Minato-Ku, Tokyo 107, Japan.

Geos also run courses for non-native English speaker teachers in January in the UK.
Contact: **Geos English Academy,** Teacher Training Department, 55-61 Portland Road, Hove, Sussex BN3 5DQ. Tel: 01273 73975.

inlingua (250 schools worldwide)
inlingua adopts the direct method of teaching (see p182). Their in-house teacher training courses qualify teachers to work for inlingua schools. inlingua teach using their own specially designed coursebooks. The school prefers graduates of British or Irish nationality.
Contact: **inlingua Pedagogical Dept.,** UK Branch, Essex House, 27 Temple Street, Birmingham B2 5DB Tel: 0121 643 3472 or: **inlingua,** Weisenhausplatz 28, 3011 Berne, Switzerland.

LINGUARAMA (35+ school worldwide)
This international chain runs both intensive introductory teacher-training courses for non-experienced graduates and in-house training programmes for Linguarama teachers already employed. The one-week introductory courses are run monthly in Birmingham and Manchester and consist of 40 hours' theory and short teaching practice sessions. Linguarama frequently recruit teachers for their international school network from these courses. Only native English speakers are accepted.
Contact: **Linguarama,** Queen's House, 8 Queen Street, London EC4N ISP.

MULTILINGUA
Multilingua is part of the General Education Group, a teacher training and recruitment organisation, and provides its own introductory courses throughout the year. All courses can be attended on a full or part-time basis. Multilingua places teachers from its courses in schools across the world. Applicants do not need a degree or teaching experience, but must pass an aptitude test. In addition Multilingua provide courses for non-native English speakers and courses in teaching business English. All courses are run in the UK.
Contact: **Multilingua Administration Centre,** St. Michael's House, 53 Woodbridge Road, Guildford, Surrey GU1 4RF.

SALISBURY SCHOOL
Salisbury School recruits teachers for Sweden on behalf of the British Centre, run by Folk University in Stockholm. The British Centre recruit in January and September, and Salisbury School run free introductory EFL courses for successful candidates before they go to Sweden.
Contact: **The Salisbury School of English,** 36 Fowlers Road, Salisbury, Wiltshire SP1 2QU, UK. Tel: (01722) 331011.

A number of schools train their teachers in their own in-house method.

Multlingua places teachers from its courses in schools across the world.

'The Qualifications awarded by both Trinity and RSA Cambridge are recognised worldwide and ... are the ones students should focus interest on' **The Guardian.**

Trinity College *London*

Setting Standards...

Spoken English Examinations
EFL Teacher Qualifications

FOR STUDENTS OF ENGLISH

Graded Examinations in Spoken English for Speakers of Other Languages *(ESOL)*

- *An examination which offers Choice, Relevance and Flexibility*
- *The only examination which focuses **entirely** on Spoken English skills*
- *Available 'on demand' in the UK, Europe and worldwide*

FOR TEACHERS

Certificate in the Teaching of English to Speakers of Other Languages *(CERT TESOL)*

- ***First Choice** for many who are entering the profession*
- *A first qualification for those with little or no previous experience*
- *Qualifies the trainee to teach both adults and children*
- *Available to both native and non-native English speakers in the UK and elsewhere*
- *Courses available at over **70** validated centres in the UK and overseas*

Licentiate Diploma in the Teaching of English to Speakers of Other Languages *(LTCL TESOL)*

- *The **Advanced** professional qualification for those with at least two years' teaching experience*
- *Recognised by the British Council and by teaching institutions worldwide*
- *Courses offered include **Distance Learning Modules***

To: Jane Davey, Trinity College London, 16 Park Crescent, London W1N 4AP, UK *Telephone* 0171 323 2328. *Fax* 0171 323 5201

Please send syllabus and details of your:

- ☐ **Graded examinations in ESOL**
- ☐ **Certificate in TESOL**
- ☐ **LTCL TESOL Diploma**

I am a: ☐ Student ☐ Teacher

Name ....

Address ....

....

....

....

EFL Guide 95

Oxford House College

London W1

TRINITY COLLEGE CERTIFICATE IN TESOL COURSES

(for those with no previous experience of teaching English)

- Courses in London and Barcelona
- Full-time and part-time programmes
- Pre-course task
- Jobs counselling and placement
- One of Trinity College London's largest centres
- Over 800 trainees have qualified through us

TRINITY COLLEGE DIPLOMA IN TESOL COURSES

(for those with substantial experience of teaching English)

- Flexible distance-learning to prepare for written examination
- Short London block to prepare for practical examination
  OR take the practical in your own school
- Dedicated Diploma Coordinator to help you with any academic problems

For a brochure, please contact Teacher-training Dept, Oxford House College. 28 Market Place, London W1N 7AL

Tel 0171 580 9785 or Fax 0171 323 4582

Oxford House College teacher-training qualifications are validated/ examined by Trinity College London. Always take a validated course.

Oxford House is recognised by the British Council for the teaching of English as a Foreign Language.

Oxford House is a member of Arels, the Association of Recognised English Language Services.

Your First Class

You've got the job. It's Monday morning, your first class. Your class might be children, adult beginners, elementary or advanced. Here's some advice to help you get through your first hour.

The aim should be to encourage students to speak in English as much as possible.

Read the teacher's book

You can carbon date teachers by which teacher's book they learned to teach from. For teachers in the sixties, it was probably *First Things First* and *Kernel Lessons*; in the seventies, *Strategies*, and in the eighties; *Cambridge English Course* and *Headway*. The point is that all teachers, even if they have a certificate, find their feet in the classroom by following a teacher's book. So find a course book and read the teacher's notes before you start.

Learn their names

Learn your pupils' names and start using them. Use charts on your desk or United Nations style name cards propped up in front of the student - but learn them. After a couple of weeks it becomes embarrassing to ask a student's name and you may risk ignoring them as a result - to their detriment.

Get them talking

It's important for the class to talk, not you. Try and minimise TTT (Teacher Talking Time). Ask questions to elicit information rather than explaining at length. Ask questions that elicit short answers: 'yes, he did'/ 'no, he didn't', questions that elicit simple sentences: 'where do you work?', 'At the Post Office', and open questions: 'what are you doing?'.

The worst thing to do is to try and answer when you are unclear yourself.

As soon as possible get the class talking to each other. If the class are elementary level or thereabouts get them to work in pairs, finding out each other's names, nationality and maybe job, and get them to introduce their partner to you. You can initiate the process by writing clues on the board - name, country, town, job - and then by engaging one student in a dialogue as a model. For example:

What's your name?	My name's...
	I am...
Where are you from?	I'm from...
Where do you live?	I live in...
What's your job?	I'm a...(student)

Try to get students to practice talking to each other, preferably in small groups, as much as possible.

Find out what they know

By getting your class talking, you will know what their real level is (their ability to communicate may be well below or well above their test scores or their grammar level) and be able to identify their most common mistakes. Have a pad of paper by you to take notes.

Error correction

New teachers are unsure if they should stop students and correct them every time they make a mistake. The tendency now is to concentrate on fluency and only to correct mistakes that can be corrected without interrupting the speaker's train of thought. Make a note of major errors and come back to them when the student has stopped speaking or include a discussion of major grammatical errors as part of a special grammar presentation later on.

Translation?

There was a time when translation into the learner's mother tongue was anathema in the classroom. This view has changed. Most teachers now believe that all a learner's resources are important in helping them to learn a language and that translation is one of those resources. The aim should be to encourage students to speak in English as much as possible, but, if translation helps the teacher to briefly explain a word or concept, then translation should be used. In any event, try not to rely upon translation.

Answering questions

A source of terror for new teachers is being asked the meaning of a word, or the difference between two words or tenses, when you don't know the answer. The worst thing to do is to try and answer when you are unclear yourself. You'll end up talking too much and confusing the student. The best thing to do is to say you'll deal with the answer in the next class - and make sure that you do! Arm yourself with a couple of survival manuals, a good learner's dictionary - the *Longman Dictionary of Contemporary English*, the *Oxford Advanced Learners Dictionary* or the *Collins Cobuild Dictionary* - and a good grammar - *Practical English Usage*

(Oxford University Press) or *English Grammar in Use (Cambridge University Press)* and go to work.

Pronunciation

New teachers worry, 'Which accent shall I use?'. The answer is, if you are a native speaker of English, your own. It's the best model for the student. If you are not a native speaker of English, then your model is still the best for the students, but you may want to supplement it by using tapes of native speakers from ELT courses.

The stages of a lesson

Most lessons progress through stages - from controlled presentation and practice of language to spontaneous use of that language in the student's own situations.

The three stages are:
PRESENTATION IN SITUATION
(pre-presentation of key vocabulary and language patterns followed by comprehension of a short dialogue on tape or video or in the textbook)

CONTROLLED PRACTICE
(identification of key language to be learned, followed by repetition or drill practice, or practising and acting out the dialogue)

FREE STAGE
(students' own opportunity to use the new language through discussion, role-play, reading and writing)

Planning your lesson

For a 45 minute or one hour lesson you should always have a written plan to serve as an 'aide memoire', not only in case you get distracted, but also to help you pace the lesson and to make sure you cover the points you intended to make. Keep successful plans, as they can be the basis of new lessons later on.

A lesson plan should contain the following:
-the aim of the lesson
-the texts or aids you expect to use (reading comprehension, tape, video or objects)
-the key vocabulary you expect to teach
-key comprehension points and questions you need to ask
-the key practice activities you will carry out
-the free stage activities you will carry out

It's worth spending time on it as it will help you feel more confident in the classroom. For a one hour class, plan three to five activities. These may be different activities based on a single text or grammar point to provide better cohesion for the lesson.

Activities may include the following:

Lesson Plan

1 A warm up
Saying hello, learning people's names
2 Vocabulary work
Teach and practice
3 New Language
Presentation and practice of some new grammar through a text.
4 Free stage
Role playing similar dialogues, understanding information in an advertisement or notice, or writing a note to someone else in the class.
For example:
Hello, I'm Juan. I'm from Spain
Hello, I'm Fatima. I'm from Turkey.
5 Summary/Skills work
Taking students through examples of homework activity or a light-hearted game or song.

A game such as Hangman to revise vocabulary is a good idea.

Put the first letter of a word on the board and put dashes for the other letters
e.g. L _ _ _ _ _
The class suggest the other letters. If they are right, write in the appropriate space. If they are wrong, begin drawing a gallows, like this:-

Can the class guess the word before the man is hanged? They have ten guesses.
When the class have got the idea they can think of words and draw the hangman.

In Conclusion

Be friendly, smile, encourage your class (Say 'Good'!), don't criticise, keep eye contact (not too much, if they're Japanese), learn and use their names and you'll do fine. Have fun!!

For a 45 minute or one hour lesson you should always have a written plan to serve as an 'aide memoire'.

Keep successful plans, as they can be the basis of new lessons later on.

You want **flexibility?** You want **variety?**
You want it *now?* You want...
Photocopiable Resource Packs
from Heinemann
Ready when you are!

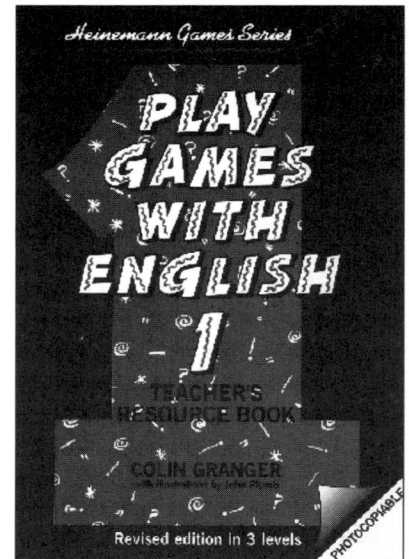

Book 1 Available now Book 2 May 1995

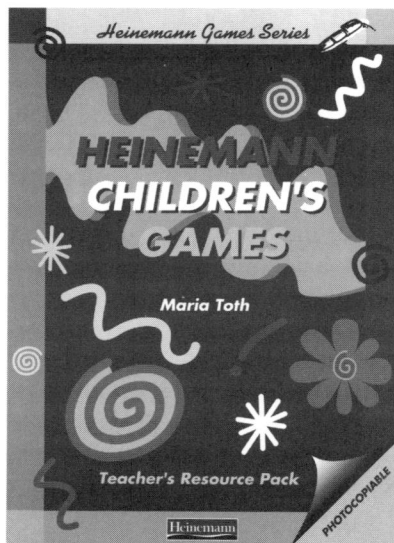

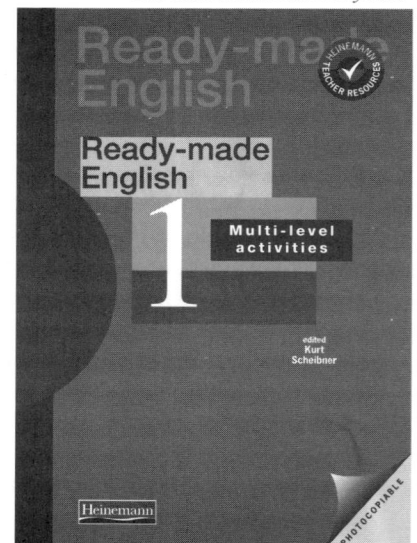

Don't forget our other best selling photocopiable titles
Word Games With English and *English Puzzles*
Watch for more new photocopiables coming throughout 1995

*For further information, please contact
Paul Zbihlyj, Heinemann ELT,
Halley Court, Jordan Hill, Oxford OX2 8EJ.
Tel: (01865) 314292 Fax: (01865) 314193*

Heinemann
ENGLISH LANGUAGE TEACHING

Teacher's Survival Kit

Once you have your job offer or have decided to pack your bags to look for an exciting job, the last expense you will need is extra books, so we asked Andy Cowle of Keltic International to compile a list of the essential teacher's books.

This list is a personal selection and we would like to stress that there are equally suitable alternatives.

The Practice of English Language Teaching (*Longman*)
Jeremy Harmer
£11.50
A complete guide to theory, techniques and materials for teaching EFL. Provides guidance in analysing student needs and developing approaches to presenting language for essential elements of lessons: grammar, vocabulary, skills and pronunciation.

Grammar Practice Activities (*CUP*)
A Practical Guide for Teachers
Penny Ur
£10.20
A collection of 200 activities practising a wide range of important grammar points for all levels, with lesson procedure and preparation explained in full. Includes a detailed introduction to grammar teaching in the EFL classroom and guidelines for designing additional activities.

Keep Talking (*CUP*)
Communicative Fluency Activities for Language Teaching
Friederike Klippel
£9.95
A practical guide to over 100 communication and role-play activities covering all levels. Provides notes on level, time, preparation, procedure and language aims of each activity. Accompanied by worksheets at the back of the book.

Learner-based Teaching (*OUP*)
Colin Campbell & Hann Kryszewska
£8.30
Contains over 70 adaptable activities (with variations) for all levels, and covers grammar, integrated skills, writing, translation, games and examination practice. Intended as a resource when no other materials are available.

1000 Pictures for Teachers to Copy - New Edition (*Nelson*)
Andrew Wright
£11.50
Invaluable resource of 1000 simple drawings for teachers to present or elicit language. Introduces basic techniques as well as ways of using pictures in the classroom. Covers basic vocabulary, verbs, adjectives, scenes, settings and sequences.

Teaching Tenses (*Nelson*)
Ideas for Presenting and Practising Tenses in English
Rosemary Aitken
£10.00
A resource book with ideas for presenting tenses and verb patterns. Analyses form and function of each tense, and includes a review of common errors and suggestions for presentation and practice of structures in context.

Additional Recommendations

A Source Book for TEFL (*Heinemann*) £11.00
Anti-Grammar Grammar Book (*Longman*) £9.90
Communication Games (*Nelson*) - Series - £13.00 each
Vocabulary Games & Activities for Teachers (*Penguin*) £17.50

KEY TO CERTIFICATE REFERENCE ADVERTISING

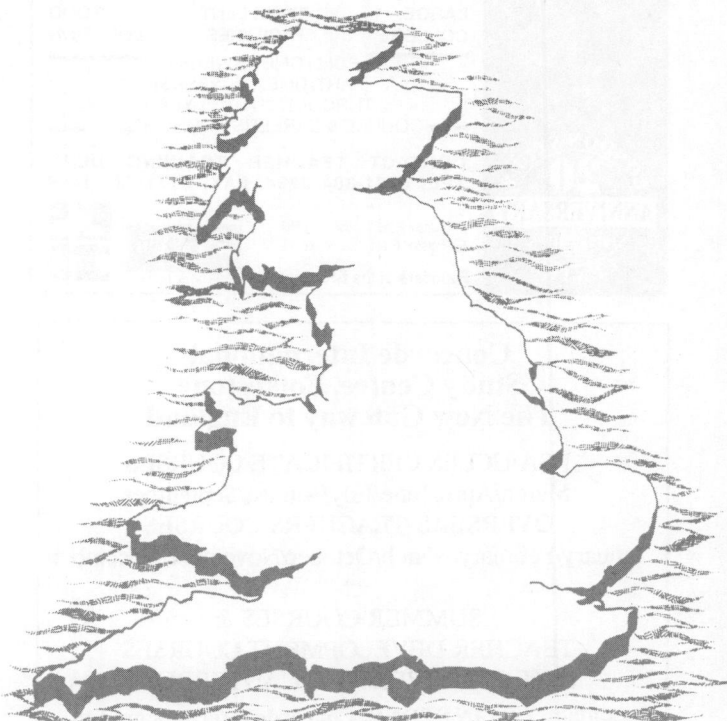

KEY TO OVERSEAS REFERENCE ADVERTISING

RELSA-Ireland - The Recognised English Language Schools Association Ireland introduced the Preparatory Certificate in Teaching English as a Foreign Language in 1992. This Certificate is the accepted short-term TEFL qualification in Ireland. Issued by RELSA, courses leading to the Certificate are offered at the undermentioned schools - the leading EFL institutions in Ireland. For details contact any of the following:

Alpha College of English
4 North Great Georges Street, Dublin 1
Telephone: 01-8747024, Fax: 01-8747031

Centre of English Studies
31 Dame Street, Dublin 2
Telephone: 01-6714233, Fax: 01-6714425

Cork Language Centre International
Wellington House, St Patrick's Place,
Wellington Road, Cork
Telephone: 021-551661, Fax: 021-551662

Dublin School of English
10-12 Westmoreland Street, Dublin 2
Telephone: 01-6773322, Fax: 01-6718451

Emerald Cultural Institute
10 Palmerston Park, Rathgar, Dublin 6
Telephone: 01-4973361 Fax: 01-4975008

English Language Education Institute
30, The Mall, Tralee, Co. Kerry
Telephone: 066-22552, Fax: 066-22368

English Language Institute
99 St. Stephen's Green, Dublin 2
Telephone: 01-4752965 Fax: 01-4752967

European Education Centre
Main Street, Templeogue, Dublin 6W
Telephone: 01-4900866 Fax: 01-4900871

Galway Language Centre
The Bridge Mills, Galway
Telephone: 091-66468, Fax: 091-64122

International Study Centre
67 Harcourt Street, Dublin 2
Telephone: 01-4782766, Fax:01-4781490

Language Centre of Ireland
45 Kildare Street, Dublin 2
Telephone: 01-6716266, Fax: 01-6716430

Westlingua Language Centre
Cathedral Building, Middle Street, Galway
Telephone: 091-68188, Fax: 091-63462

Note: Dial Codes are Int +353 +1(Dublin), 21(Cork), 91(Galway), 66(Tralee)

Finding a Job

The reason behind any training is to find a job, so this section shows you how to go about finding your first teaching job, summer job, volunteering job, going for promotion, alternatives to actual teaching and even setting up your own business. It will also give you an insight in to the ways that EFL is taught and how technology is affecting it.

How to find work

Newspapers, recruitment agencies and major employers

Newspapers

The following newspapers and newsletters regularly carry EFL, and ESP recruitment advertisements. (*available from most newsagents). See also local English language newspapers in Section Three.

Worldwide

EFL Gazette (monthly) - available for £1.50 (1 issue), £22-50-UK, £26-Europe, £30-Rest of the world (yearly subscription) from 10 Wrights Lane, London W8 6TA, UK, or from specialist bookshops in Britain.

Globetrotters, PO Box 741, Pwllheli, Gwynedd, LL53 6WA UK.

*The Guardian** (Tuesdays and Saturdays) - Education supplement (UK edition only) carries job advertisements.

Overseas Jobs Express (twice monthly) - available from PO Box 22, Brighton BNI 6HX.

*Times Educational Supplement** (Fridays).

TESOL Newsletter - available from TESOL.

*International Herald Tribune** (daily).

Ireland

*Irish Independent** (daily); *Irish Times** (daily).

Japan

The Language Teacher (monthly) - available from JALT

United Kingdom

ARELS bulletin will place free 'jobs wanted' ads and circulate them to member schools in the UK - write to Arels, 2 Pontypool Place, Valentine Place, London SE1 8QS. The Department of Employment's **Overseas Placing Unit** (OPU) has a list of vacancies in the EC, and can be contacted via any Jobcentre in the UK.

Jobshops

At the following conferences teachers are recruited:

Japan

Japanese Association of Language Teachers (**JALT**) have a job Information Centre with about 100 employers who give interviews to qualifying applicants.

USA

TESOL job shop. Contact TESOL, see p184-190

Recruitment agencies

Sending a CV to a recruitment agency may be better than approaching individual employers. Established agencies will let you know when opportunities arise. An EFL specialist agency will tell you exactly what you need to know about a particular vacancy and should offer an interview supplying all the information you will require. Since agencies generally charge employers a percentage of salary, it is in their interest that you earn as much as possible. See p184-191 for addresses unless listed below:

European Council of International Schools (ECIS). Recruit for Europe, Africa and the Far East. Mainly prefer teachers with specialist subjects to teach English in independent international schools.

English Worldwide. Recruit for Europe, the Middle East, the Far East and South America.

English and Spanish Studies (for Spain only).

Foreign Language Services. Recruit for Greece. Contact Alexis Pournatzis, Gounari 21-23, 262 21 Patras.

Central Bureau for Exchange arrange teaching exchanges in Europe. They also recruit for the Japan Exchange and Teaching (JET) scheme (see p12).

Hilderstone College. Recruit for Shumei secondary schools in Japan.

Language Matters, 4 Blenheim Road, Moseley, Birmingham B13 9TY, UK.

Nord Anglia International Ltd. Recruit for UK and abroad.

Saxoncourt (UK) Ltd, 59 South Molton Street, London W1Y 1HH. Recruit for Japan, the Far East and Europe, Eastern Europe, and Africa.

Teach Asia. Recruit for Asia and the Far East. Contact Jon Felperin, Workforce 2000 Associate, especially for vacancies in Korea and Japan, Tel/Fax: 415-585-3220. TeachAsia@AOL.com or 74204.3507@compuserve com., 55 Chumasero Drive, #9a, SanFrancisco, CA 94132, USA.

Teachers in Greece (for Greece only), Taxilou 79, Zographou, 15771 Athens, Greece.

Major employers

The following are major employers who have branches worldwide, and may be worth approaching for potential employment.

American Language Academy (USA).

ARA (UK- recruit for Middle East).

Berlitz International (USA). **Berlitz School** (UK).

Bell Educational Trust (UK - offer good conditions but prefer well-qualified teachers).

Benedict Schools (Switzerland).

British Aerospace (UK - recruit males for Saudi Arabia).

British Council (UK - for Commonwealth nationals only. Sometimes recruit locally, but well-qualified teachers are offered lucrative London contracts. Expect to be moved every three years.

Centre for British Teachers (UK - run projects in Europe, the Middle and Far East - primary and secondary EFL).

ELS International Inc (USA). **ILC Recruitment** (UK).

Inlingua (Switzerland and USA). Also **Inlingua Pedagogical Department,** UK Branch, Essex House, 27 Temple Street, Birmingham B2 5DB, UK.

International House, London (UK - have branches and affiliated schools around the world).

International Language Services (UK - for Sweden only).

Linguarama Ltd (UK).

Applications can also be made to the schools listed in the country classifications of **Section Three** (pages 67-112).

See **Keeping in Touch** (pages 180-181), **Summer Schools** (pages 55-56) and also **Volunteering** (page 59).

Working in the UK & Ireland

Job prospects, terms and conditions

The United Kingdom

Minimum salary: This varies considerably between areas - Oxford and Cambridge schools pay well while rates in London are relatively low. Try contacting three schools in the area you want to work to compare rates. You should get at least £8 per hour in the private sector; state colleges pay about twice that.

Tax and National Insurance: 25% plus 9% NI.

Visa requirements: EU nationals do not need a permit. Commonwealth citizens who have a grandparent with a British passport do not need a work permit, but need clearance first from their local British Embassy. Australians and New Zealanders under 26 can apply for a working holiday visa. Other Australians and New Zealanders as well as Americans and Canadians do not need a visa but must arrange a work permit before they enter the country. Your employer should help with this. Other nationals must apply for a visa at their local British Embassy.

Accommodation: £60-70 for a room in a shared flat in London and the south east, less elsewhere.

Other information: A certificate or a PGCE is usually considered the minimum requirement (see p13). There has always been a huge demand for teachers during the summer months when private language schools, colleges and, more recently, universities recruit for the annual influx of foreign students (see p55). Year round jobs are less frequent, with hundreds of qualified teachers returning from abroad competing for jobs, which has led to lower salaries. However, although it is hard for unqualified or newly qualified teachers to find well paid work in the UK, there is a demand for teachers with the RSA or Trinity Diploma (see p121). Non-British teachers with Qualified Teacher Status in their countries will find they can work in the primary or secondary system.

Most private school jobs involve teaching mixed nationality students of all levels, usually young adults. It is possible to teach English as a Second Language to immigrants.

There are also prospects for freelance and English for Specific Purposes teachers (see p144), some of whom can earn up to £20,000 per year. With the EU's Lingua programme and the growth of EFL in eastern Europe, there are also opportunities for teacher trainers. Geographically, London has the most language schools, but also the most competition for jobs and the highest cost of living. Oxford, Cambridge and the south coast towns also have a large EFL market, but the rest of England and Wales are becoming more popular for foreign students, so jobs are also more prevalent. Scotland is now promoting itself as an independent EFL destination. A consortium of Scottish schools and the British Council are pushing EFL in Scotland, especially in the Far East and Latin America.

State and private sector jobs in colleges and universities can be well paid, but competition for work remains fierce, with management positions being particularly scarce. If you want to progress in EFL as a career, you may increase your options if you work abroad.

There are also opportunities in the UK for spin off careers from EFL if you are an experienced teacher (see p61). For job sources in the UK see p54. For information about recognition schemes, designed to regulate the standards of schools and colleges, see p173.

Ireland

Minimum salary: Ir£8-10 per hour.

Tax and health insurance: 27% plus 7.75% social security. Be warned that if you stay for under 6 months you could be charged emergency tax after your first month - this could be up to 50%. Check with your employer.

Visa requirements: Your employer will arrange permits for non EU residents, but note that it is hard to get one unless you can convince them you are doing a job which can not be done by an EU citizen.

Accommodation: After the recent building boom in Ireland there is no shortage of accommodation. Expect to pay Ir£35-50 for a room in a shared house.

Other information: There has been a move to improve the image of language schools in Ireland after a proliferation of cowboy setups and a confusing array of teacher training certificates. For details on recognition schemes, see p173, and for recognised qualifications in Ireland, see p21. There are various staff associations and unions that teachers can approach, such as the National Association of Teachers of English as a Foreign Language in Ireland (NATEFLI). See p73 for a selection of schools in Ireland.

Students in Ireland have traditionally been southern Europeans, mostly attending courses in the summer months. Now that EFL is being more carefully regulated, however, Ireland is becoming popular for all nationalities throughout the year. Most language schools are in the Dublin area, but there has been a move to decentralise which has seen a growth in the number of schools in tourist areas such as Cork, Kerry, Limerick and Galway. Thanks also to an integrated marketing plan, which is now paying dividends, the future of EFL here looks promising. The Union of Students in Ireland (USI) arrange 9-month exchange programmes for teachers from the USA, for which no work permit is needed.

Summer Schools

There are plenty of seasonal opportunities for EFL teachers in the school holidays.

As students have the time to travel and study English during their long summer holidays, schools put on special courses. There is a boom in July and August especially in the UK, Ireland and Canada, when the European schools are on holiday. In Australia and New Zealand the busy time is between December and March, when schools in Japan and the Far East are on holiday.

Established language schools run summer courses, as do colleges and universities, but EFL agents and teachers may hire out public buildings to run their own seasonal summer school. With so many courses being run, staff are in huge demand but salaries are not that good. Often courses are split into half a day of language learning and half a day of recreation - perhaps sightseeing trips or sports activities - so courses need people to be lively administrators as well as competent language teachers.

In Britain there are courses combining English with just about everything, from horse riding to sailing. In Australia and New Zealand it is also possible to combine teaching English with activity holidays, including sports like scuba diving and even bungee jumping. So if you have any experience in such activities you may be in demand.

Summer school contracts usually run for one to two months. As with any job in EFL, some sort of TEFL qualification will ensure you get a better-paid job. Experienced teachers may also be able to become course directors or Directors of Studies. In Britain, state sector colleges and, increasingly, universities also run summer courses. Pay tends to be quite high - up to £18 per hour in some colleges. Teachers on pre-sessional courses who teach English for Academic Purposes to students going on to study at British universities should expect £250 a week, plus accommodation and all meals.

Summer courses are traditionally where newly qualified teachers have their first classroom experience. Demand for teachers is so high that unqualified people have a good chance of being taken on. The courses are usually quite intensive and cater for multinational students. If you are interested in finding out more about teaching summer courses, read *Teaching English on Holiday Courses* by Nick Dawson, part of Longman's Handbook for Teachers series. Many schools prefer teachers with primary rather than TEFL experience, as some summer courses are for young learners.

Unfortunately summer schools in Britain have often had a bad press, with stories of exploitative agents employing inexperienced teachers on inadequate premises. There has been a move to crack down on such operations, but one result of this has been to push students away from the established centres, such as the south coast of England, to the north of England, Ireland and Scotland. Students have found such areas less crowded, cheaper and friendlier. Prospective teachers can thus find potential employment throughout the British Isles. Pay conditions still vary considerably, with Cambridge reportedly commanding the top rates. London has too many teachers available to pay well and has the highest cost of living.

Some schools offer full board and accommodation on residential summer courses, which is valuable for teachers returning from abroad for the summer, but they may pay badly and you may be expected to look after the students outside class hours.

Tips for would-be summer school teachers:
- Apply early. Christmas is a good time to get an interview and secure a place at a favoured school.
- Check salary rates. Telephone a number of centres in your chosen area to get an average. Around £7 an hour should be the minimum with extra for social activities.
- Look for professionalism during the interview.
- Be prepared for a lot of hard work - often you will be living, eating and socialising with your students for the duration of the course.
- Make sure the school includes a proper training day.
- Teachers should check pay, tax and insurance conditions, especially if the school is less well-known.

Some UK schools offer full board and accommodation in residential summer schools, which is valuable for teachers returning from abroad for the summer, but they may offer very low salaries and you may be expected to look after the students outside class hours.

UK SUMMER SCHOOLS DIRECTORY
(R = recognised)

Abon Language School (R) 25, St John's Road, Clifton, Bristol BS8 2HD. Tel: (01179) 730354.
Anglo Continental (R), 33 Wimborne Road, Bournemouth. Tel: (01202) 557414, ext 213.
Anglolang (R), 20 Avenue Road, Scarborough, N Yorkshire. Tel: (01723) 367141. Fax (01723) 378698.
AST School of English (R), Perth Aerodrome, Scone PH2 6NP, Scotland. Tel: (01738) 52311 Ext 241.
Bedford Study Centre (R), 95/96 Midland Road, Bedford MK40 1QE. Tel: (01234) 36-4161.
Bell Educational Trust (R), 1 Red Cross Lane, Cambridge CB2 2QX. Tel: (01223) 247242.
Berkeley School of English 43/45 Queens Road,

Clifton, Bristol. Tel: (01179) 290604.

Bournemouth Teaching Service, 139 Charminger Road, Bournemouth. Tel: (01202) 521355.

Brighton and Hove School of English (R), 7-9 Wilbury Villas. Hove, East Sussex. BN3 6GB. Tel: (01273) 738182.

Buckswood Grange (R), Uckfield, East Sussex TN22 3PU. Tel: (01825) 761666.

Cambridge Academy of English (R), 65 High Street, Girton, Cambs CB3 OQD. Tel: (01223) 277230.

The Cambridge School of English (R), 8 Herbrand Street, London WCIN IHZ. Tel: 0171 734 4203.

Channel School of English (R), Bicclescombe Park, Ilfracombe, Devon, EX34 8JN. Tel: (01271) 862834.

Churchill House (R), 40-42, Spencer Square, Ramsgate, Kent CT11 9LD. Tel: 01843 593630.

Clark's International Summer Schools (R), 28 Craiglockhart Drive South, Edinburgh EH14 IHZ. Tel: (0131) 443 3298.

Concord College (R), Acton Burnell Hall, Shrewsbury, Shrops SY5 7PF. Tel: (016944) 631.

Concorde International (R), Arnett House, Hawks Lane, Canterbury, Kent CT1 2NU. Tel: 01227 451035.

Devon English Centre (R), 1 Victoria Rd, Exmouth EX8 IDL. Tel: (01395) 265068.

Eastbourne School of English (R), 8 Trinity Trees, Eastbourne BN21 3LD. Tel: (01323) 721759.

Edinburgh School of English (R), 271 Canon Gate, The Royal Mile, Edinburgh EH8 8BQ. Tel: (0131) 5579200.

Edinburgh Tutorial College (R), 29 Chester St, Edinburgh EH3 7EN. Tel: (0131) 225 9888.

EF International School of English (R), 1/2 Sussex Square, Brighton BN2 IFJ. Tel: (01273) 571780.

ELCO (R), Lowlands, Chorleywood Road, Rickmansworth, Hertfordshire. Tel: 01923 776731.

ELS (R), 3 Muirfield Crescent, Mill Harbour, London E14 9SZ. Tel: 0171 512 0600.

English and Cultural Studies Centres (ECSC) (R), 40 Village Rd, Enfield, Middx EN1 2EN. Tel: (0181) 360 4118.

English in Chester (R), 9\11 Stanley Place, Chester, CH1 2LU. Tel: (01244) 318913/314457.

English Language Centre (R), 44 Pembroke Road, Bristol, BS8 3DT. Tel: (01179) 737216.

English Language Systems (R), The Old Rectory, Church Lane North, Old Whittington, Chesterfield, Derbyshire S41 9QY. Tel: (01246) 450503.

Essex House School of English (R), 4 Church Road, Clacton-on-Sea, C015 6AG, Essex. Tel: (01255) 423465.

Euro-Academy Ltd (R), 77a George St, Croydon, Surrey CRO 1LD. Tel: (0181) 681 2905.

Eurocentre Brighton (R), Huntingdon House, 20 North Street, Brighton BNl 1EB. Tel: (0273) 24545.

Eurocentre Lee Green (R), 21 Meadowcourt Road, London SE3 9EU. Tel: (0181) 318 5633.

Frances King School of English (R), 3 Queensberry Place, South Kensington SW7 2DL. Tel: (0171) 584 6411.

Functional English (R), 5 Chubb Hill, Whitby, N Yorks Y021 1JU. Tel. (0947) 603933.

Greenwich School of English (R), 2/3 Turnpin Lane, London SE10 9JA. Tel: (0181) 305 0370.

The Greylands School of English Ltd (R), 315 Portswood

Road, Soton, S02 ILD. Tel: (01703) 550633.

Harrow School of English, 4 Gosling Close, Mill Green, Lyme Regis, Dorset, DT7 3PH. Tel: (012874) 3042.

Harven School of English (R), The Mascot, Coley Ave, Woking, Surrey GU22 7BT. Tel: (01483) 770969.

Hastings English Language Centre (R), St Helens Park Rd, Hastings, Sussex TN34 2JW. Tel: (01424) 437048.

House of English (R), 24 Portland Place, Brighton BN2 lDG. Tel: (01273) 694618.

Hurtwood House School (R), Holmbury St Mary, Dorking, Surrey RH5 6NU. Tel: (01483) 277416,

International Community School (R), 10 York Terrace East, Regents Park, London NW1. Tel: (0171) 935-1206.

International Homestays Programmes Ltd, 37 Park Road, Bromley, Kent BR1 3HJ. Tel: (0171) 464 6925.

International House, Hastings (R), White Rock, Hastings, Sussex TN34 1JY. Tel: (01424) 720100.

International Language Institute (R), County House, Vicar Lane, Leeds LS1 7JH. Tel: (01132) 428893.

The International School (R), 1 Mount Radford Crescent, Exeter EX2 4EW. Tel: (01392) 54102.

ISCA School of English (R), PO Box 15, 4 Mt Radford Crescent, Exeter, Devon, EX2 4JN. Tel: (01392) 55342.

ITS English School (R), 44, Cambridge Gardens, Hastings, East Sussex TN34 1EN. Tel: (01424) 438025.

Kent School of English (R), 3 Cranville Road, Broadstairs, Kent. Tel: (01843) 868207.

King's School of English (R), 25 Beckenham Road, Beckenham, Kent BR3 4PR. Tel: (0181) 650 5891.

Lake School of English (R), 14B Park End Street, Oxford OX1 lHW. Tel: (01865) 724312.

LTC International College of English (R), Compton Park, Compton Place Rd, Eastboume, Sussex BN21 1EH. Tel: (01323) 727755.

Mayfield College of English (R), 24 Holland Road, Hove, Sussex BN3 1JJ. Tel: (01273) 779231.

OISE (R), Youth Language Centres, 1 King's Meadow, Ferry Hinksey Road, Oxford OX2 ODP. Tel: (01865) 792702.

The Oxford Academy (R), 18 Bardwell Road, Oxford OX2 6SP. Tel: (01865) 512174.

Oxford Study Centre Ltd (R), 17 Sunderland Ave, Oxford OX2 8DT. Tel: (01865) 515243.

Penzance Language School, 21 Regents Square, Penzance PRI8 4BG. Tel: (01736) 67760/68520.

Pilgrims Language Courses (R), 8 Vernon Place, Canterbury, Kent. CT1 3HG. Tel: (01227) 762111.

Regent Summer Schools (R), 3rd Floor, 19-23 Oxford Street, London WIR IRF. Tel: (0171) 734 1137.

RLC International, 27-28 George Street, Richmond TW9 1HY. Tel: (0181) 948 3333.

Richmond School of English, 6 & 8 Oxford Rd, Moseley, Birmingham B13 9EH. Tel: (0121) 449 7748.

St Godric's College (R), 2 Arkwright Rd, London NW3.

Swandean School of English (R), 7 Oxford Rd, Worthing, W. Sussex BNll 1XG. Tel: (01903) 31330.

Woking and Chertsey Adult Education Institute, Danesfield Centre, Grange Road, Woking, Surrey. Tel: (01483) 721425.

Yorkshire International School, 12l St Helens Gardens, Leeds LSI6 8BT. Tel: (01132) 611603.

Working in North America

Job prospects and conditions in the USA and Canada.

USA

Minimum salary: This inevitably varies from state to state, but expect around $20-50 per hour in the state sector and as little as $10-25 per hour in private language schools. There is also a distinction between publicly funded institutions, and public institutes. Community colleges pay quite well and offer full benefits for as little as ten teaching hours. Other public universities have extension programs which are economically self-sufficient and thus pay a more competitive wage; benefits are sometimes included.

Tax and health insurance: Based on total income, ranging from 15-38% for federal taxes alone. Many states also charge an income tax which can be as high as 11% (California). Social security taxes are about 8.5%. Private health insurance is almost always provided free or with a small co-payment in the public and private sectors for full-time instructors. The problem is that fewer and fewer jobs are full-time. Public K-12 schools always provide full benefits.

Visa requirements: You should have a green card of permanent residence or a work permit, although it is often possible to work while on a student or cultural visa. There are two types of visa. The J1 visa is for 'Researchers, Teachers and Professors'. Obtaining it is a lengthy process; you must contact the head of a school, who will give you a form to return to the Foreign Student Department - who in turn will tell you which consulate to approach for the J1 visa. The H1B (working) visa can only be obtained if you are sponsored by a US company, and it is processed by the Immigration and Naturalisation service, as well as the Department of Labour.

Accommodation: From $500-600 per month in Manhattan to below $350 in rural areas. Allow around $30 per month for bills.

Other information: There is a huge number of immigrants in the United States who need to learn English. Although qualified US citizens should have no problem gaining employment, for non-Americans it is harder to get employment teaching EFL/ESL. You do not need to be a citizen to work in a public school and emergency credentials or alternative credentialing programs are available in many states. As well as the differences in language, the RSA and Trinity certificate qualifications are not very widely recognised, though many employers will treat the diploma as equivalent to an MA (see p121). It is unwise to try to work illegally, as there are stiff financial penalties for employers.

Education is decentralised, so conditions vary from state to state. There is no accrediting agency specifically for ESL programs, although in some states, programs must meet certain requirements. There are state sector teaching possibilities in public schools where ESL is taught from kindergarten to twelfth grade. Jobs tend to be well paid and secure, but you need to be certified as a teacher from a training establishment within the state you wish to work. There are many community-based organizations that hire ESL teachers for VESL programs. Public adult education programs hire people who can qualify to teach ESL: a BA/BS and relevant experience or training, including RSA type schemes, qualify one for a position. Unqualified teachers may also be used. The Amnesty Program was set up for immigrants in order to improve their standard of English, so that they could qualify for citizenship. Amnesty is offered if they attend an English language class - so the numbers attending such courses are enormous.

Many trade schools or semiprofessional training schools and programs are also hiring ESL/EFL teachers these days to meet the increasing demand for foreign students who wish to enter programs designed for native English speakers. In all cases, neither credentials nor MAs are required and the pay is $20-$30 per teaching hour.

Canada

Minimum salary. Canadian $20/hour in the private sector, and about $35/hour in state schools.

Tax and health insurance: The federal government and the local province income tax averages at 30%. Health care is free for residents in most provinces. There are insurance plans for those not covered by public schemes.

Visa requirements: Unless you emigrate, it is very hard for non-residents of Canada to obtain a work permit. Under immigration laws, you must demonstrate that you are more suitable than Canadian candidates for any prospective jobs. As there are so many highly qualified teachers in Canada, this rarely happens.

Accommodation: This is easy to find, although it can be expensive in Toronto and Vancouver.

Other information: If you do get a work permit, the standard of living in Canada is high. As a result of Canada's official bilingualism and its strongly multicultural character, teaching English as a Second Language (ESL) is a huge industry. Canada's open immigration policies are accompanied by publicly funded intensive ESL training for immigrants for up to six months, resulting in a huge demand for ESL teachers in the larger cities.

Conditions vary from province to province. ESL training takes place mainly in post-secondary colleges and adult education departments. State schools also teach ESL, and tend to offer the highest salaries. Many universities also offer ESL and advanced English for Academic Purposes (EAP) courses. The federal and provincial governments offer in-house ESL training for francophone employees.

The Council of Second Language Programmes in Canada runs courses all year. For information on teaching on these programmes, contact **Council of Second Language Programmes in. Canada, 151 Slater Street, Ottawa, Ontario, Canada KlP 5Nl.**

Working in Australia/NZ

Job prospects, terms and conditions in Australia.

Australia

Minimum salary: A national award negotiated by the Independent Education Union of Australia covers salaries for those teaching English Language Intensive Courses for Overseas Students (ELICOS See p183-189) in private schools. Rates of pay are scaled according to qualifications and experience, and a full-time salary for a teacher with minimum qualifications for ELICOS is A$27,738. The casual rate ranges from A$127 to A$179. These rates include a loading for preparation time and sick leave. University ELICOS centres are covered by the award conditions of their staff association. Salaries for Directors of Studies are not covered by an award and vary from school to school, ranging between A$40,000 and A$50,000 a year.

Tax and Health insurance: Tax rates for those with a tax file number average 30%. If there is no tax file number, the percentage of tax increases to the marginal rate of 48%. If you have an overseas student visa, you will be required to take out Overseas Student Health Cover, and payments for a single person are as follows:

3 month A$ 63   9 months A$179
6 months A$126   12 months A$231

Permanent residents and those on working holiday visas will have a levy deducted from their pay as a contribution to the government's Medicare health plan.

Visa Requirements: In order to work in Australia, you need either resident status, a working holiday visa or a full time overseas student visa, which allows you to work up to 20 hours per week. Permanent residents are assessed for immigration on a points system, and part of the assessment is based on whether the profession is 'needed'. EFL teaching is not at present a 'needed' occupation among immigrants and so does not earn any points on the assessment.

It is relatively easy for British teachers to obtain a working holiday visa which is valid for a year. In order to obtain a work permit you should be between 18 and 26 years of age, and the visa allows you to work for each employer for up to three months. Because of the restriction on the period of work, it is relatively unusual for teachers on working holiday visas to gain employment in public sector ESL programs, and if they do it is usually as casual relief teachers. However, it is possible to obtain work in the ELICOS sector and on study tours, which cater for tourists who wish to combine English language studies with their holiday (See page 23).

Accommodation: Costs are considerably higher in Sydney than in other cities. A room in a shared flat will cost around A$90-110 per week in Sydney, and accommodation is plentiful. In other capital cities it varies, but is likely to be about A$60-70 per week.

Other information: Australia's TESOL Industry is divided into two sectors: the ESL sector, which provides government-funded courses for permanent residents of non-English speaking backgrounds, and the private EFL sector. Permanent residents have access to English courses provided by the Adult Migrant Education program in each state and the Department of Technical and Further Education (TAFE). Teachers in the Adult Migrant Education Services have union representation through the Teachers Federation, and are covered by an award. The policy on minimum qualifications is similar to that required in the private EFL sector (see p23).

ELICOS teachers can be employed on a casual hourly basis for relief work and for short periods of time; for teachers employed for more than 4 and less than 40 weeks the award states that they must have what is termed a sessional contract. This provides some continuity of employment, and includes some provision for sick leave and recreation leave.

Teachers who already have postgraduate qualifications in TESOL or linguistics and who have a minimum of 5 years experience with adult TESOL may be eligible for a position as senior teacher or Director of Studies. These positions are not plentiful and most schools will give preference to those with local experience. If you have an overseas qualification and intend to apply for teaching or Director of Studies positions, it is advisable to have your qualification formally assessed for equivalence. This can be done through the National Office of Overseas Skills Recognition, Commonwealth Department of Employment, Education and Training (Tel: 06-276 8111, Fax: 06-276 7636).

New Zealand

Minimum salary: NZ$20-27.50 per hour, NZ$25,100 per year.
Tax and health insurance: 24%, rising to 33% on earnings over NZ$33,000. An accident compensation levy is paid by employees and employers. All visitors require private health insurance.

Visa requirements: No work permit required by Australian citizens. People under 27 of other nationalities can obtain a working holiday visa from their local New Zealand embassy. If you are over 27, you must have a letter of employment before applying for a work visa, which will only be issued if New Zealanders are not available to do the work. This can be done within the country. Temporary work permits are available for teachers with exceptional qualifications/experience. Well qualified teachers might find emigration to be their best route.
Accommodation: NZ$80-100 for a shared flat in Auckland. NZ$60 for Christchurch. Teachers are expected to find their own accommodation, but this is not usually a problem
Other information: Since 1990 the value of export education in NZ has risen fourfold. Qualified teachers are in great demand, and most vacancies arise in February-May and July-August. Auckland tends to be the best place to find work. State schools may have vacancies to teach (ESL). Polytechnics run well-paid ESL and/or EAP programs. Food is very cheap, general living costs are lower than in Europe.

Volunteering

Voluntary and aid organisations - working in the developing world

There are various organisations that recruit people to work as English teachers overseas, often in the developing world. Most developing countries are realising the importance of using experienced and qualified volunteers for their needs, and the days when people could simply take off for a year's adventure with most voluntary organisations have gone.

Today volunteers' average age is 30. Most organisations prefer to recruit teachers with at least two years' experience. Graduates have sometimes found that two years' experience volunteering has revitalised their career, with head teachers keen to take them on in the state sector when they return. The British Council are sometimes interested in former volunteers, and OXFAM and the ODA (who fund VSO) often recruit people who have worked in the developing world. Volunteering is also a way into teacher training and materials development. If you are interested in volunteering, contact the following organisations (addresses p190-196).

Voluntary Service Overseas (VSO)

VSO have over 1500 volunteers operating in 50 developing countries, but only recruit British and Irish teachers. They have an acute shortage of volunteers for 1995, especially for China, the Solomon Islands and Eritrea. VSO usually offer two-year contracts, and volunteers can choose which area of the world they would like to work in. Furnished accommodation should be provided, along with medical and insurance cover and paid national insurance contributions. Airfares will also be paid - but usually only at the beginning and end of your contract. In between expect to pay for your own flights. Salaries are at local rates, so your living standard will not be high. As a volunteer, you do not have many rights or benefits, and only those committed to their work helping a particular country are advised to go.

VSO has English teachers in: Cambodia, China, Dominican Republic, Guinea-Bissau, Hong Kong, Indonesia, Laos, Mongolia, Namibia, Pakistan, Sri Lanka, St Vincent and the Grenadines and Vietnam. Contact VSO for other destinations.

United Nations Volunteers (UNV)

VSO recruit and sponsor volunteers to work through the United Nations multinational programme, the UNV. Work tends to be specialised, but allowances are larger and UNVs may be posted with their spouse and up to two children.

East European Partnership (EEP)

EEP is a branch of VSO, set up to contribute to the development of Eastern European countries. They are particularly interested in recruiting child carers and ELT/secondary level teachers for their projects in Albania, Bulgaria, the Czech and Slovakian Republics, Hungary, Poland and Romania. A TEFL qualification is preferred for their teacher training projects and teachers with specialist knowledge are in demand to teach English for Specific Purposes (ESP). As with VSO, EEP volunteers are paid a local salary, but are provided with accommodation and free medical services. Posts are for one to two years.

Peace corps

Peace corps volunteers are particularly active in Eastern Europe. Returning volunteers are now offered state teaching jobs in the USA while they study for MEds.

WorldTeach

WorldTeach is a programme of Harvard University's social service organisation in America, and they have operations in Africa, Asia, Central America and Eastern Europe. Most volunteers teach EFL on a one-year contract. Volunteers do not need any qualifications except a degree. Volunteers pay a fee of around $3000 to cover insurance, airfares and support services. They are then paid a local salary, and get free accommodation.

Useful organisations

If you want to talk to former volunteers, there are various recruiting agencies who will put you in contact with those in your area. **Returned Volunteer Action** (RVA) have an information pack, *Thinking about Volunteering?*, and also run 'Questioning Development Days' when you can meet former volunteers. Contact: **Returned Volunteer Action** (RVA), Amwell Street, London EC1R IUL.

Other voluntary organisations

Catholic Institute of International Relations, 22 Coleman Fields, London NI 1UL, UK.
Designers for Development Ltd., Campden Hill, Ilmington, Shipston-on-Stour, Warwickshire CV36 4JF UK. Fax: 01608 82643. (Min. 3 month contracts in Vietnam).
Skillshare Africa, 3 Belvoir Street. Leicester LE1 6SL UK. Tel: 01533 540517.

Graduates have sometimes found that two years' experience volunteering has revitalised their career.

OXFAM and the ODA often recruit people who have worked in the developing world.

Developing a new career

Working as an EFL teacher can lead to many other job opportunities. Here are some ways of using your valuable experience.

If you are feeling jaded with teaching, there are opportunities for moving up in the EFL world, as well as using your experience to secure managerial positions in training and personnel departments of companies far removed from EFL.

Management

The traditional route for advancement in EFL is by going into school management. As teachers become more senior, they are given special responsibility for certain areas, and they may be made Assistant Director of Studies, Director of Studies and finally Principal. If a teacher stays abroad, he or she could become Director of Studies within four years. In anglophone countries competition will make such a move slower, but, in comparison to other industries, promotion to management in EFL tends to be rapid. It can therefore provide a useful springboard to management in other sectors. The communication skills gained within EFL are now recognised by recruiters in all sectors as a positive asset.

The communication skills gained within EFL are now recognised by recruiters in all sectors as a positive asset.

As the EFL industry becomes increasingly professional, management skills are becoming more sought-after. The sort of problems a Principal or Director of Studies finds him or herself dealing with range from declining enrolments, to staff pay increase demands. These are not usually areas covered on an academic course. In order to combat this, some TEFL- or Linguistics-orientated Master of Arts degrees (MAs) are now introducing a management component (see Section Four). Another alternative is for EFL teachers to take the Masters Degree in Business Administration (MBA).

IATEFL (The International Association of Teachers of English as a Foreign Language) has a Special Interest Group which produces newsletters and sets up conferences to share information about management. Members are usually in middle management, but for those interested in making the move into management, the service shows what possibilities are available. For more information contact: Sue Leather, The IATEFL Management Special Interest Group (see p181).

There is a great demand for teacher trainers, especially in eastern Europe.

Lecturing

It is possible to use your TEFL experience to become a university or college lecturer in a related field. This can be a rewarding move, but competition for posts is fierce.

Jobs tend to be available to younger people with a Ph.D and EFL experience, or to older people with considerable practical experience, probably at a high level in a college.

Getting into lecturing can be a question of chance, so carefully consider what sort of person they are looking for. For example, a university may want a lecturer with specialist experience in teaching children. A candidate with this experience who also shows strong academic potential and initiative, has a better chance of getting the job. Writing articles on the specialist subject for an educational journal could help to prove that you have this potential.

It may be easier to get your first lecturing post in a non-anglophone country. Often a college that requires a Ph.D from a local candidate may accept a Masters from a native English speaking candidate.

Teacher training

Teacher trainers are in great demand, especially in eastern Europe, and particularly in the growing area of primary English. Make sure that you are really interested in teacher training before you make a commitment, and be aware that it is a stressful occupation. Try to talk to teacher trainers for advice before making your decision.

The advantages, however, include the potential for moving into quasi-management, as an in-service trainer or Head Teacher, for example. The post also offers you the opportunity to travel widely, to attend workshops and conferences, and perhaps to have your articles published in educational journals.

Teacher trainers should have a good deal of teaching experience with all levels and nationalities. If you are prepared to advise other teachers, you need to have experienced anything they are likely to encounter. To prepare yourself, read *The Teacher Trainer, A practical journal for Modern Language teacher training*, (available from Pilgrims); the CUP series on Teacher Training and Development by Adrian Doff, Tessa Woodward and Michael Wallace; or the IATEFL Special Interest Group for Teacher Training newsletter (see p181 for addresses).

In the UK there are several courses in Teacher Training (see p148-149 for details).

Spin-off Careers

Teaching EFL can lead to many other related careers.

Few EFL teachers switch careers overnight. They usually begin by freelancing in a related field while still teaching, before they make the break. If you are interested in broadening your career outlook within EFL, you could consider the following options.

Becoming an examiner
Marking exam papers can provide a welcome income supplement for teachers especially during the school holidays. Suitably qualified teachers may become a marking or setting examiners for one of the EFL examining boards. Pitman Examinations Institute, UCLES, Trinity College London and the University of Oxford Delegacy welcome applications from experienced EFL teachers.

Working as an Agent
Many EFL teachers who represent schools as a sideline find it so rewarding that they decide to pursue it as a career. EFL teachers have direct access to the students that schools in anglophone countries are trying to target, so they are ideally placed to act as agents.

Start by writing to schools which advertise frequently, as they are probably the most keen to expand. Explain what you can offer them and ask for a commission of at least 10%. Some schools will work on an informal basis, paying you as and when you recruit students, but others may expect more commitment. Beware of contracts which tie you to only one school.

Reading for EFL publishers
Independent assessment is vital for publishers, who need good teachers, trainers and advisors to review new material. Projects for review are sent to readers, who are paid according to the amount of work they do. Publishers usually choose readers they know, but they are sometimes on the look-out for potential course-users to work as reviewers. You may try contacting publishers you are particularly interested in.

Becoming an editor
If you have taught EFL but have no previous editorial experience, the way in to being an editor of EFL books and course materials is via secretarial work, trialling new books in your school, or by doing freelance work as a reader or proof-reader. Previous editorial work, perhaps with a local newspaper overseas, will give you a head start over applicants who have only EFL experi-

ence. There are also a number of courses in the UK which contain an editorial or production element such as the Diploma in Printing and Publishing Studies at the London College of Printing and Distributive Trades, Elephant and Castle, London SE1.

Lexicography
This is the skill of dictionary writing. A possible way into the field is by working as a part-time freelance lexicographer while you are still teaching EFL. There are frequent vacancies for free-lancers which may suit part-time teachers or those with young families. It may be possible to work from home if you have computing facilities. The market for EFL-related dictionaries has been fiercely competitive in recent years, and dictionary writing is a booming business for publishers.

There is a scarcity of people with dictionary experience, and publishers are often looking for people with some EFL experience. Obviously recruitment varies from publisher to publisher, but a Master of Arts (MA) in linguistics or a TEFL qualification would stand you in good stead. Some publishers will then short-list candidates and give you a test to check your lexical aptitude You will be expected to show that you can make language pedagogically valuable.

Most lexicographers can expect on-the-job training, though Longman offer a 2-3 week training course after a year on a particular project. A career in lexicography may lead on to project management, or into other areas of publishing.

Sales representatives
The sales rep must know the publisher's list inside out, and must build up contacts with schools and bookshops in the area they represent. This may be in their native country but plenty of sales jobs can involve travelling to or living and working in a country overseas. For this you will need fluency in one or more languages other than English - ideal for teachers who have been working abroad.

You may also be required to give presentations at conferences or at schools, as well as organising stands and displays for your publisher at trade fairs. You may need to arrange school visits for authors, commissioning editors or publishers and entertain your visitors during their stay. You could be able to make a move from sales into marketing or promotions.

A career in lexicography may lead on to project management, or into other areas of publishing.

Sales jobs can involve travelling to or living and working in a country overseas.

Starting your own language business

Those of you with an entrepreneurial spirit may be interested in the opportunities that EFL presents as a small business. Consider these main points before you start your market research.

Many experienced EFL teachers - as well as a few business entrepreneurs - have seen how lucrative it can be to open their own language teaching business. You may even decide to set up you own educational consultancy which requires less investment.

Starting a language school

If you are considering opening a language school remember that you can expect at least a two-year slog before your school is likely to break even. Many schools in the UK have not survived this period, partly because of the British Council's recognition scheme. Only private language schools which have been operating for two years are considered for recognition. Without this it could be difficult to attract students. Once you reach the two-year limit, make sure you meet the recognition standards (see p173).

If you are considering opening a school abroad, check out the legalities first.

Make sure you have the financial backing to survive the first few years. Consult an accountant to see how much money you will need to get going. You will need money for market research and advertising and you must pay rent, the teachers' salaries, your own salary, tax, and bills. Check your cash-flow - some clients may take up to 120 days to pay invoices.

Recent changes in VAT laws relating to EFL operations could help you to cut your tax bill by a hefty sum. A specialist accountant will advise you on the newest EU regulations. Education is normally VAT-exempt so if your school only supplies EFL tuition you will not have to pay VAT. However, if you are running residential courses and have to buy in travel services it is mandatory to use the Tour Operators Margin Scheme (TOMS) to work out your VAT bill. The EFL element of courses is VAT-exempt while excursions, accommodation and catering carry a 17.5% VAT rate. Transport is currently zero-rated, but from January 1996 it will be liable for VAT.

Make sure your best clients are taught by your best teachers.

If you are considering opening a school abroad, check out the legalities first. In Greece, for example, it is hard for a foreigner to open a school unless they at least have a Greek partner, although if you are an EU citizen, this is technically illegal.

Do your market research before you make a final commitment. Find out what competition you have from other schools in the area, and try and offer something none of them have - Business English or classes for younger learners, for example.

Think carefully about how to make your business efficient. Investing in a good PC will ease administration, and a laser printer will ensure top quality copies for classroom use and help you to do your own professional advertising. Choose suppliers you can trust. Try to arrange discounts on bulk orders of office and teaching materials. If you offer excursions or study trips, make sure your tour operator is reliable.

You must also consider how you will recruit teachers. If you want to recruit from a native English speaking country, will it be worth offering to pay their airfare? Will you recruit highly-qualified teachers, knowing they will expect higher salaries? Will you be strictly 'legal' and pay their tax and insurance contributions, or will you find loopholes to avoid this? All these factors will affect your prices, and the quality of your school.

Decide on a marketing campaign to attract clients. Mailshot your list of contacts and try the personal approach by following it up with a telephone call or a visit. It is helpful if you can offer to tailor your courses to fit clients' exact requirements, Make sure that your most important clients are taught by your best teachers.

Educational consultancies

If your budget does not run to equipping school premises, but you have the contacts to teach a large number of clients, it may be worth starting an educational consultancy. In this way you will only need an office, from which you can deal with your clients and your teachers.

Consultancies supply businesses or individuals with teachers at the client's premises. Investment will be less for a consultancy than for a school, but the same principles of research, marketing and recruitment will apply. Once you have a reputation for supplying quality teachers, an agency can be a sound business.

Financial Advice

Advice on tax, investments and insurance if you are planning to work abroad.

The idea of being able to find work wherever takes your fancy is very attractive. However, such a lifestyle has inherent financial disadvantages unless simple arrangements are made prior to departure. Below are the areas which could have a fundamental effect on your financial well-being. Most of this information applies to teachers of all nationalities, but, where specific details are mentioned, non-British teachers should consult their relevant authorities.

Financial reward is not the first objective which comes to mind when considering a career in EFL. If you are approaching your first job abroad, the chances are you will not be earning a fortune. However, many teachers find that if they are working in a country with a low income tax, they can save considerable sums of money. This may be because their living expenses are very low, or because on completion of their contract they are entitled to a surprisingly generous bonus payment. These payments may be taxed in the country where they are earned, or they could be taxed on the teacher's return to their native country even if the bonus is tax-exempt in the country in which it was earned.

Taxation

For teachers to avoid unnecessary tax payments on income earned abroad, they must establish their personal status. First see if the country where you are going to work has a reciprocal agreement with your country - contact your local tax office. If this is not the case, taking the UK as an example shows just how intricate tax laws can be and how great the need for expert advice is in this field.

Under UK law, if you are away for at least 365 days, and visits to the UK are less than 62 consecutive days (or one-sixth of a total period abroad), you are eligible for exemption, but you are not considered to be non-resident. To obtain non-resident status, you must work full time abroad for more than a whole tax year (i.e. from April to April) without visiting the UK for more than three months per annum.

The difference between non-resident status and exemption is that non-residents are not liable for tax on unearned income arising overseas (such as interest on offshore bank accounts) and capital gains. However, non-resident status does not exempt you from all UK tax by any means. Most non-residents are still considered to be domiciled in the UK as determined by the courts. This means that income obtained in the UK is still taxable, and that your estate - in other words your worldwide assets - is liable to UK inheritance tax.

Remember also to keep a record of any payments you have made whilst abroad - this will ensure you are not taxed again on your return to your native country. See also the Inland Revenue leaflet IR6-Double Taxation Relief.

National Insurance / Health Insurance

While you are working abroad, you may lose your entitlement to social security if your fail to keep up your contributions. To qualify for a full UK state retirement pension, you must have paid the minimum contribution each year for at least 90% of your working life.

If you are from the UK, obtain leaflet NI38 (SA29 if you will be working within the EU) from the Overseas branch of the Department of Social Security (Tel. 0191 213 5000). This explains the effect on benefits of working abroad.

If you are working in a country with a reciprocal agreement with the UK for a certain period, you will be subject to the UK social security scheme for that period, and will have to pay Class 1 contributions. After this period you can pay Class 2 (self-employed) or 3 (voluntary) contributions to the UK scheme and remain eligible for benefits.

If you are working in a country with a permanent reciprocal agreement with the UK, you must pay contributions to that country's scheme - which could be substantially higher than the scheme in the UK. Check these figures before you go.

Medical Advice

If you are planning to teach overseas, one of the things you should think about is providing for your health.

If you are an EU citizen, you and your family are entitled to the same level of medical cover as the nationals of any other EU country

Teaching abroad is stimulating and exciting, but coping with different climates, political and economic situation can put people under great psychological stress, as well as exposing them to physical risks. "What has to be considered are the different facilities, or lack of such facilities when abroad. In addition there are language complications, and although one of the family may be fluent in several languages, it does not always follow that the spouse and children will have that same expertise," says Neil Horseman of BUPA.

Pre-departure check-ups

You must take some general health precautions before going to work abroad. You should have a full medical and dental check-up. A visit to the optician for an eye test or change of glasses is also advisable. You must of course be up to date with all injections and vaccinations. If not, do not leave them to the last minute. Vaccination programmes should be started at least six weeks prior to departure. If the family are travelling with you, don't forget to make sure the children have been vaccinated against the usual infections and illnesses, eg, rubella, measles and tetanus.

European Union

If you are an EU citizen, you and your family are entitled to the same level of medical cover as the nationals of any other EU country in which you are staying. In order to take advantage of this reciprocal arrangement, you must obtain the relevant form prior to your departure. In the UK, it is known as Form E111 and is available from the Department of Health and Social Security.

Travel Packages

There are a number of 'extended stay' travel insurance packages available, which are often adequate, but you may be better covered at a lower premium under a tailor-made policy.

Private medical insurance

Having private medical insurance can take the worry and uncertainty out of health care abroad. It gives you control over where you are treated and ready access to treatment when you need it. If you are taking out private medical insurance make sure you understand what you are paying for and be certain that you are sufficiently covered for your circumstances. Most schemes provide a generous annual maximum for the costs of hospital accommodation, specialists' fees, in-patient charges such as x-rays, drugs and dressings, and out-patient consultations and treatment.

Some schemes limit the number of nights spent in hospital for eligible treatment in any one year. Also there are others that have restrictions on sporting activity cover, so it is important to check the details. If your employer does not provide cover, you should consider taking out your own policy, and if your employer does offer this benefit, check the scheme to ensure that it provides adequate cover

New options

Low-cost options have been introduced which do not include out-patient benefit and are approximately 20 per cent cheaper than standard schemes. They provide the same comprehensive cover for in-patient and day-case treatment as well as all the other benefits of the standard schemes.

Most insurers will now tailor schemes to provide cover for additional health care costs, such as General Practitioner consultations, emergency dental treatment, and professional nursing care in your own home.

Evacuation cover

An important service that can also be provided is optional evacuation cover with 24 hour emergency service. Many people think of this service as one of helicopters and air ambulances flying the sick and injured to hospitals from remote areas. But it has other features, such as the fact that the subscriber is never more than a telephone call away from multilingual medical help. A telephone call will put you in touch with doctors and specialists who could advise you on exactly what to do depending on the medical emergency.

They may suggest the nearest medical Centre if that will meet the needs. It may be necessary to move the patient to another hospital or even to evacuate them to another country. The policy also allows the patient's spouse to accompany them, or a parent to travel with their child if necessary on medical grounds.

Being ill can be a worrying thing in a foreign Country. Be sure that you go adequately prepared, not just for the job and new lifestyle but for your health as well.

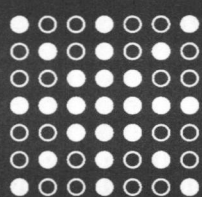

World English

This section is for EFL teachers looking for work outside their native country and for people seeking English training. There is general information about English language training in each country, teachers' pay, visa requirements, etc. Where possible, this is followed by a list of training establishments that have been put forward by independent sources. Training managers are advised to contact a number of schools in their area and refer to Section One before making a decision. Job seekers are advised to apply to a selection of schools in the area in which they wish to work and contact any local organisations for further information.

The European Union

EU nationals no longer require a work permit in order to take up employment in another member state. Non-EU passport holders may not work in the European Union without a work permit, which must be obtained before entry to the country, and is applied for by the employer. If the job could be done by an EU national, you may get a refusal, and many work permits are for a fixed period of time, so economic changes may mean that it will not be renewed.

Austria

Minimum salary: 150-200 schillings per hour, 15,000 schillings per month on contract. (US$ = approximately 10 schillings)

Tax and health insurance: Income tax is charged at the rate of approximately 40% of your salary.

Visa requirements: January 1995 heralded a change in visa requirements following Austria's membership of the European Union. EU nationals are to be afforded the same opportunities as Austrians when applying for a job and work permits are no longer required. Within three months, foreigners are required to apply for an identity card for citizens of the EU at the Austrian Immigration Office. For detailed information, contact your local Austrian embassy or consulate.

Accommodation: About 6,000 schillings per month for a one-bedroom flat in Vienna or Salzburg - slightly cheaper elsewhere. Apartments are difficult to find, but agencies can help.

English language newspaper: *New Gazette* (M).

Other information: Teachers in Austria are civil servants and therefore teaching posts used to be restricted to Austrian citizens. By law it is now possible for citizens of EU members to be employed as teachers in Austrian state schools or universities. Knowledge of German is a basic entry requirement for such posts. Many other opportunities exist for temporary employment as assistant teachers or under exchange schemes.

For further details, contact:
Bundesministerium fur Unterricht und Kunst, Minoritenplatz 5, A-1010 Wien (Tel: 0222 531 200).
Central Bureau for Education Visits and Exchanges (CBEVE), Seymour Mews House, Seymour Mews, London W1H 9PE (Tel: 071 486 5102).
inlingua (Birmingham) teacher service for Austria (Tel: 021 643 3472).

There are a reasonably large number of private language schools which tend to be very well organised and are often prepared to take on unqualified teachers - as long as they have a degree or equivalent. There is also a strong demand for in-company business English, but a knowledge of German has always been a prerequisite for teaching in this area. Food is expensive in Austria, although restaurants and drinks are relatively cheap.

List of schools in Austria

American International School, Salmannsdorferstrasse 47, A-1190, Wien.

Amerika-Institut, Operngasse 4, 1010 Wien.

Austro-American Society, Stallburggasse 2, 1010 Wien.

Austro-British Society, Wickenburggasse 19,1080 Wien.

Berlitz Sprachschulen Gesmbh, Graben 13, 1010 Wien.

Berufsforderungsinstitut, Kinderspitalgasse 5, 1090 Wien.

Business Language Center, Trattnerhof 2, 1010 Wien.

Danube International School, Gudrunstrasse 184, A-1100, Wien.

Didactica Akademie Fur Wirtschaft Und Sprachen, Schottenfeldgasse 13-15, 1070 Wien.

English For Kids, 232 Vienna, A-Baumgartner-Str 44a/7042, 1230 Wien. Tel: 0222/6674579.

English Language Centre Hietzing, In Der Hagenau 7, 1130 Wien.

Graz International Bilingual School (GIBS), Marschallgasse 19-21, A-8020, Graz. Tel: 0316/97 10 50. Fax: 97 10 50 4. Bilingual state school. Languages of instruction: English and German. Students' age: 10 to 18. Admission requirements: mother tongue English or German.

inlingua Sprachschule, Neuer Markt 1, 1010 Wien.

Innsbruck International High School, Schönberg 26, A-6141, Innsbruck.

Institut Cef, Garnisongasse 10, 1090 Wien.

International House Vienna, Schwedenplatz 2/55, 1010 Wien.

The International Montessori Preschool Vienna, Mahlerstrasse 9/13, A-1010 Wien.

Jelinek & Jelinek Privatlehrinstitut, Rudolfsplatz 3, 1010 Wien.

Kindergarten Alt Wien, Am Heumarkt 23, A-1030, Wien.

Linzer International School Auhof, Aubrunnerweg 4, A-4040, Linz.

Mini-Schools & English Language Day Camp, Postfach 160, 1220 Wien.

Salzburg International Preparatory School, Moosstrasse 106, A- 5020 Salzburg.

Sight & Sound Studio Gesmbh, Schubertring 12, 1031 Wien.

Spidi-Spracheninstitut Der Industrie, Lotringerstrasse 12, 1031 Wien.

Sprachstudio J-J Rousseau, Untere Viaduktgasse 43, 1030 Wien.

Sprachinstitut Vienna, Universitätsstr. 6, 1090 Wien.

Super Language Learning Sprachinstitut, Florianigasse 55, 1080 Wien.
Verband Wiener Volksbildung, Wiener Volkshochschulen, Hollergasse 22, 1150 Wien.
Vienna International School, Strasse Der Menschenrechte 1, A- 1220, Wien.

Belgium

Minimum salary: 550 francs per hour or 45-50,000 francs per month (US$ = approximately 30 francs).
Tax and health insurance: Employers pay tax and health insurance if you have a contract. Freelance rates vary according to salary.
Visa requirements: Non-EU nationals can apply to their local embassy. Proof of employment must be shown.
Accommodation: With Brussels being one of the major EC centres, expect to pay 15,000 francs per month, 10,000-12,000 francs outside the capital.
English language newspaper: *The Bulletin* (W).
Other information: There are many American, British and Belgian language schools. Degrees and TEFL qualifications preferred. The voluntary-run Community Help Service in Brussels has a list of schools on 02 647 6780.

The standard of living in Belgium is high, though food is generally cheap. Despite the on-going tension between the Flemish and French languages, which has forced the country to have two distinct semi-autonomous districts, English is quietly becoming more prevalent. This is likely to continue with the importance of Brussels as an EC centre.

List of schools in Belgium

Access Bvba Taalbureau, Atealaan, 5, 2200 Herentals.
Access Taal & Commumicatie, Abdy Van Tongerlo, Abdystraat 40, B-2260 Westerlo.
Belgo - British Courses, 21 Rue D'ecosse, 1060 Brussels.
Berlitz Language Centre, 28 Rue Saint Michel, 1000 Brussels.
Berlitz Language Centre, Westinform 17-19, Monnikenwerve, 8000 Brugge.
Berlitz Language Centre, 172 Leuvenselaan, 3300 Tienen.
The British School Of Brussels, Leuvensesteenweg 19, 3080 Tervuren.
Brussels Language Centre, 55 Rue Des Drapiers, 1050 Brussels.
Crown Language Centre, 9 Rue Du Beguinage, 1000 Brussels.
The English Institute, 77 Rue Lesbroussart, 1050 Brussels.
inlingua School Of Languages, 62 Limburgstraat, 9000 Gent.
Institute of Modern Languages and Communications S.A., 20 Av De La Toison D'or, Bte 21, 1060 Brussels.

Institut Pro Linguis SC, Place De L'eglise, 6717 Thiamont.
May International, 40 Rue Lesbroussart, 1050 Brussels.
Mitchell School Of English, 156 Rue Louis Hap, 1040 Brussels.
Peters School, 87 Rue Des 2 Eglises, 1040 Brussels.
Practicum, 24 Reep, 9000 Gent.
School Voor Europese Talen, 28 Charlottalei, 2018 Antwerpen.

Denmark

Minimum salary: Salaries vary according to teachers' qualifications and the type of institution they work for.
Tax: 52%.
Visa Requirements: Virtually impossible for non-EU nationals.
Accommodation: In and around Copenhagen, the cost of accommodation averages out at 8,000-10,000 kroner per month. Elsewhere it can be considerably less, and standards are high.
Other information: Danish state teachers enjoy some of the highest salaries in the EU, primarily attributable to the fact that they are expected to be able to teach any subject to students of any age. As a result, the majority of Danish teachers have a very high standard of proficiency in English, with little need for native English speakers.

With local unemployment running at an average of 11%, the prospects of finding a teaching post in Denmark are currently very poor, particularly as the number of children of school age continues to decrease, and schools, universities and teacher training colleges alike cut back on staffing.

Accustomed to free education, the private schooling sector continues to be small, and the problem of finding posts in the Danish public sector is only exacerbated by the need for non-native teachers to possess a sound knowledge of Danish.

Some opportunities may be found in institutes running part-time courses and evening classes, particularly in business English, and it is in this area where job-hunting efforts should be concentrated.

List of schools in Denmark

Access, Hamerensgade 8, 1267 Copenhagen K - branches in Odense & 4 other cities.
Activsprog, Rosenvægets Alle 32, 2100 Copenhagen - also Odense, Ärhus & Aalborg.
Ais Language Training Centre, Kongevejen 115, 2840 Holte - also Odense, Silkeborg, Esbjerg.
Aktiv Sprogservice I/S, Lindevej 9, 1877 Frederiksberg C.
Babel Sprogtræning, Vordingborggrade 18, 2100

Copenhagen - also Fredericia.
Berlitz International, Vimmelskaftet 42a, 1161 Copenhagen - also Äalborg.
Bls Sprogskole, Rolfsvej 14-16, 2000 Frederiksberg.
Cambridge Institute, Vimmelskaftet 48, 1161 Copenhagen - branches in 40 centres. Tel: 33133302.
Elite Sprogcentret, Hoffmeyersvej 19, 2000 Frederiksberg.
Erhvervs Orienterede Sprogkurser, Betulavej 25, 3200 Helsinge.
European Education Centre Aps (Inlingua), Lyngbyvej 72, 2100 Copenhagen.
Ibl Sproginstitut, Rosenvængets Alle 32, 2100 Copenhagen - also Arhus, Äalborg, Esbjerg, Kolding, Odense, Vejle.
Linguarama, Hvilevej 7, 2900 Hellerup.
Master-Ling, Sortedam Dossering 83, 2100 Copenhagen.
Praktisk Sprog Træning, Faksegade 13, 2100 Copenhagen.
Sprogklubben, Vendersgade 6, 1363 Copenhagen.

Finland

Minimum salary: A minimum of 6,800 markka per month, but can rise as high as 10,000 markka depending on qualifications and experience (US$ = approx 4.5 markka). Some employers pay airfares.

Tax and health insurance: Tax is 20-30%, while employers are entirely responsible for paying towards the comprehensive social security system..

Visa requirements: A letter of employment must be submitted to any Finnish Embassy. An academic qualification is needed. Permits will initially be renewable after three months. It is possible to enter on a tourist visa, find employment, and then leave the country to apply for a work and residence permit.

Accommodation: Expect to pay 1,200-1,500 markka per month, which includes heating, a real bargain during the long, cold winters. Some employers may pay your rent.

Other information: Most language schools and commercial colleges (Kauppaloulu) are concentrated in Helsinki and the south of Finland, usually offering evening courses to supplement state school English. Business English in particular is in great demand. Many employers offer English language learning as a perk for their employees. As a result, many private English language schools arrange in-company work. Private in-company work is also possible.

Teaching qualifications are not necessary, but it is better to have some experience. There have been reports of schools neglecting unqualified teachers' legal rights. Eating and drinking out are very expensive.

List of schools in Finland:

The Federation of Finnish-British Societies, Puistokatu 1bA, 00140 Helsinki, Tel: 639625. This school recruits qualified teachers all year round.
Lansi-Suomen opisto, (Private School) 32700 Huittinen. Tel: 8 3267866.
Richard Lewis Communications plc, 107 High Street, Winchester, Hants SO23 9AH, UK - recruits Business English teachers.

France

Minimum salary: Salaries for teachers vary immensely in France and will usually be considerably lower in the provinces than in Paris due to the lower cost of living. In universities the hourly rate may be as high as FF230, but paid three months later and with no long-term guarantee of work. Private language schools vary, but the lowest rate currently stands between FF50-100 per hour (US$ = approximately 5 francs).

Tax and health insurance: English language teachers in France fall into two categories - a "salarié" (employee) or a "travailleur indèpendent" (self-employed). Status implies different rights and obligations. As a "salarié", social security contributions are deducted by your employer before you receive your pay slip and you are entitled to sick leave, holiday pay and certain other advantages. "Travailleurs indèpendants" are paid in "honoraires" (fees) which should be set significantly higher than salaries, due to the fact that social security contributions are paid separately. If you only teach a few hours a week you may not be covered by the French social security system.

Visa requirements: EU nationals need a "carte de Séjour de ressortissant de la CEE", which should be applied for within three months of arrival in France, or as soon as you find work. Non-EU residents will need different documentation and should check with the relevant sources before setting off.

Accommodation: From around FF3,500 per month for a one-bedroom flat in Paris, about FF1,800 in rural areas. It is fairly cheap to live outside Paris.

English language newspapers: *International Herald Tribune* (D); *Paris Passion* (US magazine).

Other information: Since 1971, the majority of French companies have been required by law to spend a fixed percentage of turnover on vocational training, with many allocating a large percentage to the development of their employees' English language skills, given the rapid developments within the European Community. Business English and English for Special Purposes (ESP) are two areas of opportunity, while the best paid jobs are often found at the Chambre de Commerces who do much of the training (including English teaching) for smaller firms.

It is also possible for teachers to pick up bits of work as a part-time "vacateur", especially in the big EFL centres such as Paris, Toulouse and Strasbourg. For all English teaching, although a degree is often enough, a TEFL qualification is preferred and most schools will expect a good knowledge of French.

Legislation at EU level is forcing developments within the French public teaching sector, opening access to a number of posts for non-nationals. For those wishing to keep in touch with these rapidly changing developments, it is advisable to obtain the *Bulletin Officiel du Ministère de l'Education Nationale*. An additional source of useful information on working and teaching in France is the "Centre d'Information et Documentation Jeunesse" (CIDJ). In Paris, the English Teaching Resource Centre aims to provide support to English teachers on a membership basis, and provides a sound base of materials and ideas.

List of schools in France

AABC, 20 Rue Gonot de Mauroy, 75009 Paris. Tel: 1 42661311.
Academie des Langues Appliquees, 60 Rue de Laxou, BP 3736-54098 Nancy.
Alexandra School, 32 Rue Amiral de Grasse, 66130 Grasse.Tel: 93368801.
Alpha Formation, 51 Rue Saint-Ferreol, 130001 Marseille. Tel: 91330072.
The American Centre, Belomeau, Avenue Jean-Paul Coste, Paris. Tel: 1 42384238.
Arc Langue, Chemin de la Haie, 64100 Bayonne. Tel: 59550566.
Audio-English, 44 Allees de Tourny, 33000 Bordeaux. Tel: 56445405.
BEST, 24 Bd Beranger, 37000 Tours. Tel: 47055533.
British Connection International, 279 Rue Crequi, 69007 Lyon. Tel: 72730255.
BTS Language Centre, 226 Route de Philipeville, 6001 Marcinelle. Tel: 71313076.
Collegium Palatinium, Dept EFL/CP, Chateau de Pourtales, 61 rue Melanie, 67000 Strasbourg. Tel: 88310107.
English Apart, 82 rue Jean Jaures, 29200 Brest.
The English Institute, 24 Rue Vieux Marche aux Vins, 67000 Strasbourg. Tel: 88325136.
English International, 8 Quaie Jules Courmont, 690021 Lyon.
The English Study Centre (TESC), 16 Rue Manuel, 13100 Aix-en-Province. Tel: 42380754.
Executive Language Services Group, 25 Boulevard Sebastopol, 75001 Paris Tel: 1 2366255.
Forum, 66 Rue Bretonnerie, 45000 Orleans. Tel: 38625245.
France Europe Consultants, 49 Rue Du Petit Bois, 35235 Thorigne. Tel: 99838934.
IFS, 23 Bis Boulevard de Louvain, 13008 Marseille Tel: 91792503.
ILIC, 12 Rue Letellier, 75015 Paris. Tel: 1 45751962.
Info Langues Tassin, 169 Avenue Charles de Gaulle, 69160 Tassin. Tel: 78361111.
ISES, 70 bis Avenue Maignot, 37100 Tours (mainly ESP).
ITS Langues, 21 bis rue des Plantes, 75014 Paris. Tel: 1 40449848.
Language Studies System, 23 Rue Sommeiller, 74000 Annecy. Tel: 50528756.
Rapid English, BP410, 27404 Louviers. Fax: 32402256.

Riviera Plus, 22 Boulevard Dubouchage, 06000 Nice.Tel: 93626062.
Rothman Institute, 21 Avenue du Major General Vanier, 1000 Troyes. Tel: 25803041.
Sarl Executive Language Service, 25 Bld Sebastopol 75001, Paris.
School Cool, 1c Chemion Etrer, 60270 Gouvieux. Tel: 44571504.
Wood Language Studies, 33 Cours De La Liberte, 69003 Lyon. Tel: 78601560.

Germany

Minimum salary: On contract, 2,400-3,000 DM, which is 1,600-2,000 DM net. Hourly rates vary from 20-45 DM per 45-minute lesson depending on the school and type of class. Business English classes pay up to 60DM per hour. (US$ = approximately 1.5 DM)
Tax and health insurance: EU nationals pay about 13% in social security contributions, but can work tax-free for the first two years. You are liable for back tax on your first two years' salary if you stay beyond this period, at 33%. Freelances should take out a private health policy.
Visa requirements: Non-EC residents must get a job before entering the country to get a permit - usually difficult.
Accommodation: 750-1,000 DM per month for a room in a shared flat, through rents vary from city to city. Accommodation is very difficult to find, except in the former East Germany, where it is cheaper but of a lower standard.
Other information: Germany's unification has slowed economic growth. Teachers new to Germany may find the conditions very tough, pay in schools is low and there are only a few full-time contracts available.

There is a core of contracted teachers working for the major schools. Probably up to 90% of teachers work on a freelance basis, working in *Volkshochsculen* (Adult Education Centres), private companies and smaller schools. It is a hostile and competitive market, and many unqualified teachers work for low wages.

Prerequisites for success as a freelance include initiative, a high level of spoken German and being prepared to work early mornings and late evenings. There is considerable demand for Business English and English for Special Purposes (ESP), with government grants ensuring much lucrative in-company work.

Demand for teachers in the former East Germany continues to be high, although many Russian teachers have been retrained to fill English teaching posts. Conditions in the former East Germany are still difficult on the whole and racism is to be expected.

The International Language Institute in Munich, is drawing up proposals for two-month courses in specialised areas such as banking, finance, and tourism, and consequently native English speakers continue to be in demand.

Transport is reasonably inexpensive while being fairly efficient and Germany's federal capitals are pleasant, relatively uncrowded places to live. A smart appearance may be expected if you want to make a good impression. You are advised to take about 6,000 DM with you for initial expenses.

Applications for work can be sent to The Central Placement Office of the Federal Department of Employment, who process overseas applications. Contact Zentralstelle fur Arbeitsvermittlung Feuerbachstrasse 42, D-6000 Frankfurt am Main 1.

List of schools in Germany

Administration Office for Examinations Ltd, Platanenstr 5, 07549 Gera. Tel: (365) 388519. Fax: (365) 388536. Representing the London Chamber of Commerce and Industry Examinations Board in Germany.
Anglo-German Institute, Christopherstr 4, 70178 Stuttgart. Tel: (711) 60 38 58. Fax: (711) 640 99 41. Official examination centre for Oxford, Cambridge, LCCI and Institute of Linguists. Staatl anerk Berufsfachschule fur Wirtschaftskorrespondenten.
ASK Sprachenschule, 1 Kortumstr 71, 44787 Bochum. Tel: (234) 12910.
Barnsley College, Str Des Friedens 35, 03222 Lubbenau, Brandenburg. Tel: (03542) 44407. Fax: (03542) 44408. Intensive English training from native speakers; in-company Business English, commercial English with modern telecommunications. Schools in Frankfurt/O, Cottbus & Spreewald.
Benedict School, Gurzenichstr 17, 50667 Koln. Tel: (221) 212203.
Berlitz, Friedrich-Wilhelm-Strasse 30, 47051 Duisburg. Tel: (203) 27168.
Christopher Hills School of English, Sandeldamm 12, 63450 Hanau. Tel: (49) 6181 15015. Fax: (49) 6181 12121. Professional English language training in Germany and England. Long-term posts with good career prospects for experienced teachers.
Collegium Palatinum, Adenauerplatz 8, 69115 Heidelberg. Tel: (06221) 46289. Fax: (06221) 182023. University courses in English during the academic year. Accommodation on campus or with guest families. Cultural and activity program.
Didacta, Hohenzollernring 27, 95440 Bayreuth. Tel: (49) (921) 27555.
English Language Centre, Altonaer Chausee 89, 22869 Schenefeld. Tel: 830 2421.
English Language Institute, Sprachenchule 4, Ubersetzer Am Zwinger 14, 33602 Bielefeld. Tel: (521) 69353. Also Alter Kirchenweg 33A, 22844 Norderstadt. Tel: 405251660.
Europa-Universitat Viadrina, Sprachenzentrum, Grosse Scharrnstr 59, 15230 Frankfurt (Oder).
European Language School, Hansastrasse 44, 44137 Dortmund. Tel: (231) 579496.
Euro-Sprachscule, Am Plarrer 6, 90429 Nurnberg.
Eurozentrum Koln, Sedanstrasse 31-33, 50668 Koln. Tel: (221) 720831.
FBD Schulen, Katharinenstr 18, 70182 Stuttgart. Tel: (711)

21580.
GLS, Sprachenzentrum, B Jaeshke, Pestalozzistr 886, 10625 Berlin. Tel: (30) 3135025.
Hallworth English Centre, Frauenstrasse 118, 89703 Ulmponau. Tel: (731) 22668.
Helliwell Institute of English, Markt 15, 50321 Bruhl. Tel: (2232) 12893.
inlingua Sprachschule, Konigstrasse 61, 47051 Duisburg. Tel: (203) 341334; Kaiserstrasse 37, 60329 Frankfurt. Tel: (69) 231021. Fax: 234829; Knapper Strasse 38, 58507 Ludenscheid. Tel: (2351) 20275; Schildern 8, 33098 Paderborn.
inlingua Sprachschule Gmbh, Heinrichstr 4a, 36037 Fulda.
Intercom Language Services Muggenkampstr 38, 20257 Hamburg.
Knowledge Point, Hohenzollernstrasse 26, 80801 Munchen. Tel: (089) 33 34 05.
Linguotek Institut, Schlueterstrasse 18, 20146, Hamburg. Tel: (40) 459520.
Modernes Lernstudio, Prinzenstr 1, 30159 Hannover. Tel: (511) 321861.
Neue Sprachschule, Rosastrasse 1, 79098 Freiburg. Tel: (761) 24810/32026.
NSK Language and Training Services (language courses for industry), Comeniusstr. 2, 90459 Nurnburg. Tel: (911) 441552.
Sprachschule Griffin, Reilstrasse 8, 06114 Halle (Saale), Tel: (345) 503422.
Sprachstudio Lingua Nova, Thierschstrasse 36, 80538 Munich. Tel: (89) 221171.
Stevens English Training, Ruttenscheider Strasse 68, 45130 Essen.
Vorbeck-Schule, 77723 Gengenbach. Tel: (7803) 3361.
Wirtschaftwissen-schaftliche Fakultat Ingolstadt, Auf der Schanz 49, 85049 Ingolstadt (for lecturers in business English only).

Greece

Minimum salary: Salaries for EFL teachers in Greece are low (around £4/$6 per hour). You should never accept less than 1,500 drachmas per hour for junior classes, or 1,800 for seminars. Many teachers supplement their income with private lessons, which are usually easy to arrange at 2,000-3,000 drachmas per hour, although some schools may discourage this or expect a cut of your pay. Most schools provide a generous bonus at the end of each term, but do not pay during the summer holidays. It is advisable that all teachers insist on a written contract before commencing employment, and pay close attention to the terms and conditions (US$ = approximately 230 drachma).
Tax and health insurance: Teachers are required to pay tax and social security (IKA), which is compulsory for the first year. On a salary of around 150,000 drachmas per month (£400/$600), for example, these would amount to around 28,000 drachmas (£80/$120).
Visa requirements: As Greece is an EU country, EU nationals have the right to work but will need a work/

residence permit. The employer is responsible for obtaining these but sometimes teachers may be paid "off the payroll" without papers. For non-EC nationals, a work permit will be arranged by your school, which will require a translated copy of your degree certificate (cheaper if done at a Greek consulate than in Greece itself). You may also require a doctor's certificate of good health. Permits take up to two months, though in practice you may find your contract is over before your papers actually arrive. You may find it very hard to get a full residence permit unless you can claim *omogenesis* - being of Greek descent.

Accommodation: Prices can be high, especially in the Athens areas where a typical one-bedroom flat may cost £200/$300 per month. Landlords often require two or more months' rent as a deposit and this is not always returned. A phone is a great advantage, as the waiting list for installation is around 10 years, and the phone provides an invaluable source of communication, particularly if you intend to focus on private classes.

English language newspaper: *The Athens News* (D).

Other information: Greece has a huge EFL market and there are over 4,000 *frontisteria* (educational institutes). Most of these teach children aged 8-18, up to Proficiency in the larger schools. Around 70,000 students take Cambridge exams each year. Most lessons are in the evening, when students have finished their state lessons.

The recession, together with the introduction of English in state primary schools, have reduced the number of children attending *frontisteria*, but there is a new emphasis on Adult courses, particularly in ESP.

Teachers need a degree, preferably in English, to be eligible for a work permit, but TEFL qualifications are not necessarily required. Unqualified teachers will be paid less, but language schools are sporadically checked to ensure that everything is above board. Despite EU legislation, the government is attempting to protect local teachers' employment making it virtually impossible for non-Greeks to own language schools.

Eating and drinking out are still cheap, but other costs are high. Foreign-registered cars are prohibited if you work in Greece. Be warned that Athens has a chronic pollution problem, and that winters in Greece can be bleak, particularly in the north.

Note that schools in Greece recruit teachers for the whole academic year. Recruitment is normally made in May-June or in early September and there is little point in applying for posts mid-way through the year. The normal pattern is for teachers to approach schools in person as most teachers are taken on locally rather than from overseas. *The Athens News* carries job advertisements.

List of schools in Greece

Alpha Abatzolglou Economou, 10 Kosma Etolou St, 54643 Thessaloniki. Tel: 31 830535.
A Andriopoulou, 3, 28 Octobrio, Tripolis.
Athens College, PO Box 65005, 15410 Psychico, Athens. Tel: 1 6714621.

English Tuition Centre, 3 Pythias Street, Kypseli 1136, Athens.
Enossi Foreign Languages (The Language Centre), Stadiou 7, Syntagma, 10562 Athens. Tel: 3230 356/ 3250081. Also 8 centres (6 in Athens, 1 in Larissa & 2 in Salonika).
Eurocentre, 7 Solomou Street, 41222 Larissa.
Hambakis Schools of English, 1 Filellinon Street, Athens. Tel: 1 3017531/5.
Hellenic American Union, 22 Massalias Street, GR-106 80 Athens.
Homer Association, 52 Academias St, 10677 Athens. Tel: 1 3622887.
International Language Centre, 35 Votsi Street, 26221 Patras.
Institute of English, French, German and Greek for Foreigners, Zavitsanou Sophia, 13 Joannou Gazi St, 31100 Lefkada. Tel: 64524514.
Institute of Foreign Languages, 41 Epidavrou St, 10441 Athens. Tel: 1 5142397.
ISIAA 93, Lamia 35100. Tel: 23 121028.
Makri's School of English, 2 Pardos G Olympion St 60100 Katerini. Tel: 35122859.
G Michalopolous School of English, 24E Antistasis, Alexandria, 59300 Imathias, Thessaloniki. Tel: 333 322890.
New Centre, Arkarnanias 16, Athens 11526.
Peter Sfyrakis' School of Foreign Languages, 21Nikiforou Foka St, 72200 Ierapetra, Crete. Tel: 84228700.
Protypo English Language School, 22 Deliyioryi Street, Volos 38221.
School of English, 8 Kosti Palama, Kavala 65302.
School of Foreign Languages, 12 P Isaldari St, Xylokastro, 20400 Korinth. Tel: 74324678.
The Director, SILITZIS School of Languages, 42 Koumoundourou, 412 22 Larissa.
The A Trechas Language Centre, 20 Koundouriotou St, Keratsini. Tel: 1 432 0546; 34 Argostoliou St, Egaleo, Athens. Tel: 1 5617263.
Zoula Language Schools, Sanroco Square, Corfu. Tel: 66139330.

Ireland

Please see page 54 for full details of the market in Ireland and working conditions.

List of schools in Ireland

Education Through English, 68 Merrion Square, Dublin 2, Tel: +353 1 6765431 Fax: +353 1 661 3866. High School/academic year programmes throughout Ireland since 1988. International summer programmes/residential camps (Irish/foreign). Member of FIYTO and RELSA.
Galway Cultural Institute, Lowstrand House, Flood Street, Galway, Tel: +353 91 68300 Fax: +353 91 68301. Quality year-round adult school. Summer junior pro-

grammes. **English for non-native teachers. TEFL courses. Accommodation, sports and social programmes organised. Westlingua Language School, Cathedral Building, Middle Street, Galway. Tel: +353 91 68188 Fax: +353 91 63462.**
Westlingua is a small, but busy, school offering high quality teaching and the RELSA Teacher Training Certificate course.

Italy

Minimum salary: Salaries range from 1.2 million lira per month as a University "lettori", with contracts of a limited duration, to 1.5 million lira in some private sector schools, but an average figure of around 1. 4 million lira per month can be expected. Many teachers supplement their income with private lessons, translations. Expect to earn 20-30,000 lira for work on an hourly basis (US$ = approx. 1700 lira).
Tax and health insurance: 25-30% tax if you are on contract, plus 19% VAT if you are freelance. Private schools and universities should deduct tax and national insurance equivalents, and it is important to check that they do. Although your employer may pay health insurance, extra cover is desirable.
Visa requirements: For EU nationals, no visa is required. Work permits are issued by the police, which means the process is often slow and tiresome. Non-EC nationals will find it difficult to get a work permit unless they are of Italian descent. It is essential to have employment before entering the country to get a work permit.
Accommodation: A typical flat now costs 1 million lira per month in cities (less in rural areas), and as a result, flat sharing is increasingly common. Accommodation is difficult to find in the major cities and foreigners will often have to pay higher rents than the locals.
Other information: There are hundreds of private schools in Italy, as the state system is disorganised and the demand for English is huge. However, the recession has meant a decrease in student numbers and fiercer competition for jobs. Some schools will take on any native English teachers, but conditions are better if you are qualified, particularly if you have a TEFL Diploma. Although housing costs more than in the UK, transport and food costs are lower.

The *Associazione Italiana Scuole di Lingua Inglese* (AISLI) at Via Campanella 16, 41100 Modena regulates the conditions in its member schools, so AISLI schools are generally recommended.

There are sometimes opportunities to work as university lecturers, but foreign lettori's salaries have dropped, pay is often delayed and classes are overcrowded.

Private lessons are actually illegal if you hold a contract, but self-employed teachers should be able to get plenty of in-company work as the business community increasingly needs English. A knowledge of Italian would be an asset.

Italy is expensive in the north. Government reports say that the small industrial cities in the north and centre offer the best standard of living but those with an appetite for Mediterranean living might prefer the south.

List of schools in Italy

ABC English School, Via San Rocco 7, 23017 Morbegno (SO).
Academy Lord Byron, Via Sparano 012, Bari.
Academia Britannica, Via Bruxelles 61, 04100 Latina. Tel: 773 491917.
Anglo American School, Piazza S. Giovanni in Monte 9, 40124 Bologna.
Anglocentre, Via A de Gasperi 23, 70052 Bisceglie (BA).
Arlington Language Services, cp99, 29100, Piacenza.
Bari Poggiofranco English Centre, Viale Pio XII 18, 70124 Bari.
Benedict School, Via Sauro 1/2, Bologna.
Berlitz, Via delle Asole 2, Milano.
British Institute, Fontane 109, Rome. Tel: 6491979. Fax: 64815549; Via Marghera 45, 20149 Milan. Tel: 2 48011149.
The British Institute of Florence, Palazzo Feroni, Via Tornalbuoni 2, Florence. Tel: 55 298866.
The British Language Centre Via Piazzi Angolo Largo Pedrini, 23100 Sondrio. Tel: 342 216130.
The British Language Centre, Via Piazza Roma 3, 20038 Serengo.
The British School of Bari, Via Celentano 27, 70121 Bari. Tel: 080 5247335. Fax: 080 5247396.
Callan, Via Garibaldi 1, 40124 Bologna.
Cambridge Academy, P. Castelnuovo 50, Palermo.
Cambridge School, Via S Rochetto 3, Verona. Tel: 458003154. Fax: 458003154.
The Cambridge School, Pal. Casa, Bianca Via Origlia 38, 84014 Nocera Inferiore, Salerno.
Canning School, Via San Remo 9, 20133 Milano.
Centro di Lingue, Via Pozzo 30, Trento. Tel: 461981733. Fax: 461981687.
Centro Internazionale di Linguistica Streamline, Via Piave 34/b, 71100 Foggia. Tel: 039 88124204.
Cento Lingue di Vinci Antonella, Via San Martino 77, Pisa.
Centro Lingue Tradint, Via Jannozzi 8, S Donato Milanese (N1). Tel: 25231312.
Centro Studi Drago, P. Drago 18, 30017 Jesolo Lido (VE).
Chandler, Viale Aventino 102, 00153 Roma.
Conner Language Services, Via Macchi 42, Milano.
Devon School, Contra Porti 4, Vicenza.
Dialogue International, Corso Re Umberto 61, 10128 Torino.
Elite, Corso De Gasperi 46, Torino.
English Centre, Via Promis 8, 11100 Aosta. Tel: 0165 235416. Fax: 0165 238381. Courses for children, adolescents and adults of all levels, Business English, ESP and exam preparation. British Institutes Affiliated.
The English Centre, Via Dei Mille 18, 07100 Sassari, Sardinia. Tel: 79 232154.
The English Connection, Via Ferro 1, 30027 San Dona di Piave (VE).
The English Institute, Corso Gelone 82, Siracuse, Sicily.

Tel: 931 60875.

English House, Via Roma 177, 85028 Rionero, Potenza.

The English Language Studio, Via Antonio Bondi 27, 40138 Bologna. Tel: 51347394. Fax: 51505952.

Eurolingue, Via Chiana 116, 00198 Roma.

European Language Institute, Via IV Novembre 65, 55049 Viareggio (LU).

Filadelfia School, Via L. Colla 22, 10098 Rivoli.

Home School, Via F. Malvotti 8, Conegliano (TV).

inlingua, Piazza XX Settembre 36, Civitanova Marche (MC).

inlingua, Corso Vittorio Emanuel II 68, Torino.

inlingua, Via Leoncino 35, 37121 Verona.

inlingua, Via Monte Piana 42, Venezia.

International House, Via Manzoni 64, La Spezia.

International Language School, Via Tibullo 10, Rome. Tel: 66547796. Fax: 66547796.

Language Centre, Via Milano. 20, 21100 Varese. Tel: 0332 282732.

Language Centre, Via G Daita 29, 90139 Palermo.

Lb Linguistico, Centro Insegnamento, Lingue Staniere, Via Caserta 16, 95128 Catania, Sicily.

Lions School, Via sale 9, Udine.

Lingua Due Villa, Pendola 15, 57100 Livrono.

Living Languages School, Via Magna Grecia, 89100 Regio Calabria. Tel/Fax: 39 965330926.

Lord Byron College, Via Sparano 102, 70121 Bari. Tel: 80 232696.

Managerial English Consultants, Via Sforza Pallavicini 11, 009193 Rome. Tel: 6 654 2391. Fax: 6 6871159.

Modern English School, Via Giordano Bruno 6, 45100 Rovigo. Tel: 425 200266.

Modern English Study Centre, via Borgonuova 14, 40125 Bologna. Tel: 51 227523.

Multimethod, I Go Richini 8, 20122 Milan. Tel: 2583042. Fax: 289401235.

Oxford Inst Italiani, Via Senato 28 20121.

Oxford School, San Marco 1513, Venice. Fax: 415210785.

The Professionals, Via F Carcona 4, 20149 Milan Tel: 2 48000035. Fax: 2 4814001.

Regency School, Via Arcivescovado 7, 16121 Turin. Tel: 11517456. Fax: 11,541845.

Regent International, V.U. Da Pisa 6, Milano.

Regent International, Corsa Italia 54, 21047 Saronno.

The RTS Language Training, Via Tuscolana 4, 00182 Roma.

Scuola The Westminster, Via Tevere 84, Sesto Fiorentino (FI).

Spep School, Via della Secca 1, 40121 Bologna.

Studio Linguistico Fonema, via Marconi 19, 50053 Sovigliana-Vinci (Fl). Tel: 571 500551.

Studio professionale Apprendimento Linguistico Programmato, Via Ferrarese 3, Bologna. Tel: 051 360617. Fax: 051 368413. Full Immersion - Programmed learning. English, French, German, Spanish, Italian for Foreigners.

Unimoney, Corso Sempione 72, 20154 Milano.

Victoria Language Centre, Viale Fassi 28, 41012 Capri.

Wall Street Institute, Piazza Combattento 6, 4100 Ferrara. Tel: 532200231; Corso V. Emanuele 30, 20122 Milan. Tel: 2 76013959.

Luxembourg

If you want to work in this tiny country, your opportunities are limited to two private schools, the English Language Centre and the International Language Centre. The state-controlled Centre de Langues also runs English courses (80 Boulevard George Patton, 23-16 Luxembourg Tel: 403914).

English language newspaper: *Luxembourg News Digest* (W).

Other information: English language teaching is nearly all done in the state system. There are no universities in the principality, so Luxembourg residents must take a BA in the UK or the USA to be able to teach - hence the high level of English teaching. The British Luxembourg Society is promoting an English language movement and has ties with the British Council. For information contact the British Council in Brussels - Tel: (02) 193600.

Netherlands

Minimum salary: 1,900 guilders per month (US$ = approximately 1.6 guilders).

Tax and health insurance: Around 30%.

Visa requirements: Arranged by employer.

Accommodation: Availability of housing in the Netherlands is a particular problem and it can be very expensive. Rented accommodation is often advertised in local newspapers from 350 guilders per month, but you can also contact the Netherlands Estate Agents Federation for suitable agents who deal with rented property.

Other information: As a full member of the European Community, all EU nationals have the right to live and work in the Netherlands without a work permit. UK nationals working in the Netherlands have the same rights as nationals of that country with regard to pay, working conditions, access to housing, vocational training, social security and trade union membership. Moreover, families and immediate dependents are entitled to join them and have similar rights. British nationals are free to enter the Netherlands for up to three months to look for work or set up in business. Visitors, even if looking for work, may be asked to prove that they have adequate means for the duration of their stay and that the cost of their return journey is secured.

Most Dutch people are fluent in English because of their excellent state system, and as a result opportunities to teach EFL are limited mainly to business English or English for Specific Purposes. In the state system teachers must be fluent in Dutch. Organisation in the private system is fairly chaotic.

List of schools in the Netherlands

Alenpracticum Almelo, Nieuwstraat 171, 7605 Ad Almelo.

Amerongen Talenpraktikum, De Kievit 1, 3958 Dd Amerongen.

Asa Studiecentrum, Kotterstraat 11, 1826 Cd Alkmaar.

Asco, Nassauplein 8, 1815 Gm Alkmaar.

AVC, Oringerbrink 43, 7812 Jr Emmen.

Avoc Teleninstituut, Heugemerweg 2d, 6229 As Maastricht.

Bell College, Afd English LanguageTraining, Stationsstraat 17, 6221 Bm Maastricht.

Berlitz Language Centre, Rokin 87-89, 1012 Kl Amsterdam.

Bltc, Keizersgracht 389, 1016 Ej Amsterdam.

B N M, Heinsbergenstr 27, 502 Cd Uden, Flinckstraat 1/Keet, 1506 Lk Zaandam, Niow, Boslaan 6, 3701 Cj Zeist.

Boerhave Opleidingen, Hoogstraat 118, 801 Bb Zwolle.

Bressler's Business Language, Buiksloterdijk 284, 1034 Zd Amsterdam.

Class International, Bijlwerffstr 28b, 3039 Vh Rotterdam.

Dinkgreve Handelsopleiding, Wilemsparkweg 31, 1071 Gp Amsterdam.

Dutch College, P Calandlaan 42, 1065 Kp Amsterdam.

Educational Holidays, Beukstraat 149, 2565 Xz Den Haag.

Eerste Ned Talenpraktikum, Singel 355, 3311 He Dordrecht.

Eerste Nederlandse Talenpraktikum, Kalverstr 112, 1012 Pk Amsterdam.

Elseviers Talen, Jan Van Galenstraat 335, 1061 Az Amsterdam.

Elseviers Talen, Westelijke Parallelweg 54, 3331 Ew Zwijndrecht.

Erasmus College, Planetenlaan 5, 2024 Eh Haarlem, Hendrik Ido Ambacht.

Esp, Laan V Meerdervoort 834, 2564 As Den Haag.

Europa Talenpraktikum, Vosselmanstraat 400, 7311 Cl Apeldoorn.

Fikkers Handelsinstituut, Anna Paulownastr 37a, 2518 Bb Den Haag.

Gebo, Boelekade 36-38, 2806 Al Gouda.

Gouwe College, Turfsingel 67, 2802 Bd Gouda.

Instituut Meppel, Tav Dhr J G Rijpkema, Postbus 263, 7940 Ag Meppel.

Instituut Schoevers, Markt 17, 5611 Eb Eindhoven.

Instituut Schoevers, Postbus 10486, 5000 Jl Tilburg.

Interlingua Taalsupport Bv, Wijnhaven 99, 3011 Wn Rotterdam.

Interlingua Talenpraktikum, Burg van Royensingel 20 - 21, 8011 ct Zwolle.

International Studiecentrum, voor de Vrouw Concertgebouwplein 17, 107 LM Amsterdam. Tel: (020) 6761437.

Interphone Opleidingen, St Jorisstraat 17, 5361 Hc Grave.

Language Partners, Wtc Beursplein 37, 3011 A Rotterdam.

Leidse Onderwijsinstelling, Tav Mr Wirtz, Leidsedreef 2, 2352 Ba Leiderdorp.

Linguarama Nederland, Wtc Strawinskylaan 507, 1077 Xx Amsterdam.

Linguarama Nederland, Venestraat 27, 2525 Ca Den Haag.

Linguaphone Instituut, Peperstraat 7, 6127 As Grevenbicht, Huis Van Bewaring, de Koepel Afd Onderwijs, Harmenjansweg 4, 2031 Wk Haarlem.

Meab Onderwijs-Instituut Bv, Herengracht 4, 2312 Ld Leiden.

Mieke Boot Instuitut, Waterbergseweg 13, 6815 Al Arnhem.

Notenboom, Kerkakkerstraat 34, 5616 Hc Eindhoven.

Onderwijsinstituut Netty Post, Haverstraat 2, 1447 Ce Purmerend.

Scholengem. G K Van Hogendorp, Postbus 290725, 3001 Gb Rotterdam.

School Of English, Eerste Wormenseweg 238, 7331 Nt Apeldoorn.

Stichting Volwasseneducatie Deventer, Afd English Language Training, Postbus 639, 7400 Ap Deventer.

Talenpraktikum Twente, Tav Dhr P De Wit, Ariensplein 2, 7511 Jx Enschede.

Telencentrum Dordrecht, C De Wittstraat 50, 3311 Kj Dordrecht.

Trait D'union, Argonautenlaan 24a, 5631 Ll Eindhoven.

Zeeuwse Volksuniversiteit, Afd English Language Training, Postbus 724, 4330 As Middleburg.

Portugal

Minimum salary: 120,000-160,000 escudos per month, with the average rate of pay on an hourly basis estimated at approximately £12. A number of schools offer end of term bonus schemes (US$ = approximately 150 escudos).

Tax and health insurance: Not all schools offer health insurance and a minimum of class 3 NI is recommended. The first 1,500,000 escudos of salary are tax free, but after that, the rate varies between 5-30%, depending on how much is earned above the threshold. Because a one-year contract covers two tax-years, however, most teachers are entitled to hefty tax-rebates.

Visa requirements: Work permits and residents permits should be arranged by employers. A lot of schools are reluctant to hire non-EU nationals, because of the extra paperwork involved. Even EU citizens should be prepared for a lot of bureaucracy and waiting around.

Accommodation: There is a severe housing shortage in Lisbon, while rents in Porto and the university town of Coimbra have also escalated dramatically. Expect to pay in the region of 40,000-70,000 escudos per month in a shared flat in these cities, less in smaller towns.

English language newspapers: *The Portugal Post* (W); *The Anglo-Portuguese News* (W); *The Algarve Gazette* (M).

Other information: Although Portugal is now no longer the EC's poorest country, its rapid economic growth and corresponding demand for English has slowed down. Student numbers have tailed off and competition for jobs is keen.

There are probably more opportunities for teachers prepared to work in the smaller private language schools in the provinces, but pay is unlikely to be very high. The cost of living has also risen, and is comparable with northern Europe for many essentials (though eating and drinking out are still cheap). Housing is generally of low quality.

If you pay local health insurance, you are entitled to Caixa (basic medical treatment), but expect to wait several days for an appointment. A private health insurance policy is worth considering.

Ensure your timetables avoid a split shift, or your days will be very long. Travelling around Lisbon and Porto can take some time, and you will probably have to spend at least one hour a day commuting as it is.

A degree is necessary to obtain a work permit, but in many schools qualifications are not essential. Such schools may expect you to work long hours. Others may offer you "green receipts", which in effect means you are self-employed and excluded from sick pay, holiday pay and bonuses. If this is the case, make sure you are paid enough to compensate. Private lessons are easy to find, especially for business English, and in-company work is lucrative.

The government are now promoting English at primary level, and there may be openings in the state sector. Teachers of young adults, particularly at exam level, are also constantly in demand. Portuguese students' English is generally of a high standard.

The Portuguese climate is warm but expect a lot of rain in the winter. Northern Portugal is cheaper and generally friendlier than the south, but the weather is unreliable all year. In the Algarve, English is widely spoken and there is a large residential English population. Prices are higher here to reflect this.

Madeira

There are several private language schools on this island resort, especially in the capital, Funchal. The island has no beaches, but is very scenic and stays warm and humid all year.

List of schools in Portugal

Berlitz, Av Conde Valbom 6-4, 1000 Lisboa.
Big Ben School, Rua Moinho Fanares 4-1, 2725 Mem Martins.
Cambridge School, Avenida de la Liberdade 173-4, 1200 Lisboa. Tel: 352 74 74, Fax: 353 47 29. Courses: CTEFLA, Business, Companies, Juniors, UCLES exams. Employment: EC citizens, BA, CTEFLA/TESOL. Portugal's largest teaching chain - 7 locations.
Casa de Inglaterra, Rua Alexandre Herculano 134, 3000 Coimbra.
Celfibocage, Av Luisa Todi, 288-2, 2900 Setubal.
CENA-Cent. Est. Norte Americanos, Rua Remedios 62 c/ v, 1200 Lisboa.
Centro de Estudos IPFEL, Rua Edith Cavell 8, 1900

Lisboa.
Centro de Instruçao Tecnica, Rua Da Estefania 32-10Dto, 1000 Lisboa.
Centro Internacional Linguas, Av Fontes P de Melo 25-1Dto, 1000 Lisboa.
Centro de Linguas de Alvide, Rua Fonte Nino, Viv Pe Americo 1, Alvide, 2750 Cascais.
Centro de Linguas Estrangeiras de Cascais, Av Marginal BI A-30, 2750 Cascais.
Centro de Linguas Intergarb, Tv da Liberdade 13-1, 8200 Albufeira.
Centro de Linguas de Quarteira, Rua Proj 25 de Abril 12, 8125 Quartiera.
Centro de Linguas de Queluz, Av Dr Miguel Bombarda 62-1E, 2745 Queluz.
Centro de Linguas de Santarem, Lg Pe Francisco N Silva, 2000 Santarem.
CETI, Av Duque de Loule, 71-2, 1000 Lisboa.
CIAL-Centro De Linguas, Av Republica 14-20, 1000 Lisboa, Tel: 351-1-3533733, Fax: 351-1-3523096.
Class, Rua Gen Humberto Delgado 40-1, 7540 Santiago Do Cacem.
Clube Conversaçao Inglesa 3M, Rua. Rodrigues Sampaio 18-3, 1100 Lisboa.
Communicate Language Institute, Praceta Joao Villaret 12B, 2675 Povoa de Sto Adriao.
Curso de Linguas Estrangeiras, Rua Dr Miguel Bombarda, 271-1, 2600 Vila Franca De Xira.
Ecubal, Lombos, Barros Brancos, Porches, 8400 Lagoa
ELTA, Av Jose E Garcia 55-3, 2745 Queluz.
Encounter English, Rua Letes 42-2, 8000 Faro.
English at PLC, Praça Luis de Camoes 26, Apartado 73, 5001 Vila Real.
English Institute Setubal, Av 22 Dezembro 88, 2900 Setubal.
The English Language Centre, Rua Calouste Gulbenkian 22-r/c C, 3080 Figueira Da Foz.
The English School of Coruche, Rua Guerreiros 11, 2100 Coruche.
English School of Loule, Rua Jose F Guerreiro 66M, Galerias Do Mercado, 8100 Loule.
Escola de Linguas de Agueda, Rua Jose G Pimenta, 3750 Agueda.
Escola de Linguas de Ovar, Rua Ferreira de Castro 124-1 A/B, 3880 Ovar.
Eurocenter Instituto de Linguas, Av de Bons Amigos 4-1, 2735 Cacem.
Gab Tecnico de Linguas, Rua Hermenegildo Capelo 2-2, 2400 Leiria.
GEDI, Pq Miraflores Lt 18-lA/B, 1495 Alges.
IF - Ingles Funcional, Rua Afonso Albuquerque 73-A, 2460 Alcobaca.
IF Ingles Funcional, Rua Com Almeida Henriques 32, 2400 Leiria.
IF Ingles Funcional , Av Vidreiro, 95-2, 2430 Marinha Grande.
INESP, Rua Dr Alberto Souto 20-2, 3800 Aveiro.
INLINGUA, Campo Grande 30-1A, 1700 Lisboa.
INPR, Bernardo Lima 5, 1100 Lisboa.
Instituto Britanico, Rua Cons Januario 119/21, 4700 Braga.

Instituto Britanico, Rua Municipio Lt B - 1 C, 2400 Leiria.

Instituto Britanico, Rua Dr Ferreira Carmo, 4990 Ponte De Lima.

Instituto Franco-Britanico, Rua 5 de Outubro 10-1Dto, 2700 Amadora.

Instituto Inlas do Porto, Rua S da Bandeira 522-1, 4000 Porto.

Instituto de Linguas, Rua Valverde 1, 2350 Torres Novas.

Instituto de Linguas do Castelo Branco, Av 1 Maio, 39 S - 1 E, 6000 Castelo Branco.

Instituto de Linguas de Faro, Av 5 de Outubro, 8000 Faro.

Instituto de Linguas do Fundao, Urb Rebordao Lt 17-r/c, 6230 Fundao.

Instituto de Linguas de Oeiras, Rua Infante D Pedro 1 e 3-r/c, 2780 Oeiras.

Instituto de Linguas de Paredes, Av Republica, Casteloes Cepeda, 4580 Paredes.

Instituto Nacional de Administracao, Centro de Linguas, Palacio Marquus de Oeiras, 2780 Oeiras.

Instituto Sintrense de Linguas, Rua Dr Almeida Guerra 26, 2710 Sintra.

Interlingua, Lg 1 de Dezembro 28, 8500 Portimao.

Interlingua, Rua Dr Joaquim Telo 32-1E, 8600 Lagos.

International House, Lisbon, Rua Marques Sa Da Bandeira 16, 1000 Lisboa - Branches throughout Portugal.

International Language School, Av Rep Guine Bissau, 26-A, 2900 Setubal.

Inter Way, Po Jose Fontana 11 -1Dto, 1000 Lisboa.

ISLA, Bo S Jo de Brito, 5300 Bragan A, Manitoba,C Com Premar, l-72, 4490 Povoa De Varzim.

Know-How, Av Alvares Cabral 5-300, 1200 Lisboa.

Lancaster College, Rua C Civico, Ed A Seguradora 2, 6200 Covilha.

Lancaster College, Pta 25 Abril 35-1E, 4400 Vila Nova De Gaia.

Language School, Rua Alm Candido Reis 98, 2870 Montijo.

Linguacoop, Av. Manuel da Maia 46-10 D, 1000 Lisboa.

Linguacultura, Rua Dr Joaquim Jacinto 110, 2300 Tomar.

Linguacultura, Lg Sto Antonio 6-1 Esq, 2200 Abrantes.

Lisbon Language Learners, Rua Conde Redondo 33-r/cE, 1100 Lisboa.

Lusodidacta, Av Ant Augusto Aguiar 24-7D, 1000 Lisboa.

Mundilingua, Rua Dr Tefilo Braga, Ed Rubi-1, 8500 Portimao.

Mundilinguas, Rua Miguel Bombarda 34-1, 2000 Santarem.

The New Institute of Languages, Urb Portela Lt 197-5B-C, 2685 Sacavem.

Novo Instituto de Linguas, Rua Cordeiro Ferreira 19 C-1D, 1700 Lisboa.

PROLINGUAS, Rua Saraiva Carvalho, 84 - Pt2, 1200 Lisboa.

Royal School of Languages, Av Dr Lourenco Peixinho 92-2, 3800 Aveiro. Tel: (034) 2956. Fax: (034) 382870. Also schools in Agueda, Ovar, Guarda, Porto.

Tell School, Rua Soc Farmaceutica 30-1, 1100 Lisboa.

Tjaereborg Studio, Av Liberdade 166-4F, 1200 Lisboa.

Weltsprachen-Institut, Qta Carreira 37 r/c, 2765 Sao Joao do Estoril. TEL: 4684032. Branch: Rua Dr Brito Camacho 22-A-1, 7800 Beja.

Whyte Institute, Lg das Almas 10-2E/F, 4900 Viana Do Castelo.

World Trade Centre - Lisbon, Av Brasil 1-5e8, 1700 Lisboa.

Spain

Minimum salary: The rates of pay for EFL teachers range from 130,000 to 160,000 pesetas. A minimum salary should not be less than 105,000 pesetas net per month (for 25 teaching hours per week). Some employers may pay a fixed salary for 10-14 hours and give the rest cash in hand on an hourly basis. Before agreeing to these terms, check holiday and sick pay, and whether the minimum salary is guaranteed should the school be unable to offer you the number of hours agreed (US$ = approximately 130 pesetas).

A teacher can also charge up to 2,500 pesetas an hour for a private class on a one-to-one basis. However, due to the large number of EFL teachers entering Spain, it is essential that you are prepared to put considerable effort into finding work.

Tax and health insurance: Up to about 6% taxation on gross salary, deducted at source. If your salary is quoted net, make sure that your employer is covering your tax and national health insurance contributions. All foreigners legally employed are entitled to medical treatment, but private medical insurance is no more or less necessary than it is in Great Britain.

Visa requirements: Non-EC nationals still require visas and work permits, which you must apply for personally in your own country with a written offer of employment. A work permit can then be obtained within Spain through your employer, but the papers are expensive and not easy to obtain, so employers tend to favour applications from EC nationals, who no longer need them.

Accommodation: The average price of accommodation in a shared 2-3 bedroom flat in the centre of a provincial town is about 50,000 pesetas, rising to 90,000 in Madrid, Barcelona and San Sebastian.

Other information: Spain's education system is undergoing *La Reforma*, the introduction of more modern teaching methods into the state system. English is also now taught at primary level, which has made it harder for teachers to find work in the private sector, especially given the high rates of unemployment. Although the boom in EFL in Spain is slowing down, and competition for school work is fierce, there is still scope for freelance private and agency work. Perhaps now there is a greater demand for trained primary and secondary school, rather than straight EFL, teachers, in International or Bilingual day-schools. Coming out to Spain to try and find work is, these days, essential. It is highly unlikely that a teacher will get anywhere by sending a CV out to schools here from Britain.

Schools usually recruit in September and January, when many teachers have left because of the often surprisingly cold winters (especially in Northern towns such as Avila, Burgos and Vitoria). June is also a good time for teachers to come out, as it coincides with the end of the academic year. Qualifications and experience are an invaluable asset. English and Spanish Studies, 26-40 Kensington High Street, London W8 4PF recruit for teachers to work in Spain. Tel: (0171) 937 3110. Fax: (0171) 376 2714.Try also the English Educational Services, C/ Alcala 20-2, 28014 Madrid. Tel: 341 531 4783. Fax: 341 531 5298.

List of schools in Spain

Academia Andaluza de Idiomas, Crta El Punto 9, Conil, Cadiz.

Academia Britanica, Rodriguez Sanchez 15, 14003 Cordoba.

Academia Saint Patricks, Calle Caracuel 1, 17402 Girona.

Academia Wellington House, Guiposcoa 79, 08020 Barcelona.

Acento - The Language Company, Ruiz De Alarcon 7, 21, 41007 Sevilla.

Afoban, Alfonso Xii 30, 41002 Sevilla.

AHIZKE/CIM, Loramendi 7, Apartado 191, Mondragon Guipuzcoa.

Alce Idiomas, Nogales 2, 33006 Oviedo. Tel: 85 254543.

Aljarafe Language Academy, Crta Castilleja-Tomares 83, Tomares, Sevilla.

American Institute, El Bachiller 13, 46010 Valencia.

Apple Idiomas, Aben al Abbar 6, 46021 Valencia. Tel: 362 25 45.

Audio Jeam, Pza Ayuntamiento 2, 46002 Valencia.

Augusta Idiomas, Via. Augusta 128, 08006 Barcelona.

Aupi, Jesus 43, 46007 Valencia.

Berlitz, Gran Via 80-4, 28103 Madrid. Tel: 1 542 3586. Also schools around Spain.

Berlitz, Edif Forum 1 Mod, 3 Av Luis Morales, S/N 41018 Sevilla.

Big Ben College, Plaza Quintiliano 13, Calahorra 26500 La Rioja.

Brighton, Rambla Catalunya 66, 08007 Barcelona.

Britannia School Of English, Juan Diaz De Solés 9, Bl 2 41010 Sevilla.

Britannia School, Leopoldo Lugones 3-1B, 33420 Lugones, Asturias. Tel: 85 26 2800. Also Raset 22, Barcelona 08021. Tel: 3 200 0100. Fax: 414 4699.

British Language Centre, C/Bravo Murillo 377, 28020 Madrid. Tel: 1 733 07 39.

Callan Method School of English, Calle Alfredo Vicenti 6 bajo, 15004 La Coruna.

Centre of English Studies, Jai Alai 5, 46010 Valencia.

Centro Atlantico, Villanueva 2apdo, 28001 Madrid. Tel: 1 435 3661. Fax: 1 578 1435.

Centro Britanico, Republica De El Salvador 26-10m, (Edificio Simago), 15701 Santiago De Compostela, La Coruna. Tel: 8159 7490.

Centro Cooperativo De Idiomas, Clavel 2, 11300 La Linea, Cadiz.

Centro Estudios Norteamericanos, Aparisi y Guijarro 5, 46005 Valencia.

Centro de Estudios de Ingles, Garrigues 2, 46001 Valencia. Tel: 352 21 02.

Centro De Idiomas Liverpool, Libreros 11-10, 28801 Alcala de Henares, Madrid. Tel: 1 881 3184.

Centro De Ingles, Tejon Y Marin, S/N 14003 Cordoba.

Centro de Ingles Luz, Passage Luz 8bajo, 46010 Valencia. Tel: 361 40 74.

Centro Linguistico del Maresme, Virgen De Montserrat. Tel: 35 55 5403 (Jenifer Grau).

Centro Superior de Idiomas, Tuset 26, 08006 Barcelona.

Chatterbox Language Centre, Verge de l'Assumpcio 21, Barbera del Valles.

CLIC (Centro de Lenguas é Intercambio Cultural), Santa Ana, 1141002, Sevilla. Tel: 34-5-437 4500/438 6007. Fax: 437 18 06.

Collegium Palatinum, Calle de Rodriguez San Pedro 10, 28015 Madrid. Tel: 1 446 2349. Fax: 1 593 4446. English Courses during the academic year combined with university courses. Accommodation off campus, cultural and activity program offered.

"Communication", Academia De Idiomas, Sociedad Cooperativa Andaluza, C/ Camilo José Cela 12-1a, 11160 Barbate, Cadiz.

The English Academy, Cruz 15, 11370 Los Barrios, Cadiz.

English Activity Centre, Pedro Frances 22a, 07800 Ibiza. Tel: 7131 5828.

The English Centre, Apdo de Correos 85, 11500 El Puerto De Santa Maria, Cadiz. Tel: 34 56 850560, Fax: 873804. English/Spanish school for teens/adults wishing to combine language-learning experience with sun & sea.

The English Centre, San Francisco 10, 33400 Aviles, Asturias. Tel: 8554 5933.

The English College, c/ Andalucia 2/4, Gijon 33208, Asturias.

English Language Centre, Jesús Maria 9-1d, 14003 Cordoba.

English Studies, SA Avenida de Arteijo 8-1, 15004 La Coruna.

English Way, Platero 30, San Juan De Aznalfarache, Sevilla.

Epicenter, Niebla 13, 41011 Sevilla.

Eurocentre, Puerta De Jerez 3-1, 41001 Sevilla.

Eurolingua, San Felipe 3, 14003 Cordoba.

European Language Studies, Edificio Edimburgo, Plaza Nina, 21003 Huelva. Tel: 34 59 263821. Fax: 34 59 280778. Modern Centre, Homologated with University of London, with twenty teachers who have conversational Spanish and experience in all ages.

Fiac School, Mayor 19, 08221 Terrassa, Barcelona.

FLAC, Escola D'Idiomes Moderns Les Valls, 10 2/0, 08201 Sabadell, Barcelona.

Glossa English Language Centre, Rambla De Cataluna 9, 78 20 2A 08008 Barcelona.

Idiomas Oxford, Calvo Sotelo 8-1, 26003 Logrono. Tel: 4124 41332.

Idiomas Progreso, Plaza Progreso 12, 07013 Palma De Mallorca. Tel: 7123 8036.

Idiomaster, Los Maristas, 2 Lucena, Cordoba.

inlingua Idiomas C/o Greforio Fernandez 6, 47006 Valladolid.

inlingua Idiomas, Maestro Falla 5, 2,12, Puerto del Rosario, 35600 Fuerteventura, Canary Islands.

inlingua idiomas, Tomas Morales 28, 35003 Las Palmas de Gran Canaria. Tel: 2836 0671.

inlingua idiomas, Ribera 13, 46002 Valencia.

The Institute of English, Santiago Garcia 8, 46100 Burjasot (Valencia).

Interlang, Pl Padre Jean de Mariana 3-2, 45002 Toledo.

International House, Canovas Del Castillo 33, 11001 Cadiz.

International House, Rodriguez Sanchez 15, 14003 Cordoba.

International House, C/Hernan Cortes 1, 21001 Huelva. Tel: (959) 246529.

International House, Pascual y Genis 16, 46002 Valencia. Tel: 352 06 42.

John Atkinson School of English, Isaac Peral 11 y 13, 11100 San Fernando.

Key School Princes, 3-1, 36001 Pontevedra.

Language Study Centre, Corredera Baja 15 Bajo, Chiclana De La Frontera, Cadiz.

Lawton School, Cura Sama 7, 33202 Gijon, Asturias. Tel: 8534 9609.

Lexis, Avenida de la Constitucion 34, 18012 Granada.

Linguasec, Malaga 1, 14003 Cordoba.

London House, Baron de S Petrillo 23bajo, 46020 Benimaclet.

Manchester School, San Bernado 81, 33201 Gijon, Alicante. Tel: 8535 8619. Fax: 8535 6932.

Modern School, Gerona 11, 41003 Sevilla.

Nelson English School, Jorge Manrique 1, Santa Cruz, Tenerife.

Ten Centro de Ingles, Caracuel 24, Jerez de la Frontera. Tel: 324707.

The New School, Calle Sant Joan 2, 2a Reus Tarragona.Tel: 77 330775.

Number Nine English Language Centre, Sant Onofre 1, 07760 Ciutadella De Menorca, Baleares. Tel: 7138 4058.

Onoba Idiomas, Rasco 19-2, 21001 Huelva.

Oxford Centre, Alvaro de Bazan 16, 46010 Valencia.

Oxford House, San Jeronimo 9-11, Granada.

The Oxford School, Maron Feria 4, 41800 Sanlúcar La Mayor, Sevilla.

Passport to English, Segura 14 - 16, 41001 Sevilla.

Piccadilly English Institute, Los Chopos 8, 14006 Cordoba.

Preston English Centre, Edif El Carmen Chapineria 3, Jerez De La Frontera, Cadiz.

Principal English Centre, Aptdo 85, Puerto De Santa Maria, Cadiz.

Ripolles, Adriano 3, 41001 Sevilla.

Rolleston, Melliza 1, Dos Hermanas, Sevilla.

San Roque School, Plaza San Roque 1, Guadalajara.

Skills, Trinidad 94, 12002 Castellon. Tel: 6424 2668.

Stanton School of English, Colon 26, 03001 Alicante. Tel: 65207581.

St Patrick's Caracuel, 1 Jerez De La Frontera, Cadiz.

The Tolkien Academy, Juan Bautista Erro 9, 20140 Andoain.

Top Class, Plaza del Chofre 20, 20001 San Sebastian.

Tower Centre, Asuncion 43, 41011 Sevilla.

Trafalgar idiomas, Avda Castilla 12, 33203 Gijon, Asturias. Tel: 85 332361.

Trinity School SL, C/ Golondrina (Plaza Jardines) 17 Bajo, 11500 Puerto De Santa Maria, Cadiz. Tel: 34-(9) 56-871926. Fax: 541918.

Wall Street Institute, Av República Argentina 24 P12 D, 41011 Sevilla.

Warwick House Centro Linguistico Cultural, Lopez Gomez 18-2, Valladolid 47002.

Welcome, Avenida Guipuzcoa 2, 20300 Irun.

Westfalia, Chapineria 3, Edificio El Carmen, Modulo 310, 11403 Jerez de la Frontera.

William Halstead School of English, Camilo Jose Cela 12, 11160 Barbate de Franco.

Windsor School of English, Virgen De Loreto 19-1, 41011 Sevilla.

Yago School, Maria De Molina 40-l, 28006 Madrid.

York House, English Language Centre, Muntaner 479, 08021 Barcelona. Tel: 32 113200.

Sweden

Minimum salary: Every language school employer pays union rates, even if none of the employees is a union member. At present this works out at just over 130 krona per 45 minute lesson. This can be supplemented with private lessons. Expect about 15,000 krona before tax for a full-time job.

Tax and health insurance: Tax currently stands at 32%. Only 2% of a hefty social security bill is met by your employer - check how much you will have to pay on top.

Visa requirements: A work permit must be obtained before you enter Sweden. To get one takes about six weeks and it will be initially valid for nine months. Permits are not possible to obtain for private language schools. International Language Services, based at the Salisbury School of English, arrange visas for the teachers they recruit for Folk University in Stockholm. The Folk University places teachers in its network of adult institutions, known as the British Centres, throughout the country.

Accommodation: 2,000 Krona per month for a shared flat, probably a third of your income. Finding accommodation can be a real problem, especially in Stockholm. Make sure your employer helps you find somewhere. The standard of housing is invariably high.

Other information: Swedish children learn English from age 10. General English courses were subsidised by council grants, but cut-backs have made lessons more expensive. As a result, schools have had a drop in numbers. Nevertheless, joining the EC has maintained demand, especially for business English. Many companies now have language departments. Adult education is also very popular in Sweden. Eating out and drinking is very expensive. Sweden is good for the outdoor life, but the winters are long.

The Rest of Europe

The disintegration of the Soviet Bloc has led to enormous economic disparities amongst the countries of eastern and central Europe. Most of the expanding economies are applying to join the European Union and job prospects in these countries are very good, whilst in other countries the economies have stagnated and the only work easily found is voluntary.

Albania

Despite years of isolation, the general level of English is quite good, especially in Tirana, perhaps because English offers Albanians a means of leaving the country. They are going through an uneasy transitionary period at the moment, which has resulted in a short supply of food and books. Tertiary demand for English is huge, though college entry requirements are strict. Should you wish to work in this interesting, but unstable country, contact the British Council resource centre in Tirana or Fakulteti Histori-Filogogja, Universiteti Tiranes, Tirana.

Bulgaria

Minimum salary: Currently Bulgarian EFL teachers charge an average of 100 Leva per private lesson (45 minutes), which is about £2.25. It should be noted that prices in Bulgaria are subject to constant growth as a consequence of the increasing inflation rate.

Tax and health insurance: The majority of teachers will be required to pay income tax. The rate of tax varies and is progressively increased. Its highest annual rate of 52% is applied to an annual income of 270,000 Bulgarian Leva which is equivalent to about £6,000. Health insurance is still not developed in Bulgaria apart from the general social security system. It is advisable to take out a private health insurance policy.

Visa requirements: All non-Bulgarian citizens need to obtain an entry visa, which may be obtained from the Bulgarian Consular Service in any country. Within 48 hours of arrival, all foreigners are required to make an address registration with the respective Visa and Passport Office of Police. If your employer is Bulgarian you will be issued with a "labour visa", which permits residence for up to a year. In its present application, the authorities are rather lenient towards employees originating from the EC and US. However, as the system evolves, it may become more stringent.

Accommodation: Prices vary, depending on location, size and type of building. Renting prices are currently US$ 5-15 per sq. metre. However, accommodation is often provided free with your contract of employment.

Other information: Air fares are usually paid for and some contracts may include free flights for your family. Conditions continue to be hard and inflation is still very high. Expect food shortages and fuel rationing, especially in winter. Other basic necessities are often unobtainable. However, Bulgarians are highly motivated in their desire to learn English. As a teacher, expect to have a high profile in the community. Bulgaria has a surprisingly developed ELT structure.

The Central Bureau for Educational Visits and Exchanges arrange for EFL teachers to work for the Bulgarian Ministry of Education in local ELMS. There are EFL opportunities in language centres such as the Institute for Foreign Students in Sofia which runs intensive courses for professionals. The British Council have recruited lecturers for Bulgarian universities, but generally need teacher trainers. The East European Partnership (EEP) also recruit volunteers to teach in Bulgaria.

List of schools in Bulgaria

Alliance, Centre for Teaching of Foreign Languages, 3 Slaveikov Square, 1000 Sofia.
Centre for Language Qualification, National Palace of Culture, Administrative Bldg., 2nd Floor, Room 131, Sofia.
Institute of Tourism, Park Ezero, 8000 Bourgas.
Meridian 22, 6 Dimiter Blagoev Street, Sofia.
Pharos Ltd., 2 S.Vrachansky Street, Vasrajdane Square, Sofia.

Croatia

Minimum salary: Rates vary from DM600-DM1000 (US$400-650) per month depending on if the school is private or state-run. Native speakers are paid more only in some private schools according to the teachers' qualifications and experience and the size and reputation of the school.

Tax and health insurance: Paid by the employer, so teachers receive a net salary.

Visa requirements: A visa is not required for British citizens and a work permit will be arranged by the employer on arrival in Croatia without problem.

Accommodation: Average rent is 300-500 DM per month for a one-bedroom flat. Flats are not easy to find and landlords ask for rent be paid in foreign currency.

Other information: There is a shortage of English teachers throughout Croatia, but schools generally require their teachers to have a university degree and a teaching diploma. The British Council in Zagreb advises teachers who want to work in Croatia to contact them first to establish working conditions. Inflation and exchange rates are now stable. Croatia was always a pleasant place to live and work for native speaking English teachers. Things are now looking brighter now that the political and economic situation caused by the war is beginning to stabilise.

List of schools in Croatia

Centar za strane jezike, Vodnikova 12, 4100 Zagreb and Trg republike 2, 58000 Split.
Class, Jankomirska 1, 41000 Zagreb.
The English Workshop, Medulinska 61, 52000 Pula.
Interlang, Krisaniceva 7, 51000 Rijeka
Lancon, Jurisiceva 1, 4000 Zagreb.
Linguae, Radiceva 4, 51000 Rijeka.
LS Lukavec, Skolska 27, 41409 Donja Lomnica
Narodno sveuciliste, Skola za strane jezike, Trg Matice Hrvatske 3, 41430 Samobor
Octopus, Savska 13, 41000 Zagreb.
Radnicko sveuciliste, Bozidar Maslaric, 5400 Osijek.
Skola za strane jezike, Varsavska 14, 41000 Zagreb
Svjetski jezici, Varsavska 13, 41000 Zagreb
Verba, M. Gorkog 5, 51000 Rijeka.

Cyprus

Minimum salary: Salaries vary significantly, with no minimum guidelines. Private institutes may in some cases pay only hourly or weekly and not at all during holiday periods.
Tax and health insurance: It is advisable for all non-Cypriot nationalities to take out personal insurance against illness and accident. Information on income tax rates can be obtained from the Ministry of Finance, Department of Inland Revenue, Nicosia.
Visa requirements: All non-Cypriots require work permits before taking employment in Cyprus. These are not normally granted by the government of Cyprus unless the vacant position cannot be filled by a Cypriot. It is the responsibility of the prospective employer to obtain a work permit for the applicant before engaging their services. Travel to Cyprus is inadvisable before a work permit has been issued.
Accommodation: Rented accommodation in the large towns is plentiful and is comparatively inexpensive. The rent of a furnished, three-bedroom house for example, in a respectable area should cost C£350-500. Unfurnished flats of a similar size and situation cost C£150-180, and shared accommodation is also widely available and inexpensive.
English language newspapers: Advertisements in the local English language newspapers may be helpful in finding employment and include *The Cyprus Mail* (P.O. Box 1144, Nicosia) and the *Cyprus Weekly* (Archbishop Makarios III Avenue, Mitsis Building 3, Office 216, Nicosia).
Other information: As a former British colony, English is widely spoken and the state system is fairly efficient. There are a number of private language schools which may recruit native English speakers. English is taught in the last years of state primary schools and in secondary schools but many students take private lessons and sit for a number of English examinations. The Ministry of Education normally requires teachers to have a degree in the subject being taught and it is therefore advisable for prospective teachers to clear their qualifications with the Ministry of Education.

List of schools in Cyprus

Ashley Janice, Arch Makarios III Avenue, Kanika Street,
CDA Coaching Centre, 5 Akritas Street, Larnaca.
Europa Language Centre, 3 Kypranoros Street, Nicosia.
Forum Language Centre, 47a Prodromou Street, Strovolos, Nicosia.
G.C. School of Careers, PO Box 5275, Nicosia
Language Centre, 49 Kennedy Avenue, Nicosia
Linguaphone Institute, 21 P Katelari Street, Nicosia.
Masouras Private Institute, D Lipertus Street, Zenia Zoe Court, Flat 103, Paphos.
PASCAL Institute, 3c Pantelides Street, Strovolos, Nicosia.
Proodos Institute, 2 Asopios Street, Nicosia.
Richmond Institute, 9 Chr Kannaouros Street, Dasoupolis, Nicosia.
Themis Tutorial, 6a Einar Gzerstad Street, Larnaca.
Thomas Michaelides, 52 Golgon Street, Limassol. Limassol.

The Czech Republic

Minimum salary: Foreign teachers are paid on the same basis as Czech teachers, which is about 5,000 Czech crowns per month after tax. Private lessons pay up to 200 crowns per hour.
Tax and health insurance: Medical insurance is usually paid by employers. Tax is charged at the rate of 15-20%, although you may be able to claim some of this back if you are on a short-term contract.
Visa requirements: Not necessary for EU nationals, but other nationalities should apply to their Czech Embassy. Work and residence permits will usually be arranged by your employer. Teachers under contract will qualify for a residence permit which is necessary for any kind of employment. It is best to apply for this long-term residence permit prior to entry at any Czech Embassy. Application may also be made upon arrival as a tourist. When applying for the permit you will be asked to present your contract, as well as confirmation of housing arrangements, and that you hold no police record in the Czech Republic.
Accommodation: This may be subsidised or arranged by your employer - often with a local family or student hostel. Central Prague is short of housing and outlying areas tend to be drab concrete estates. Expect to pay 1,500 to 4,000 crowns a month in Prague. You must be prepared to travel fairly long distances to work.
Other information: The Czech Republic is the wealthier half of former Czechoslovakia, and enjoys a fairly stable

political environment. There is a thriving EFL market, particularly in Prague and Brno. English is becoming more popular than German as the second language to learn. Teaching may well involve travelling to give in-company lessons. Expect to work 14-22 hours per week, mainly early morning or early evening. Private lessons are easy to come by and there are numerous private language schools - some more reputable than others. The Bell School in Prague and ILC in Brno are two major international organisations now established in the Czech Republic. There are also many opportunities to work in the state sector in secondary schools. Although these offer competitive salaries and free accommodation, teachers are expected to pay their own travel expenses. Since 1992, 21 Upper Vocational Schools have been created.

The Academic Information Agency (Tel: + 42 2 24229698. Fax: + 42 2 24229697) helps foreign teachers find jobs at local schools. Foreign teachers are not expected to speak Czech and will tend to teach conversation classes, although you may also be required to teach grammar.

Outside the main cities there are still shortages of many essential food items, particularly fruit and vegetables. Books are expensive and in short supply. Transport and eating out are cheap, though in Prague restaurants tend to be busy.

Addresses

Academic Information Agency, Dum zahranicnich styku MSMT CR, Senovazne namesti 26, 111 21 Praha 1.
The British Council English Language Teaching Centre, Narodni 10, 125 01 Praha 1.
Ministry of Education, Karmelitska 9, 11000 Prague 1 - recruit for general state schools.
Pedagogicky Ustav Prahy, Na Porici 4, 11000 Prague 1 - recruit for state schools in the Prague area.
Pro-English, Mala Strana, 5 Hellichova (4th Floor), Prague.

Hungary

Minimum salary: 15-25,000 forints per month for c. 20 hours/week in the private sector (15,000 in the state sector). Private lessons pay 300-800 forints an hour and are easy to find.
Tax and health insurance: 62%.
Accommodation: In Budapest there is a housing shortage and you should expect to pay 15-30,000 forints per month - potentially more than your basic salary. State sector and many private sector schools subsidise or provide free accommodation. Student hostels are a short-term solution.
Visa requirements: To prevent another glut of unemployed teachers, regulations have been tightened. You must have a job offer before entry. You will then be issued with a one-month permit (costing $20), which can be extended at your local police station.
Other information: EFL is big business in Hungary and native speakers are needed in private schools, state schools and universities. English has replaced Russian as

a requirement for university entrance. There are over 300 private language schools, many of which belong to The Chamber of Language Schools - a recognition body. For a fee of $20 they put teachers on a database which is circulated to members; contact: Eva Vajda, Nyelviskolak Kamaraja, Rath Gyorgy u.24, 1122 Budapest. Tel: 155 4664.

Teaching standards are generally high in Hungary. The larger private schools will expect good qualifications, but state primary and secondary schools take on unqualified assistants, which is a good way to get some experience, but not a great income. The state sector has no formal recruitment policy, so jobs are difficult to track down - try IATEFL Hungary. In secondary schools, you may need to speak Hungarian.

The East European Parnership (EEP), the Fulbright Program and the US Peace Corps recruit for voluntary work in Hungary (see p59). The Central Bureau in London recruits for summer camps.

Addresses:

The Budapest Pedagogical Institute, Horveth Mihaly Ter 8, Budapest 8 - recruits for schools in Budapest.
The English Teachers' Assoc. of the National Pedagogical Institute, Bolyai u.14, 1023 Budapest.
IATEFL Hungary, Kecskemet, Akademia Korut 20.L.31, 6000 Budapest.
IH Budapest, POB 95, Budapest 1364.
recruits for schools outside Budapest.
RLC International, 27-28 George Street, Richmond, Surrey T9 1HY, UK - recruits for Hungary.

Iceland

Minimum salary: 80,000-90,000 krona per month.
Tax and health insurance: The only tax rate is 39.85%.
Visa requirements: Your employer must arrange a work permit before you enter. You will also need to be issued with an identity card and National Registration Number.
Accommodation: 20,000-30,000 krona per month for a one-bedroom flat, often part of a contract, otherwise hard to find.
Other information: Because of its limited population and high general level of English, EFL work is limited, especially in the current recession. Expect a harsh climate but if you enjoy outdoor living, thermal springs and volcanic landscape, this could be the place for you. Most foreigners work in the fish processing industry.

List of schools in Iceland

Ministry of Education and Culture, Sölvhólsgötu 4, 150 Reykjavík
Enskuskólinn hf, Túngötu 5, 101 Reykjavík
Málaskóli Halldórs Thorsteinssonar, Midstraeti 7, 101 Reykjavík
Máloskólinn Mímir, Ananaustum 15, 107 Reykjavík

Malta

Minimum salary: 3,300-3,500 Maltese pounds per year.
Tax: 30%.
Visa restrictions: Work permits will be arranged by your employer.
Accommodation: 60 Maltese pounds per month for a bedsit.
English language newspaper: *The Times (D)*.
Other information: EU Commission discussions with Malta on accession could begin in mid-1997 as the country has made important progress in aligning its economy with those of the EU. English is the official language on this tiny Mediterranean island. In theory, only Maltese nationals can teach here, but the surprisingly large EFL market, especially in the summer when foreign students take advantage of its relatively cheap courses and nice climate, often means a shortage of qualified teachers. Business English is also big. The Federation of English Language Teaching Organisations in Malta (FELTOM) monitors standards of schools on Malta.

List of schools in Malta

AM Language Studio, 14 Tigne St., Sliema. Tel: 318673.
inlingua, 9 Fawwara Lane, Off Tower Lane, Sliema.
Institute of English Language Studies, Manoel Court, Parisio St., Sliema. Tel: 335367.
NSTS English Language Centre, 220 St Paul St., Valletta.
Revival English Language Institute, Trinity Hall, Taliana Lane, Gzira. Tel: 331853.

Norway

Minimum salary: 95 krona an hour, up to 400 krona for business English. (US$ = approximately 6 krona)
Tax and health insurance: 35-40%.
Visa requirements: Very hard to obtain unless you live with a Norwegian or have a specialised skill, such as in EAP.
Accommodation: 2,500 krona a month for a one-bedroom flat in Oslo, 2,000 krona elsewhere.
Other information: Children learn English from age 9, but English language tuition tends to be informal evening classes. With possible entry into the EC, there has been a growth in business English. There is fierce competition for jobs, and unemployment is high.

Poland

Minimum salary: Average salary when working for a state school is about 1,500,000 zloty (about US $80) a month for about 18 contact hours a week. Some schools may offer 'extra hours' and may pay more for this. The basic salary may be slightly more in 'social schools', which are funded by the Ministry of Education and parents (60%), and local regional authorities (40%). Private language schools pay more - 120,000-150,000 zloty per hour.
Tax and health insurance: No taxation for two years. Health insurance, if paid by the school, amounts to 48% of total salary. However, schools are very reluctant to cover this, and it is generally advisable to obtain your own insurance cover from your native country.
Visa requirements: Visas have been abolished and there is no need for them if a teacher comes for a short period of time (say a month). Any period longer than this will require the school to apply, on a teacher's behalf, for a work permit to Wojewodzke Urzad Pracy, 44 Czerniakowska Street, 00-717 Warszawa. It usually takes a about a month to come through. A teacher with employers' sponsorship may also get a "working visa" before departure from their local Polish consulate.
Accommodation: About 2,000,000-3,000,000 zloty for a one-bedroom flat - less with a family or when a school arranges it. If you work in the state sector through a scheme or voluntary organisation, like the VSO or Teachers for Poland, you will be offered accommodation with board or its equivalent. Finding accommodation in the large cities is not easy and is often expensive, and it should be remembered that gas and electricity are expensive. In order to live at a reasonable standard in a large city in Poland, expect to spend an average of 8-10 million zloty per month.
Other information: If you want to find a state post in a school on your own, contact: The Ministry of National Education, Department of International Cooperation, Mrs Katarzyna Malec, Al. I Armii Wojska Polskiego 25, Warszawa, Poland (Tel:+ 297241 ext. 655).

Conditions are improving quickly in Poland. With the collapse of communism and the move to a market economy, there has been a huge demand for English and an increase in the number of private language schools. Poland is now probably the fastest growing market for EFL. The Polish Association for Standards in English (PASE), monitors schools in Poland. Native English speaking teachers are in demand, and qualifications are not always essential. Now that Britain has lifted visa restrictions to Poles visiting the UK, British English has the edge on US English. There is a need for business English, and in-company work can be extremely lucrative. The British Council and the Peace Corps have invested heavily in Poland. There are opportunities for teachers in the state sector, although pay is likely to be low.

The Central Bureau and EEP also recruit for Poland.

List of schools and addresses

ABC, Uslugi Jezykowe, ul ZWM 6 m 29, Warszawa.
AJM, ul Klaudyny 30 m 100, 01-684 Warszawa.
American English School, Oddzial Warszawa-Cztery, Kondratowicza 25a m 33, 03-285 Warszawa.
Angloschool, ul Elblaska 65/84, Warszawa.
AS, Studio Jezykow Obcych, ul M L Kinga 13, 75-016 Koszalin
Bakalarz, Prywatne Studium Jezykowe, ul Rakowiecka 45/25, 02-528 Warszawa. Tel: 489 889
Best, Prywatna Szkole, Jezyka Angielskiego, ul Wiktorsga

99, Warszawa.

Beyond 2000, Szkola Jezykow Obcych, ul Szuberta 39/5, 02-408 Warszawa.

British Council English Language Centre, Warsaw Technical University, ul. Filtowa 2, 00-611 Warszawa. Tel: 25 82 87.

The British School of Warsaw, Sp z o o, ul Zielona 14, 05-500, Piaseczno

Business and Educational English, ul Conrada 10 m 57, 01-922 Warszawa.

Compact School of English, Spolka Cywilna, Nowogrodzka 78/24, 02-018 Warszawa.

Discovery, Osrodek Nauczania Jezykow Obcych, Klub WAT-u, ul Kaliskiego 25a, 01-489 Warszawa.

Dominet, ul Pulawska 33, 05-500 Piassaczno

The Eagle English Centre, Al Stanow Zjednoczonych 26 m 25, 03-965 Warszawa.

Elan, Mokotowska 9 m 6, Warszawa. Tel: 25 19 91.

Elite Language School, ul Dunikowskiego 10 m 56, 02-784 Warszawa.

English is Fun, Warchalowskiego 2/13, Warszawa.

The English Language Academy, ul Narbutta 9 m 3, 02-564 Warszawa.

English Language School, ul Gleboka 49, 43-400 Cieszyn

English Language Studio, ul Jadzwingow 1 m 34, 02-692 Warszawa.

English Unlimited, Osrodek Jezyka Angielskiego, ul Podchorazych 41/2, Warszawa.

Falaland, Osrodek Nauczania Jez Obcych, Margerytki 52, 04-908 Warszawa.

Fast, Firma Prywatna, Jezyk Angielski-Lektoraty, Ewa Maszonska-Pazdro, ul Mickiewicza 74/58, 01-650 Warszawa.

Greenwich School of English Poland, ul Zakroczymska 6, 00-225 Warszawa.

Human, Agencja Jezykow Obcych, ul Swietokrzyshka 20 pok 317, 00-002 Warszawa.

Junior Art-Language Studio, ul Gwardzistow 8 m 5, 00-422 Warszawa.

Kajman, ul Felinskiego 15, 1 LO pokoj 57 (parter), 01-513 Warszawa.

Konwersatorium, Jezykow Obcych, Grojecka 40a m 13, 02-320 Warszawa.

Kozlowski I Rejman, Kusocinskiego 2, 31-300 Mielec

International House - Bydgoszcz, Pl Piastowski 5, 85-012 Bydgoszcz. Tel: 22 35 15.

Langhelp, Al Jerozolimskie 23/34, Warszawa. Tel: 21 44 34.

Lektor, Prywatna Szkola, Nauczania Jezykow Obcych, ul Sadowa 1, Warszawa.

Lexis College of Foreign Languages, ul Danilowiczowska 11m 18, Warszawa.

Lingua, Studium Jezykow Obcych, ul Moniuszki 4a, Lodz

Lingwista, ul Saska 59, 03-958 Warszawa, and Janowskiego 50, 02-784 Warszawa.

Mosak, ul Bonifacego 83/85 m 87, Warszawa.

Omnibus, Pl Wolnosci 5, 61-738 Poznan. Tel: 52 79 08.

The Orlik Language Centre, ul Rogalskiego 2 m 49, 03-982 Warszawa.

Perfect, Naucanie Jezykow Obcych, ul Wolnosci 2 bl 13 m 14, Maciej Musiala, Zielonka

Perfekt, Firma Oswiatowa, ul J Kaden-Bandrowskiego 2/16, 01-494 Warszawa.

Poliglota, Biuro Uslug Jezykowych, ul Dzialdowska 6, 01-184 Warszawa.

Prima, Osrodek Nauczania Jezykow Obcych, ul Rozana 7 m 3, 15-669 Bialystock

Promotor, Szkola Jezykow Obcych, Agencja Oswiatowa, Kraszewskiego 32a, 05-800 Pruszkow

Prymus, ul Jasna 2/4 pok 209, 00-950 Warszawa.

Pygmalion, Szkola Jezyka Angielskiego, ul Saska 78, Warszawa.

Success, ul Batalionow Chlopskich 14/50, 94-058 Lodz

Surrey Business and Language Centres, ul Gwardzistow 20, 00-422 Warszawa.

Studio Troll, Wrzeciono 1/22, Warszawa.

Urszula, Biuro Organizacji Kursow, Dworcowa 1 pok 13, 10-431 Olsztyn

Warsaw School of Commerce, Kursy Handlowe, al Chlodna 9, Warszawa.

Warsaw Study Centre, Osrodek Jezykowo-Szkoleniowy, ul Raszynska 22, 02-026 Warszawa.

World, ul Basztowa 17, 31-143 Krakow. Tel: 22 91 61.

Worldwide English School, ul Stoleczna 21 paw 24, 01-530 Warszawa.

Yes, ul Chelmonskiego 6 m 18, Lodz. Tel: 43 95 26.

Romania

Conditions remain difficult - inflation is high without pay increases to match. Although there is a lack of resources to develop English training, there is a great deal of interest in the language and Romanian schools have always taught two foreign languages from the age of seven. Nearly all opportunities are in the state sector with local salaries. The British Council has a local operation, the Soros Foundation has set up a school Timisoara and the EEP sends volunteers (see p79).

Addresses:

ABB Power Ventures Ltd, CS-MR/PS, PO Box 8131, CH-8050 Zurich, Switzerland - recruits for in-company teachers in Romania.

Technical University, Timisoara - funded by the Soros Foundation.

Serbia and Montenegro

Minimum salary: Average rates of pay for EFL teachers range from DEM 150-200 monthly in private language schools.

Visa requirements: Contact your local Embassy for details.

Accommodation: For a flat of approximately 40 sq. metres, it will cost roughly DEM 150 per month.

Other information: Many private language schools in Yugoslavia will welcome EFL teachers, as there continues to be a high demand for such teachers.

The Republic of Macedonia

Minimum salary: An average ofDM300 per month
Accommodation: A small apartment will cost about DM200 per month.
Other information: The Republic of Macedonia is still struggling for international recognition. The economy is unhealthy and it is an expensive place to live. Despite the volatility of the region and the low rates of pay, the British Council reports growing interest in its resource centre in Skopje. There is not much TEFL activity, though there are a number of Macedonian-run private language schools. There are opportunities for voluntary work through the European Partnership. For more information on teaching contact The Embassy of the Republic of Macedonia, 10, Harcourt House, 19a, Cavendish Square, London W1M 9AD.

Slovakia

With a weaker economy than the Czech republic, conditions are much more difficult. The capital Bratislava's proximity to Vienna has led to a demand for German and private English schools are scarce. English is more popular in the eastern town of Kosice. The EEP and the Peace Corps recruit teachers on a voluntary basis (see p79).

Slovenia

Minimum salary: £7/hour freelance, £500-600 a month net (21 teaching hours/week).
Tax and health insurance: Income tax of 20%, social security charges of 22.6%. Foreigners have the same right to health services as Slovenes for a nominal charge.
Visa requirements: A work permit is required. Contact your local embassy/consulate.
Accommodation: One room - about £180/month; two bedroom apartment - about £300/month, plus bills.
Other information: As this was the first state of the former Yugoslavia to gain independence, it is the most stable. Most foreign teachers work freelance and schools will usually expect teachers to have a degree in English. Slovenia is a very pleasant place to live and the standard and cost of living are high. It is frequently likened to Austria and resembles countries in the West rather than the East. The Slovenians are anglophiles and English is spoken by people under 40, although German is more widely known.

List of schools in Slovenia

ACCENT on Language, Ljubljanska 36, 61230 Domzale. Tel: 061 712 658.
Babylon, Komenskega 11, 61000 Ljubljana. Tel: 061317980
CTJ, Vilharjeva 21, 61000 Ljubljana. Tel: 061 317 865.
CZT, Gospodarska zbornica Slovenije, 69252 Radenci. Tel: 069 65 059.

Switzerland

Minimum salary: 30-38 Swiss francs per hour, up to 125 SF in some schools. Teaching higher level classes is better paid (US$ = approximately 1.2 francs).
Tax and health insurance: Basic of 18-20%. This varies from canton to canton. Contact the local canton, which should have an office that deals with foreign workers. Some cantons levy a church tax, although this can be claimed back. A 35% 'withholding tax' is levied on interest from bank accounts, so it is advisable to invest money elsewhere.
Visa requirements: This is a problem. Although your employer should arrange a work permit, processing it is particularly rigorous. You must have employment before you enter the country. However, those in the country on a student visa are allowed to work a few hours a week.
Accommodation: 1,800-2,000SF per month in Geneva for a two-bedroom flat, less elsewhere.
Other information: Because of the work permit situation, most native English speakers tend to be married to Swiss nationals or teach part-time in addition to other employment. Teaching conditions vary between the 26 autonomous education departments, but state-run schools and colleges require Swiss qualifications. Because the Swiss must learn the other languages of the country before English at school, many go to private schools for English tuition, therefore teaching opportunities tend to be in private shools teaching general EFL. The RSA and Trinity certificates are becoming more widely recognised.

Although riddled with bureaucracy and one of the most

expensive countries in Europe, employers are usually generous about maternity leave and sick pay. English Teachers Association of Switzerland (ETAS) publish a booklet entitled *Legally Lost? Brief Information for English Teachers Working in Switzerland,* available from Silvia Dingwall, Stermenstr.7, 5415 Nussbaumen, Switzerland.

List of schools in Switzerland

Alpha Sprachstudio, Freidstrasse 72, 8032 Zurich.
Bell School, Zurich Todistrasse 1, 8002 Zurich. Tel: 1 2810781.
Collegium Palatinum, c/o American College of Switzerland, CH-1854 Leysin. Tel: (25) 34 22 23. Fax: (25) 34 13 46. English courses during the year combined with university courses. Accommodation full-board on campus. Sports and cultural programme.
Ecole Club Migros Geneve, 3 rue du Prince, 1204 Geneva. Tel: 22 286555.
Ecole Club Migros Lausanne, Place de la Palud 22. Case Postale 313, 1000 Lausanne 17. Tel: 21 202631.
Ecole Club Migros Neuchatel, 3 rue du Musee, 2001 Neuchatel. Tel: 38 258348.
ELCRA-BELL, Chemin des Sports 8 1203 Geneva. Tel: 22 3441225.
Migros Klubschule Aarau, Herzogstrasse 26, 5000 Aarau.Tel: 64 246431.
Migros Klubschule Baden, Hochhaus Hotel Linde, Hellingerstr. 22, 5400 Baden. Tel: 56 226206.
Migros Klubchule Basel, Jurastrasse 4, 4053 Basel.Tel: 61 350066.
Migros Klubschule Bern, Marktgasse 46, 3011 Bern.Tel: 31 222021.
Migros Klubschule Luzern, Schweizerhofquai 1, 6004 Luzern. Tel: 41 515656.
Scuola Club Migros Lugano, Via Pretorio 15,6900 Lugano. Tel: 91 227621.
TASIS, The American School in Switzerland, CH 6926 Monagnola-Lugano. Tel: 91 546471.

Turkey

Minimum salary: A CTEFLA teacher can expect a salary of about £400-500 month (in lira) in a private language school, and slightly more in a private secondary school in Istanbul. Rates are slightly lower in Ankara (a cheaper city) and you may be poorly paid in Izmir. Provincial rates vary, but are generally less than Istanbul and Ankara. All Turkish salaries are quoted net of tax, normally in Turkish Lira. University ELT posts can be very well paid indeed by Turkish standards, but there is a correspondingly long queue of applicants.
Tax and health insurance: Salaries are quoted net of tax. There is a legal requirement for schools to register their teachers under the state social security scheme (if the teacher requests it). It is not necessary to have a work permit to be registered. However, the service provided is generally considered to be very inadequate. It is worth investing in private health insurance policies and visits to private health centres can be very reasonably priced. Dentists are very expensive. There are health schemes available for Turkish insurance companies, and some organisations are beginning to offer them as part of the overall package. Be sure to discuss this point at interview.
Visa requirements: Visas and work permits are necessary. A work visa must be obtained from a Turkish Consulate in your country before departure. There is a charge for this service. The necessary documents for this should be provided by the Turkish employer. Residence permits are arranged on arrival. Owing to the length of time it can take for schools in the provinces to get teachers' qualifications processed (a necessary condition for the issuing of a work visa), many schools ask their prospective teachers to come in on a tourist visa and arrange work visas after arrival. The school pays a fine regularly until the documents are processed, as the teacher is technically working illegally. The legal responsibility for acquiring working permission rests with the teacher (even though all schools do the work for their teachers), so a foreign teacher has no legal defence against breach of contract by the school.
Accommodation: Most schools provide accommodation for their teachers, often in shared flats. Accommodation in Istanbul costs 50% more than other areas. Most flats in Turkey are unfurnished - your employer should help you find furnished accommodation.
English language newspaper: *Turkish Daily News* (D)
Other information: Turkey has a huge and growing EFL market as it tries to shift closer to the European Community. Unqualified teachers are not in great demand and generally a degree, plus an RSA or Trinity Certificate in TEFL will be the minimum requirement in order to obtain a work permit.

The 18-25 age group is growing fast, and with it a demand for English. The English medium secondary schools and colleges generally offer better terms and conditions than private language schools.

With national unemployment of around 15%, your pay may be 2-3 times the rate of a local university professor, even if by western standards this is a moderate wage. Inflation fluctuates dramatically, so check that wages are adjusted.

Istanbul is the most popular destination, and is relatively expensive - and polluted. Recent riots among rival Muslim factions may be a prelude to further unrest, as Islamic fundamentalism becomes more widespread. Istanbul, Izmir and Ankara, are fairly western orientated, however, further east, in addition to the Kurdish unrest, life is still fairly traditional and is also predominantly Muslim, so women may find conditions difficult. Dealing with sex, politics and religions should be avoided in the classroom.

List of schools in Turkey

Akademi School of English, PK 234, 21001 Bahar Sokar No 2, Diyarbakir. Tel: (90) 83242297. Fax: 83217908.
Ankara University, Rektorlugu, Beslevler, Ankara. Tel: 41234361.

Best English, Mesrutiyet Caddesi no 2/8, Ankara. Tel: 4172536.

Dilko English Centres, PO Box 152, Kadilkoy, 81300 Istanbul. Tel: 1 3380170.

Elissa English, Ihsaniye Mah 41, Sokak 48, Bandirma, Balikesir.

The English Centre, Rumeli Cad. 92/4, Zeki Bey Apt., Osmanbey, Istanbul. Tel: 1 470983.

English Fast, via Mr. K. Humphries, 9 Denmark Street, London WC2H 6LS, UK.

Evrim, Ozel Evrim Yabanci, Dil Kurasi, Cengiz Topel Caddesi 8/2, Camlibel, Mersin. Tel: 74121893.

International School, Eser Apt.A Blok Kasap, Sokak 1617, Esentepe, Istanbul.

Istanbul Turco-British Association, Suleyman Nazif Sokak 68, Nisantasi, 80220 Istanbul. Tel: 1 132 8200.

Istanbul University, Rektorlugu Beyarzit, Istanbul. Tel: 1 522 1489.

Kumlu Dersanerleri, Bursa Merkez, Basak Caddesi, Bursa. Tel: 241 20465.

Kent English, Mithatpasa Cad. 46/3, Kizilay, Ankara.

New Kent English, 1477 No. SK 32, Alsancak, Izmir.

Countries of the Former USSR

The Baltic States

As Estonia, Latvia and Lithuania re-establish independence, tax systems remain minimal or non-existent. Accommodation remains a real problem, so if it is part of your contract it will be a huge bonus. Otherwise you may find yourself in a student hostel. English is in demand, and there are a number of private language schools being set up, often by cooperatives of state teachers who work in them in the evenings. Universities are also crying out for teachers.

In Latvia and Lithuania, the English syllabus is part of the school curriculum which is being rewritten, but expect local salaries if you work in the state system. Experienced local teachers within the state system survive on a salary of little more than US$60-70 per month. Private companies with overseas funding can pay more lucrative rates of US$400-500 per month for Business English. Private lessons pay quite well, possibly even in hard currency. Non-qualified teachers can also find work giving conversation lessons. Conditions are changing quickly in the Baltics, but books remain in short supply. Nevertheless, motivation is high and the level of English is surprisingly good. The Peace Corps are active in the Baltics.

Estonia

Minimum salary: 1,500 kroone per month (around $100).

Visa requirements: None for UK passport holders, but the situation varies for other EU citizens. For most nationalities the procedure to obtain work permits is relatively easy.

Other information: Because of Estonia's close ties with Finland, it is better off economically and English is widespread. Private language schools are crying out for teachers. The Soros Foundation has a centre in Tallin, where the British Council plans to open a resource centre. There are a number of other private language institutes in Tallin. Arrive before the onset of winter in November.

Latvia

Minimum salary: 8,000 roubles per month (about $45). Experienced teachers could earn up to 50,000 roubles with in-company work.

Visa requirements: Work permits are easy to obtain and visas can be purchased.

Other information: Teaching material is scarce, although the government is trying to get publishers to print using local materials. The government are keen to promote English signs, which were in Russian and Latvian, and are now in English and Latvian, but Russian remains the second language.

The British Council has resource centres in Lazaetes, Lela and Riga, but economically the country is in a mess. Qualified teachers can contact the teachers' association in Latvia. Write to LATE, PO Box 194, Riga 047, Latvia.

Lithuania

Minimum salary: Expect the equivalent of $50 a month.

Visa requirements: As Estonia.

Other information: Qualified teachers can contact the Ministry of Education. The country's currency problems mean materials and foreign expertise are hard to come by. The Soros Foundation has a centre in Vilnius, where the British Council has a resource centre.

Georgia

Minimum salary: 5,000 roubles per month (the equivalent of $15).

Tax and health insurance: Tax is at source and quite low. Private health insurance is recommended.

Visa requirements: Entry visas are issued on arrival. Work permits can be obtained by your employer.

Accommodation: Usually part of a contract, or expensive for foreigners.

Other information: Conditions are difficult in Georgia, and there is civil war in the north west. Inflation is very high, but English is in demand and some private lessons may pay in hard currency. Take your own materials as these are very scarce. There are also fuel shortages, hence little heating and public transport.

The British Council in Tbilisi will give advice to those who are tempted by this adventurous, but cultured and friendly country, where teachers are warmly appreciated. Contact David Rowson at the British Council centre. Tel: Tbilisi 78832 230232. Fax: 78832 983250.

Russia

Minimum salary: Expect about US$10 per hour in the private sector, a nominal sum in the state sector.

Tax: There are plans to tax foreigners at 40% of hard currency earnings, but if paid a local salary, this will not affect you. Tax laws change frequently and are often retroactive. Private health insurance is strongly recommended. For the International Department of the Education Committee (for those interested in working in the state sector), a health certificate, a certificate of EFL qualification and references from previous employers are required.

Visa requirements: Single entry visas only can be obtained from your local embassy (£10-15). Laws on work permits are being revised, so check with the embassy.

Accommodation: Usually provided, but often in student hostels. A bedsit in Moscow will cost at least $200 a month, but foreigners often pay much more. In St. Petersburg expect to pay US$300-1000 for a small flat.

English language newspapers: *The Moscow Times, The Moscow Tribune*, and *The Moscow News*.

Other information: The rouble has plummeted in value, as the Russian economy faces hyper-inflation. Russia, like the other former states of the USSR, is desperate for English teachers but lacks the resources to meet demand. The local salary quoted above would require teachers in Moscow and St. Petersburg to give private lessons to supplement this basic income. It is probably best to arrange some employment before going and hope you can find private students through contacts when you are there, although this could prove difficult with no knowledge of Russian. There is quite a demand for teachers of young learners. Most native-English speakers are only taken on as language assistants. Teaching methods are still traditional and a knowledge of Russian helps. The Linguistic Association of Teachers of English at the University of Moscow (LATEUM) and the Moscow Association of Applied Linguistics (Maal) aim to provide cooperation between English teachers inside Russia and abroad.

English language newspapers, available free at international supermarkets, carry classifieds and you may find work through them. Finally, be prepared for a culture shock when you arrive in Moscow. Although the heart of the city has a fairly modern feel with international shops, offices and restaurants like any other big northern capital, the picture is very different out in the suburbs. Most foreigners working in Moscow receive home country-based salaries, and it is highly unlikely that you will enjoy the same standard of living on a teachers' wages. Russia relies heavily on imported goods from food and drink to electronics, and prices for most of these are similar to those in the west; so be warned.

List of institutions in Russia

Anglo-American School, Penkovaya Ul. 5, St. Petersburg
Benedict School, Pskovskaya Ul. 23, St. Petersburg
Centre for Intensive Foreign Language Instruction, Sparrow Hills, Building 2, Moscow 119899.
Intense Language Business Centre, PO box 38, Ulitsa

Gilyarovskogo 31/2, Moscow 125183
International Education Centre, School No. 56, Kutuzovski Prospekt 22, Moscow
Language Link School, BKC London-Moscow, Kashirskoe Shosse 54, Moscow 115409
Marina Anglo-American School, Leninsky Prospekt 39a, Moscow 117313
Moscow International School, 2nd Ulitsa Maryinoy Roshchi 2a, Moscow
Moscow MV Lomonosov University, Sparrow Hills, Moscow 117234.
Polyglot International School, 22 Volkov Pereulok, Flat 56, Moscow
St Petersburg University, Universitetskaya, Naberezhnaya 7/9 B-164, St Petersburg 199164.
St Petersburg University of Humanities and Social Sciences, Ulitsa Fuckhika 16, St Petersburg 192238.
RISC Language School, Ulitsa Dekabristov 23a, Moscow
Russian Academy of Sciences, Universitetskaya Naberezhnaya 5, St Petersburg 199034.

Ukraine

Minimum salary: The equivalent of $1 an hour. The official minimum salary is the equivalent of $8 a month.

Tax: Paid by your employer if you are on contract, otherwise a complex system of six different taxes.

Visa requirements: If you are invited by an employer, you do not need a work permit. Visas are issued on arrival.

Accommodation: The equivalent of $50 a month for a modest flat.

Other information: There are many private language schools in the Ukraine and teachers should find work easily. Business English is lucrative and foreign teachers can have a good standard of living. The British Council are setting up a centre in Kiev. The Slavonic Center runs business and children's classes and plans to run a summer camp. Contact Eugeny Samartsev, The Slavonic Center, 16 Rozi Luxemburg, 252021 Kiev. Fax: 2779797.

Latin America

Despite the diversity of schools in this huge area, the best opportunities for native speaker teachers are with the established organisations, such as the Culturas, the LAURELS schools or the Bi-national centres. International House and ELS also have large Latin American operations. The Latin American British Cultural Institutes (LABCI) have centres in Argentina, Brazil, Uruguay, Mexico and Paraguay. These Cultural Institutes (Culturas) have close ties with the British Council. Some have British Council postings.

Culturas are non profit-making and generally have better conditions than private language schools. Culturas will usually offer teachers a rent allowance for at least the first six months, and help find accommodation. Private health schemes are also offered. They mainly recruit locally and prefer teachers with the RSA certificate. In Mexico and Brazil the Culturas may run RSA Diploma courses. Other centres may be prepared to take on and train unqualified teachers.

The Latin American Union of Registered English Language Schools (LAURELS) was founded in Brazil in 1987 and is an association of private self-regulating language schools throughout South America. The schools are thus reputable and offer good conditions.

The recent devaluation of the Mexican currency and the subsequent economic collapse in Mexico are having a negative knock-on effect on the economies in the rest of Latin America. Foreign investment is being withdrawn, but this may be only a temporary setback. At the time of going to press it is difficult to predict the extent of the economic repercussions in the region, and we strongly advise you to double-check inflation rates, salary rates and terms and conditions of employment before you decide to leave for Latin America.

Throughout Latin America, telephone calls are cheap locally, but expensive externally. Numbers frequently change. Remember also that the Latin American academic year runs from February to December.

Argentina

Minimum salary: Pay depends on qualifications and experience. It is common practice to pay teachers per course (usually 10-12 hours per month for each course), and earnings vary between $100-300 per month for this work. Expect to earn the equivalent of about $1000-1,500 for 25 hours teaching per week.

Tax and health insurance: Local medical care is expensive. Private medical insurance is recommended.

Visa requirements: No visa is required to enter Argentina and employers can arrange a work permit. The process of obtaining a permit is lengthy and bureaucratic, sometimes taking up to eight months. Teachers will be more attractive to an employer if they obtain a permit through the Argentine Consulate in their home country. The government welcomes qualified immigrants, especially Brits (despite the Falklands conflict). You can apply for a residence permit after two years.

Accommodation: Averages at a third of your salary and hard to find.

English language newspapers: *Buenos Aires Herald (D).*

Other information: The Argentinian economy is relatively healthy and inflation is low by Latin American standards. There is a demand for Cambridge exams, which private schools have offered since the British Council closed during the Falklands Crisis. The Council now runs teacher training courses. The standard of English in Argentina is generally high, so few teachers are recruited from outside the country. You will be more in demand if you are qualified and speak Spanish.

List of schools in Argentina

Colegio Peralta Ramos, Maipu y Salta, 7600 mar de Plata, Buenos Aries.
The Franklin Institute, Vicente Lopez 54, Salta 4400.
IELI, Alberti 6444, San Jose de la Esquina, Santa Fe 2185.
Instituto Cultural Argentino-Britanico, Calle 12, No 1900, La Plata.
Instituto Rush, La Prida 820, Tucman.
Liceo Superior de Cultura Inglesa, Italia 830, Tandil, 7000 Pica de Buenos Aries.
St John's School, Recta Martinoli 3452, V Belgrano 5417 Cordoba, Pica de Cordoba.

Bolivia

Opportunities occasionally arise in Bolivia, one of Latin America's poorer countries. Positions are usually in English-medium secondary schools or with voluntary organisations (see p64).

Brazil

Minimum salary: Varies depending on experience, qualifications and type of school. A graduate in TEFL or applied linguistics can earn up to the equivalent of UK£18,000 per year, while an unqualified native speaker could expect upwards of £220 per month (£2,640 per year).

Teachers are paid 13 months in the year. Many teachers supplement their income with private classes which can be quite lucrative. Inflation is high so check that pay is adjusted and issued regularly.

Tax and health insurance: Health insurance can be taken out locally with different rates for different levels of cover. There are a number of other benefits offered by well-established institutes, including contributions to private medical insurance schemes. Members of the middle class take out private medical insurance and the recommended schemes are: Golden Cross, Bradesco Saude, Sulamerica, Itau and Unimed. Tax is levied at around 25% of the salary, which includes a contribution to the national medical scheme.

Visa requirements: At least six months should be set aside for getting a working visa. According to the Brazilian consulate in London, it is the sole responsibility of the individual to find employment and arrange a working visa. Work can be obtained illegally by visitors on tourist visas, but is obviously not to be recommended.

Good schools are unlikely to take the risk of employing such a teacher. It also leaves the teacher vulnerable to exploitation and the possibility of an eight day deportation order. Teachers should contact: Dr Paulo Cavalcant Pessoa, Chefe do Setor de Estrangeiro, Departamento de Policia Federal, Av Martin Luther King - 321, Cais do Apolo, Recife - PE, 50080-090. Tel: + 55 081 424 1444.

Accommodation: Some schools provide free accommodation.

English language newspaper: *Brazil Herald* (D).

Other information: Contributing to the huge demand for fee-paying English courses in Brazil is the poor teaching in the state sector, caused by crowded classrooms, under-funding, poorly paid teachers and a maximum of only two hours a week on the timetable, adding up to insufficient input in the state sector. The secondary level timetable is devised in such a way that a child studies in either the morning or the afternoon, but not both. This leaves plenty of time that both child and parent want to fill in a constructive manner.

The recession has made competition for jobs even more intense and a foreign language qualification is a definite advantage on your CV. One of the most noticeable features of the commercial sector is the large number of well-trained non-native speakers. They are certainly needed as the requirements for obtaining visas for foreign teachers are lengthy and bureaucratic. As the UK has a large pool of itinerant EFL teachers, it is frustrating for British schools not to be able to employ more of them.

Qualified teachers are guaranteed as much work as they want, but are most probably put off by the negative effect of inflation on living standards, and tales of violence. In fact Brazil is a safe and professionally rewarding country in which to work. Teachers will not save a great deal, but they can certainly enjoy a reasonable standard of living in a country which is seldom dull. Brazil is highly susceptible to American cultural influences and English is perceived as the key to membership of an international culture club.

Much is made of the activities of criminals by expatriates, the local media and foreign press. Care should obviously be taken not to flash money or display expensive cameras, watches or bags.

Some useful background reading can be found in the *South American Handbook* and Fodor's *Guide to Brazil*. Internal flights within Brazil are extremely expensive and if you intend to travel a lot on your own account it is worth investigating air passes, which are only issued by airline companies outside Brazil.

List of schools in Brazil

Britannia Schools, Rua Garcia D'Avila 58, Ipanema, Rio De Janeiro RJ, 22421-010. Tel: (55 21) 511-0940. Fax: (55 21) 511-0893. Six high quality schools - Rio, Sao Paulo, Porto Alegre - general English, executives, public exam preparation. Further education scheme for teachers.

Britannia Special English Studies, Rua Dr Timoteo, 752 Moinhos De Vent, Porto Alegre Rs.

Britannia Special English Studies - Juniors, Rua. Barao da Torre 599 - Rio de Janeiro, CEP 22411-003, Rj. Tel: 55 21 239-8044. Fax: 55 21 286-0861. Special English classes for children aged 4 and above, and adolescents, small groups, modern classroom resources, video classes, trips to England. Preparation for PET , CCSE 1 Cambridge exams.

Britannia Executive School, Rua Barao De Lucena 61, Botofogo, Rio de Janeiro 22260.

Britannic English Course, Rua Joao Ivo Da Silva 125, Recife Pe.

Cambridge Sociedade Brasileira do Cultura Inglesa, Rua Piaui 1234, Londrina 86020 320 Pr. Tel: 043 324 - 1092.Fax: 324-8391. University of Cambridge authorised Centre for PET, FCE, CAE, CPE and Oxford/ARELS Oral Examinations.

Casa Branca, Rua Machado De Assis 372 Boqueirao, Santos Sp.

Ccli, Rua Dr Silvio Henrique Braune 15, Nova Friburgo Rj.

Ccli, Rua Dr Silvio Henrique Braune 15, Nova Friburgo Rj.

Cel-Lep, Av. Cidade Jardin 625, Sao Paulo - Sp.

Centro de Enseñanza P.L.I., Rua de Octubro, 1234 Conj 4, Porto Alegre, RS 90000.

Centro De Cultura Inglesa, Av Guapore 2.236, Cacoal - RO, CEP 78 975-000. Tel: 55 (69) 441-2833. Fax: 441-5346. Always pioneering. Not only an English learning centre, but also a teaching training centre since 1981 in a town founded 22 years ago.

Centro De Cultura Inglesa, Rua 12 De Outubro 227, Cuiaba Mt.

Cultura Inglesa, Rua Mamanguape 411, Boa Vigem, Recife Pe.

Cultura Inglesa, Rua Goias 1507, Londrina Pr,

School House, Rua 4, No. 80 Esq. Rua 3, Goiania Go.

Cultura Inglesa, Av Bernardo Vieira De Melo 2101, Jaboatao Pe.

Cultura Inglesa, Rua Natal 553 V. Municipal, Arianopolis, Manaus -Am.

Cultura Inglesa, Visinde De Alburquerque 205, Madalena, Recife Pe.

Cultura Inglesa, Goiana, Rua 86 No.7 - Setor 74083-330 Goiana - Go. Tel: 55 62 241-4516, Fax: 241-2582. Member Brazilian Association of Culturas Inglesas, PET, FCE, CAE, CPE, CEELT centre, Communicative Learner-centred approach. Teamwork highly valued.

Cultura Inglesa, Rua Ponta Grossa 1565, Dourados Ms.

Cultura Inglesa, Av. Barao De Maruim 761, Aracaju, Sergipe 49015-040. Tel: 55 97 224-7360/4637. Fax: 221-1195. Member ABCI. Centre for Cambridge and Oxford EFL exams. Self-access centre with multi-media computers. Student body of 900.

Cultura Inglesa, Av Ouze 1281, Ituiutaba Mg.

Cultura Inglesa, Rua Eduardo De Moraes 147, Bairro Novo Olinda Pe.

Cultura Inglesa, Av Tiradentes 670, 36300 Sao Joao Del Rei MG. Tel: (032) 371-4377, Fax: (032) 371-4377.

English Forever, Rua. Rio Grande Do Sul, 356, Pituba, Salvador - Ba.

Ibi, Sep Sul Entrequadra 710/910, Brasilia Df.

Inst Academico De Cultura Inglesa, RuaConde De Porto Alegre 59, Duque De Caxias Rj.

Instituto Britanico, R. Dep Carvalho Deda 640, 49025-070 Salgado Filho, Aracaju SE. Tel: 079-23-2791. Fax: 079-27-2645. University of Oxford accredited centre, LAURELS member. Top salaries, fringe benefits.

International House-Matriz, The School House, Rua 4, 80 Se Goiania 74110-140, Goais.

Liberty English Centre, R Amintas De Barros 1059, Curitiba Pr.

Sbci, Casa Forte, Av 17 De Agosto 223, Recife Pe.

Sbci, Av Dos Andradas, 536 Juiz De Fora Mg.

Sbci, Rua Antonio De Alburquerque 746, Belo Horizonte Hg.

Sbci, Rua Do Progresso 239, Recife Pe.

Sbci, Rua Raul Pompeia 231, Rio De Janeiro Rj.

Sbci, Ponta Verde, R Eng Marion De Gusmao 603, Maceio Al.

Sbci, Rua Marechal Deodoro 1326, Franca Sp.

Sbci, Rua Visc De Inhauma 980, Ribeirao Preto Sp.

Sbci, Rua Julia Da Costa 1500, Curitiba Pr.

Sbci, Rua Humberto De Campos, Campo Grande Ms.

Sbci, Pca Rosalco Ribeiro 10, Maceio Al.

Sbci, Rua Joao Pinheiro 808, Uberlandia Mg.

Sbci, Av Rio Grande Do Sul 1411, Joao Possoa Pb.

Sbci, Av Guilherme Ferreira 650, Uberaba Mg,

Sbci, Rua Maranhao 416, Sao Paulo Sp.

Sbci, Rua Acu 495, Petropolis, Natal Rn.

Sbci, Rua Plinio Moscoso 945, Jardim Apopema, Salvador Ba.

Sbci, Rua Ana Bilmar 171, Aldeota, Fortaleza Ce.

Sbci, Rua Jeronimo Coelho 233, Joinville Sc.

Sbci, Av Simoa Gomes 400, Garanhuns Pe,

Sbci, Seps 709/908 Conjunto B, Brasilia Df.

Sbci, Rua. Sao Sebastiao 1530, Sao Carlos - Sp.

Sbci, Rua Mal Floriano Peixoto 433, Blumenau Sc.

Sbci, Av Rio Branco 17, Haringa Pr.

Sbci, R Paula Xavier 501, Ponta Grossa Pr.

Sbci, Praca Mauricio Cardoso 49, Porto Alegre Rs.

Sbci, Av. Gov. Jose Malcher 1094, Belem Pa.

Seven Language & Culture, R. Bela Cintra 898, 01415-000, Sao Paulo - Sao Paolo. Experience in a wide range of courses (children to Business English) and a wide range of methods (communicative, T.P.R., Silent Way)

St. Peter's English School, Rua Berilo Guimaraes, 182 Centro Itabuna, Bahia.

Universitas, R Gongalves Dias 858, Belo Horizonte Mg.

Chile

Minimum salary: An average of 150,000-200,000 pesos per month. Inflation is reasonably high. Private lessons will pay 1,000-3,000 pesos per hour. One-to-one lessons in multi-national companies are in demand and are potentially lucrative.

Tax and health insurance: Payable by employer.

Visa requirements: These are easy to obtain at any time for British or Irish nationals, but are harder for US nationals. Your employer should be able to arrange work permits. Temporary work and residence permits are issued for one year, when they can be extended to become permanent permits.

Accommodation: 60,000-70,000 pesos per month for a studio flat in the main cities. Sharing is difficult unless you have contacts.

Other information: It is not recommended to go to Chile without having a firm offer of employment unless you have contacts in the country. English is more in demand in the new "democratic" Chile, and private schools have mushroomed.

The British-linked Culturas and North American Cultural Institutes are major employers throughout Chile, although outside Santiago and Vina del Mar there are few, if any, opportunities for private school work. In the two main cities expect a mixture of in-class and in-company teaching. Santiago is well stocked with English language bookshops, and the Instituto Chileno Britanico has a good library of teaching material.

The Chileans consider themselves "the English of South America", and they feel a bond to the English language. They are not very flamboyant and value privacy. Chile is one of the most wealthy and stable of the South American countries.

List of schools in Chile

Andree English School, Principe de Gales 7605, La Reina, Santiago.

Instituto Chileno-Britanico De Cultura, Castilla 2607, Concepcion.

Colombia

Minimum salary: The average monthly salary ranges between 825,000 and 1,120,000 pesos per month. Inflation is routinely above 20% per month. The British Council and many other institutes pay 14 salaries per year.

Tax and health insurance: With a normal work visa teachers will pay tax according to their salaries and this could be anything from 8% upwards. If the employer is not in a private health scheme, it is strongly recommended for you to join one, since the public health service is poor, and medical treatment is very expensive.

Visa requirements: All non-Columbian teachers are required to hold a permit. The British Council arranges a Service Visa for its employees. Any reputable institute will obtain a work permit and visa for its teachers. If an institute is reluctant or unable to obtain such papers, it is probably not a very reliable concern.

Accommodation: In Bogota and most other cities, expect to pay about 250,000 pesos for a one-bedroom flat in a reasonably exclusive area of the city.

Other information: Red tape is a problem and delays in issuing of visas and work permits must be expected. Colombia's bad reputation is exaggerated. However, problems do exist and the British Embassy does put certain travel restriction on British Council employees from time to time and certain areas of the country are best avoided. It is also advisable to register with your appropriate Embassy on arrival.

In all major cities prospects for EFL teachers are good, as there are plenty of jobs available. However, it should be pointed out that the quality and conditions of these jobs is variable.

There is a growing professional class that needs English in Colombia, and despite low wages, teachers can have a good standard of living. There are English Medium International Schools, Centro Americanos and British Council centres in Bogota and Cali.

The British Council are coordinating the Colombian Framework of English and English Language Teaching Officer training scheme with the ODA, which will help establish more ELT resource centres. However, most opportunities are in private language schools. Many of these have difficulty in getting work permits unless teachers are qualified and experienced, and can be poorly paid. American English may be preferred.

A fascinating country, but some areas are definitely no-go. Check with your Embassy before you go to remote locations. It is not advisable to take children as kidnappings are possible. The main cities have bad traffic problems and water and electricity cuts are common. Electrical goods and cars are expensive.

List of schools in Colombia

Academia Ingles Para Niños, Calle 106 No 16-26, Bogota.

Advanced Learning Service, Transversal 20 No 120-15, Bogota.

Aprender Ltda, Calle 17 No 4-68 Ql. 501, Bogota.

Aspect, Calle 79a No 8-26, Bogota.

BBC De Londres, Calle 59 No 6-21, Bogota.

Babel, Avenida 15 No 124-49 Cf. 205, Bogota.

Bi Cultural Institute, Avenida 7 No 123-97 Of. 202, Bogota.

Britanico Americano De Idiomas, Avenida 13 No 103-62, Bogota.

Carol Keeney, Carrera 4 No 69-06, Bogota.

Centro Audiovisual De Ingles Chelga, Calle 137 No 25-26, Bogota.

Centro Colombo Andino, Calle 19 No 3-16 Of. 203, Bogota.

Centro De Ingles Lincoln, Calle 49 No 9-37, Bogota.

Centro De Idiomas Winston Salem, Calle 45 No 13-75, Bogota.

Centro De Lengua Inglesa, Calle 61 No 13-44 Of. 402, Bogota.

Coningles, Calle 63 No 13-24 Of. 502, Bogota.

English For Infants (John Dewey), Diagonal 110 No 40-85, Bogota.

English Language & Culture Institute (Elci), Calle 90 No 10-51, Bogota.

Escuela De Idiomas Berlitz, Calle 83 No 19-24, Bogota.

Genelor International, Avenida 78 No 20-49 Piso 20, Bogota.

I.C.L., Calle 119 No 9a-25, Bogota.

Ingles Cantando Y Jugando, Calle 106 No 16-26, Bogota.

Instituto Anglo Americano De Idiomas, Carrera 16a No 85-34 Of. 204, Bogota.

Instituto Electronico De Idiomas, Carrera 6 No 12-64 Piso, Bogota.

Instituto Meyer, Calle 17 No 10-16 Piso 80, Bogota.

Interlingua Ltda., Carrera 18 No 90-38, Bogota.

International Language Institute Ltda, Carrera 11 No. 65-28 Piso 3, Bogota, Tel: 571 235-8152/72. Fax: 310-2892. Or: Carrera 13 No. 5-79, Castillo Grande, Cartagena, Tel: 956-651-672. Or: Carrera 7a No 7-17 Neiva, Tel: 988-728-057. Eleven years offering general, conversation, business and intensive English; Spanish and French for adults and children. Personalised and communicative methodology.

International System, Transversal 6 No 51 A 33, Bogota.

K.O.E De Columbia, Calle 101 A No 31-02, Bogota.

Life Ltda., Transversal 19 No 100-52, Bogota.

The British Council, Calle 87 No 12-79, Bogota.

Oxford Centre, A.A. 102420, Santate de Bogota.

Ways' English School, Calle 101 No 13 A 17, Bogota.

Boston School of English Ltda, Carrera 43 No 44-02, Barranquilla.

California Institute Of English, Carrera 51 No 80-130, Barranquilla.

Centro De Lenguas Modernas, Carrera 38 No 69 C 65, Barranquilla.

Esquela De Ingles, Calle 53 No 38-25, Barranquilla.

Idiomas-Munera-Cros Ltda, Carrera 58 No 72-105, A.A. 52032, Barranquilla.

Instituto De Lenguas Modernas, Carrera 41 No 52-05,

Baranquilla.

Instituto Experimental De Atlantico, "jos Celestino Mutis", Calle 70 No 38-08, Barranquilla.

Instituto De Ingles Thelma Tyzon, Carrera 59 No 74-73, Barranquilla.

Avc, Carrera 45 El Palo 52-59, Cali.

Centro De Idiomas Winston Salem, Avenida La Ceste No 10-27, Santa Teresita, Cali.

Instituto Bridge Centro De Idiomas, Carrera 65 No 49 A 09, Cali.

Centro De Idiomas Y Turismo De Cartagena, Popa Calle 30 No 20- 177, Cartagena.

Ceico, Calle Siete Infantes, San Diego, Cartagena.

International Language Institute Ltda, Carrera 13 No 5-79 Castillogrande, Cartagena.

Instituto De Ingles, Calle 42 B No 48-45, Ibagu.

Business Language Centre Ltda., Carrera 49 No 15-85, Medellin.

Centro De Idiomas Winston Salem, Transversal 74 No C2-33 Laureies, Medellin.

Easy English, Carrera 45 A No 34 Sur 29 Torre No 4, Portal Del Cerro , A. A. 80511, Envigado, Medellin.

El Centro Ingles, El Poblado Carrera 10 A.No 36-39, Medellin.

Centro Anglo Frances, Carrera 11 No 6-12, Neiva.

International Language Institute Ltda, Carrera 5a No 21-35, Neiva.

Boston School Of English Ltda, Carrera. 43 No 44-02, Barranquilla.

Costa Rica

Minimum salary: The equivalent of $300 per month.
Tax: 10%.
Visa requirements: Rarely a problem.
Accommodation: $100-200 a month for a shared flat.
Other information: One of the safest but most expensive Latin American countries. There are many private language schools, but often with huge classes of mixed ability and poor facilities. Qualified teachers who speak Spanish could work in the private bilingual schools. Qualified teachers enjoy a reasonable standard of living in a beautiful, friendly and diverse country.

For further information contact: **The Instituto Britanico,** Apdo. 8184 San Jose 1000.

Cuba

Minimum salary: The state system has a set wage. The private sector pays a small salary in dollars which is convertible on the black market.
Tax and health insurance: No tax, free health insurance, but private cover is advisable.
Visa requirements: There is a restricted immigration policy,

so it is hard to get a work permit. Apply to the local Cuban embassy, or contact the British Council in Havana.
Accommodation: Difficult to find.
Other information: Cuba is facing economic difficulties now that Russia no longer helps its economy. However, the growing tourism market may cause growth in the demand for English.

List of schools in Cuba

Universidad de Cienfuegos, Departamento de Inglés, Carretera a Rodas, Km 4, Cuatro Cam. Cienfuegos 55100.

Ecuador

Minimum salary: The equivalent of $350-1000 per month.
Tax and health insurance: Everyone who is employed (legally or not) is subject to a 7% tax retention on any money earned. You are advised to take out health insurance in your home country.

In all major cities prospects for EFL teachers are good, as there are plenty of jobs available. However, it should be noted that the quality and conditions of these jobs is variable.
Visa requirements: All foreigners are required to have a residence visa and a work permit in order to be employed. They should be sponsored by their employer before they enter. However, in practice, many private language schools employ native speakers either illegally or for a short term only. A tourist visa lasts three months and cannot be changed to any other kind of visa.
Accommodation: Apartments are available for $125-250 per month depending on size and location.
Other information: There are many private language schools in Quito which vary greatly in quality. It is not difficult for native English speakers to obtain work, but rates of pay are often poor and most teachers take on additional private students. The British Council has two teaching centres in Ecuador, which pay well, but they recruit through their central offices in London and not locally.

Inflation is very high, but Ecuador is more stable and generally cheaper than many of its neighbours. There are around 20 private schools in Quito, many of which take on unqualified teachers. There are also opportunities in the coastal business centre, Guayaquil, but this is more expensive than the capital.

List of language schools in Ecuador

Benedict, 9 De Octubre 1515, Y Orellana, Quito.
Lingua Franca, Edificio Jerico, 12 De Octubre 2449 y Orellana, Casilla 17-2-68, Quito. Tel: 546075. Fax: 593-2-568664.
Quito Language And Culture Centre, Republica De El Salvador, 639 Y Portugal, Quito.

Guatemala

Minimum salary: The equivalent of $3-4 per hour. The average teaching week is 25 hours of classes.

Visa requirements: Work permits are usually difficult to obtain unless you can prove that a Guatemalan cannot do your job. Most teachers work illegally on a tourist visa. The authorities tend to turn a blind eye to this, and some schools have teachers giving classes to government employees without work permits.

Other information: Guatemalans now need an advanced level of English to graduate from university. There is a general awareness of the importance of learning the language, and student motivation is high. Schools rarely recruit externally, preferring to find teachers locally as the need arises.

Mexico

Minimum salary: In the state sector, expect 2000-4000 new pesos at University level (US$ = approximately 6.5 new pesos). The private sector pays up to 50 new pesos per hour. Private teaching is possible to supplement basic pay. The economy is very unstable, following the recent collapse of the stockmarket, so check pay against rates of inflation.

Tax and health insurance: Taxation is about 25- 35%, but it varies according to salary, as does the cost of health insurance, which is not cheap.

Visa requirements: It is illegal for a foreigner to work in any capacity without a work permit, and this is difficult and expensive to obtain. Very few institutions are prepared to offer a contract for a foreigner and scarcely any will do so without a personal interview. This applies to both private and public sector entities. Take originals of qualifications or an authorised copy. Where a work permit is needed, your employer in Mexico will handle everything through the Mexican government, who will advise your local embassy when work permit clearance is received. For further information contact: Simon Brewster, Director of Operations of the Instituto Anglo Mexicano de Cultura, Rio Nazas 116, Col. Cuauhtemoc, Mexico, DF.

Accommodation: Shared accommodation will cost about $150 per month. Furnished accommodation is rare, so check with your employer who should be able to help.

Other information: Mexico City has a severe pollution problem and is not recommended for children. Although Mexico has joined the free trade agreement with Canada and the USA (NAFSA), and demand for English should thus increase, the economic crisis is far from over, so it may be some time until the positive effects of the accord reach the ELT market.

Some schools are prepared to employ teachers without a work permit and it is easy to get work illegally - people become "phantom-names" on the school's books. Expect lower salaries in the provinces.

List of schools in Mexico

Univ. Autonoma De Aguascalientes, Rio Tamesis 438, 20100 Aguascalientes, Ags.

Universidad Autonoma De Baja California Sur, Carr. Al Sur. Km. 5.5, 23080 La Paz, Bcs.

Univ. Aut Del Carmen, Fac. De Ciencias Educativas, 24170 Cd. Del Carmen , Camp Alabama 2401, Quintas Del Sol, 31250 Chiuahua, Chih.

Universidad Autonoma De Chiapas, Apdo. Postal No. 933, 29000 Tuxtla Gutierrez, Chis Cipresses No. 12, Fracc. Los Laureles, 30780 Tapachula, Chis.

Univ Aut De Coahuila, Depto. De Idiomas, Hidalgo Y Gonzalez Lobo, Col. Republica De Oriente, 25280 Saltillo, Coah.

Universidad De Colima, Escuela De Lenguas Extranjeras, Josefa Ortiz De Dominguez S/N, 28950 Villa De Alvarez, Col.

Univ. Aut. De Guerrero, Av. Lazaro Cardenas 86, 39000 Chilpancingo, Gro.

Universidad De Guanajuato, Centro De Idiomas, Lascurian De Retana 5, 36000 Guanajuato , Gto.

Universidad Autonoma De Hidalgo, Centro De Lenguas, Carr. Pachuca/Tulancingo S/N, 42000 Pachuca, Hgo.

Universidad De Guadalajara, Esc Superior De Lenguas Modernas, Apdo. Postal 2-416, 44280 Guadalajara, Jal.

Univ Autonoma Del Edo De Mexico, Centro De Ensenanza De Lenguas, Rafael M. Hidalgo No. 401 Pte., 50130 Toluca, Edo De Mexico.

Universidad Michoacana De Sn. N.H., Apartado Postal 225-C, 58260 Morelia, Mich.

Universidad Autonoma Del Edo De Morelos, Centro De Lenguas, Rayon 7b- Centro, 62000 Cuernavaca, Mor.

Universidad Autonoma De Neuvo Leon, Fac. Filosofia Y Letras, Apdo. Postal 3024, 64000 Monterrey, Nl, Mil Cumbres No. 4853, Col. Villa Mitras, 64170 Monterrey, Nl

Univ Aut Benito Juarez De Oaxaca, Centro De Idiomas, Armenta Y Lopez 700, Centro, 68000 Oaxaca De Juarez, Oax.

Universidad Autonoma De Puebla, Dpto Lenguas, 4 Sur 104, 72000 Puebla, Pue.

Universidad Autonoma De Queretaro, Escuela De Idiomas, Cerro De Las Campanas, 76010 Queretaro, Qro.

Universidad Autonoma De San Luis Potosi, Centro De Idiomas, Zaragoza No. 410, 78200 San Luis Potosi, S.L.P.

Universidad De Sonora, Idiomas, Rosales Y Blvd. Luis Encinas, 83000 Hermosillo, Son, Av Universidad, Centro De Ensenanza Idiomas, Zona Cultura , 86000 Villahermosa, Tab.

Universidad Autonoma De Tlaxcala, Depto De Filosofia Y Letras, Carretera A San Gabriel S/N, 90000 Tlaxcala , Tlax.

Universidad Veracruzana Udih, Fac. De Idiomas, Fco Moreno Esq Ezequiel Alatriste, 91020 Xalapa, Ver.

Universidad Autonoma De Yucatan, Fac. De Educacion, Calle 61 No 525 (Entre 66 Y 68), 97000 Merida, Yuc.

Universidad Autonoma De Zacatecas, Centro De Idiomas, Alameda 422, 98000 Zacatecas, Zac.

Nicaragua

Teaching posts at universities offer good conditions. The Nicaragua Solidarity Campaign may recruit and help with airfare, as do the Peace Corps (see p59). Thieving is common. A knowledge of the political situation will help you integrate with the local people who are very hospitable.

Visa requirements: UK citizens do not require a visa to enter the country. To stay for a maximum of three months, you must show return tickets and have at least $300. Other nationalities require a tourist visa, available by sending passports to their respective Nicaraguan embassies. Work permits must be obtained before entering Nicaragua. Schools must submit a work permit request to the respective Nicaraguan embassy.

Peru

Minimum salary: Depends on qualifications, and crucially, the type of contract you get. Rates are good if you are recruited for English medium secondary schools. Some qualified teachers charge up to the equivalent of $10 an hour. Inflation is rife, but expect the equivalent of $4 an hour for a 30-hour week.

Tax: 25%, payable by your employer, usually deducted at source.

Visa requirements: A contract in advance enables teachers to obtain a work permit, though people can enter Peru on a tourist visa for up to three months and approach the Ministry of the Interior for a permit once employment has been found. Obtaining permits can take over a year, and can be difficult to obtain unless you can prove a Peruvian cannot do your job. Take originals of qualifications or an authorised copy if you wish to work legally. Many people work illegally on a tourist visa.

Accommodation: One-third of your salary for a shared flat. Furnished accommodation is rare - your employer may be able to help.

English language newspapers: *Lima Times* (W).

Other information: It is not advisable to go on spec without at least a contact in Peru. There are grave economical difficulties and some parts are still no-go areas because of terrorists.

Uruguay

The standard of EFL teaching in Uruguay is very high, and few schools recruit externally, but if you are there, you may find work from the list below.

List of schools in Uruguay

British Schools, Maximo Tajes esq Havre, Carrasco, Montevideo.

Dickens Institute, 21 De Setiembre 3090, Cp 11300 Montevideo.

English Studio Centre, Obligado 1221, Montevideo.

Instituto Cultural Anglo-Uruguayo, Casilla de Correo 5087 Sec.1, San Jose 1426, Montevideo.

London Institute, Caramuru 5609, Av. Brasil 2846, Montevideo.

St Patrick's College, Av J.M. Ferrari 1307, Montevideo.

Venezuela

Minimum salary: The average rate of pay is the equivalent of about $500 - $1,200 per month.

Visa requirements: It is very easy to enter on a tourist visa, but to work you need a "transeunte", which must be issued outside Venezuela. This takes a long time to come through, since your employer will need to have it authorized by the government. It is possible (but illegal) to work as a language teacher on a tourist visa, but even this is proving more and more difficult.

English language newspaper: *The Daily Journal* (D), written primarily for the American reader.

Accommodation: Flats are expensive, and rates depend very much on inflation, so check before you go.

Other information: Although the oil boom has declined somewhat, there is still a great demand for English, although American English is more common. Remember that this is one of the most expensive and cosmopolitan countries in South America, and salaries should reflect this. Caracas is generally dry, warm and sunny thoughout the year, but temperatures and humidity elsewhere vary with altitude.

Thanks to its beautiful Caribbean coastline, plains full of wildlife and spectacular jungle, the tourism industry is growing rapidly. As the vast majority of tourists are American, this should result in demand for English for Tourism.

List of schools in Venezuela

Berlitz Escuela de Idiomas, Av. Madrid, Urb. Las Mercedes, Caracas 1060.

The British Council, Torre La Noria, Piso 6, Paseo Enrique Eraso, Urb. Las Mercedes, Aptdo. 65131, Caracas 1065.

Centro Venezolano-Americano, Av. Principal Jose Marti Urb. Las Mercedes, Caracas 1060.

English Lab, Quinta Penalba, Av. Venezuela, Urb. El Rosal, Caracas 1060.

Instituto de Ingles Britanico, Av. Avila No. 52, Urb. San Bernadino, Caracas 1011.

Instituto Loscher-Ebbinghaus SRL, Quinta Magal, Av. Venezuela, Urb. El Rosal, Caracas 1060.

Instituto Venezolano-Britanico, Quinta Guaricha, Avenida Los Manguitos, Urbano Sabana Grande, Caracas 1050.

The Far East

Brunei

Minimum salary: About 2,400 Brunei dollars per month. You must have a degree and at least two years' teaching experience. Top salary is up to B$70,000 per year. Most posts are recruited by the Centre for British Teachers who recruit for the Ministry of Education (see p53).

Tax and health insurance: Normally no personal income tax. Health insurance is usually part of the package offered by most employers.

Visa requirements: The Brunei High Commission will supply a visa with proof of job offer - either before or after your arrival. Your passport is stamped on arrival for a period decided at the discretion of the immigration officer. The work permit application form is filled in by your employer and submitted to the Commissioner of Labour in Brunei. If the job offer comes from the private sector, the company must obtain a labour licence before they can apply for a work permit.

Accommodation: Usually provided or subsidised as part of the job package, otherwise prohibitively expensive - 1,500 Brunei dollars a month. At least a three-month deposit is demanded.

English language newspapers: *Borneo Bulletin (D)*.

Other information: The standard of living is similar to northern Europe in this wealthy country. Have a medical and dental check-up before you go. Public transport is limited and most schools insist that teachers have a clean driving licence and buy a car out there - fuel is very cheap. Some kind of car loan scheme is usually offered. Brunei is a Muslim country, so teachers are advised to dress "modestly". Take enough shoes - it is difficult to buy over English size five.

Cambodia

Minimum salary: The equivalent of £18,000 unless accommodation is provided.

Tax and health insurance: Probably no tax. Take out private health insurance.

Visa requirements: Visas will be arranged by your employer.

Accommodation: The equivalent of £1,500 per month for a two-room villa in Phnom Penh. The shortage of accommodation for aid workers has forced prices up dramatically.

Other information: Because the UN are virtually running the country, English is very popular, especially business English. CFBT and VSO recruit teachers and teacher trainers (see p58 and 64). However, the Khmer Rouge are still active and many parts of Cambodia remain dangerous.

Hong Kong

Minimum salary: HK$150-200 per hour, though qualified teachers should get double this.

Tax and health insurance: 15%.

Visa requirements: UK nationals can get a work permit in Hong Kong. Other nationalities must be sponsored before they can get a permit.

Accommodation: Expect to pay a minimum of HK$1,500 for a shared, very small flat. Many teachers stay in hostels. Accommodation is larger in outlying islands, such as Lamma and Cheung Chau, but these are becoming more expensive.

English language newspapers: *Hong Kong Standard, International Herald Tribune, South China Morning Post(D)*

Other information: There are enough people needing private lessons to be a full-time freelance teacher. English is becoming more important as Chinese control approaches. Qualifications are not essential, and native English speakers are needed to give conversation lessons in box-rooms around Chung King Mansions (40 Nathan Road). Some schools also offer coffee-shop-style conversation classes to up to 20 students. Generally a degree is preferred, and a diploma will give you the cream of the jobs, such as working for the state island schools. Contact the Hong Kong Government Office, 6 Grafton St, London W1X 3LB (UK) for secondary school opportunities. The British Council in Hong Kong is the largest in the east and is a good source of information. Many teachers find extra work with publishers or do voice-overs for films.

List of schools in Hong Kong

First Class Language Centre, 22a Bank Tower, 351-353 King's Road, North Point. Tel: (5) 887 7555.
Hong Kong English Club, Ground floor, 176b Nathan Road, Tsimshatsui, Kowloon. Tel: (3) 722 1300.
Josiah's Institute of English, 2nd and 3rd floors, 88 Lockhard Road, Wanchai.

China

Minimum salary: Varies considerably but expect around 700-1,000 yuan per month for a lesser qualified "foreign teacher", while "foreign experts", who are required to have an MA, can expect about 1,400-3,500 yuan a month. Negotiate before you go to China.

Tax and health insurance: Tax-free, and free health care.

Visa requirements: You must get a letter of invitation from your prospective employer to take to your local Chinese

Embassy to receive a visa. You have to undergo a medical examination, including an HIV test, before you are allowed into China. Get it done before you go or you may have to have additional, more risky, tests within China. You can apply for a residence permit after three months.

Accommodation: Usually provided by employer, and varies in quality from poor to inadequate. Expect sporadic heating and hot water. South of the Yangtse river there may be no heating as it is "warmer", although the winters are bleak.

English language newspaper: *China Daily* (D).

Other information: Chinese institutions employ two types of foreign teachers. The first is a "Foreign Expert", who should have an MA in a relevant discipline and some experience of teaching at the tertiary level. Chinese institutions will pay the salary, airfares, accommodation costs and some baggage costs for such teachers. The second type of teacher is a "Foreign Teacher", whose salary is considerably lower (often less than half) than that of the "Foreign Expert", and air fares are not paid. Qualifications required vary, ranging from just native English speaker to several years' experience. For both types of post, applications should be made to the State Bureau of Foreign Experts, Friendship Hotel, Beijing 100873, or to the Education Section of the Embassy of the Peoples Republic of China, 5-13 Birch Grove, Acton, London W3 9SW, or directly to an institution in China.

Applications can also be made in February to the British Council, Overseas Educational Appointments Department, 15 Medlock Street, Manchester M15 4AA. VSO also recruits English teachers, mainly for teacher training colleges in China.

There are no private language schools in China, although some hotels and large companies have their own language training facilities, for which they normally recruit locally.

Living conditions tend to be harder living away from Beijing, where western food is available. The Chinese are highly motivated and interested in foreigners, but expect traditional learning methods and there are few, if any, facilities such as cassettes, books and photocopiers. Nevertheless, China is slowly opening up, especially with the influx of western technology, which has brought satellite television into the country. For further details get the following book, which includes a list of Chinese colleges and universities: *Living in China - A Guide to Teaching and Studying in China including Taiwan,* published by China Books and Periodicals Inc, 2929 24th St., San Fransisco, CA 9410 USA.

Indonesia

Minimum salary: Rp3 million ($1,500) per month in Jakarta, less outside the capital, depending on qualifications and experience.

Tax and health insurance: Most language schools have some kind of health insurance policy for teachers, but it is advisable to arrange cover privately before arriving in Indonesia. Generally though medical services are poor and many EFL teachers fly out to Singapore.

Visa requirements: Officially work permits and visas are required to teach in Indonesia. There are two main types of visa: DINAS, a six month visa issued to many EFL teachers, and KIMS, under which you pay a much lower rate of tax. Many prospective EFL teachers arrive in Indonesia on tourist visas, and once they have found a job, go to Singapore to obtain a business visa, which can subsequently be changed to KIMS or DINAS. It is worth bearing in mind that passports do have to be surrendered at regular intervals, sometimes for as long as six weeks at a time, while visas are being renewed.

Accommodation: Usually provided by employers, mostly in bungalows or houses. If not, it is becoming increasingly expensive, especially in Jakarta, where rent for a small house near the centre is $5,000 a year. For a larger-style house the average price is nearer $10,000. Landlords usually expect expatriates to pay two years' rent in advance, and it is advisable to seek legal advice to ensure your lease is in order if you do pay in advance. Employers may be prepared to offer you an initial loan.

English language newspaper: *The Indonesian Times, Indonesian Observer,* and the *Jakarta Post* (D).

Other information: English is booming in Indonesia, and most opportunities for teachers are in Jakarta, Surabaya and Bandung. North American and Australian EFL teachers dominate the area. Qualified teachers can command far higher rates than unqualified staff, and business English is the key area of demand growth. Language schools, which are "Yayasans" or foundations, are able to compete commercially with one another and appear to be doing well. Indonesia's growing economy has sharpened people's awareness of the importance of English language learning, and increased demand for classes.

Public transport tends to be poor, over-crowded and dangerous, and most foreign nationals find they prefer to spend the extra on taxi fares, which are still relatively cheap. Women should dress discreetly. Jakarta is very dirty and non-violent crime is common. New shopping malls have opened in Jakarta in recent years and provide a comprehensive range of services, including facilities for making international telephone calls and for sending faxes. Most western products can be obtained in supermarkets in Jakarta, although these products command a premium.

List of schools in Indonesia

ALT (American Language Training), Jalan R.S. Fatmawati 42a, Keb Baru, Jakarta Selatan. Tel: 769 1001. Five schools.

EEC (English Education Centre), Jalan Let Jen S.Parman 66, Slipi, Jakarta Barat. Tel: 567 1144.

EEP (Executive English Programs), Jalan Wijaya VIII 4, Kebayoran Baru, Jakarta Selatan. Tel: 722 0812. Branch in Bandung.

ELS International, Jalan Tanjung Karang 7 c-d, Jakarta Pusat. Tel: 323211.

ELTI (English Language Training International),
Complex Wijaya Grand Centre, Blok f83, 84a &b, Jalan
Wijaya II, Keb Baru, Jakarta Selatan. Tel: 720 2957.
Branches in Yogyakarta, Semarang and Solo.

IALF (Indonesia-Australia Language Foundation),
Wisma Budi, Suite 503, Jalan HR Rasuna Said Kav c-6,
Kuningan, Jakarta Selatan 12940. Tel: 521 3350. Branch in
Bali.

ILP (International Language Programs), Jalan Panglima
Polin IX/2, Kebayoran Baru, Jakarta Sealtan. Tel: 722
2408. Branch in Surabaya.

SIT (School for International Training), Jalan Hayam
Wuruk 120c-d, Jakarta Pusat. Tel: 629 3340.

TBI (The British Institute), Setiabudi Building 2, Jalan
HR Rasuna Said, Kuningan, Jakarta Selatan. Tel: 512 044.
Branch in Bandung.

Japan

Minimum salary: Since it is difficult to get a visa, many
schools offer teachers just enough to get them one.
Monthly pay therefore begins at around 250,000-300,000
yen per month for between 25-30 contact hours per week.
Better schools pay more. Expect less outside Tokyo.

Tax and health insurance: Income tax is around 10% and
local tax is about 5%. The Japanese health insurance
system is complicated, with some places running a local
health scheme which may cover up to 70% of your medical
costs, based on your previous year's salary - so initially it
is for a minimal fee. Some prefectures will not allow
foreigners to join the local scheme, however, and private
medical insurance is strongly advised. Larger schools will
often offer a private insurance scheme, which you may be
able to join.

Visa requirements: Japanese law requires teachers to have
a valid work visa, and it is impossible to apply for a work
visa unless you are sponsored by an employer. The
application process is lengthy, and usually involves a wait
of up to three months before the visa is granted.
Consequently teachers intending to work in Japan are
strongly advised to arrange employment before they arrive.
It is illegal to work on a tourist visa, even if a work visa is
being processed in the meantime. Students are entitled to
work on a part-time basis if they have an official student
visa. In order to get a visa, you need various documents
including a guarantee of monthly salary in excess of 260,000
yen. Although it is illegal to work on a tourist visa, it is
possible to use such a visa to solicit and secure a firm
offer of employment. However, if you find work in this
way, you will need to leave the country and re-enter with
sponsorship from your employer, getting the change of
status endorsed by an overseas Japanese embassy. You
cannot change your status without leaving Japan.

Accommodation: Finding a flat is a big problem in Japan
and many Japanese landlords are reluctant to rent to
foreigners, so it is worth getting a Japanese intermediary
to help you. Most landlords require six months rent in
advance, four months of which is non-returnable "key-

money". Most good schools will help teachers find suitable
accommodation with rents varying from 60,000-85,000 yen
per month for a small one-bedroom unfurnished flat, 80,000
yen in Tokyo.

English language newspaper: Monday's edition of *The
Japan Times* carries the best selection of teaching jobs.
Also the *Asahi Evening News*, the *Daily Yomiuri*, and the
Mainichi Daily News (D).

Other information: Despite the recession, Japan remains
a massive EFL market, with a large proportion of children's
work (you may teach children as young as two!). Travelling
to and from work can be long and arduous; the climate is
oppressive in the summer. The Japanese have a strong
work ethic, which is reflected in teachers' contracts (25-30
hours per week is the norm, with often only 10 days holiday
a year, not including public holidays). Most work takes
place in the afternoons and evenings.

State education concentrates on reading and writing, so
private language schools which concentrate on
"conversation" are popular. There remains no regulation
of language schools, which means that standards vary.
However, the economic downturn in Japan has meant that
many of the worst schools have closed, and the better
schools have significantly improved their teaching
standards. The Japan Association of College English
(JACET) is aiming to improve state education, especially
at primary level.

Foreigners are known as "gaijin" and it is estimated to
take at least six months to adjust culturally and
economically. Japan is generally safe, but teachers,
especially women, should not allow themselves to be lulled
into a false sense of security, as sexual and racial
harassment is becoming increasingly frequent.

The best time to look for work is March - just before the
start of the Japanese academic year in April. September is
another possibility. The government is clamping down on
illegal workers, but the National Union of Workers and
Kanto Union Teachers' Federation will help legal teachers
know their rights.

See ELS (USA), Hilderstone College and information on
the JET scheme (p12) for details of their recruitment
schemes to Japan.

List of schools in Japan

Aeon Institute of Foreign Languages, 7f Nihonseimei
Building, 7f 1-1 3 Shimoishii Okayama-shi 700.
Attorney Foreign Language Institute, Osaka Ekimae
Daiichi Building, 1-3-1 Umeda Kita-ku, Osaka.
American Academy, 4-1-3 Kudan Kita Chiyoda-Ku,
Tokyo 102.
American School of Business, 1-17-4 Higashi Ikebukuro
Toshima-Ku,Tokyo 170.
Azabu Academy, 401 Shuwa-Roppongi Building, 3-14-12
Roppongi Minato-ku, Tokyo 106.
Berkley House Gogaku Centre, 4-2 Go-bancho
Chiyoda-ku, Tokyo 102.

Berlitz Schools of Languages (Japan) Inc., Kowa Bldg. 1,5f, 11-41, Alasaka 1-chrome, Minato-ku, Tokyo 107.

Bernard Group, 2-8-11 Takezono, Tsukuba City, lbaraki-Ken, 305 (recruit for British-owned schools).

Cambridge English School, Dogenzaka 225 Building, 2-23-14 Dogenzaka Shibuya-ku,Tokyo 150.

Cambridge School of English, Kikumura 91 Building1-41-20 Higashi, Ikebukuro Toshima-ku, Tokyo 170.

Cosmopolitan Language Institute, Yashima B Building, 4f 1-8-9 Yesu Chuo-ku,Tokyo 104.

CIC English Schools, Kawamoto Building, Imadegawaagaru Nishigawa Karasuma-dori, Kamigyo-ku, Kyoto.

DEH, 7-5 Nakamachi, Naka-ku, Hiroshima 730.

David English House, 2-3f Nakano Building 1-5-17 Kamiyacho Naka-ku, Hiroshima 730.

EEC Foreign Languages Institute, Shikata Building, 2f 4-43 Nakazald-Nishi 2-chrome, Kita-ku, Osaka 530.

ELEC Eigo Kenkyujo (The English Language Education Council), 3-8 Kanda Jimbo-cho Chiyoda-ku,Tokyo 101.

Executive Gogaku Centre (Executive Language Centre), 1 Kasumigaseki Building, 12F 3-2-5 Kasumigaseki, Chiyoda-ku,Tokyo 100.

FCC (Fukuoka Communication Centre), Dai Roku Okabe Building, 5f Hakata Eki Higashi, 2-4-17 Hakata-ku, Fukuoka 812.

F L Centre (Foreign Language Centre), 1 Iwasaki Building, 3f 2-19-20 Shibuya-ku,Tokyo 150.

Gateway Gakuin Rokko, Atelier House, 3-1-15 Yamada-cho Nada-ku, Kobe.

ICA Kokusai Kaiwa Gakuin (International Conversation Academy), l Mikasa 2 Building, 1-16-10 Nishi Ikebukuro Toshima-ku, Tokyo 171.

IF Foreign Language Institute, 7f Shin Nakashima Building, 1-9-20 Nishi Nakashima Yodogawa-ku, Osaka.

Kains English School in Gakko, 1-5-2 Ohtemon Chuo-ku ,Fukuoka 810.

Kyoto English Centre, Sumitomo Seimei Building, Shijo-Karasuma Nishi-iru Shimogyo-ku, Kyoto

Kobe Language Centre, 3-18 Wakinoharnacho, 1-chome, Chuo-ku, Kobe 651.Tel: (78) 2614316.

Language Education Centre, 7-32 chome Ohtemachi Nakaku, Hiroshima-shi 730.

Matty's School of English, 3-15-9 Shonan-takatori, Yokosuka 234. Tel: (468) 658717.

Mobara English Institute, 618-1 Takashi, Mobara-shi Chiba-ken 297. Tel: (475) 224785.

Plus Alpha, (Agency) 2-25-20 Denenchofu, Ota-Ku, Tokyo 145.

Queens School of English, 3f Yuzuki Bldg, 4-7-14 Minamiyawata, Ichikawa 272.

Pegasus Language Services, Sankei Building 1-7-2 Otemachi Chiyoda-k, Tokyo 100.

REC School of Foreign Language, Nijojo-mae Ebisugawasagaru Higashihorikawa-dori Nakagyo-ku, Kyoto.

Royal English Language Centre, 4-31-3-2 Chyo Hakataku, Fukuoka 812.

Seido Language Institute, 12-6 Funado-cho Ashiya-shi, Kyoto.

Sun Eikaiwa School, 6f Cherisu Hachobori Building, 6-7 Hachoubori Naka-ku, Hiroshima-shi 730.

Shane Corporation, 4f Kimura Building, 4-14-12 Nishi Funa Funabashi Shi Chiba, Ken 273.

Shane Corporation, Yutaka Dai-2 Building, 4f Higashi Kasai 6-2-8 Edogawa-Ku, Tokyo.

Shane English Schools (Head Offices):
Fujisawa, 251 Fujisawa Homon Building, 6f , Fujisawa 484-25, Fujisawa-shi, Kanagawa-ken 251.

Kimura Building, 4f, Nishifuna 4-14-12. Funabashi-shi, Chiba-ken 273.

Maehara Building, Sakuragi-cho, 2-455-2, Omiya-shi, Saitama-ken 331.

Stanton School of English, 12 Gobancho Chiyoda-ku, Tokyo 102.

Chunichi Bunka Centre, 4-5f Chunichi Building 4-4-1 Sakae Naka-ku, Nagoya 460.

Smith Ohokayama Eikaiwa School, 2-4-9 Ohokayama Meguro-ku, Tokyo 152.

Ten'noji Academy of Business and Languages, 2-9-36 Matsuzaki- cho Abeno-ku, Osaka.

Tokyo YMCA College of English, 7 Kanda Mitoshiro-Cho Chiyoda-ku, Tokyo T-101.

Tokyo Language Centre, Tatsunama Building, 1-2-19 Yaesu, Chuo-Ku, Tokyo 103.

Tokyo English Centre, (TEC) 7-9 Uguisudai-cho Shibuyaku, Tokyo 150.

Toefl Academy, 1-12-4 Kundankita, Chiyoda-ku, Tokyo 102. Tel: (3) 2303500.

World Language School Inc., Tokiwa Soga Ginko Building, 4f 1-22-8 Jinnan Shibuya-ku, Tokyo 171.

Yoko Ishikawa, 480 GO, Takaatano, Anjo, 730.

Malaysia

Minimum salary: Malaysian $3,000-4,000 per month.

Tax and health insurance: 17-20%. Some employers will arrange health insurance. If not, take out a private policy. Local doctors are inexpensive.

Visa requirements: Visa and work permit regulations are very strict. Teachers must have a work permit to work either privately or in the public system. Permits are only issued for jobs for which no suitably-qualified Malaysian is available. As a result there are almost no expatriate teachers in the public sector and few in the private system, irrespective of the subject offered. Those teachers who do obtain employment often do so through entering the country on a tourist visa, securing a post, and then leaving the country to get their work permit.

Accommodation: The price of flats has risen steeply. Expect to pay Malaysian $1,000-1,200 for a flat in Kuala Lumpur or Petling Jaya where accommodation is scarce. Elsewhere, the price is considerably reduced.

English language newspaper: *Malay Mail*, *The Borneo Post, New Straits Times*, and *The Star* (D).

Other information: The Prime Minister is promoting English and demand is high in the business community, and the state and private sectors. Economic growth has meant high inflation, but clothes, food and restaurants are relatively inexpensive. Public transport is generally good, although trains are slow. EFL books are readily available. Women should dress modestly outside the big cities, especially on the more conservative east coast, and it should be noted that Malaysia is predominantly Muslim.

The Malaysian Ministry of Education, Pusat Bandar Damansara, Blok J, 50604, Kuala Lumpur, sometimes recruits experienced teachers for lucrative university posts. The Centre for British Teachers and ELS also recruit.

List of schools in Malaysia

The English Language Centre, 1st Floor, Lot 2067, Block 10, K.C.L.D., Jalan Keretapi, PO Box 253, 93150 Kuching, Sarawak.
The Kinabulu Commercial College, 3rd & 4th Floors, Wisma Sabah, Kota Kinabulu, Sabah.

Nepal

Current opportunities for TEFL in Nepal are not good, due to stringent visa restrictions. However, with the unquestioned demand for wider access to the English language, the medium-to-long term outlook is fairly promising.
Visa requirements: Unless you are employed by an official organisation such as the British Council, a Diplomatic Mission or a UN Agency, it is impossible to secure anything more than a tourist visa for Nepal. The tourist visa is usually valid for one month on entry and can be extended for two additional months but further extensions beyond a total initial stay of three months are never approved. A tourist visa does not entitle you to work legally during your stay. At present, none of the bi-lateral or multi-lateral donors are involved in EFL/ESL programmes though there are signs that this position may change within the next two years. This means that it is unlikely that you could obtain employment and hence a non-tourist visa through an official organisation.
Other information: There are a myriad of private language schools in Kathmandu which are run as businesses by enterprising Nepalese. Some of these (illegally) recruit tourists as teaching staff and are generally unable to assist in the process of changing the visa status of their employees from "tourist" to "non-tourist". These schools are usually poorly resourced, and do not pay a living wage to those who work for them.

The British Council has a small Direct Teaching Operation in Nepal which at present is staffed almost entirely by part-time teachers, as the volume of work does not yet justify more than one contract post. They do hope to expand however, and the possibility of the creation of an additional post is likely during the next two years. The minimum qualification for a teacher at the British Council is the RSA/UCLES CTEFLA (or equivalent) with at least two years relevant experience, but an RSA/UCLES DTEFLA (or

equivalent) is preferred. Contact address: The British Council, Kantipath, P.O. Box 640, Kathmandu, Nepal (Tel: + 2213 05/2237 96/2226 98).

The American Language Centre runs courses for Nepalese intending to study in the USA under US Government Scholarship schemes and also teaches business-oriented language courses for employees of local companies. Contact address: Mr Chris Gamm, The Director, P.O. Box 58, Kathmandu, Nepal.

Singapore

Minimum salary: Singapore $2,000-2,500 per month.
Tax and health insurance: 12%. There is a kind of savings tax (the Central Provident Fund) which you can opt out of if you have some kind of social security in your home country.
Visa requirements: Many teachers arrive on a Social Visit Pass (SVP), a kind of tourist visa, and scout around for jobs. If they find a job, the SVP is converted into an employment pass without them having to leave the country.
Accommodation: Singapore $700-1000 per month for a room in a shared flat.
English language newspapers: *Business Times. Straits Times, The New Paper* (D).
Other information: Singapore is a modern but conservative country. Terms of student and work visas require that applicants state that they have no political interests and no intent to get involved in political activities. The Singapore High Commission in London have a recruitment office linked to the National University of Singapore. Tel: 0171 235 4562. Teachers in government schools and colleges should have a relevant qualification and preferably five years' experience, but are rewarded with a salary of Singapore $5,000 tax free. International House and the British Council can supply details of other language schools.

South Korea

Minimum salary: 1,400,000 won per month, more for qualified and experienced teachers.
Tax and health insurance: Tax-free with a contract for two years, but very high after this period - most teachers leave at this time. Private medical insurance is recommended.
Visa requirements: Obtainable from your local Korean embassy, who will want to see sponsorship from an employer before you can get a work permit. Many teachers work illegally with a tourist visa.
Accommodation: 250,000 won per month for a one-room flat in Seoul, 150,000 won elsewhere. Rates may be lower if you put down a large deposit.
English language newspapers: *Korean Herald, Korean Times* (D).

Other information: English is essential for university entrance and state school English is poor, so students are very keen in private schools. It is easy to find work, particularly in Seoul and Pusan. English for Academic Purposes (EAP) and business English are popular and lucrative. Some places prefer American English - many students are keen to live there. Public transport, including an underground, is good in the huge capital, Seoul.

Taiwan

Minimum salary: New Taiwanese $8,500-$9,000 per month, or $370 an hour.
Tax and health insurance: 20% tax. Proof of tax payment will help you get a visa extension. Take out a private health insurance policy.
Visa requirements: These have been tightened and you must now have sponsorship and a degree to obtain a work permit. If you enter on a tourist visa and find work, you must leave the country to apply for a work permit. You also need a health certificate, including an AIDS test.
Accommodation: New Taiwanese $7,500 per month for a room in a shared flat, cheaper outside central Taipei. Most landlords will want three months' rent in advance.
English language newspapers: *China Post, China News, China Daily News (D).*
Other information: Since the government clamped down on illegal teachers, some schools have found that they have been unable to get permits for their staff. Salaries have remained high for qualified teachers. Check your school can guarantee a permit. With low unemployment and a healthy economy, there is plenty of in-company and private work, and falling rates may rise again now some of the cowboys are being forced out. This should compensate for the high cost of living, especially in Taipei. Some schools prefer American English, and there is also a demand for teachers of children.

List of schools in Taiwan:

ELS (see p53) have branches in Taipei and Kaohsiung.
Hess Language School, 51 Ho Ping East Road, Sec 2, 1f Taipei. Tel: 7031118.

Thailand

Minimum salary: Rates of pay vary greatly. Private sector language schools pay 225 Baht ($9) per hour, and teachers tend to work about 25-35 hours per week. Terms for full-time staff vary widely and should be verified.
Tax and health insurance: Teachers may have to submit their own return - awkward for non-Thai speakers. However taxation rates are generally quite low and may be nil if you are on a one-year fixed contract. Health insurance is available locally. Ensure that you are covered for dental as well as medical treatment. Booster innoculations can be done cheaply at the Pasteur Institute in Bangkok.
Visa requirements: Still under revision. Teachers should have work permits and some employers will help arrange these. Most teachers are on a 60 or 90day non-immigrant visa and have to leave the country every few months to get a new visa. The nearest places to do this are Malaysia or Laos; the trip takes about three days and costs about 2-5,000 baht, depending on the degree of comfort you prefer.
Accommodation: Rents are cheap away from Bangkok, particularly if you share. Expect to pay about 3,000 Baht monthly for a one-bed flat in the provinces, while in Bangkok similar accommodation will cost 3,000-6,000 Baht.
English language newspapers: *Bangkok Post,* and *The Nation* (D).
Other information: There is no body which oversees private language schools. The academic year is June-March with a break in October. University staff get 15 days holiday per year. The local English teachers association in Thailand - TESOL - is fairly active. Contact through: AUA, 179 Rajdamri Road, Bangkok 10330, or the British Council.

The rapid growth of the middle classes has meant an increased demand for higher education. There are now English medium universities and colleges and a drive to improve teacher training. However, few posts are advertised outside the country and many schools remain poorly equipped. Many teachers are unqualified, and get employment (well-paid by local standards) whilst "passing through" on their travels. Few schools offer teachers anything in the way of board, insurance, or transport allowance. Bangkok is hot, noisy and polluted. Unless you want to spend at least three hours a day on buses, buy a motorcycle. Shopping is excellent, but electrical goods are expensive. Cleanliness and respect mean a lot to Thais, who are Buddhist.

Bangkok is the main centre for EFL. Chiang Mai in the north also has some work, including at the Chiang Mai University. World Teach and VSO also recruit for Thailand.

List of schools in Thailand

ECC, 430/19-20 Chula 64, Siam Square, Bangkok 10330. Tel: 2551856.
The English Language Schools, 26/3, 26/9 Chonphol Lane 15, Bangkok 10900. Tel: 25110439.
Training Creativity Development in Languages (T.C. D Co. Ltd.), 28 Soi Kasem (24) Suhkumvit Road, (Opposite Ariston Hotel) Bangkok 10110. Tel: 2587036.
LCC Language Institute, 8/64-67 Ratchadapisek-Larprao Road, Bangkhaen, Bangkok 10900.

Vietnam

Lifting of US sanctions may soon change the economic climate of Vietnam. However, at the moment, opportunities are almost completely restricted to volunteering or teacher training, although demand for English is very strong.

The Rest of Asia and the East

Teaching opportunities elsewhere in Asia and the east are generally limited to voluntary or aid work, mainly because these countries are either too poor to afford to pay privately for non-native teachers, the political situation is prohibitive, or because English is the official language anyway. However, there are possibilities in the following countries:

Indian sub-continent

English is the official language, though mainly spoken only by the elite ruling classes. There are some private schools and British Council centres in India and Bangladesh, but apart from these limited (mainly teacher training) opportunities, most work is on a volunteer basis. VSO are active in Bangladesh, Bhutan, Pakistan and Nepal (see p59).

Maldives

Minimum salary: 10-20 rufiya per hour in the government-subsidised private schools, slightly less in the state system.

Tax and health insurance: No tax, and medical consultation is free. A private health insurance policy is recommended.

Visa requirements: You must get a sponsor to get a work permit, but this is not usually a problem. Write, with details of your educational background, to the Ministry of Education, Male, Republic of Maldives. Tel: (960) 323836.

Accommodation: Usually provided with your contract.

Other information: The Maldives comprise of 1,200 islands and atolls, 200 of them inhabited. The English medium school system uses British exams, so British teachers are in demand. The Maldives are a developing country and living standards for teachers are modest, but your contract may include a return air fare, and bicycles are often provided. Most work is in the capital and main island, Male.

Mauritius

Minimum salary: Average rates of pay are between Rs 6,000-13,000 per month for graduates.

Tax and health insurance: The taxation rate for income is levied at the rate of 30%, but this only applies for income above Rs 6,000, after the deduction of any personal allowances.

Visa requirements: It is unlikely that foreign nationals will be given permits to work in Mauritius, and a work permit is a prerequisite for all foreign nationals.

Accommodation: Accommodation is expensive and can range from anything from Rs 6,000-8,000 per month, for a furnished flat or small house or more depending on size and location.

Other information: In Mauritius, the medium of education at both primary and secondary levels is English and opportunities for EFL are restricted. There are in fact no private English language schools.

Mongolia

Mongolia is now a free-market economy. As the country opens up to western influence, English has joined Chinese, Japanese and Russian as the main foreign languages being learned. The huge demand for English far exceeds the supply of teachers, in a country where 75% of the population is under 35. Retrained Russian teachers have attempted to cope with the introduction of English in the huge secondary school sector. Projects are also being carried out with the help of the UN, VSO, the British Council, CFBT, the Peace Corps and the Bell Educational Trust. These are mostly in English for Specific Purposes and teacher training.

Although Mongolia is the size of western Europe, its population is just two million, and it is considered the world's most remote country. Transport is scarce and food supplies unreliable. At present only ministry officials and senior bankers speak any English, and there is a severe shortage of paper and English textbooks. Many aid and charitable organisations are already moving in. For further information contact: Mongolian Embassy, 7 Kensington Court, London W8 5DL, UK. Tel: 071 937 0150.

Papua New Guinea

English is an official language in Papua New Guinea - education is all in English. However, with over 800 language groups, English is only loosely the second language. Jobs exist mainly in the secondary sector, and few are purely EFL posts. Teacher training is fairly advanced. Salaries are not high, although taxes are.

Visa requirements: Teachers must secure a job before applying for a working visa. The employer has to lodge an application with the authorities in Papua New Guinea and the prospective employee must apply to the immigration department of any Papua New Guinea High Commission.

Other information: The locals are excellent linguists. Although a beautiful country, their High Commission in London say it is not a suitable destination for "those of nervous disposition", and some areas are controlled by bandits.

VSO and the UN also recruit volunteers to work in Papua New Guinea (see p64).

Addresses:

University of Papua New Guinea, Allude, for teacher training.
Papua New Guinea University of Technology, Lae, for tertiary EFL.

Sri Lanka

Minimum salary: 10,000 rupees per month.
Tax and health insurance: Free for the first year, although private health insurance is recommended.
Accommodation: 3,000 rupees per month in a shared flat.
Visa requirements: Enter on a tourist visa. Your employer will arrange a work permit.
English language newspapers: *The Island, Daily News* (D).
Other information: English has become important in Sri Lanka, where the government are trying to diffuse the political and cultural tension between the Tamils and the Sinhalese, who each have their own languages. Native English speakers are in demand and for those working for international organisations in the capital, such as the British Council and the Colombo International School, living standards are high. Most work outside Colombo is on a volunteer basis (see p64). The civil war is confined to the north and east of the country and violence is declining. Coursebooks are hard to obtain - take your own.

Addresses:

International English Language Services (PVT) Ltd., 292/1 Galle Road, Colombo 4. Tel: (94) 1 590707.

A warning

Because of the cultural, economic or political troubles in some countries, it is advised that you proceed with great caution should you decide to work in them. Conditions change around the world all the time and the following list is inevitably not exclusive. However, if you obtain employment in the following countries, it is advisable to contact your embassy first. (See also relevant country guides):

Algeria, Burma, East Timor, Egypt (certain parts only), El Salvador, Georgia, Guatemala, Iran, Iraq, Lebanon, Liberia, Libya, Mozambique, Papua New Guinea, Peru (certain parts only), Somalia, Sudan, Yemen, the states of the former Yugoslavia, Zaire.

North Africa and the Middle East

For the past 20 years a significant demand for EFL training has been sustained in much of North Africa and the Middle East, despite political and religious unrest, and war. Oil is still the driving force behind economic development in the area -English and the petro-dollar are the language of the oil business. Visitors should be aware of the political and religious environment. Women, in particular, have to restrict their lifestyle in some states, which may offer work permits only to men. Good qualifications and previous experience of living in a Muslim country will improve employment prospects. Teachers often leave the Gulf states with significant savings, thanks to contractual bonuses and low taxation.

Algeria

The British Council Algiers reports that English has grown in popularity due to a reaction against French. English is now a primary school option. There has been a great deal of civil unrest recently with the rise of Islamic Fundamentalism, and several foreigners have been murdered. Consult your Foreign Affairs department before taking a post.

Bahrain

Minimum salary: Salaries range between BD 520-580 (CTEFLA or equivalent), and BD 580-700 (DTEFLA/MA). The rate for part-time work varies between BD6-8 per hour.
Tax and health insurance: No tax is charged and basic health cover can be obtained locally for approximately BD 125 per annum, and many recognised western insurance companies are established in Bahrain. More comprehensive health cover is recommended for those who are not 100% fit. The health facilities available are more than adequate.
Visa requirements: Visas are not required for British nationals born in the UK. Those not born in the UK might have to get their employers to obtain a NOC (no objection certificate), before entry into Bahrain, although usually they can get a 3- or 5-day visa on arrival and the employer can sort out the arrangements in this period. Work permits are required and are obtained by the employer soon after the employee's arrival. In order to obtain a work permit, new employees must have a medical check-up in a certain health centre in Bahrain soon after arrival.
Accommodation: Varies from BD 140-300 per month for a studio or a 1/2 bedroom flat.
Other information: There is not a vast amount of EFL work in Bahrain. Some companies and ministries have language units within training departments (including the Ministry of Education). The University has an ELC, and there are a number of private institutes which teach English.

Bahrain is a very easy, relaxed place to live. There is plenty of nightlife (including alcohol), although the salaries are not as good as in the neighbouring countries and the cost of living is higher. Bahrain is one of the most pro-Western of the Gulf states.

List of schools in Bahrain

ACCESS, Tel: 722898.
The British Council, Tel: 26555.
IPE, Tel: 290028.
Polyglot Schools Ltd., Tel: 271722.

Egypt

Minimum salary: Rates of pay vary greatly, but normally range between LE10-27 per hour, while the British Council pays LE 30,000-40,000 per annum. Other schools often pay less but may pay a dollar supplement.
Tax and health insurance: Teachers do not currently pay local tax. It is advisable to take out your own insurance policy in addition to your employer's provisions, particularly those who are employed on a part-time contract.
Visa requirements: Work permits are required and these are normally arranged by the school after arrival. A visa can be obtained from ports of entry.
Accommodation: A two-bedroom flat costs around LE 800-1,500 per month, or LE 300-400 for a good quality shared flat - less outside Cairo or it may be included in your contract.
English language newspaper: *Egyptian Gazette* (daily).
Other information: Although salaries may seem low, Egypt is very cheap and teachers are able to maintain a good standard of living on this type of wage. One of the most pro-Western Arabic countries, English is widely spoken and there are many private language schools around Cairo, which usually recruit internally. Despite problems with Islamic Fundamentalists, English is still popular, particularly amongst wealthy Egyptians.

List of schools in Egypt

American University in Cairo, Room 108, Division of Public Service, Falaki Street, Cairo.
El Kawmeya International School, Horreya Avenue, Bab Sharki.
El Manar School, Amin Fikry Street, Ramleh Station, Cairo.
El Pharaana School, El Pharaana Street, Bab Sharki.
ILI, 2 Muhammad Bayoumi Street, Heliopolis, Cairo. Seven or eight courses a year. Maximum 12 trainees on each course. Accommodation and airport pick-up arranged. Tel: (202) 2291 9295. Fax: (202) 291 2218.
ILI School (KG), Ziziniah, Alexandria.
International Centre for Idioms, (behind Wimpy Bar), Dokki.
International Language Institute Soafeyeen (ILI), 3 Mahmoud Azmi Street, Madinet El Sohafayeen, Embaba, Cairo.
International Language Learning Institute, Pyramids Road, Guiza.
Living Language College, Heliopolis.
October Language Schools, 13, Saad El Ali Street, Mohandesssin.
Port Said School, 7, Taha Hussein Street, Zamalek 3403435.
Schutz American School, Cairo. Tel: 5701435/5712205.
The London Business Institute, Dokki.
The British Broadcast College, Dokki.

Iran

There has been a resurgence in the demand for English in Iran, with a huge growth in candidates sitting Cambridge exams. Although the government is becoming more and more moderate, work possibilities for westerners remain limited unless you are a Muslim.
English Language newspaper: *Teheran Times* (D).

Israel

Minimum salary: The average rate of pay is 40 NIS per class contact hour.
Tax and health insurance: 25%.
Visa requirements: Jews are eligible for automatic citizenship and work permits. For non-jews of any nationality, your employer should arrange visas and permits. It is possible to work on a tourist visa. National insurance contributions are low, and non-jews have to arrange their own health insurance.
Accommodation: At least $300-$400 mth for a shared flat.
Other information: The recent liberalisation of Eastern and Central Europe has led to a large influx of immigrants, most of whom are keen to assimilate by learning English as well as Hebrew. It is becoming harder to obtain a work permit for Israel because of rising unemployment. However, the demand for English is high and there are many private

language schools that are prepared to take on unqualified native English speakers.

Israeli Occupied (Palestinian) Territories

Minimum salary: The average rate of pay is 35 NIS per class contact hour.
Tax and health insurance: No taxation. Take out medical insurance.
Visa requirements: Teachers working for the British Council do not normally get a working visa, but generally get a tourist visa which must be renewed every three months.
Accommodation: In East Jerusalem it is expensive and rent for an ordinary flat for one month costs approximately $500. For a shared flat the going rate is about $300/month - less in Gaza and Nablus.
Other Information: The British Council is the only well-known English language school. Teachers are advised to expect to work under pressure, as circumstances are very stressful. Interestingly, demand for English has increased recently, as it is seen as potentially liberating. Living conditions are still difficult, and the "intifada" has crippled the economy.

Jordan

Minimum salary: At the British Council, the basic teacher's salary is currently JD 826 per month, plus increments for relevant qualifications and experience and a JD 200 housing allowance.
Tax and health insurance: Taxation rates are very informal and a teacher earning a salary at the above rate would pay JD 93 per month in tax.
Visa requirements: Entry visas are required for Jordan and temporary visas are obtainable at the airport. To work there legally it is necessary to have both work and residence permits.
Accommodation: Accommodation is often hard to come by and sharing seems to be the best option.
English language newspaper: *The Jordan Times* (D).
Other information: Opportunities for TEFL are limited, although a few private schools are in need of teachers to teach English examination syllabuses. However, most do not guarantee serious professional support and a reasonable salary. The American Language Centre employs only Americans. Traditionally one of the more tolerant and stable Middle Eastern countries, Jordan's economy is recovering after Gulf War setbacks.

List of schools in Jordan

Amman Baccalaureate School, Amman, Tel: 624872.
The Ahliyyeh School for Girls, Amman. Tel: 624872.

American Language Center, Amman. Tel: 659859.
British Council, First Circle, Jebel Amman, P.O. Box 634, Amman 11118.
The National Orthodox School, Amman. Tel: 685393.
New English School, Amman. Tel: 827154.
Yarmouk Cultural Centre, Amman. Tel: 671447.

Kuwait

Minimum salary: KD 650-700 per month. Most expatriates manage to save well over half their salary.

Tax and health insurance: At present, all salaries are tax free. However, with the present national budget imbalance, there has been talk of foreign nationals being taxed at a future date. Similarly, at present medical treatment in Kuwaiti governmental clinics and hospitals is free for British nationals, but the government is currently considering the imposition of charges for non-Kuwaitis. Some teachers take out private health insurance but several big EFL employers arrange financial support for medical expenses.

Visa requirements: Once in Kuwait, a series of medical tests are required before a full working visa, or residency as it is known in Kuwait, is granted. This includes a compulsory HIV test. Prospective teachers may choose to have a test in their home country, as anyone proving to be HIV positive is immediately deported, and no attempt is made at counselling. Unlike some other Gulf countries, you cannot enter Kuwait without a "sponsor" who is responsible for obtaining your visa. It is not possible to come on a visitor's visa to search for employment. Airlines will not allow anyone to fly into Kuwait without presenting firm evidence of having obtained a visa.

Accommodation: In virtually all cases, the employer provides accommodation free of charge for expatriate EFL staff in Kuwait, although this may involve sharing with one or more colleagues. Such accommodation may or may not include free water and electricity - an important point worth clarifying in advance. Accommodation is also furnished.

English language newspaper: *Kuwait Times* (D), *Arab Times* (D).

Other information: As most EFL teachers come on one- or two-year contracts and leave without renewing, there is a constant demand for EFL staff in Kuwait. This has increased since the invasion brought home to many Kuwaitis the need to learn to speak more English themselves and to start their children learning as early as possible. It should be noted that EFL staff with experience of teaching young learners, age 6+ are particularly in demand.

Kuwait is a very small, relatively Islamic country with limited possibilities for social and recreational activities. Most EFL teachers come to amass capital rather than expecting or hoping to play a full part in the life of the country. It could be an excellent career move if one intended to study for a distance qualification, such as an MA. The government is keen to promote English and ties with the west. It is the working language of many Kuwaiti companies. ILC Hastings and English Worldwide recruit for Kuwait.

List of schools/organisations in Kuwait

American International School, Tel: 5318175.
ELU, The Kuwait Institute of Banking Studies, PO Box 1080, Safat 13011 (ESP teachers only).
Fahaheel English School, Tel: 3711070.
Gulf English School, Tel: 5629215.
Kuwait English School, Tel: 5629356.
Language Centre, PO Box 2575, Safat 13026.
Pitman Secretarial and Business Studies Centre, Tel: 2544840.

Libya

Despite trade sanctions, the economy is healthy. Although the British Council warns teachers to "proceed with caution", oil and private companies occasionally recruit teachers. Contact AFMENCO (UK) Ltd, 39 Marsh Green Road, Exeter EX2 8PN.

Morocco

Minimum salary: Terms and conditions vary widely and full-time contracts are not common, with teachers tending to be paid on a hourly basis. This ranges from 6,000-10,000 dirhams per month for 24-25 contact hours, with the hourly rate in the region of 50-120 dirhams, depending on qualifications

Tax and health insurance: The taxation rates are complex, but depending on the monthly income, tends to vary between 17-30%. Tax may be deducted at source, but in some cases teachers are expected to pay their own. A private health insurance policy is recommended.

Visa requirements: Entry visas are not required by British nationals, who are entitled to stay for up to three months without a residence permit. Employers generally arrange work permits for their expatriate teachers and original copies of your birth certificate, degree, and teaching qualification will be needed. Other nationals should apply well in advance to their local Moroccan embassy, or alternatively contact Ministere de l'Emploi, Quartier des Ministeres, Rabat, Morocco.

Accommodation: Usually unfurnished and a flat in one of the main towns will cost between 1500-3000 dirhams a month. If acquired through an agent, a fee of one month's rent is charged.

Other information: Qualified teachers should easily find employment. It is however, much easier to find employment from within the country than by postal application. Transport is good in the main cities and, despite high levels of inflation, eating out is inexpensive. In general the cost of living is relatively cheap however items of clothing and footwear tend to be more expensive. Morocco is currently liberalising its exchange regulations and foreign residents may now transfer 50% of their salaries in addition to payments into pension funds and foreign social security. A knowledge of French is useful.

List of schools in Morocco

American Language Center, 4 zankat Tanja, Rabat 9 other centers.
The British Council Language Centre, 36 rue de Tanger, B.P. 467, Rabat
Business and Professional English Centre, 74 rue Jean Jaures, Casablanca.
ILC, Rabat. Tel: 70-97-18.
The London School of English, 10 ave des Far, Casablanca.

Oman

Minimum salary: 600-700 rials per month.
Tax: Tax-free.
Visa requirements: Employer's sponsorship required for a permit, which can take some time.
Accommodation: Often provided; if not, 250 rials per month.
English Language Newspaper: *Oman Daily Observer* (D), *Times of Oman* (D).
Other information: It is a popular destination, but less well paid than its neighbours. Most jobs are in Muscat. Conditions are relatively good for women and buying alcohol is permitted. Contact **CFBT** (see p53) or the **English Language Teaching Dept.,** Ministry of Education, PO Box 3, Ruwi.

Qatar

Minimum salary: The equivalent of about $22,000 a year. Teachers usually receive a low salary and a huge bonus.
Tax and health insurance: Tax-free.
Visa requirements: UK nationals can enter on a tourist visa. Employer's sponsorship is required for a work permit.
Accommodation: Free or at minimal, subsidised rate.
Other information: This tiny Gulf state offers some of the best salaries in the area.

Saudi Arabia

Minimum salary: Salaries vary widely, but good employers will pay around 9,000 Saudi Riyals per month at the mid-point of their salary scales, with actual starting salary depending on qualifications. Packages will vary however, from between SR 5,000-10,000 per month. Some employers will offer a 13-month bonus and all will offer a gratuity payment of half a month's salary for each completed year of service.

Tax and health insurance: There is no taxation or other deduction from gross salaries. Employers will normally provide health insurance as part of the employment package. If not, cover would be required for all normal medical requirements as clinics and hospitals are private. An HIV negative certificate is required to obtain an entry permit.
Visa requirements: Most foreign teachers will require a work visa, which will only be issued when the formal application is backed by documentation from a sponsoring organisation. At least four weeks should be allowed for the issue of the visa, but it may take longer. Tourist visas are not issued for Saudi Arabia, and you cannot go there in order to seek work.
Accommodation: The housing market is volatile and prices are currently rising steadily. For a single prerson, expect to pay between SR 20,000-40,000 per year, and a married couple would probably need to spend between SR 60,000-100,000. Expatriates tend to live on compounds. The quality of accommodation is particularly important for families, since women are very restricted and cannot drive or generally work. Many employers will provide an allowance equivalent to anything up to three months' salary, while some may provide accommodation free with the contract.
English language newspaper: *Arab News* (D).
Other information: There are relatively few language schools, but a great number of Saudi-based companies which have large in-house English language training programmes. These provide the major employment opportunities in Saudi Arabia for EFL teachers.

The Saudi environment is very demanding, both climatically and culturally - all forms of public entertainment are banned except sports. The cost of living is relatively low, and teachers can save a considerable proportion of their salary. Employment opportunities for women are substantially more limited than for men.

It is not really recommended for families, or for periods of about more than three years. Couples will have the best opportunities of meeting people locally - otherwise male and female students are strictly segregated. If you are offered work as a couple (and you must be married), ensure that you can both obtain work permits - women are often refused these even with a job offer. Women are also prohibited from driving.

Despite the drawbacks, many teachers love working in Saudi and find the desert landscape uniquely beautiful. Others find the prospect of being able to earn enough to retire early or set up their own business more than compensates for a few years in an alien but fascinating culture.

List of schools in Saudi Arabia.

The British Council, Direct Teaching Operation, PO Box 58012, Riyadh 11594.
Education, End of Jareer Street, Malaz, Riyadh.
English Language Centre, King Adulaziz University, PO Box 1540, Jeddah 21441.
Girls' College of Arts - General Presidency for Female Institute for Languages and Translation, c/o King Saud

University, PO Box 2465, Riyadh 11451.
Inst. of Public Administration, PO Box 205, Riyadh 11411.
King Fahd University of Petroleum and Minerals, English Language Centre, Dhahran 31261.
Riyadh Military Hospital-Training Division, PO Box 7897, Riyadh 11159.
Saudi Airlines - Saudia cc:452, PO Box 167, Jeddah 21231.
Saudi Language Institute, PO Box 6760, Riyadh 11575.
SCECO-East Central Training Inst., PO Box 5190, Damman 31422.
Yanbu Industrial College, PO Box 30436, Yanbu Al Sinaiyah 21477.

Syria

Minimum salary: Salaries can be expected to be in the region of SL 20,000 per month.
Tax: Tax-free.
Visa requirements: A visa can be obtained from any Syrian Embassy, but the foreign teachers will need a sponsor. Upon arrival in Syria, a resident permit can be obtained, and only after that can a work permit be secured.
Accommodation: For reasonable accommodation in a one- or two-bedroom flat, you can expect to pay approximately SL 20,000-50,000 per annum.

List of Schools in Syria

Al Razi, Damascus. Tel: 457301.
American Language Center, Damascus. Tel: 2247236.
Dimashk al Lughawi, Damascus. Tel: 454615.

Tunisia

Minimum salary: It is possible to find work on either a part-time basis paid hourly or on a full-time contracted basis. Average pay depends on the school and ranges from 400-1000 dinars per month.
Tax and health insurance: Under the state health scheme (CNSS), a contribution of 6.25% is made (employer adds 18%), and 1.75% for non-compulsory health cover (COMAR), where the employer adds 6.25%. Many teachers do, however, take out private health insurance and it is recommended. The tax rate lies between 10-15%, dependent on level of income.
Visa requirements: EC nationals usually enter Tunisia on a three-month tourist visa which is given on arrival. The employer will then put in an application for a work permit and this involves a considerable amount of paper work and organisation. Original degree certificates and original birth certificates are required. While your permit is being processed you will probably receive a temporary work permit or a letter from your employer saying that you work for them, which is also sufficient for temporary identification. The official work permit is normally valid for 1-2 years, depending on your contract.
Accommodation: Many teachers choose to live in the expatriate belt of coastal suburbs where rents for two bedroom flats are around 250-300 dinars per month. In the less fashionable areas rents are cheaper.
Other information: Tunisia is one of the Arab world's most liberal nations and has a rich cultural heritage. Although officially classed as a developing country, this is not apparent in the cosmopolitan and predominantly European capital. Tunisians are on the whole highly motivated to learn English which is slowly replacing French in business dealings within the capital. As most Tunisians speak French as a second language, a knowledge of French is more or less essential for survival. Much teaching takes place in the evenings and while general English is the mainstay, an increasing amount of work is being done in companies off site. Most of the EFL activity is in the capital, although small private language schools are springing up in the provinces.

List of schools in Tunisia

English Language Training Centre, British Council, 47 Avenue Habib Bourguiba, Tunis.
IBLV, 47 Avenue de la Liberte, Tunis.

United Arab Emirates

Minimum salary: 5-10,000 dirhams per month
Tax and health insurance: Tax-free. Health card: 300 dirhams.
Accommodation: Usually provided, otherwise expensive. A single flat costs 20-35,000 dirhams, a double 35-50,000.
Visa requirements: Tourist visa issued readily. You need a sponsor to be able to live and work in the UAE. Rules about visas change at short notice, so contact your local UEA embassy before departure.
English language newspapers: *Emirates News, Gulf News, Khaleej Times* (D).
Other information: With the growth of tourism, there is a growing demand for both male and female EFL teachers. Both Abu Dhabi and Dubai are cosmopolitan, relaxed cities, without the restrictions normally associated with the Gulf. Try contacting the **Abu Dhabi National Oil Co. (ADNOC),** PO Box 898, Abu Dhabi.

Yemen

Minimum salary: 200,000 rilas/month. You may get a hard currency supplement.
Tax: Tax-free.
Visa requirements: It is usually easy to obtain a tourist visa from your local Yemen embassy. Application for a work permit can be made before or after entering the country.
Accommodation: Usually free with contract.
Other information: Not being an oil state, conditions in Yemen are very different to the other Gulf states. It is a traditional Arab country with a recent history of political instability.

Sub Saharan Africa

Botswana

Minimum salary: Salaries for a graduate teacher with a PGCE begin at around 22,000 Botswana Pula (P) per year, but this varies according to qualifications and experience
Tax and health insurance: Tax is about 8-10% depending on income.
Visa requirements: Tough entry restrictions are in place requiring an entry visa or permit to be obtained merely to visit Botswana. Visitors can usually obtain a permit valid for a maximum of only thirty days - but only if they have a return ticket and evidence of sufficient financial support. All non-national teachers in the private sector require work permits from the Department of Labour, which are valid for only a limited period and must be renewed. Since employers are required to give preference to Botswana nationals, work permits are becoming increasingly difficult to obtain. For those employed in the public teaching sector, a combined residence and work permit is generally issued by the Immigration Department.
Accommodation: Most state schools subsidise accommodation and it is normally charged at a rate of 15% of salary. There is an acute shortage of housing and, in Gaborone in particular, teachers can expect to spend the first few months in a hotel while waiting for a house or flat to be allocated. There is a wide range of housing each with its own rental scale. A two-bedroom flat for example, costs P400-P650 as Government housing, while renting a similar flat privately would cost between P1,500-P2,500 per month.
Other information: The demand for EFL teachers in Botswana is fairly low, given that English is the official language and medium of instruction in schools. However, native English speakers are in demand as teachers of English as a formal subject within the curriculum. Since most teachers are employed through the Teachers for Botswana Recruitment Scheme (TBRS), administered by The British Council in Manchester and the Department of Teaching Service Management in Botswana, these are the key sources to contact for further up-to-date information and advice on teaching in this country. Qualified teachers are recruited twice a year for two-year contracts throughout Botswana.

Cameroon

Minimum salary: Average rate of pay CFA 400,000 per month plus any allowances.
Tax and health insurance: Tax is charged at an average rate of 10%. Health problems are generally associated with malaria, typhus and stomach ailments, and although there are good clinics and pharmacies, a private health insurance policy is advisable.
Visa requirements: Visa and work permits are required for all non-nationals.
Accommodation: Accommodation is reasonable and a furnished two-bedroom flat will cost between CFA 120,000-150,000 per month.
Other information: Teaching institutes tend to rely on Cameroonians or locally available native English speakers. Prospects are not great in the short term, due to the current economic crisis and unstable political situation. Teachers wishing to teach in Cameroon should contact the Embassy and the British Council before doing so for an update on the social and political situation. Camaroon is a beautiful and potentially rich country, and the people are generous and hospitable. A knowledge of French is desirable.

List of schools in Cameroon

The American Cultural Centre, BP 817, Yaounde. Tel: (237) 23 14 37.
The British Council, Avenue Charles de Gaulle, BP 818, Yaounde. Tel: (237) 21 16 96.
The Presidency Bilingual Centre, BP 7239, Yaounde. Tel: (237) 22 18 11.

Kenya

The ODA have eight English resource centres in Kisii, Bubngoma, Embu, Kwale, Nyahururu, Garissa, Eldoret and Migwnani as part of the Secondary English Language Project (SELP). The British Council has a DTO in Nairobi specialising in business communication, and support a biannual ELT newsletter. Prospective teachers should contact the National Association of Teachers of English.

Lesotho

There are no specialised EFL schools in Lesotho.
Visa requirements: Visas are not required by UK nationals for visits of less than 30 days. Visitors intending to stay longer should make an application for extended stay to the Director of Immigration and Passport Services in Maseru. This can normally be done after arrival.
Other information: Two official languages are taught and used in schools - English and Sesotho. Greetings are an important social ritual and it is worth learning the basic pleasantries in Sesotho. English is widely understood, particularly in urban areas. Lesotho is a relatively healthy

country, free from many of the diseases found in tropical Africa such as malaria, bilharzia and meningitis, and medicines are freely available. Postage facilities and telecommunications are fair, and it is possible to make direct international calls to most countries, although there are few public telephone boxes.

Namibia

Most opportunities are in teacher training. Education has been conducted in English rather than Africaans since Namibia won independence in 1990. You could try contacting the Namibian Ministry of Education. See also Volunteering, (p59).

South Africa

Minimum salary: 1,800 rand per month, R20 per hour.
Visa requirements: You must have employment before you can obtain a work permit. This can be done within the country.
Accommodation: R400 for a flat, less for a furnished room.
Other information: The economic is in decline with 40% (largely black) unemployment. Language schools are flourishing to cater mainly for Europeans on study holidays. 35% of native whites speak English as a first language. State education is poor in black towns and is often funded by the ODA. English is the official language of the ANC and is much in demand.

List of schools in South Africa

Bloemfontein School of Languages, Bloemfontein.
Cape Town School of English, Claremont 7700. Cape Town. Tel: (021) 61 7635. Same address for information on South African Federation of English Language Schools.

Swaziland

Opportunities for EFL teachers in Swaziland are limited. There are no private sector language schools, but there is an international school which employs expatriate teachers called Waterford Kamhlava United World College, P.O. Box 52, Mbabane. Currently about 20% of secondary school teachers are non-Swazis, and most of these come from other African countries, though there are one or two foreign EFL teachers. Details of employment opportunities can be obtained from: The Teaching Service Commission, P.O. Box 39, Mbabane. The University of Swaziland has an Academic Communications Skills Unit, and offers rather better terms and conditions than the Ministry. There are a few European expatriate staff on local contract. Details from: The Registrar, University of Swaziland, Private Bag, Kwaluseni.

Uganda

Uganda is an English speaking country, in which English is the medium of education. It does not therefore have English language schools. There are a number of private schools however which may offer opportunities. We have no salary guidelines at present.
Tax and health insurance: You should consider taking out health insurance which covers emergency repatriation to your home country.
Visa requirements: All foreigners now require an entry visa to visit Uganda, with single entry visas costing about $30, and multiple entry visas lasting six months costing $50. As for work permits, your employer should lodge an application for a work permit before you arrive. It takes time and bonds or a deposit air ticket may be required. You should register with the appropriate Consul soon after arrival.
Accommodation: Supply in the housing rental market has improved tremendously over the last year, and many new houses have been completed and are currently available for immediate letting. Most houses are unfurnished and a furnished house may cost $200-300 extra to furnish. Typical average monthly rents for an unfurnished two-bedroom house will be from $400 to well over $1,000 in the major urban areas.
Other information: Security risks do exist, so sensible precautions are necessary. You should carry some ID with you at all times.

Zimbabwe

Minimum salary: Starting salary for a graduate with a teaching diploma is the equivalent of $1,600 per month.
Tax and health insurance: Tax is charged at a rate of 25-30% on such a salary and Public Services Medical Aid Insurance costs $25 per month.
Visa requirements: All teachers whether in private or state schools, are controlled by the Ministry of Education P.O. Box 8022, Causeway, Harare, from whom a Temporary Employment Permit (TEP) must be obtained. This is granted for two years initially, and may be renewed annually up to a maximum of five years. It is a Catch 22 situation as you require a TEP to get a job, but a TEP is for a specific appointment to a specific school, and may not be transferable. Some recruitment is carried out by the Zimbabwe High Commission in London.
Accommodation: A rural school will provide one room in a shared house for $20 per month. A one-bedroom flat in Bulawayo costs $300-500 per month and in Harare between $500-1,000 a month.
Other information: Teaching posts in Zimbabwe are not easy to obtain. As English is the medium of instruction throughout the educational system (officially at least), specialised EFL appointments do not exist. It is possible to pick up some part-time low-paid EFL work, and the fact that this is illegal is normally ignored. Contact Speciss College, 2nd floor, Speciss Annex, PO Box 2713 Harare.

Professional Development

In order to progress through the hierarchy of ELT, you need a mixture of experience and training, so there is a wide range of courses available; from specialised weekend courses to Masters degrees and PhDs. Once you are on the first rung of the ladder, this section you how to choose courses that will ensure your steady climb to the top.

So, you want to do a further qualification?

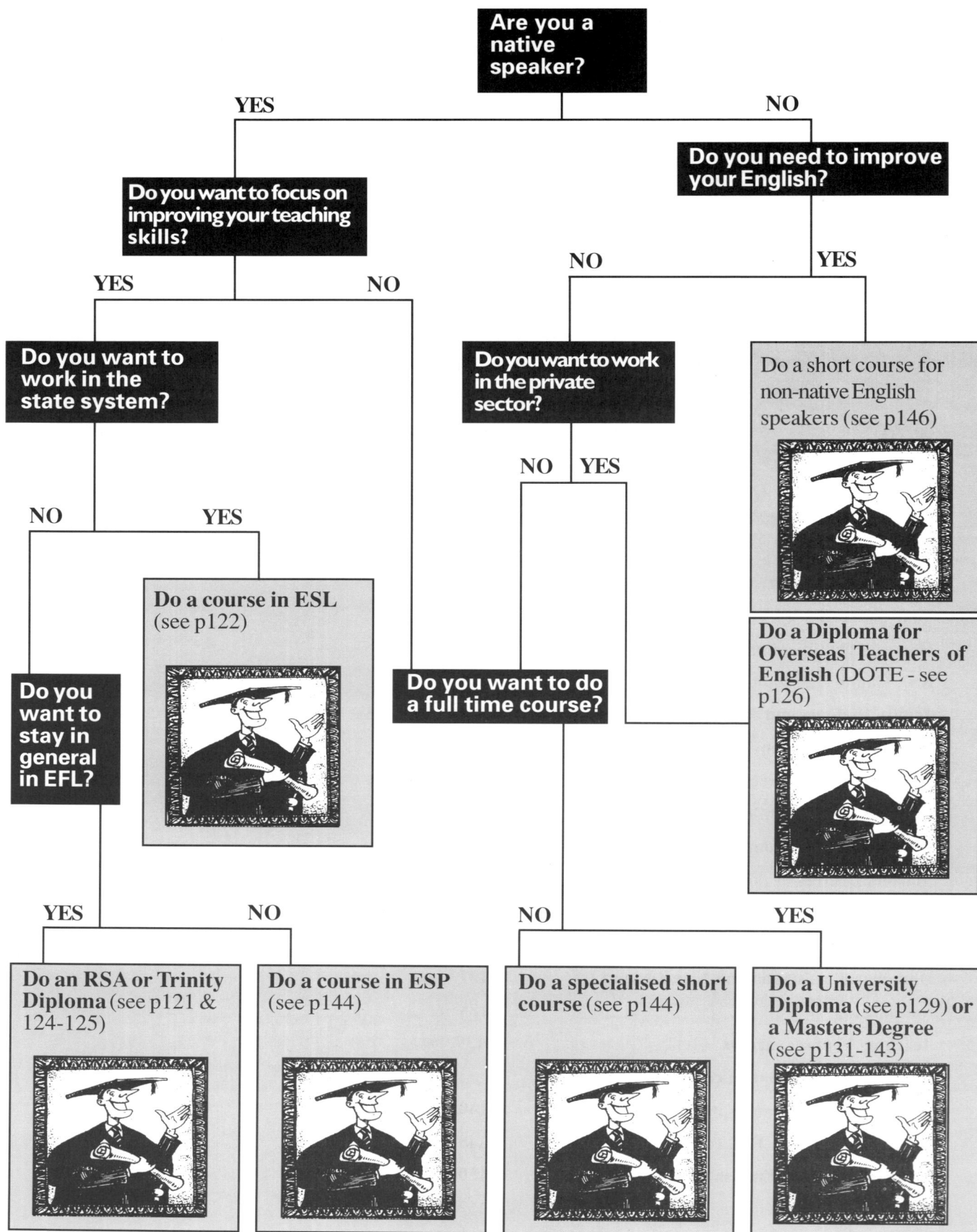

Are you a native speaker?

YES / **NO**

NO →

Do you need to improve your English?

YES →

Do you want to focus on improving your teaching skills?

YES / **NO**

NO / **YES**

Do you want to work in the state system?

NO / **YES**

Do you want to work in the private sector?

NO / **YES**

Do a short course for non-native English speakers (see p146)

Do you want to stay in general in EFL?

Do a course in ESL (see p122)

Do a Diploma for Overseas Teachers of English (DOTE - see p126)

Do you want to do a full time course?

YES / **NO**

NO / **YES**

Do an RSA or Trinity Diploma (see p121 & 124-125)

Do a course in ESP (see p144)

Do a specialised short course (see p144)

Do a University Diploma (see p129) or a Masters Degree (see p131-143)

Your Career Path

Everyone has different career objectives, but your choice may depend upon qualifications. Broaden your horizons and consider the most popular options outlined here.

Although its emphasis is on successful classroom methods, Teaching English as a Foreign Language is still an academic discipline and it is important that you take time out to continue studying and researching as your career develops. Academic qualifications will definitely be a factor in obtaining high profile jobs, especially in the public sector.

Let's suppose you start with a university degree and an RSA/Cambridge or Trinity Preparatory Certificate, obtained by doing a short training course, as discussed in Section One. (For short courses see p140-147).

An EFL Diploma

Some teachers may choose immediately to study for a recognised EFL diploma, for example, the RSA/Cambridge or Trinity Diploma. This exam contains both written papers and a practical, two lessons, each with a different class, taught by you, observed by an examiner and marked accordingly. Many teachers prefer to have practical teaching experience for up to a year before entering for a diploma. A diploma course may take up to three months' study.

A distance learning RSA Diploma has also been offered for many years by International House. However, to take the examination you will need to be registered with a recognised school.

A diploma is a recognition of your practical application of the theory and practice of Teaching English as a Foreign Language. You will probably find it necessary if you wish to continue in classroom teaching for any longer than two years.

Experienced teachers with two years or more classroom experience behind them may proceed directly to the Diploma in Education, specialising in EFL. This is also a one-year university degree course, that is equivalent to the general Postgraduate Diploma in Education (DipEd). It qualifies teachers in other subjects to teach in secondary schools.

The Master of Arts (MA)

Academically, EFL is an application of linguistics and many teachers choose to do a one-year MA in Applied Linguistics. As part of your MA course you will have to do research for a short

dissertation. This may allow you to pursue areas of special interest, for example the use of media or the use of video in ELT. If this is the case, you should look for colleges that have a special interest in this area, such as the University of Westminster or the Language Centre at Brighton Polytechnic.

Doctorate in Philosophy (PhD)

Either as a manifestation of your academic interest or because you intend to undertake a university teaching career, you may wish to study for a doctorate. Doctorates involve researching and writing a dissertation on your chosen area of research and can last from between two years (full-time research) and what sometimes seems like a lifetime (part-time). The subject for your doctoral research must be agreed by a university at the outset and a research supervisor will be assigned to you. Some universities - London is one - offer a one-year MPhil (Masters in Philosophy) which counts towards the full doctorate. This might be appropriate for a practising teacher who has done the Diploma and wants to approach doctorate work without doing the MA.

English for Specific Purposes (ESP)

If you have some EFL teaching experience, you can do a course in ESP. A specialist background, in business for example, will make you particularly suitable to teach ESP, which is teaching English towards a specific objective. If your students want to be doctors or pilots, they will need specialised English, so ESP is job- rather than exam-orientated. ESP courses analyse the needs of such students, looking at syllabus design and materials development. (For course details see p144 and p146-153).

English for Academic Purposes (EAP)

EAP courses are generally run for non-native English speakers who wish to attend anglophone higher educational establishments. Courses give students the language skills to understand lectures or write essays, for example. Probably the best way into EAP is to do a related short course and apply for a support service position with a university in a non-anglophone country. This will give you the academic background. If you succeed in this competitive field, senior university positions and their respective salaries will follow.

Academic qualifications will definitely be a factor in obtaining high profile jobs, especially in the public sector.

A specialist background, such as in business, will make you particularly suitable to teach ESP.

English as a Second Language (ESL)

In the United States ESL refers to teaching English to all foreign students in the country. In the UK, Australia, Canada and New Zealand ESL or E2L refers to teaching English to immigrants. Unlike general EFL students, immigrants' main needs are how to integrate into the country's educational system, work environment and general social culture. ESL is taught to children and adults, with courses often run by state schools and colleges.

A move into ESL can offer EFL teachers the opprtunity to stay in their native country.

A move into ESL can offer EFL teachers the opportunity to stay in their native country in a job with a clearer career structure. Although levels of pay are not particularly high, ESL teaching may, perhaps, offer you more social satisfaction.

In the UK the National Association for the Teaching of English and Other Community Languages to Adults (NATECLA) has been campaigning for more bilingual and non-native teachers in ESL, particularly those who speak the languages of the Indian subcontinent, Vietnamese, Turkish, Arabic or Greek. Courses in ESL in the UK include the RSA/Cambridge Certificate in TESL for Adults and the Diploma in Further Adult and Community Education.

International Equivalence

If you intend to work in another country in the national education system it is important to check that your qualifications are comparable to the qualifications in the country in which you intend to work. For example, in some countries a British MA is considered equivalent only to a first degree. If you intend to settle down in a foreign country for the duration of you career and work within the national education system, you should seriously consider studying for the teaching qualifications that pertain in that system. It could avoid all kinds of problems.

Go East!

You will have a better opportunity to clinch many EFL jobs if you have travelled.

You will have a better opportunity to clinch many EFL jobs if you have travelled. The reason is simple - if you are working with foreign students, experience of their cultures and countries will enrich you and the institution you are working for. If you have the opportunity of spending a couple of years teaching in a country outside Western Europe, it will be even more of an employment advantage.

Publish and be saved!

All academic progress is enhanced by publishing and EFL is no exception. EFL lives on the interchange of ideas between teachers and several magazines and journals are devoted to making this happen.

You don't have to be a university researcher to carry out your own classroom research. In recent years academics have stressed the importance of teachers carrying out informal research into what works and doesn't work for their students. Teachers can carry out their own classroom research into methodology or materials and write up the results for any one of a number of journals such as ELTJ (English Language Teaching Journal), MET (Modern English Teacher) or local journals. Also there is the opportunity to present your observations and research at conferences, which can in turn be the source of more seminar work or even of publishing contracts. More details of journals and conferences are on p186 'Keeping in Touch'.

EFL is an astonishingly varied career. As well as travel throughout the world, it offers opportunities in children's and adult education, in the corporate sector and at university, as well as in publishing and the media. It may even spur you to start your own small business by opening a school or teaching agency of your own. Decide where you want to go in EFL and get moving!

STARTING AGAIN

Many teachers in the State educational system retire early or decide at a late stage to begin a new career in EFL. Similarly an increasing number of people retiring early or made redundant in other careers are looking into EFL as a possible alternative. Some healthy retired people have chosen to spend their early retirement years doing voluntary work in with VSO (Voluntary Service Overseas) or other charity organisations (see p59).

It's important to stress two things. First, in the UK and USA competition for jobs is fierce at the moment. Second, EFL teaching is different from school teaching in that the stress is not so much on imparting information as on helping learners to develop a skill.

For these reasons, whatever your background and qualifications, retraining as an EFL teacher is essential before you go into the classroom. A 4-week preparatory certificate course will help you find out if you are suited to the hands-on teaching approach required, but don't be put off if you find it personally quite testing and that you are not totally successful immediately! Not everybody excels in a new discipline in four weeks. As for new teachers, a diploma will be an essential part of your job-seeking armoury and you may choose to do the twelve-week course first. It's not cheap but it will be immensely worthwhile. Regard this as an investment in a new and fulfilling career.

How Will Qualifications Help Me?

I am an experienced native English speaking teacher of EFL but I have no qualification. What should I do?
It is a good idea to get a qualification. You do not necessarily need to do a certificate course, which is the course most teachers of EFL will initially take. If you want to work in the private sector and you have more than two years' experience, you could do an RSA or Trinity Diploma (see p 125). Note, however, that some centres may prefer you to do the RSA Certificate before they will let you do the Diploma. If you want to work in the state system, you must achieve Qualified Teacher Status. With two years' teaching experience you can do a Masters degree or a diploma. A recent report showed that 50% of people studying for Masters courses had no EFL qualifications.

Does any qualification guarantee a job?
There is a popular myth that if you do a Masters degree, you will automatically get a better job. This is not necessarily true. Although jobs which require MAs generally pay well, there are not many of them around and far too many teachers with MAs chasing them. There is, however, a shortage of experienced teachers with diplomas.

Is a university diploma equivalent to an RSA or Trinity Diploma?
It can be equivalent if it contains teaching practice, but generally it is a completely different qualification (see p127).

Are MAs much the same price?
The cost of MAs does vary from country to country. In general, MAs in Australia and Canada are relatively cheap. In the EU, most countries have comparable costs. MAs for overseas teachers - i.e. non-residents - are more expensive. Be warned also that if you are a British teacher who has been overseas for a long time, you could be classed as an overseas teacher in the UK.

Are all MA courses similar?
Not really. Because some universities are inevitably better equipped with staff and materials in some fields, MA courses at such universities will also be stronger in those fields (see p135,137,141).

I am interested in computers/ literature/drama. What should I do?
There are courses that focus on a specialised area of teaching. You can choose from a range of subjects as diverse as video, audio and computers in teaching to English through theatre or designing and creating materials (see p144 - 157).

How can I pay for any further training that I do?
If you are an EU citizen, you may be eligible for a Career Development Loan - ask your college. If you do a course in Australia, you have automatic, limited work rights, whatever your nationality. In the US and Canada you can only legally work on the college campus.

Can I do a further training course while I am working?
Yes. You can do an RSA Cambridge or Trinity Diploma while you are working. Also, some MAs can be taken as distance learning courses (although these tend to suit only experienced teachers) and others can be taken on a modular basis.

I want to train to get into management. What should I do?
You could do an MBA (Masters in Business Administration). Many EFL teachers are now turning to this qualification as a way of either getting into management within EFL, or of broadening out of EFL into general management (see p77 and p125). Bristol University, in conjunction with International House, run a management stream. West Sussex University also run a management course. Some other British MAs also incorporate management training elements. IATEFL (the International Association of Teachers Of English as a Foreign Language) has a Special Interest Group (SIG) dedicated to management (see addresses p168).

I want to teach English as a Second Language (ESL) in the UK. What should I do?
Many EFL teachers change to ESL as an opportunity to have a clearer career structure. It also offers the means to remain teaching in your native country in the primary or state sector (see p148).

I want to teach English for Specific Purposes (ESP). What is the best thing to do?
Teaching English in specific specialised subjects such as English for Banking is a growing area. If you have a specialist background you could be in demand (see p148 and p157). Training courses in ESP, although not obligatory, are a common requirement for teaching ESP.

I am a primary specialist. Which is the best course for me?
There are various short courses that incorporate such experience (see p149 - 156).

Will I automatically get more money if I am better qualified?
Unfortunately not. There is no incremental system as such within the private EFL sector, and salaries can vary quite widely for teachers with the same qualifications. Only state schools and major employers, such as the British Council, have a rigid incremental system.

RSA/Cambridge Diploma (DTEFLA)

College	Course length	FT/ PT	Fees	Start dates	Entry requirements	Contact	Comments	Max no. of students
Bell Language School, Cambridge	27 wks	PT	£895 + exam fee	Oct	2 yrs exp	Sue Sheerin		15
Bell Language School, Norwich	10 wks	FT	£1,300 + exam fee	Mar	2 yrs exp	Sarah Knights		15
Bell Language School, Essex	10 wks	FT	£1,300 + exam fee	Mar	2 yrs exp	Robin Davis		15
City of Liverpool Community Coll	1 yr	PT	£700 + exam fee	Sep	As per UCLES	Diana Lane		10
Colchester Institute	10 wks	FT	£650 + exam fee	Jan	Degree + 2 yrs exp	Simon Haines		12
Eastbourne School of English	8 mths 9 wks	PT FT	£900 £1200 DL	Oct, Jan	Degree + CTEFLA + some exp	Dorothy S Rippon	Practising teachers accommodation	12
University of Edinburgh	10 wks	FT	£1,397	Mar	Degree/Teaching Qual + exp	Secretary IALS		8
GLOSCAT, Cheltenham	1 yr	PT	£600	Sep	EFL exp, interview	Beth Grant		15
Greenhill College, Harrow	1 wk 1 yr 3 mths	FT PT FT	£150 £480 £125 pw	Throughout year; Sep	Substantial TEFL exp FCE level	Judith Haigh Sheila Tracey		10
Hammersmith & West London Coll	1 yr	PT	£550	Sep	CTEFLA + 2/3 yrs exp	Course Information Centre	Apply before June	15
Hilderstone College, Broadstairs	9 mths	PT	£950 + exam fee	Oct	High level educ + 2 yrs exp; Native speaker	Valerie Horne		12
Kings College, London	8 mths	PT	£850	Sep	Degree + CTEFLA + 2 yrs exp	Jennifer Jenkins		12
International House, London	8 wks 8 mths 5.5 mths	FT PT DL	£1200 + exam fee £350	Mar on appl Jan	Degree + CTEFLA + 2 yrs exp RSA/TEFLA int re-sit	Secretary		
Intl. Lang. Centres, Hastings	8 wks	FT	£1228 + exam fee	Mar, Oct	CTEFLA + 2 yrs exp	Adrian Underhill	Accom. Service available	12
ITTC, Bournemouth	8 wks 8 mths	FT PT	£1,237 + exam fee	Oct, Feb, Apr	Degree + 2 yrs exp	Annette Harwood		18
Mid-Cheshire College, Northwich	1 yr	PT	on appl	Sep	Degree + 2 yrs exp	Peter Main		18
Moray House, Edinburgh	3 mths	FT	£1,375	Jan	Degree or equiv + 2 yrs exp	The Registrar		12
Northumbria Uni, Newcastle	2 yrs	PT	£650 + exam fee	Sep	Degree/Teaching Qual or equiv	Dept Office Hist & Crit Studs	Flexible exit and entry pts	15
Skola Teacher Training, London	8 wks 10 mths	FT PT	£1,250 + exam fee	Jul	CTEFLA + 2 yrs exp	Lyndel Sayle	8 wks UK; DL. Exams o'seas	15
Stevenson Coll, Edinburgh	30 wks	PT	£800	Sep	Degree + some exp	David Gibson		12
UTS Oxford Centre, Oxford	9 mths	PT	on appl	Oct	CTEFLA + Degree + 2 yrs exp	Mark Bartram		10-14
Waltham Forest College, Essex	9 mths	PT eves	£500 + exam fee	Sep	Currently in EFL + 2 yrs exp	Course Tutor	Apply from May	15

Trinity Licentiate Diploma in TESOL

College	Course length	FT/PT	Fees	Start dates	Entry requirements	Contact	Comments	Max no. of students
Aberdeen College of FE	Varous	PT	On app.	Various	2 yrs exp.	Anne Bain		
Farnborough College of Tech	1 yr	PT	£460 + moderation fee	Sep	Native and non-native speakers	A Ashwell	Career advice given	16
International Language Institute	9 mnths 8wks	FT PT	£1250	Sep Mar	2 yrs exp	Steven Procter		10
ITS English School, Hastings	1 yr	PT	£1,250	Aug	2 yrs exp	John Palim		6
Oxford House College, London	Flexible	DL	£950	Anytime	TEFL Cert + 2 yrs exp	Chris Polatch	DL + 2 week "London Block".	-
Sheffield Hallam University	4 wks 40 wks	FT DL	£1200 £900	Aug	Degree + CTEFLA or teaching exp	Gill King		40
South East Essex College	Varies	FT PT	on appl	On req	On appl; Interview	Marketing		-
Surrey ACE Serv, Woking	4 terms	PT	£450 + fee	Oct	Degree + 2 yrs exp	Ursula Over		16
Waltham Forest College	9 mnths	PT	£350	Sep	2 yrs exp + teaching exp	Course Tutor		12

Overseas Trinity Licentiate Diploma in TESOL

College	Course length	FT/PT	Fees	Start dates	Entry Requirements	Contact
ECS Abu Dhabi	8 mths	PT DL	On req	Oct	Degree or equiv; 3 yrs exp	Kate MacFarlane
ECS Dubai	8-10 mths	PT DL	On req	May, Oct, Mar, Sep	Degree or equiv; 3 yrs exp	Charles Boyle
RELC, Singapore	On appl	FT PT	On req	On appl		SEAMEO Lang Centre

Diploma for Overseas Teachers of English (DOTE)

College	Course length	FT/PT	Fees	Start dates	Entry requirements	Contact	Comments	Max no. of students
Bilkent University, Turkey	2 yrs	FT	TBA	Oct	Min 2 yrs exp CEELT pref	Simon Phipps	CEELT 2 Taken in first year	12
Instituto Anglo-Mexicano de Cultura	6 mnths	PT	4,500M	Oct	EFL qual + 2 yrs exp	Paul Sellers		18
Instituto Chileno-Britanico	14 mnths	PT	£500	Mar	FCE + 500 hrs teaching	Anthony Adams		20
Klubschule Migros, Switzerland	2 yrs	PT	SFR 7950	Sep	Practising teacher & Cambridge Prof	Peter Holland	Special Prospectus	15
METU, DBE Turkey	2 yrs	PT	£250	Oct	3 years teaching exp, fluent english	Suna Yazar		12
Study Space, Thessaloniki	18 mths	PT	£1050 + exam fee	Jan	2 yrs exp + Degree interview	Chrissie Taylor	Practising teachers only	8

Overseas RSA/Cambridge Diploma (DTEFLA)

College	Course length	FT/ PT	Fees	Start dates	Entry requirements	Contact	Comments	Max no of students
Australian TESOL Centre, NSW	8 wks 28 wks	FT PT	A$2,990 A$2,990	Feb,Sep	Degree or equiv + 2 yrs exp	Gloria Smith		12
Bilkent Univ., Turkey	9 mths	PT	$1,000	Oct	2 yrs exp CTEFLA	Simon Phipps		12
British Council, Hong Kong	18 wks	PT	HK$ 21,000	Sep	Degree, CTEFLA + 2 yrs exp; Eng prof	Cecilia Chan		15
British Council, Milan	9 mths	PT	2.2m ITL	Oct	Degree + 2 yrs exp	David Gibbon	Fridays	14
British Council, Naples	9 mths	PT	3.0m ITL	Sep	CTEFLA + 2 yrs exp	F C de la Motte	Practising teachers	6
British Council, Singapore	9 mths	PT	S$4500	Sep	Degree or teaching qual; screening	Vickie Tang	Teaching Adults OR Youngsters	18
British Council Warsaw	10 mths	PT	£750	Oct	As per UCLES	British Council		20
British Institute of Florence	9 mths	PT	2.4m ITL	Oct	CTEFLA pref.	Sarah Ellis		12
British Institute in Paris	30 wks	PT	on appl	Oct	Practising teacher, several yrs exp pref	Eng Dept Sec TEFL	Incl teaching practice	12
British Language Centre, Madrid	2 mths 7 mths	FT PT	240,000 PTS	Oct, Jul	Degree + CTEFLA pref	Alastair Dickinson	Help with accomm	15
British School of Milan	8 mths	PT	2.1m ITL	Sep	Degree + substantial exp	Susan Swift	Need exp at all levels	14
Cambridge School, Verona	8 mths	PT	2.280m ITL	Oct	Degree,CTEFLA + 2 yrs exp pref	Anne Parry		15
International House, Barcelona	8 wks 6 mths	FT PT	on appl	Jul, Oct	Degree or equiv + 2 yrs exp	Jenny Johnson	Help with accomm	18
International House, Budapest	8 wks	FT	£950	Oct	CTEFLA + 2 yrs exp	Frances Hughes	For teachers in Budapest	12
International House, Lisbon	6 mths	PT	260,000 Esc	Sep	CTEFLA + 2 yrs exp	Kathryn Gordon	Interview	12
International House, Madrid	9 mths	PT	225,000 PTS	Oct	CTEFLA + 2 yrs exp	Steven Haysham		15
International House, Rome	120 hrs	PT	2.4m ITL	Oct	As per UCLES	Director		14
International House, Vienna	9 mths	DL	on appl	Oct	Training Qual + 2 yrs exp	Head of Training		5
Language Centre of Ireland, Dublin	8 mths	PT	on appl	Oct	Pre-course interview	Tom Doyle		14
International Language Centre, Japan	156 + hrs	PT	Y395,000	Oct	Min 2 yrs EFL exp RSA/cam cert or equiv	Mark Rossiter		12
Instituto Anglo-Mexicano de Cultura	6 mths	PT	4,500MP	Oct	2 yrs exp + Teaching qualification	Paul Sellers		18
Klubschule Migros, St Gallen	2 yrs	PT	SFR7,950`	Sep	Teaching exp + Camb prof or equiv	Peter Holland		15
Language International, NZ	30 wks	PT	$NZ4500	Sep	CTEFLA + 2 yrs exp	Graig Thaine		12
Study Space Thessalonica	18 mths	PT	£1050 + exam fee	Jan	Degree + 2 yrs EFL teaching	Christine Taylor		8

UK University Courses

Pre-experience certificates, post-experience certificates, diplomas and Masters degrees.

There are too many EFL teacher training courses offered by universities to list here, but the following information describes courses leading to certificates, advanced certificates and diplomas. Remember that there are many new universities, as changes in legislation have enabled British polytechnics to run degree courses and become universities.

Pre-experience certificates

The term 'certificate' generally refers to a short course between three and six months in length. Most certificates in the UK are initial teacher training courses open to native and non-native speakers. It is possible to take a university certificate in most Anglophone countries instead of the more widely known RSA/Cambridge or Trinity Certificates (see p13). However, if you take a university course, make sure it includes teaching practice with foreign students and not just peer teaching with other teachers on your course. Many employers will not recognise such a qualification unless it includes teaching practice.

Post-experience certificates

These are usually called 'advanced certificates' and last three to six months. They are designed for people who either have experience but no previous qualifications, or who have training and need further qualifications without having the time to do a full Masters degree. Recently there has been a growth in advanced certificates for experienced teachers wishing to specialise in ESP or teacher training, for example.

Postgraduate diplomas

These are usually a year in length, and are for experienced native or non-native English speakers. They are not automatically seen as equivalent to the RSA/Cambridge or Trinity College Diplomas (see p13) unless they include teaching practice with EFL students.

The advantage of such courses is that they have easier entry requirements to the Masters programmes, and they should be more practical and less academic - although this is not always the case. The disadvantage of such courses is that too many universities offer exactly the same courses for diplomas or Masters. Either check the contents of the course carefully, or make sure that you opt for a course that allows you to move over from a diploma to a Masters if you do well enough.

There is also an infinite variety in academic level between one diploma and another. This is partly because there is no validation scheme for diplomas in the UK. Universities validate their own degrees, and while control of degree awards such as Masters are strictly regulated by mastership committees, diploma status seems to be more easily conferred. In effect a diploma is any course that is not a Masters, although the British Association of Applied Linguistics (BAAL) is trying to rectify this.

Masters degrees

Teachers of EFL/ESL in the United States generally hold an MA in TESL or Applied Linguistics as a minimum qualification, largely because there is no widely recognised equivalent to the RSA/Cambridge or Trinity Certificates (see p13). The only problem with this system is that many MA courses offer theoretical tuition with too little practical guidance. For this reason, teachers are not adequately prepared to teach in the classroom. It is therefore vital to check the Masters degree has a solid teaching component.

Elsewhere, teachers of EFL tend to take a Masters degree as a way up the career ladder (see p131 - 134). Remember that there are now a great number of EFL teachers who hold a Masters degree, far more than there are jobs that require them. For this reason, it may be more useful to do the RSA/Cambridge or Trinity College Diplomas (see p115).

For details of university courses, see p122 - 124.

If you take a university course, make sure it includes teaching practice with foreign students.

Make sure that you opt for a course that allows you to move over from a diploma to a Masters if you do well enough.

College	Course Title	Course length	FT/ PT	Fees	Start dates	Entry requirements	Contact	Comments
Aston University	Cert in Principles of ESP	1 term	FT	£1957	Oct, Jan,	Degree + 2 yrs exp	Course Secretary	
	Advanced Cert in Principles of TEFL	6 mths	DL	1100	Jan	Teaching qualification + 2 yrs exp	Course Secretary	EFL exp. not necessary
Blackpool and the Fylde College	EFL	36 wks	PT	On applic	Sep		Information Officer	
Canterbury Christ Church College	Cert. TEFL	1 term	FT	£345 EC £1715 non EC	Sep, Jan	Native speaker and teaching exp	Steven Bax	
College of St Mark & St John, Plymouth	Cert in TESP Cert ELT	3 mnths	FT	£2,600 £2,600	Jan, Apr	Teaching Qual or 3 yrs exp	Director, Intl Ed Centre	
University of Edinburgh	Advanced Cert in ELT	10 wks	FT DL	£1,397 £1,190	Oct May	Higher Ed + 3 yrs exp	Ian McGrath	2 wk res in July. Help with accomm.
	Advanced Cert in TESP	10 wks	FT	1397	Jan	Higher Ed; 3 yrs exp; Eng comp	Ian McGrath	Intensive
University of Exeter	Cert Adv Prof Studies ELT	3 wks 10 wks	FT PT	On applic	Oct Jun, July	Teaching Qualification/ Degree & Teaching exp	Prof. Stud Office	
University of Hertfordshire	TEFL training Ling TEFL	14 wks	PT	None £95	Feb	Level 3 degree	Dr T Parke	
Goldsmith's College, London	Cert. in Lang Teaching to Adults	1 yr	PT	£350	Oct	Degree or equiv; Good English	L Arthur	Apply early
University of Luton	Summer Cert. TEFL	4 wks	FT	£600	Jul	Degree or equiv; Good English	Sidney Griffin	
University of Liverpool	Cert TEFL/ ESP	6 wks 6 mths	FT PT	£920	Jul Jan	Degree	Gill Richardson	Accomm available
Manchester University	First Cert. in TEFL	4 wks 4 mths	FT PT	675	Jul Feb	Degree	Debbie Cash	Apply early
Portsmouth University	Cert. TEFLA	1 yr	PT	£510	Oct	Uni entrance level	Course Secretary	Tues + Sats
	PostGrad Cert Appl Linguistics + TEFL	1 sem 2 sems	FT PT	£2270 EC £5057 non EC £645 PT	Oct	Degree or Teaching Qual or equiv + exp	Dr Paul Rastall	
University of Wales Aberyswith	Course within PGCE	30 hrs	FT	On applic	Sep	Initial Degree	PGCE Secretary	Available to PGCE students0.
University College Swansea	Cert. TEFLA	4 wks	FT	£830	Througho year	Degree + native speaker	Director, TEFL Training	Member of BATQI
University Of Warwick	Specialist Cert Developing ELT	10 weeks	FT	£894 EC £2122 Non EC	Oct	Initial Degree + training exp	Julia Khan	
University of Wales, Cardiff	Cert. TEFL	10 wks	FT	£750	Oct	Degree or equiv	Ms C Wilkinson	..Incl Teaching practice
	Cert. in Applied Lings for ELT	10 wks	FT	£753 EC £1850 non EC	Jan	Degree + some exp	Dr P Tench	Teaching practice avail

UK University Diplomas

College	Course Title	Course length	FT/PT	Fees	Start dates	Entry requiremen	Contact	Comments
Aston University	Dip TE/TESP	6 mths / 1-2 yrs	FT / FT / DL	£1,440 EC £3,175 non EC £2,520	Oct, Jan	Degree + 3 yrs exp	Course Secretary	CTEFLA useful
University of Brighton	Dip TEFL	1 yr / 2 yrs	FT / PT	£950 £700	Sep	Degree + exp or Initial TT	Zamy Alibhai	Inc Practise Teaching
University of Bristol	Dip/ MEd TEFL	1 yr / 2-5 yrs	FT / PT	£2,000 EC £5700 non EC	Sep, Oct, Jan	On application	Arlene Gilpin	Gd research & training
Canterbury Christ Church College	Dip TEFL	3 terms	FT / PT	£260 EC per module £5,145 non EC	Oct	Degree or Cert + teaching exp	Steven Bax	
Chichester Institute, Bognor Regis	Dip ELT	6 wks	FT	£450 EC £1,240 Non EC	Oct, Jan	Hons degree or equiv + 3 yrs exp	Jean Hardy	
University of East Anglia	PostGrad Dip ELT & App Lings	8 mths	FT	£2,350 EC £5745 non EC	Sep	Degree or EFL training	Dr Jeremy Fox	No exp required
University of Exeter	B PHIL ed in Lang teaching Adv Prof Studies ELT	1 yr / 3 wks / 10 wks	FT / FT / PT	on request	Oct	Teaching qualification	Further Prof studies office Marion Williams	Degree awarded with 'Merit'
University of Essex	Dip TEFL	9 mths	FT	£2,260 EC £5550 non EC	Oct	Degree + 2 yrs exp	D Meyer	
University of Hull	Dip Applied Lang & New Tech	9 mths / 21 mths	FT / PT	£2,260 EC £5550 non EC £630 PT	Oct	Degree pref.	Language Centre	
Leeds University	Advanced Dip in ELT B A TESOL	9 mnths	FT	£2,200 EC £5870 non EC £5770 non EC	Oct	Degree + 3 yrs exp or 5 yrs exp	Hywel Coleman Lynne Cameron	
Manchester University	Dip TESOL	1yr / 1-6 yrs	FT / PT / DL	£2,350 EC £5,700 Non EC	Sep, Oct, Apr, Jan	first degree or equiv + 2 yrs exp	The Secretary	Progression to Med TESOL
St Brelade's College	Dip TESOL	4 wks	FT	£1000 + exam fee	Sep	2 yrs FT TESOL teaching	Mr Donald Brown	
University of Newcastle upon Tyne	Dip Advanced Ed Studies	1 yr	FT	£2,260 EC £5550 non EC	Oct	Teaching Qual + 2 yrs exp	The Director	Day-time course
University College of North Wales, Bangor	Dip/MA Linguistics	1 yr	FT	£2,260 EC £5550 non EC	Oct	Degree in rel subject	Secretary	
	Dip/MA Theoretical Lings	1 yr	FT	£2,260 EC £5550 non EC	Oct	Degree in rel subject	Secretary	
	Dip/MA Ling Research	1 yr	FT	£2,260 EC £5550 non EC	Oct	Degree in rel subject	Secretary	
University of Portsmouth	PostGrad Dip Appl Linguistics & TEFL	2 sems / 4 sems	FT / PT	£2400 EC £5057 non EC £590 PT	Oct	Degree or equiv + Teaching Qual + exp	Dr Paul Rastall	
University of Reading	Dip ELT	9 mths / 1-3 yrs	FT / PT	£3400 EC £5700 non EC	Oct, Jan, Apr	Degree + Teaching Qual + 3 yrs exp	Course admin CALS	
St. Mary's College	Dip in App Ling & ELT	2 yrs	PT	£2,195	Sept	degree + 2yrs exp	Secretary	
Sheffield University	Dip Modern English Lang & App Linguistics	1yr / 2yrs	FT / PT	£2,260 EC £5550 non EC £565 PT	Sep	Degree or equiv	Secretary	

UK University Diplomas

College	Course Title	Course length	FT/PT	Fees	Start dates	Entry requirements	Contact	Comments
University of Stirling	PostGrad Dip TESOL	9 mths	FT	£2,260 EC £5450 non EC	Sep	Degree + 2 yrs exp	Mrs C Tytler, CELT	
University of Strathclyde	Dip Prof Studies in Education (TEFL)	24 wks	FT	£4,500	on appl	Qual + 2 yrs exp or 5 yrs exp	Paul Curtis	Modular, award-bearing course
University of Wales, Cardiff	Dip TEFL	9 mths	FT	£1,695 EC £4160 non EC	Oct	Degree or equiv + exp	Ms C Wilkinson	Teaching practice avail
University of Warwick	Dip TEFL & Administration	9 mths	FT	£5,780	Oct	Degree or Teaching Qual + exp	Julia Khan	
University of York	Dip Linguistics & ELT	9 mths	FT	£2,260 EC £5550 non EC	Oct	Degree or Teaching Qual + exp	Sec, Grad admissions	Taught course with project

UK University Degrees

College	Course Title	Course length	FT/PT	Fees	Start date	Entry requirements	Contact	Comments
University of Bristol	BEd TEFL	2 yrs	FT	£5,700 non EC	Oct	Teaching Qual + 3 yrs exp	BEd Sec	Overseas Teachers only
College of St Mark & St John, Plymouth	BEd ELT	2 yrs	FT	£5,320 p.a.	Oct	Teaching Qual + 3 yrs exp	Dir, Intl Ed Centre	Serving Teachers
University of Exeter	BPhil(Ed) Lang Teaching	1 yr	FT	on appl	Oct	Teaching Qual	Further Prof Studs Sec	Assessed by written assignments
University of Leeds	BA (Hons) TESOL	2-3 yrs	FT	£5550 p.a.	Oct	TT + 5 yrs exp	Course Dir Intl Ed	In-service course.
Moray House, Edinburgh	BEd ELT	11 mths	FT	£2,950 EC £5725 non EC	Oct	Teaching Qual + 3 yrs exp	Registrar	In-service
Moray House, Edinburgh	B Ed(Hons) TESOL	2 yrs	FT	£5,645	Oct	Post sec QT Dip+ 3 Teaching exp	The Registrar	
University of Newcastle-upon-Tyne	BPhil (Ed) TESOL	1 yr	FT DL	£2,260 EC £5550 non EC	Oct	Teaching Qual + 2 yrs exp	Director	Day-time course
University of Stirling	BEd TEFL	12-16 mths	FT	£900 EC £5550 non EC	Sep	on appl	Dr Hawkes	Both UK & overseas teachers
University of Stirling	BA TEFL BA Tesol	3 yrs 1-18mnt	FT	On applic	Sep	University entrance qualification	Mrs Stephany Tytler	
University of Strathclyde	BEd TEFL	26 wks	FT DL	£6,000	on appl	Teaching Qual + 2 yrs exp or 5 yrs exp	Paul Curtis	Modular In-service
University Of Warwick	BA (Hons) ELT	2 years	FT	£2,300 EC £5,700 Non EC	Oct	Initial Degree +3 yrs exp	Julia Khan	

MAs in North America

North America is famous for its choice of Master's programs. Here is a selection.

In the last twenty-five years, TESOL or the Teaching of English to Speakers of Other Languages, has grown into an international profession with its own association. The overwhelming concern for training qualified practitioners has led to the establishment of the MA degree as a standard professional qualification.

With such a dazzling array of MA degree training options available it is very difficult to know which one best suits your needs. Start with your interests and whether or not you intend to teach abroad. TESOL has a large number of special interest groups, some of which run courses in such diverse subjects as research and administration, materials development, testing, classroom teaching, Second Language Acquisition (SLA), English for Specific Purposes (ESP), Computer Assisted Language Learning (CALL), and Adult Literacy.

The core of MA programs in the US contains a series of competencies geared toward developing effective teaching skills. They include: English linguistics, psycholinguistic and sociolinguistic processes, pedagogy and testing, cultural study and a teaching practicum. The nearly 200 MA programs offered in the United States emphasize one or more of these areas.

English linguistics refers to the nature of language, linguistic descriptions, contrastive analysis among other languages and such aspects as grammar, phonology and semantics. The University of Pittsburgh, UCLA, Colorado at Boulder, Ball State, Illinois at Chicago all have good programs; Harvard and MIT have well-known programs in pure linguistics.

Psycholinguistic and sociolinguistic processes refer to how we learn languages, factors that affect language learning, differences in learning styles and other social determinants. The University at Southern California, UC Santa Cruz, San Francisco State University, UCLA and The University of Hawaii at Manoa all have a reputation for second language acquisition specialities; The University of Alabama and Hunters College in New York are known for learning style research.

Pedagogy and testing refer to the methods of teaching, lesson planning and assessment. Teachers College New York, the School for International Training, University of San Francisco, and Minnesota are quite strong in pedagogy; The University of Hawaii, UCLA, Georgetown University and Michigan are strong on testing.

Cultural studies include knowledge of the cultural influences on learning, study of intercultural communication theory, and sociocultural issues that effect second language learning. The universities of Colorado at Denver, Brigham Young in Utah, The Monterey Institute of International Studies in California and The School for International Training at Battleboro, Vermont all excel in cultural studies.

Teaching practice includes guided observation, group feedback and supervised teaching practice. All of the better known programs now contain this component. The University of Hawaii, Teachers College New York and San Francisco State University are particularly strong.

Many MA programs require the study of a foreign or second language concurrently with other studies, usually second language acquisition. Multimedia applications in language teaching are being introduced as new course elements, such as how to explore the internet for language resources via e-mail.

MA degrees are generally offered under many different university departments and in very diverse subject areas in the US. Teachers College of Columbia University in New York offers both an MA and MEd in TESOL under the Languages, Literature and Social Studies in Education Department. Georgetown University in Washington DC, offers MA degrees in TESL and TESL and Bilingual Education under the Department of Linguistics. San Francisco State University offers an MA in English with a concentration in ESL/EFL under the Department of English. Finally, Azusa Pacific University near Los Angeles offers an MEd in ESL or an MA in TESOL under the Department of International/Inter-cultural Studies.

When choosing a particular program keep in mind the school location and whether it has access to a wide range of non-native speakers. Although all universities that offer MA degrees have ESL programs for foreign students, those programs situated in multiethnic regions in the United States offer many more opportunities to gain broader teaching experience.

Bilingualism is the speciality of many Canadian programs, with Concordia and McGill, both in bilingual Quebec, taking the lead. The University of British Colombia is doing pioneering work in the area of content-based instruction.

Multimedia applications in language teaching are being introduced as new course elements.

Bilingualism is a speciality of many Canadian programmes.

College	Course Title	Course Length	FT/ PT	Fees	Application Dates	Entry Requirement	Contact
Adelphi University	TESOL	3 sems	FT	$252 per credit hour	any sem	degree	B. Robbins
University of Alabama	TESOL	6 sems	FT	$1,004 ps inst. $2,258 ps outst.	any sem	-	C. Davies
American University	Linguistics, TESOL	4 sems	FT/PT	$451 per credit hour	any sem	-	J. Schillinger
University of Arizona	ESL	1-2yrs	FT	$914 res, $2790 non-res	any sem	good degree	D. Adamson
Arizona State University	TESL	1-2yrs	FT	$914 res, $2790 non-res	Aug, Jan	degree	Sheila Moore
Azusa Pacific University	M.Ed ESL	4 sems	FT/PT	$220 per unit	any sem	degree	M. Mardock
Ball State University	Linguistics, TEFL / TESOL	3 sems	FT/PT	$1,140 ps inst. $2,680 ps outst.	any sem	degree + 2 yrs exp.	L.M. Davis
Biola University	TESOL / Applied Linguistics	4-5 sems / 4 sems	FT/PT	$240 per semester unit	Aug	degree	H.C. Purnell
Boston University	M.Ed	3 sems	FT/PT	$7,975 ps	any sem	degree	S.J. Molinsky
University of California, Davis	Applied Linguistics	3-6 qrts	FT/PT	$0 pq inst. $895 pq outst.	May	degree	DoS
University of California, Los Angeles	TESL	6 qrts	FT	$969 pq inst. $3,535 pq outst.	Jan	good degree	C.O. Kramer
California State University, Dominguez Hills	English, TESL option	2-4 sems	FT/PT	c.$500 ps	any sem	degree + 1yr foreign lang. study	A. Yamada
California State University, Fresno	Linguistics, TESL/TEFL	3-4 sems	FT/PT	$549 ps inst. $3,501 ps outst.	Feb,Aug	-	V. Samiian
California State University, Fullerton	MS Ed with TESOL	30 sem units	FT/PT	$554 ps inst. $800 ps outst. (1-6 units)	Mar	degree + 2yr foreign lang. study	N. Baden
California State University, Long Beach	Linguistics, TESL/TEFL	3-4 sems	FT/PT	c.$500 ps	Aug	good degree	S.B. Ross
California State University, Northridge	Linguistics (TESOL Track)	2 sems + thesis	FT/PT	$564 ps inst. $438 ps outst. (7+ units)	Feb,Sep	good degree	F. Hallcom
California State University, Sacramento	English, TESOL option	3 sems	FT/PT	$530 ps inst. $246 pu outst.	any sem	degree	F. Marshall
University of Colorado at Boulder	Linguistics	3-4 sems	F/T	$1,260 ps inst. $4,806 ps outst.	Sept	degree, knowledge of foreign lang.	A. Bell
Colorado State University	English, TESOL	4 sems	FT/PT	$1,069 ps inst. $3,419 ps outst.	Mar	degree	DoS

College	Course Title	Course Length	FT/PT	Fees	Application Dates	Entry Requirementss	Contact
University of Delaware	Linguistics, concentration ESL	3 sems	FT/PT	on appl	Jul, Dec	degree	I. Vogel
East Carolina University	M.Ed English, TESOL	3 sems	FT/PT	on appl	Mar, Jun, Oct	good degree	C.W. Sullivan
Eastern Mennonite University, Harrisonburgh	M.ED, TESOL Literacy	12 mnths	FT/PT	$328 p.cr hr	Oct	bachelor degree	Dr Mark Hogan
Eastern Michigan University	TESOL	5 sems	FT/PT	$89.50 pchr inst. $212 pchr outst.	Apr, Aug, Dec	degree + 1yr foreign lang. study	J. Aebersold
Florida International University	MS in TESOL	33 sem hours	FT/PT	$800 ps inst. $2,400 ps outst.	any sem	degree	C.U. Grosse
Fordham University at Lincoln Center	MS Ed, TESOL	2.5 sems	FT/PT	$352 per credit	any sem	degree + 2yrs teaching exp.	A. Carrasquillo
University of Georgia	MEd, TESL	4 qrts	FT/PT	$692 pq inst. $1,840 pq outst.	any qrtr	on application	C.J. Fisher
Georgia State University	MS, TESL	4 qrts	FT/PT	$625 pq inst. $2,000 pq outst.	Feb, May, Aug, Nov	under grad. degree in relevant area	P. Byrd
Goshen College	ESL	24 credit hrs	PT	$9,900 FT 1 yr	Jan, Apr, Aug	Christian College	Carl Barnett
University of Hawaii at Manoa	ESL	4 sems	FT/PT	$860 ps inst. $2,620 ps outst.	any sem	degree + 1 other lang.	C. Chaudron
Hofstra University	MS, TESOL	3 sems	FT/PT	$3,816 ps	any sem	good under grad. prospects + 1 other lang.	N. Cloud
University of Houston	Applied Linguistics	3 sems	FT/PT	$1,848 ps (12 hrs)	Nov, Apr, Jun	good degree	S.C.Pena
Hunter College of the City University of New York	TESOL	5 yrs max.	FT/PT	$95 pc inst. $189 pc outst.	Mar, Oct	degree + working knowledge of 1 other lang.	D.R.H. Byrd
University of Idaho	ESL	4 sems	FT/PT	$177 ps inst. $1,100 ps outst.	any sem	good degree	DoS
University of Illinois at Chicago	Linguistics, TESOL	2 sems + the following summer	FT/PT	$1,827 ps inst. $4,298 ps outst.	Jul, Nov	degree	E. Judd
University of Illinois at Urbana-Champaign	TESOL	4 sems	FT/PT	$1,418 ps inst. $3,894 ps outst.	Mar, Oct	degree + working knowledge of 1 other lang.	E.G. Bokamba
Illinois State University	MA in Writing + TESOL	4 sems	FT/PT	$1,827 ps inst. $4,298 ps outst.	Jan, Mar, Oct	degree	W. Woodson
Indiana University	TESOL	3 sems	FT/PT	$1827 ps inst. $4298 ps outst.	Feb, Sep	degree	H.L. Gradman
Inter American University of Puerto Rico, San German	TESL	variable	PT	$110 pc	Jul, Dec	degree or equiv.	Associate Director
Inter American University of Puerto Rico, Metropolitan	ESL	2yrs	FT/PT	$110 pchr	any sem	good under grad. prospects	DoS
University of Iowa	Linguistics, TESL focus	4 sems	FT/PT	$1,158 ps inst. $3,372 ps outst.	Mar	on application	C. Ringen
University of Kansas	Applied Linguistics	2 yrs	FT/PT	$1,003 ps inst. $2,860 ps outst.	Jun, Nov	degree + working knowledge of 1 other lang.	F. Ingemann
University of Maryland, College Park	MEd TESOL	4 sems	FT/PT	on application	Mar, Nov	good degree	W.E. DeLorenzo
University of Miami	MSEd TESOL	4 sems	FT/PT	$576 pc	Apr, Jul, Nov	acceptable GPA or GPE	S. Fradd

College	Course Title	Course Length	FT/ PT	Fees	Application Dates	Entry Requirementss	Contact
MIchigan State University	TESOL	4 sems	FT/PT	$5,000 inst. $10,000 outst.	Feb	degree or equiv.	S. Gass
University of Minnesota	ESL	2 yrs	FT/PT	$1,084 inst. $2,168 outst. (7-15 credits)	Mar	degree	DoS
University of Mississippi	TESOL	3-4 sems	FT/PT	$990 ps inst. $1,581 ps ·outst.	any sem	degree	A. Schrade
Monterey Institute of International Sudies	TESOL	3 sems	FT/PT	$5,650 ps	any sem	degree	R. Larimer
Nazareth College	MSEd (TESOL)	2 yrs	FT/PT	on application	any sem	good degree	DoS
University of Nevada, Reno	TESL	4 sems	FT/PT	$66 pc inst. $1,800 ps outst. + credit fees	Jan,Jul	degree	TESL Coordinator
University of New Mexico	MEd TESOL	3 sems	FT/PT	$785 ps inst. $2,639 ps outst.	Apr,Jul,Nov	degree teaching exp. pref.	R.H. White
College of New Rochelle	MEd, TESL	3-4 sems	FT/PT	-	any sem	degree + teaching cert.	L. Lyman
State University of New York at Albany	MS, TESOL	3 sems	FT/PT	-	any sem	degree	R.L. Light
State University of New York at Buffalo	MEd TESOL	3 sems	FT/PT	$1,600 ps inst. $3,258 ps outst.	Feb	degree + knowledge of a foreign lang.	D. Rissel
State University of New York at Stony Brook	Applied Linguistics / TESOL	2-3 sems	FT/PT / FT/PT	$1,075 ps inst. $3,258 ps outst.	Mar	degree + 2 yrs foreign lang. study	DoS
Northern Arizona University	TESL	4 sems	FT/PT	$764 ps inst. $2,316 ps outst.	Feb	degree	Applied Linguistics Faculty
University of Northern Iowa	TESOL / TESOL/Modern Languages	3-4 sems	FT/PT	$1,076 ps inst. $2,746 ps outst.	AprJul,Nov	degree	TESOL Coordinator
Notre Dame College	MEd, TESL	2-5 yrs	PT	$216 pchr	any sem	degree + other language exp.	B. Arnbjornsdttir
Nova University	MS TESOL	1.5 yrs	FT/PT	$170 pshr	throughout year	on application	DoS
Old Dominion University	Applied Linguistics	33 sems	FT/PT	$165 pchr inst. $433 pchr outst.	Jul,Nov	degree	J. Bing
	MA TESOL	30 sems	FT/PT	$165 pchr inst. $433 pchr outst.	Jan<May, Aug	BA in English	J.Bing
University of the Pacific	ESL	2 yrs	FT/PT	$7,080 ps	Apr,Dec	degree	J. Milon
Pennsylvania State University	TESL	4 sems	FT/PT	$2,423 ps inst. $4,846 ps outst.	Jul,Dec	degree	P. Dunkel
Portland State University	Applied Linguistics, TESOL	6-7 qtrs	FT/PT	$1,151 pqrt inst. $1,827 pqrt outst	Jan,Apr	degree	J.R. Nattinger
University of Puerto Rico	TESL	2yrs	FT/PT	$55 pc inst.	Feb	degree, Spanish +English	DoS
Rhode Island College	MEd, ESL	2 sems + 1 summer	FT/PT	$100 pshr inst. $202 pshr outst.	any sem	degree + teaching qual.	DoS
University of Rochester	MEd, TESL	3 sems	FT/PT	$400 pchr	Feb,Nov	on application	DoS

College	Course Title	Course Length	FT/PT	Fees	Application Dates	Entry Requirementss	Contact
Saint Michael's College	TESL	3 sems	FT/PT	$176 pc	any sem	degree	Dos
University of San Francisco	TESL	2 yrs	FT		Aug	B A degree	Co-ordinator
San Jose University	TESL	3 sems	FT/PT	on application	Aug,Jan	degree + foundation	Thom Huebner
School For International Training	MA TESOL	1 yr or 2 summers	FT	$17,000 inc.	Aug,June	degree	DoS
Seton Hall University	ESL	3 sems	FT/PT	$346 pc inst.	May,Jul,Nov	degree	W.E. McCarton
University of South Carolina	TEFL	4 sems	FT/PT	$1,404 ps inst.	any sem	degree	A. Mosher
University of South Florida	Applied Linguistics, TESL	4 sem	FT/PT	$66 pchr inst. $191 pchr outst.	Apr,Aug	degree	C. Cargill
Southeast Missouri State University	English, TESOL emphasis	2-3 sems	FT/PT	on application	any sem	degree	A. Heyde-Parsons
University of Southern California	Applied Linguistics	4 sems	FT	$319 pu inst.	Mar	on application	W. Rutherford
Southern Illinois University at Carbondale	EFL/ESL	3-4 sems	FT/PT	$68 pc inst. $205 pc outst.	May/Apr	degree	P.J. Angelis
	Applied Linguistics	4-6 sems					
University of Southern Maine	MS.Ed Literacy Education, ESL	3 sems	FT/PT	$90 pchr inst. $254 pchr outst.	Mar,Oct	on application	M. Wood
University of Southern Mississippi	Teaching of Languages, TESOL	3 sems	FT/PT	$1,054 ps inst. $1,785 ps outst.	May,Aug,Dec	degree	W. Powell
Syracuse University	TESL	3 sems	FT/PT	$381 pchr	any sem	degree	J.D. Marcero
Teachers College of Columbia University	Applied Linguistics	1 yr	FT/PT	on application	any term	degree	J.A. Kleifgen
	TESOL			-	Apr,Jul,Dec		DoS
Temple University	MEd, TESOL	3 sems	FT/PT	$219 pc inst. $248pc outst.	any sem	on application	G. Moskowitz
University of Texas at Arlington	Linguistics	2-4 sems	FT/PT	$25 pchr inst.	May,Sep	degree	G. Underwood
University of Texas at Austin	Applied Linguistics TESOL	3 sems	FT/PT	on application	any sem	good degree	G. Underwood
University of Texas at San Antonio	TESL	2-3 sems	FT/PT	$20 pchr inst. $136 pchr outst.	Mar,Jun,Oct	degree	C.W. Hayes
University of Texas Pan American	ESL	1 yr	FT/PT	$38 pchr inst. $ $136 pchr outst.	Apr,Jul,Nov	degree	L. Hamilton
University of Toledo	MAEd ESL	4 qrts	FT/PT	$90 pchr inst. $194 pchr outst.	any qrt	degree	D.W. Coleman
United States International University	TESOL	4-5 qrts	FT/PT	on application	any qrt	degree + interview	E. Butler Pascoe

US Masters Degrees

College	Course Title	Course Length	FT/PT	Fees	Application Dates	Entry Requirementss	Contact
University of Utah	Linguistics	6 qrts	FT/PT	$550 pqrt inst. $1,500 pqrt outst	any qrt	degree	M. Mixco
Universtiy of Washington	MAT ESL	6 qrts	FT/PT	$1,129 pqrt inst. $2,824 pqrt outst	Jan,Apr	degree + intro course	DoS
Washington State University	English, TESOL	4 sems	FT/PT	$1,694 ps inst. $4,236 ps outst	Feb,Oct	degree, foreign lang. recommended	DoS
West Chester University	TESL	5 sems	FT/PT	$146 pshr inst. $186 pshr outst.	any sem	degree + other lang.	D.L. Godfrey
Western Kentucy University	English, ESL	33 sem hrs	FT/PT	$790 ps inst. $2,230 ps outst.	Jul	degree	R.D. Eckard
University of Wisconsin, Madison	Applied English Linguistics	2-4 sems	FT/PT	$1,512 ps inst. $4,542 ps outst.	any sem	good degree	C.T. Scott
University of Wisconsin Milwaukee	MS Curriculum, Instruction, ESL	2 yrs	FT	$1,534.15 for 12+ credits	Feb,Sep	degree	D.E. Bartley
Wright State University	Humanities, TESOL	4 qrts	FT/PT	on application	any qrt	degree	DoS

Canadian Masters Degrees

College	Course Title	Course Length	FT /PT	Entry Requirements
Concordia University	MA Applied Linguistics	33 credits+thesis	FT/PT	2 yrs experience+good GPA
McGill University	M.Ed	36 credits	FT/PT	2 yrs experience
Ontario Institute for Studies in Education	MA	8-12+thesis	FT	degree in related area+good GPA
	M.Ed	8 courses	FT/PT	
Simon Fraser University	MA	33 credits+thesis	FT/PT	degree
	M.Ed	coursework, no thesis	-	
University of Alberta	M.Ed	33 credits+thesis	FT	degree + 1 yr exp. + teaching cert
University of British Columbia	MA TESL	1 yr min.	FT/PT	degree + experience
	M.Ed TESL			
University of Calgary	MA	2 yr + 1 yr resid.	FT	degree + good GPA in Ling. & Ed.
	M.Ed	1-2 yrs	FT/PT	experience
University of Victoria	MA Applied Linguistics	24 units + thesis	on app.	degree + good GPA

MAs in the UK

Which Masters is best for you?

Masters degrees in Britain are usually intended for experienced teachers. The main reason for a British teacher to do a Master of Arts (MA), Master of Education (MEd), or Master of Science (MSc) - the distinction makes little practical difference, and does not reflect courses' contents - in ELT, linguistics or TEFL is not to get a better job (there are too few posts), nor to be a better teacher (the diploma is better - see p121), but to study more deeply in a field that interests you. Before you start out, you need to know which area you want to specialise in.

Most MAs are run by the EFL unit or the language centre of a University. Courses are usually full-time, although some, for example at the Institute of Education at the University of London (IEUL), provide for home study. The Masters course at Reading is divided into two study periods, allowing the teacher to work in the interval between them.

The first question to ask is, how much linguistic theory do I want? The main complaints people have about an MA course they have taken are that it was too theoretical, or that it was not theoretical enough. Again, some courses, like the MPhil at Cambridge and the MAs at Liverpool, Sheffield and Birkbeck, are largely research-based. So before you contemplate doing a course, you should also decide if you want a heavy academic element or if you are looking for something more practical.

Those teachers looking to MAs to get them out of general EFL will be pleased to see an increasing number of courses in specialist areas:

MAs in **Linguistics**, such as those at London's School of Oriental and African Studies (SOAS) and Reading, are highly theoretical. The courses at Aston, Nottingham, Liverpool, Stirling and Birmingham focus on **discourse analysis**, while Kent's course concentrates on **test and description**, and **lexicography** can be studied at Exeter and Birmingham. Even MAs in **Applied Linguistics** tend to be more academic than those in EFL/ELT/ESOL, although Durham offers one with special reference to English Language Teaching.

Teaching related courses are offered by IEUL, Manchester, Leicester, Wales (Cardiff), Thames Valley, York, Durham and Portsmouth (where the course also includes teaching practice). Exeter offers an MEd in **Language Teaching**. The courses at Birmingham, Stirling, Newcastle, Durham, Canterbury Christchurch College and IEUL concentrate on **Methodology**. **Testing** is strong at Leeds, Edinburgh, Lancaster, Manchester, Liverpool and Reading.

The Centre for Applied Language Studies (CALS), Reading, offers a course in **Oral-Aural skills,** as do Cambridge and Lancaster - although these courses are more theoretical.

ESL (English as a Second Language, also known as English for Immigrants) is covered at St Mary's Strawberry Hill, IEUL and in Birmingham's MA in TEF/SL. Thames Valley University offer a special course in **Language in the Multi Cultural Community. Adult Literacy** is a speciality of the University of Lancaster and the Institute of Education, while Warwick, Moray House and the School of Education all specialise in the growing field of **Teaching Young Learners**.

ESP (English for Specific Purposes) is covered in the MA at the College of St Mark and St John, and at the Universities of Warwick, Aston (this can be taken as a distance-learning programme), Southampton, Essex and Liverpool. **Literature** teachers can opt for the specialist courses at Aberdeen, Nottingham and Strathclyde. Literature also features in the MA at Southampton.

Teacher training MAs are available at Moray House, the College of St Mark and St John, Warwick and Southampton. **ELT Management** is available at Bristol and the Chichester Institute of Higher Education. Management options are also available at Birmingham, Reading, Warwick, Edinburgh and Lancaster.

Materials design is highlighted at Birmingham, Lancaster, Liverpool, Thames Valley, Canterbury Christchurch and Bangor, while Newcastle offers an MA in **Software design for EFL. Computer Assisted Language Learning (CALL)** is available at the Universities of East Anglia and Essex. And for the video buff, the University of Brighton offers an MA in **Media Language Learning.**

See pages 190 - 196 for addresses.

Those teachers looking to MAs to get them out of general EFL will be pleased to see an increasing number of courses in specialist areas.

The first question to ask is, how much linguistic theory do I want?

College	Course Title	Course length	FT/ PT	Fees	Start dates	Entry requirements	Contact	Comments
Aston University	MSc TE/TESP	1 yr 2-3 yrs	FT DL	£2,350 EC £5,550 non EC £4,300 EC PT	Oct Jan	Degree + 3 yrs exp	Sec, Lang Studs Unit	CTEFLA useful DL in specific countries
Birbeck College, London	MA Applied Linguistics	2 yrs	PT	TBA	Oct	Good first degree or equiv	Dept Secretary	
University of Cambridge	MPhil Eng & Appl Lings	9 mths	FT	on appl	Oct	Good Degree + 4 yrs exp	Susan Rolfe	
Canterbury Christ Church College	MA in TEFL MA in English Language Education		FT PT	£1,390 EC £2,710 non EC £2,400 EC £2,330 non EC	Oct	Completion Dip TEFL	A Holliday	
Chichester Institute	MA ELT Management	1 yr	FT	£2,200 EC £5,740 non EC	Oct	Degree or equiv + 3 yrs exp	Jean Hardy	Formerly West Sussex Inst.
College of St Mark & St John, Plymouth	MEd English Lang Teaching	1 yr	FT	£2,650 EC £5320 non EC	Oct	Degree or equiv + 3 yrs exp	Dir, Intl Ed Centre	Non-grad route via BPhil (Ed)
	MEd Eng Lang T/Training	1 yr	FT	£2,650 EC £5,320 non EC	Oct	Degree or equiv + 3 yrs exp	Dir, Intl Ed Centre	Non-grad route via BPhil (Ed)
	MEd TESP	1 yr	FT	£2,650 EC £5,320 non EC	Oct	Degree or equiv + 3 yrs exp	Dir, Intl Ed Centre	Non-grad route via BPhil (Ed)
University of Durham	MA Applied Linguistics/ELT	1 yr	FT	£2,350 EC £5,775 non EC	Oct	BA + teaching experience	Martha Young-Scholt	
University of East Anglia	MA ELT & Appl Lings	8 mths	FT	on appl	Sep	5 yrs exp	Dr Jeremy Fox	For exp EFL teachers
University of Edinburgh	MSc Applied Linguistics	12 mths	FT	£2,450 EC £6,220 non EC	Oct	Degree + relevant exp	Fay Oliver	Also MLITT & PhD
University of Essex	MA English Lan & Lings MA language Acquisition MA ELT MA Applied Linguistics MA Descriptive & Appl Lings	9-36 mths	FT PT	£2,350 EC £5,745 non EC	Oct	Good first degree Degree + 3 yrs exp Degree	Caroline White Susan Barrington	
University of Exeter	MEd Language Teaching	1 yr	FT	on appl	Oct	Hons Degree + Teaching Qual	Further Prof Studs Sec	Written assessment
University of Hertfordshire	MA Lings & Applications	14 wks	PT	£980 + exam fee	TBA	Degree or equiv	Dr T Parke	
University of Hull	MA Appl Lang & New Tech	1 yr 2 yrs	FT PT	£2,350 EC £5,800 non EC £730 PT	Sep	Degree + 2-3 yrs exp	Dr Aub-Buscher	
University of Kent at Canterbury	MA Applied Linguistics	12 mths	FT	on appl	Oct	Degree or equiv	Robert Veltman	Examined on coursework & dissertation
University of Portsmouth	MA/PG Dip in Appl Lings & TEFL	1-2 yrs	FT PT	£2,400 EC £6,000 non EC £540 CTFLA	Oct	Degree or equiv or teaching exp	Dr P Rastall Valerie Carter	
University of Wales, Bangor	MA Lings, Ling Research, Theoretical Lings	12 mths	FT	£2,260 EC £5,550 non EC	Sep	A good first degree or equiv		

UK Masters Degrees

College	Course Title	Course length	FT/ PT	Fees	Start dates	Entry requirements	Contact	Comments
University of Wales, Cardiff	Language & Communication Research	1 yr	FT	£2,430 EC £5,700 Non EC	Oct	Relevant first degree, IELTS 6.5	Secretary	
	Applied English Lang. Studies	1 yr	FT	£2,430 EC £5,700 Non EC	Oct	Teaching exp + degree, IELTS 6.5	Secretary	
University of Lancaster	MA Linguistics for ELT	1 yr	FT	£2,260 EC £5,550 non EC	Oct	Min 3 yrs exp	Dorothy Barber	
	MA Language Studies	12 mths 2 yrs	FT PT	£2,260 EC £5,550 non EC	Oct	Degree pref but not essential	Dorothy Barber	
University of Leeds	MA Linguistics	1 yr	FT	£2,350 EC £5,320 non EC	Oct	Degree + min 2 yrs exp	PostGrad Admissions	Modular option avail
	MEd TESOL	11 mths 2-5 yrs	FT PT	£5,770 £534	Oct, Apr, Jan	Degree + Prof Qual + 3 yrs exp	Jayne Moon	Wide range of modular options
University of Leicester	MA Applied Lings &TESOL	1 yr	FT	on appl	Oct	Degree + 2 yrs exp pref	Julie Thomson	Overseas: 6.5 IELTS/ 5.5 TOEFL
Liverpool University	MA Lang Teaching & Learning	1 yr	FT	£2,350 EC £5,661 non EC	Oct	Degree + 2 yrs exp	Geoff Thomson	Incl dissertation. Overseas: 6.5 IELTS
London University Birkbeck Coll	MA Applied Linguistics	2 yrs	PT	£1,074 EC £1,484 non EC	Oct	Degree + exp pref	Registry	Apply early
London University Inst of Education	MPhil/PhD ESOL	2-3 yrs 3-10 yrs	FT PT DL	on appl	All year	Degree	Sec, ESOL Dept	Apply early
	MA TESOL	1 yr 1-4 yrs	FT PT DL	on appl	Oct, Jan, Apr	Degree + Qual in Education	Dr Guy Cook/ Anita Pincas	DL by Computer Networking
University of Luton	MA L2 Materials Development	1 yr	FT	£2,260 EC £5,520 non EC	Sep	Degree or equiv 2 years EFL, ESL	Brian Tomlinson	
Manchester University	MEd TESOL	1 yr 2-6 yrs	FT PT DL	£2,400 EC £5,700 non EC	Jun Oct, Jan	Degree + 3 yrs exp	Debbie Cash	
	MEd Educ Tech & TESOL	1 yr 1-6 yrs	FT PT DL	£2,260	Oct, Jan	Degree + 3 yrs exp	Debbie Cash	
Moray House, Edinburgh	MA TESOL	1 yr 4-6 yrs	FT DL	£2,950 EC £5,955 non EC DL £4,1851	Oct Open	Degree or equiv + 3 yrs exp	Registrar	Modular; Optional exit pts
University of Newcastle-upon Tyne	MEd TESOL	1 yr	FT DL	on appl	Oct	Degree + Teaching Qual + 4 yrs exp	Director	Day-time courses
University College of North Wales, Bangor	MA Linguistics	1 yr	FT	£2,260 EC £5,550 non EC	Oct	Degree	Secretary	
	MA Linguistic Research	1 yr	FT	£2260 EC £5,550 non EC	Oct	Degree	Secretary	

College	Course Title	Course length	FT/PT	Fees	Start dates	Entry requirements	Contact	Comments
University of Nottingham	MA ELT	1 yr	FT PT	£5,772 non EC £2,350 EC	Oct	Degree + TEFL Training + exp	Mrs Joyce West	
University of Portsmouth	MA Applied Lings & TEFL	1 yr 2 yrs	FT PT	£2,350 EC £5,057 non EC £575 PT	Oct	Degree or equiv + Teaching Qual + some exp	Dr Paul Rastall	
University of Reading CALS	MA TEFL	12 mths 1-6 yrs	FT PT	£3,635 EC £5,700 non EC	Jan, Jul Oct	Degree + TEFL Training + 3 yrs exp	Course Admin. CALS	
St Mary's University Coll, Strawberry Hill	MA Applied Lings & ELT	2 yrs	PT	£1,685	Oct, Jan, Apr	Degree + relevant exp	Ann Brumfit	Route via Cert & Dip
	MA Linguistics in Education	1 yr	FT	£2,200 EC £5,400 non EC	Oct, Jan, Mar	Degree + teaching exp	Kevin P. Germaine	Coursework + dissertation
Sheffield University	MA Applied Linguistics	1 yr 2 yrs	FT PT	on appl	Jan, Sep	Degree + teaching exp	Secretary	Modular
	MA Modern Eng Lang & Lings	1 yr 2 yrs	FT PT	on appl	Sep	Degree	Secretary	Introductory week in Sep
University of Southampton	MA (Ed) Lang in Education	1 yr 2 yrs	FT PT	£2,350 EC £5,700 non EC £720 PT	Oct	Degree + 2 yrs exp or equiv	Asst Registrar	
	MA Applied Lings for Lang Teaching	1 yr	FT	£2,350EC £5,700 non EC	Oct	Degree + 2 yrs exp	Asst Registrar	
University of Stirling	MSc/PgDip TESOL Msc in Call TESOL	1 yr	FT	On appl	Sep	Good First Degree	Mrs Tytler CELT	
University of Strathclyde	DPhil TEFL or Linguistics	variable	FT PT DL	on appl	on appl	Higher Degree pref	Paul Curtis	
	MPhil TEFL/ Linguistics	variable	FT PT DL	on appl	on appl	First Degree	Paul Curtis	Research Degree
University of Surrey	MA Applied Linguistics	27 mths	DL	£5,000	Oct, Mar	Degree + teaching exp	MA Course Admin	Optional Modules
University of Wales, Cardiff	MPhil/PhD	1-3 yrs	FT PT DL	£2,430 EC £5,700 non EC £1,130 PT	Oct, Jan, Apr	Degree + 2 yrs exp	Dr N Coupland	
	MEd TEFL	12 mths	FT PT	£2,430 EC £5,700 non EC	Oct	Degree or equiv + 2 yrs exp	Dr P Tench	in conj with School of Education
	MA Appl English Lang Studs (TEFL)	12 mths	FT	£2,430 EC £5,700 non EC	Oct	Degree or equiv + 2 yrs exp	Dr P Tench	
University of Ulster	PG Diploma MA	9 mths 12 mths	FT PT	PG £2,350 MA £682	Sep, Jan, Apr	Degree or equiv	R Pritchard	
University of Warwick	MA ESP	12 mths	FT	£2,300 EC £5,780 non EC	Oct	Degree or equiv + 3 yrs exp	Julia Khan	
	MA in English to Young Learners	12 mths	FT	£2,300 EC £5,780 non EC	Oct	Degree or equiv + 3 yrs exp	Julia Khan	
	MA ELT	12 mths	FT	£2,300 EC £5,780 non EC	Oct	Degree or equiv + 3 yrs exp	Julia Khan	

Masters degrees in Australia and New Zealand

Australia and New Zealand provide great opportunities for studying with a difference. Here we look at the Master's programmes on offer.

Australia

Australia offers overseas students a relatively low-cost option for university study. Fees of around A$ 2,000 per year for most Humanities subjects, a moderate cost of living, and work rights which permit part-time employment all add up to an attractive package.

Most of the Australian courses can be taken either full-time or part-time, but student visa regulations stipulate that all overseas students must study full-time.

As well as Masters programs, universities in most States offer Graduate Diploma courses in Applied Linguistics, TESOL or Adult/ Multicultural Education. These Diploma programs have traditionally been most popular with teachers of English as a Second Language (ESL) in schools and migrant education centres as well as with teachers of literacy. They are now also increasingly popular with ELICOS (English Language Intensive Courses for Overseas Students) teachers: this is partly because of the growing emphasis in the language school sector on formal teacher qualifications and postgraduate qualifications, especially to enhance promotion prospects.

Several Australian Masters programs in Applied Linguistics include not only predictable linguistic and TESOL-related subjects, but also practical subjects such as curriculum design, research methods, language testing, translation, and ELT program management. However, there is still a fairly common perception in the ELICOS sector that Masters courses, even in Applied Linguistics, are theoretically rather than practically oriented. Many private sector EFL teachers in particular opt for an RSA/UCLES or comparable course, and many ELICOS employers prefer to recruit teachers with such credentials. (RSA/ UCLES courses are available at Certificate and/ or Diploma level in Sydney, Melbourne and Perth.)

Australia is also the leading centre for the study of Hallidayan Systemic Linguistics, although since Halliday's retirement from the University of Sydney a few years ago, the University of Sydney's dominant position in this area has been somewhat eclipsed by the very active School of Linguistics at Macquarie University, also in Sydney.

Another option at a number of Australian universities is correspondence study, available both to overseas students (most takers are in Asia) and to expatriate Australian teachers. The University of New England in New South Wales and Deakin University in Victoria are well known for their long history of specialization in distance education programs, but are not alone in offering TESOL or Applied Linguistics courses in this form.

Many Australian universities offer two- or three-tiered qualifications, with students having the possibility of obtaining credit as they move from one tier to the next. For example, Macquarie University's new Graduate Certificate in TESOL (one semester full-time articulates with the Graduate Diploma course (normally one year full-time or two years part-time), which in turn articulated with the Masters (normally one year full- time or two years pail-time). Both the Postgraduate Certificate and the Graduate Diploma include practice teaching, whereas the Masters does not.

New Zealand

New Zealand has a small, but growing number of Master's courses. Most students are language graduates, although teachers with extensive practical experience will be considered if they have a degree in another field or have the Diploma in TESL.

Victoria University of Wellington run the MA in Applied Linguistics, which covers language **learning theory, literary linguistics, curriculum development and English as an international language.** The University of Auckland currently runs the Diploma of English Language Teaching, but may shortly introduce an MA in TESOL.

Contact the University of Otago, Massey University, Waikato University and Lincoln University for details of their courses.

Australia offers overseas students a relatively low-cost option for university study.

Another option at a number of Australian universities is correspondence study.

Diplomas in Australia

College	Course Title	Course length	FT/PT	Fees	Entry requirements	Contact	Comments
Australian Catholic University, Victoria	Grad Dip Education	1 yr / 2 yrs	FT / PT		3 yrs Teaching Qual or equiv	Mary Fisher	Start Feb, Mar
Australian College Of English, NSW	RSA/Cam Dip TEFLA	8 wks	FT		Degree, 2 yrs Teaching Qual		
Australian National University, Canberra	Grad Dip Appl Lings	6 sems	FT / PT		Degree or equiv	Dr T. Shopen	Choice of sem units
Bond Univ, Queensland	Grad Dip TESOL	2 sems / 4 sems	FT / PT		Degree or equiv	Heidi Piper	Poss by ext studs
University of Canberra	Grad Dip TESOL	1 yr	FT	A$930	Degree + Eng prof	Dr P Denham	Incl teaching practice
Curtin University of Tech, Perth	Grad Dip TEFL	1 yr / 2 yrs	FT / PT		Degree + exp	Dr Don Yeats	Provides strong theoretical background
Deakin Univ, Toorak Campus, Victoria	Grad Dip Educ/TESOL	1 yr / 2 yrs	FT / PT		Dip Teaching or equiv + 1 yr exp	A. McKnight	Recog. by Victorian Ministry of Education
International Training Centre, Victoria	Dip TEFLA	8 weeks	FT		Degree; Teaching Qual; 2 yrs exp		
Edith Cowan Univ, Perth	Grad Dip Arts & Lang Studs	1 yr / 2 yrs	FT / PT		Degree or equiv	D. Prescott	Incl teaching practice
Macquarie Univ, Sydney	PostGrad Dip Lang Education	1 yr / 2 yrs	FT / PT		Degree + 1 yr exp	Dr A. Burns	
Monash Univ, Victoria	Grad Dip TESOL	1 yr	FT / PT		Degree or 3 yrs training + exp	Ms. Jensen	
University of New England, NSW	Grad Dip in Ed Studies/Mulicult	2 yrs / 1 yr	FT / PT		Degree or 3 yr Dip	P Shanahan	
Univ of Northern Territory	Grad Dip Applied Lings	1 yr / 2-4 yrs	FT / PT		Teaching Qual + 1 yr exp	Prof Christie	May be taken by ext studies
Phillip Inst of Tech, Victoria	Grad Dip Ed Studies TESOL	1 yr / 2 yrs	FT / PT		Degree/Teaching Dip	Dr E Vine	
St Marks Intl. College	Dip TEFL	Sep-Jun	PT		Degree/Teaching exp	Paul Mercieca	
University of South Australia	Grad Dip Educ/TESOL	1 yr / 2 yr	FT / PT	A$110	4 yrs tertiary ed, incl education	Anny Bye	
University of Sydney	Dip TEFL	1 yr	FT		Degree; 2 yrs exp	Ling. Dept	for non-native speakers
University of Technology, NSW	Dip TEFLA	9 mnths	PT		Degree; Teaching Qual; 2 yrs exp	Admissions Officer	
University of Wollongong, NSW	Dip TEFL				Degree	B Derewianka	
University of Western Australia	Grad Dip TESOL	1 yr	FT		BA in English, LOTE or linguistic	Secretary Faculty of Ed	
University of Tasmania	Grad Dip Educ Studies	1 yr / 2 yrs	FT / PT		Degree; Teaching Qual; 2 yrs exp	Val Walsh	Teaching Adults

Masters in Australia

College	Course Title	Course length	Fees	FT/PT	Entry requirements	Contact	Comments
Australian National University, Canberra	M.Litt Appl Lings	6 sems		FT PT	Degree or equiv	Dr Tim Shopen	20000 word dissertation
Bond University	MA Appl Lings	1 yr		FT	degree	Heidi Piper	Poss by ext studs
University of Canberra	MA TESL	1 yrs	A$9300	FT	Grad Dip or equiv	Dr P A Denham	
Deakin University	MA TESOL	2 yrs 4 yrs		FT PT	degree	Alex McKnight	
Edith Cowan University	MEd TESOL	2 yrs		FT PT	undergraduate degree	Dasvid Prescott	
Macquarie University	MA Appl Lings	1 yr 2 yrs		FT PT	Degree or rel exp	Dr David Butt	Avail by ext studs
Monash University	MA TESOL	1 yr		FT	4 yrs tertiary training	Marie-Therese Jensen	
University of New England	M Litt, Lings Major	2 yrs		PT	1-2yr prelim course or Lings Major	Jeff Siegal	Avail by ext studs
University of New South Wales	MEd TESOL	8 sems		FT PT	Degree + 2 yrs exp; Eng prof	David Smith	
	MA Applied Linguistics	1 yr 2 yrs		FT PT	Degree or equiv	Dr Wales	
Queensland University of Technology	Med TESOL	1yr		FT	BA in relevant field + 3 yrs exp	Coordinator Med TESOL	
University of Queensland	MA Applied Linguistics	1 yr 2 yrs		FT PT	Degree + 3 yrs exp	Dr M Wales	
University of South Australia, Adelaide	MEd Research TESOL	2 yrs	A$12,00	FT PT	4 tertiary education, 2 yrs TESOL		
	MEd TESOL	1.5 yrs		FT PT	Relevant Degree; 2 years teaching exp	Dr J Panadian	Normally by ext studies
University of Sydney	MA Applied Lings TESOL	1-8 sems		FT PT	Degree; Teaching Qual; 3 yrs exp	Diane Ferari	
	MEd TESOL	2-8 sems		FT PT	Degree; 3 yrs exp; Eng prof	Pamela Riley	Modular basis
University of Wollongong, NSW	MEd Hons Doctorate of ed	1 yr		FT	Recognised degree	Ms B Derewianka	
	MEd TESOL	1 yr		FT PT	Recognised degree	Ms B Derewianka	Poss by ext studs

Masters and Diplomas in New Zealand

Auckland College	Dip TESOL				On application	Roly Golding	
Auckland University	Grad Dip in Ed Studies	1 yr 2 yrs	FT PT		Degree; Teaching Qual; 3 yrs exp	F. Townsend	
	Dip Eng Lang Teaching	1 yr 2 yrs	FT PT		Degree; Teaching Qual; 2 yrs exp	F. Townsend	
Christchurch Poly	Dip TESOL	1 yr	FT		Degree; Teaching exp	G. Cleland	
Massey University Palmerston North	IDip in Second Lang Teaching	1 yr 2 yrs	FT PT	On appl	Degree; Teaching exp	Dept of Lings	Post Grad course
	MA (as above)	2 yrs	FT				
Victoria University	MA/PhD in Applied Linguistics	1 yr 2 yrs	FT PT		First Degree, Dip TESOL, Teaching qual		Also Post Grad Dip TESL
Victoria University of Wellington	Dip Teaching ESL	9 mths	FT	$NZ14,20	Degree; Teaching Qual; 2 yrs exp	David Crabbe	w/shops & Tutorials
	MA/ PhD Applied Linguistics	1 yr 2 yrs	FT PT	approx £5680	First Degree; Teaching exp	David Crabbe	Thesis or thesis + coursework
University of Waikato, Hamilton	MA Applied Linguistics	1 yr 3 yrs	FT PT	NZ $663 x 4 Int	First Degree, Dip TESOL	Academic Adv	Hamilton & Auckland
	PostGrad Dip 2nd Lang Teaching	1 yr 3 yrs	FT PT		Degree; Teaching Qual; 1 yrs exp		

Specialising

Short courses focusing on particular areas of EFL are a UK speciality. While universities in the USA, Canada and Australia have increased their number of courses, these countries do not have the range and variety of short courses on offer in the UK. This should help you to choose a short course that suits you.

These courses offer a convenient way of studying an area of teaching that interests you without the commitment in time and money of a full-blown academic course. However, few of these courses lead to recognised qualifications. Unlike the United States, the UK does not operate a credit system which would allow you to count such courses towards another qualification, such as an MA. Some non-native English speaking teachers might get credits from their country's state system on completing the course (check with your local Ministry of Education), but most native English speaking teachers will not.

The main reason for doing such a course is that it should interest you, rather than because it leads directly to better money or job opportunities. However, more and more employers are recognising the importance of specialist EFL teachers. Business English teachers are in great demand in northern Europe, for example. If you are not sure what area of specialisation to go into, it is best to concentrate on an area in which you already have some experience or knowledge. Established EFL teachers with experience of another field, combined with the knowledge gained during a short course, can command premium salaries.

Where can I do a short course?

A whole range of institutions offer short courses, from universities to private language schools (see p146-153). Language schools in the UK play a more important role in teacher training than in other anglophone countries. In Canada the USA and Australia most short summer courses take place at universities. In New Zealand several language schools run two- and three-week courses, some of them commencing throughout the year.

Who are they for?

Most of the courses in this section are aimed at experienced teachers. Some courses, particularly refresher courses, are designed specifically for non-native English speaking teachers. Refer to grids on the following pages. Generally, non-native English speaking teaching courses will include some work on language. In fact the Cambridge Examination in English for Language Teachers (CEELT) concentrates on language in the context of teacher's needs. (see p148).

What do they cover?

There are courses available on almost everything. Some courses such as ELT methodology or refresher courses for non-native English speakers, are more general. Others focus on specific areas such as Teaching Communicative Skills. Two of the most rapidly growing areas are Primary EFL and English for Specific Purposes.

What to look for

Before you choose a course, it is important to ask yourself the following questions:

1) What do I know about the institution offering the course?

What is their general approach? Some courses are very academic, others are practical or humanistic. The biggest number of complaints we receive about courses is that they are either too theoretical or not theoretical enough! In a short course, it is often difficult to strike a good balance of approach.

2) How well known is the institution for its work in this field?

Beware of institutions that offer courses in subjects that they either do not actually teach, or for which they do not have trainers with the right background. This is very important especially in a boom area like primary EFL where the demand for courses is greater than the number of specialist trainers available. If you want to find out more about the background to the staff on the course, do not be afraid to ask.

3) How many trainers actually work on the course?

For courses that last longer than a week or two, it is better if you have more than one trainer. This will mean you get a variety of outlooks on the subject.

4) Is the course relevant to my teaching situation?

Check that if, for example, you teach literature to 12-15 year-olds, the course deals with teaching literature to this age group.

5) How much experience does the course presuppose?

Most of the courses require teaching experience, but specialist experience is important too (see the information grids on the following pages).

6) Is my English good enough for such a course?

For a non-native English speaker, this is a vital question. Be brutally honest, particularly about your listening and speaking skills - or you will not benefit from it. Many of the courses listed on the following pages are designed for non-native speakers.

7) How can I get involved in running a short course?

IATEFL run a Special Interest Group (SIG) in short courses, as do the TESOL Teacher Education Interest Group (see p186-187). The British Council and International House also run courses worldwide.

Teaching young learners

There is a growing demand for teachers of English to children, especially in southern Europe. Here are some guidelines for newcomers.

Many people go into EFL in order to teach children. Many more teachers, especially those starting out, enter EFL via this route because of the high demand for teachers of young learners. English has become compulsory at primary level in many European countries, so teachers are required at state schools and to give private tuition. Demand is particularly high in Spain, Italy and Greece, where parents seem to sacrifice virtually everything for the education of their children. In the Far East, it is also becoming the trend to start English-language teaching at an earlier age.

Teaching children can be rewarding, but it is also very demanding. You will need to develop special skills if you are to be successful. It is worthwhile considering a specialist course if you are particularly keen on this sector. Trinity College London have designed a specific course for new teachers - the CerTEYL (Certificate of Teaching English to Young Learners) and there is a selection of short courses available for existing teachers (see pages 140-147).

If you are unable to take one of these courses, here are some practical tips which will help to keep you sane and ensure that your pupils remain attentive and progress quickly.

Children (4-12 years old)

Be patient! Children do not have the same linguistic foundations to build on as teenagers. It is normal for children to learn slowly and forget easily, so keep on activating and recycling the language you have taught in different ways.

Find ways to expand their knowledge of the real world (try pointing things out from a window), increase their conceptual knowledge, improve their social skills and enhance their general understanding.

Foster good language learning habits from the earliest stage. This is the time for you to master classroom management and instill basic discipline, especially in younger children.

Be careful not to bore children, particularly the younger ones. Win children over with games and physical activities. If possible, use songs and music with repetitive choruses and actions to involve your pupils as much as possible.

Young Teenagers (12-14 years old)

Balance your approach very carefully between being too strict and being too friendly.

Find out your students' interests. Discover what they are reading and watching on TV, if they like sport or pop music. Then try to use new materials, cuttings from teen magazines for example, to support the course book.

Do not expect pupils to cope with tasks in English that they have not yet grasped properly in their own language.

Vary activities as much as possible during the lesson. Use videos, and cassettes so that they can see and hear English in use outside the classroom. You may find certain classes respond to a certain approach better than others.

Find English language tasks for your pupils that are challenging without being over-taxing. If the task is beyond them, they'll lose their confidence and begin to think of themselves as poor language learners. They will give up trying and boredom will set in.

Do not try to do all the work yourself. Use a good coursebook and read the corresponding teacher's book carefully. With children of this age you need to get it right first time. You will have to focus your energy on what is happening in class, so you will not have the time to try to design your own syllabus.

Try not to lose sight of your teaching aim. Decide what your students will be able to do when they leave the classroom, that they could not do before that particular class. In the longer term, try to envisage straightforward communicative achievements that you would like your students to all be capable of after a series of lessons.

Keep a teacher's diary and record your successes. Consider why your activities worked, what your students enjoyed most, how they completed tasks and what exactly they learned.

All good teachers of children have their own special means of engaging their audience. These guidelines should help you to develop your own classroom style, and enable you to get the best out of your students.

Be careful not to bore children. Win them over with games and physical activities.

All good teachers of children have their own special means of engaging their audience.

College	Course Title	Course length	FT/ PT	Fees	Start dates	Entry requirements	Contact	Comments	Max. no. of student
Abon Language School, Bristol	Refresher	1-3 wks	FT	£295	Jun, Jul, Aug	Teaching Qual Non-native speakers	Daid Berrington Davies	Help with accomm	10
Anglo European Study Tours, London	Secondary Teachers' Course	2 wks	FT	on appl	Throughout year	Secondary teachers	Dir of Studs	Incl accomm	12
	Primary Course	2 wks	FT	on appl	Throughout year	Primary teachers	Dir of Studs	Incl accomm	12
AngloLang Scarborough	Eng in Britain	2 wks	FT	£580	Jun, Jul, Aug	Teaching Qual; Non-native	Jenny Clark	Incl accomm	15
	General Refresher	2 wks	FT	£580	Jun, Jul, Aug	Teaching Qual; Non-native	Jenny Clark	Incl accomm	15
	Britain Today	2 wks	FT	£580	Jun, Jul, Aug	Teaching Qual;	Jenny Clark	Fee incl full accomm	15
Basil Paterson College, Edinburgh	TEFL for Primary & Secondary Teachers	2 wks	FT	£380	Jan, Apr, Jul, Aug		Mrs B Holmstrom	Also Edinburgh Language Foundation	12
Bell Language School, Cambridge	British Studies	2 wks	FT	£730	Jul	Teachers of English	Sue Shereen		14
	Language & Literature	2 wks	FT	£730	Jul	Teachers of English	Sue Shereen		14
	Contemporaryy English	2 wks	FT	£730	Jul	Teachers of English	Sue Shereen		14
	Agregation Interne	2 wks	FT	£730	Jul	Teachers of English	Sue Shereen		14
	Primary Teaching & Language Development	2 wks	FT	£730	Jul	Teachers of English	Sue Shereen		14
	Self-Access & Ind Learnig	2 wks	FT	£730	Jul	Teachers of English	Sue Shereen		14
	Overseas Teachers Course	4 wks	FT	£1360	Jan		Sue Shereen		14
Bell Language School, Saffron Walden	Overseas Teachers Course	4 wks	FT	£760	Jan	Teachers of English	Robin Davis		14
	Tech & Method for Primary Teachers	2 wks	FT	£760	Jun,Jul, Aug,Sep Sep	Teachers of English	Robin Davis		14
	Teaching Tech for Sec Teachers	2 wks	FT	£1400	Jun,Jul,Aug	Teachers of English	Robin Davis		14
Bell Language School, Norwich	Methodology & Language Improvement	3 wks	FT	995	Aug	Teachers of English	Steve Terry		14
	Overseas Teachers Course	4 wks	FT	£1240	Jan		Steve Terry		14
	Primary Teaching & Language Development	3 wks	FT	£995	July	Teachers of English	Steve Terry		14
Bell Language School, Bath	Teachers of English Course	4 wks	FT	£1240	Jan	Teachers of English	Howard Thomas		14
Bell Language School, Geneva	Teaching Children EFL	1 wk	FT	SFR62	Aug		Sean Power		15

Short Courses

College	Course Title	Course length	FT/ PT	Fees	Start date	Entry requirements	Contact	Comments	Max. no. of students
British Council, Uni of Newcastle	Exploring Spoken English	18 nghts	FT	£1,395	July	Teachers at Secondary level	Don Salter/ Veronica Brock		
British Council, Nottingham	Literature in ELT	3 wks	FT	£1,590	Aug	Teachers & Teacher Trainers; Mats Designers	John McCrae/ Ron Carter	Residential only	
British Council, Oxford University	Extending Teachers' Experise	3 wks	FT	£1,395	July	Teachers	Katie Gray		
British Council, Warwick	Literary Translation	1 wk	FT	£1,120	Dec	Teachers; Translators	Prof Susan Bassnett	Accomm optional	
British Council, Aberdeen Univ	Literature & Language	18 nghts	FT	£1,450	July	Overseas Teachers of English; Lit & Lang teachers	Mrs Fiona Jurk	Fee includes full board accom	
British Council, Brighton Univ	Video, Audio & Comps in teaching	18 nghts	FT	£1,395	July	Exp Teachers	Prof Brian Hill		
The Language Centre Brighton University	Summer TEFL Intro to CALL MA TEFL	3 wks 2 wks 1 yr-2 yr	FT FT PT-F	£4,253	Jun, Jul, Aug, Oct	Degree or Equiv	Pip Roland Geoff Pullen		
British Council, Chester College of Higher Ed	Methodology, Mats & Resources	18 nghts	FT	£1,395	Aug	Teachers; Teacher trainers esp. ESP/EAP	Dr Gillian Porter Ladousse		
British Council, College of St Mark & St John	Teaching ESP	18 nghts	FT	£1,395	Aug	Exp teachers	Jean floyd/ Ray Williams		
British Council, Durham University	Contemporary Approaches to ELT	18 nghts	FT	£1,395	July	Teachers	Kathy Keohane/		
British Council, Dyffryn Conference Centre, Cardiff	Training the Trainer	18 nghts	FT	£1,395	July	Exp teachers and teacher trainers	Maggy McNorton		
British Council, Fitzwilliam College Cambridge	Intro to teacher training	18 nghts	FT	£1,395	July	Trainee teacher trainers	Keith Morrow		
British Council, Lancaster University	Teaching & Testing	18 nghts	FT	£1,395	July	Native & Non-native speaker teachers	Alan Waters		
British Council, Leeds University	Teaching Young Learners	18 nghts	FT	£1,395	July	Non-native speaker teachers; 3 yrs exp	Lynne Cameron		
British Council, Leeds University	Communicative Approaches	18 nghts	FT	£1,395	July	Teachers; Teacher Trainers	Niall Henderson		
British Council, Lisbon	various short courses	various	PT	on appl	Oct, Jan, Apr	Non-native speaker Teachers	Julie Tice		£10

College	Course Title	Course length	FT/ PT	Fees	Start dates	Entry requirements	Contact	Comments	Max. no. of students
University of California, Riverside	Workshop in TESOL	4 wks	FT/	$850	Jan, Feb, Mar, Jun, Aug	Ad English	Co-ordinator		
British Council Madrid	Teaching English to 8-12 yr olds	25 hrs	PT	22500 PTS	Feb, April Oct		Mario Trivino		20
British Council, Moray House Inst	Training in ELT	18 nghts	FT	£1395	June	Teachers, Managers; Teacher Trainers	Mike Wallace	Incl accomm	
British Council, Nottingham University	Invigorating Coursebooks	18 nghts	FT	£1,395	July	Teachers; TTs; Writers	Gaynor Ramsey	Incl accomm	
British Council, Unis of Oxford & Strathclyde	British Cultural Studies	18 nghts	FT	£1,495	July	Secondary level teachers	Mrs Fiona Jurk	Fee incl accomm & social acts	40+
British Council, Rome	various	10-20 wks	PT	on appl	Oct	Practising Italian State Teachers	Nancy Rossi		14
British Council, University of Stirling	Professional Development	18 nghts	FT	£1,395	July	Teachers; TT	Ian McGrath	Incl accomm	
British Language Centre, Madrid	Pre-diploma Course	8 wks	PT	40,000 PTS	Jan	Exp in ELT	Alastair Dickinson	Prep for DTEFLA	15
Cambridge Centre for Langs, Cambridge	Refresher Course	3 wks	FT	£935	July	Practising Teachers	David Ball	incl accomm, lunch & CEELT prep	12
Carleton University, Canada	Dip in EFL	4 wks	FT	CA$ 750	Aug	EFL Cert or equiv	Prof Ian Pringle	Non-native teachers	12
CELT Athens	Lang Awareness	120 hrs	PT	£600	Oct	CPE or Equiv; Non native	Course Tutor	Interview	
Chichester Inst of Higher Education, Bognor Regis	Academic Study Skills & Lang	1-3 wks	FT	£225 pw	Jul, Aug, Sep	EFL Cert or equiv	Gilly Lloyd	Formely West Sussex Institute	15
	Cert/Dip Advanced Ed Studies	5 wks	FT	£465 EC £1870 non EC	Oct, Jan,	Degree or equiv + 3 yrs exp	Jean Hardy	Formely West Sussex Institute	
Colchester Eng Study Centre	English Plus with Option	2-3 wks	FT	£155-£183 pw	Throughout Year	Lower intermediate or above	Jenny Gray	Accomm £65 per week	13
College of St Mark & St John, Plymouth	Principles & Practices of ELT	1 term	FT	£2,600	Jan, Apr	Qual Teacher; 3 yrs exp	Dir, Intl Ed Centre		15
	short ELT courses	2-3 wks	FT	£360 +	Mar, Jul, Aug	Qual exp Teacher	Dir, Intl Ed Centre		15

Short Courses

College	Course Title	Course length	FT/PT	Fees	Start dates	Entry requirements	Contact	Comment	Max. no. of students
Canterbury Christ Church College	Primary Teachers	2 wks	FT	£337	Jul	Teaching exp, knowledge of English	A Hammersley		
College of St Mark & St John, Plymouth	Teachers' Development	3 wks	FT	£540	July	Min 1-2 yrs exp	Ross Lynn	incl social excursion	16
	Teaching Young Learners (nursery)	3 wks	FT	£585	Jan, Feb		Ross Lynn		16
	Teaching Young Learners (primary)	3 wks	FT	£585	Jul		Ross Lynn		16
	Secondary & Tertiary Teachers	4 wks	FT	£680	Jan	For Teachers	Ross Lynn		16
	English for Academic Purposes	1 term	FT	£150 pw	Sep, Jan, Jul		Ross Lynn		16
	Teaching Young Learners	2 wks	FT	£341	Jan, Feb		Ross Lynn		16
	TESP	3 wks	FT	£585	Jul		Ross Lynn		16
Concorde Intl, Canterbury	Teacher Development	2 wks	FT	on appl	Jul, Aug	on appl	Colin Stone	incl accomm For Non-native	12
Cork Lang Centre International	Methodology & Culture	2 wks	FT	£350	Jul, Aug	Practising EFL teachers	Director of Studies	Fee includes accomm	15
Coventry TESOL Centre	Intensive TEFL for Overseas Teachers	2 wks	FT	on appl	July	min 1 yr exp	Christopher Fry	Refresher course for overseas teachers	15
Devon School of English, Paignton	Refresher Course	2 wks	FT	£500	Jul, Aug	Teaching exp	Joan Hawthorne	Course can be tailored	12
Eastbourne School of English	Refresher Course Courses for Closed Groups	2 wks 1+ wks	FT	£360 TBA	Jan, Jul, Aug	Teaching exp	Dorothy S Rippon	Family accomm avail	12/15
Edinburgh Language Foundation	TEFL for Primary & Secondary Teachers	2 wks	FT	£380	Jan, Jul, Aug	Upper Intermediate English		See Basil Paterson College	12
English Language Inst, British Colombia Uni, Vancouver	Eng for Eng Teachers	4 wks	FT	on appl	July	Practising teachers	Corinne Janow	Accomm avail	15
Eurocentre, Bournemouth	Refresher Course	2-4 wks	FT	on appl	Jan, Jul	Non-native teachers	Ray Bell	Can be tailored	
GEOS, Hove	Refresher Course	2-4 wks	FT	on appl	Jan, Jul, Aug	FCE English; 1-2 yrs exp	School Secretary	For overseas teachers; accomm avail	12
GLOSCAT, Cheltenham	Ad English TESOL for Overseas Teachers	2 wks	FT	on appl	Jul, Aug		Mrs B M Grant		14
Godmer House School of English	Overseas teachers Course	2-4 wks	FT	£317 pw	On appl	Practising EFL teachers	TT dept		12
Goldsmith's College, London	Cert in Language teaching to adults	1 year	PT	on appl	Sep, Jan	Degree or equiv	DCCE	Pre-service & early service	25

College	Course Title	Course length	FT/ PT	Fees	Start dates	Entry requirements	Contact	Comments	Max. no. of students
Hilderstone College, Broadstairs	Language Intensive	2 wks	FT	£544	July	Overseas Teachers	Intl Students Office	Fee incl accomm	12
	Lang & Practical Ideas	2 wks	FT	£544	Jul, Aug	Overseas Teachers	As above	Fee incl accomm	12
	For Primary School Teachers	2 wks	FT	£544	July	Overseas Teachers	As above	Fee incl accomm	12
Hull College	Refresher Course	4 wks	FT	£480	July	Proficiency English + exp	Tina Cole	Option to take CEELT	15
ICELS, Oxford	Overseas Teachers Course	5 days	FT	TBA	Jul, Aug	Overseas Teachers	Richard Haill		16
International House, Hastings	Advanced English for Teachers	2 wks	FT	£432	Jan, Jul, Aug	by application	Adrian Underhill	Poss Oxford Uni/ ARELS exam	12
	Brush up your English	2 wks	FT	£432	Jun, Jul, Aug	on appl	Adrian Underhill	For non-native teachers; Accom avail	12
	Methodology 2	2 wks	FT	£432	Feb, Jul, Aug	on appl	Adrian Underhill	Non-native teachers; Accomm avail	12
	Methodology 1	2 wks	FT	£432	Jun, Jul, Aug	on appl	Adrian Underhill	Non-native speakers; Accomm avail	12
	Lexical Approaches TEFL	4 days 5 days	FT	£228	Jan Apr	on appl	Adrian Underhill	Accomm avail	12
	Dramatic Improvements	5 days	FT	£228	Jan	on appl	Adrian Underhill	Accomm avail	12
	Designing & Creating Materials	2 wks	FT	£432	Jan, Jul,Aug	on appl	Adrian Underhill	Incl accomm	
	Mod Eng Lit & Culture	2-4 wks	FT	£456 £275	Jan, Jul,	on appl	Adrian Underhill	Incl accomm	
	Facilitating Teacher Development	5 days	FT	£228	Feb, July	on appl	Adrian Underhill	Accomm avail	12
	Skills of Academic Management	2 wks	FT	£458	Jan	on appl	Adrian Underhill	Accomm avail	12
	Teaching Pronounciation	5 days	FT	£228	Jan, Oct	on appl	Adrian Underhill	Accomm avail	12
	Presence & Performance	5 days	FT	£228	Jan	on appl	Adrian Underhill	Accomm avail	12
	6 Category Intervention Analysis	5 days	FT	£228	Jan Oct	on appl	Adrian Underhill	Accomm avail	12
	Effective Personal Interaction	5 days	FT	£228	Jul	on appl	Adrian Underhill	Accomm avail	12

College	Course Title	Course length	FT/ PT	Fees	Start dates	Entry requirements	Contact	Comments	Max. no. of students
International House, Hastings	Close Encounters	5 days	FT	£228	Jan	on appl	Adrian Underhill	Accomm avail	12
	Dramatic Improvements	5 days	FT	£228	Jan, Apr	on appl	Adrian Underhill	Accomm avail	12
	From Teacher to Facilitator	5 days	FT	£228	Oct	on appl	Adrian Underhill	Accomm avail	12
	Skills of TT	2 wks	FT	£458	Feb, Jul, Aug	on appl	Adrian Underhill	Accomm avail	12
	Communicative Lang. Teaching	2 wks	FT	£432	Feb	on appl	Adrian Underhill	Accomm avail	12
	Advanced 6 Category Intervention Analysis	5 days	FT	£228	Jan	on appl	Adrian Underhill	Accomm avail	12
	Language and Teaching Skills	4 wks	FT	£605	Jan, Jun, Jul, Aug, Sep	FCE level English			
	TEFL to Young Learners	2 wks	FT	£432	Jan, Jul	on appl	Adrian Underhill	Accomm avail	12
International House, Lisbon	TEFL to Young Learners	2 wks	FT	£280	Sep	CTEFLA + 1 yr exp	Kathryn Gordon		15
International House, London	IH Cert TEFL	4 wks	FT	£805	all year	CPE	TT Dept	Apply early	12
	Language Development		FT	£580	Jul, Aug	IH Lang Test	TT Dept	Apply early	12
	Methodology Refreshers	2 wks	FT	£355	all year	IH Lang Test	TT Dept	Selection process	12
	Short courses for teachers	2-3 days	FT	£124 £176	Jul, Aug	IH Lang Test	TT Dept	Full list of courses on appl.	12
	Language & Classroom Skills for Primary teachers	2 wks	FT	£355	Jul, Aug, Sep	IH Lang Test	TT Dept	Accom service	12
	Teaching Literature	2 wks	FT	£425	Jul	IH Lang Test	TT Dept	Accom service	12
	Background to Britain	2 wks	FT	£405	July	IH Lang Test	TT Dept	Accom service	12
	Teaching Business English	2 wks	FT	£405	Sep, Nov	IH Lang Test	TT Dept	Selection process	12
	Educational Mnagmt	2 wks	FT	£615	Aug	IH Lang Test	TT Dept	Selection process	12
	TT Skills & Approaches	2 wks	FT	£635	Aug	IH Lang Test; Substantial exp	TT Dept	Accom service	12
	Language Development for Teachers	2 wks	FT	£355	all year	IH Lang Test	TT Dept	Accom service	12
	Language Teaching Skills	4 wks	FT	£605	all year	IH Lang Test	TT Dept	Accom service	12

College	Course Title	Course length	FT/ PT	Fees	Start dates	Entry requirements	Contact	Comments	Max. no. of students
ITTC, Bournemouth	Overseas Teachers Refresher Course	2 wks +	FT	£120 P W	Jun, Jul, Aug	First cert or high intermediate level	Annette Harwood		15
International House, Rome	Teaching Young Learners	40 hrs	FT	55000 ITL	June	CTEFLA	Director	Intensive	12
International House, Goiania, Brazil	Teacher Training	4 wks	FT	TBA	Jul		Maria Brown		
ITS English School, Hastings	Overseas Teachers' Certificate in Teachers Practice	2 wks 25 hrs	FT	£210 £185	July	Practising TEFL Teachers	John Palim		£10
Globe English Centre	Teachers Refresher Course	Min 1 wk	FT	£178-£247	Throughout year	Practising TEFL Teachers	Catherine Borgen		
Lake School of English, Oxford	Practical Refresher	5 days	FT	£210	Mar, Jun, Sep	CTEFLA or equiv	Susan Kay	Between Cert and Diploma	14
	Comm Activity Workshops	1 day	FT	£55	Twice a wk	CTEFLA or equiv	Susan Kay	Practical	25
Leeds University	Training, Basic & Practice Teachers for ELT	10 wks 6 mths	FT FT	£2,850 £4275	Jan, Oct	Degree or equiv + 3-5 yrs exp	Martin Bygate	Develops training skills	8
Liberty English Centre, Brazil	Refresher Course	3 wks	FT	$100	on appl	Cambridge Proficiency	O. Belloso Riberiro		20
Living Lang Ctr, Folkestone	Refresher Course	3 wks	FT	£900 approx	Jul, Aug	High level English	Bridget Peacock	Fee incl accomm	12
LTS Training & Consulting, Bath	Developing ESP	1 wk	FT	£340	Jun, Dec	Degree or equiv + 2-3 yrs exp	Adrian Pilbeam	First Part LCCI	12
	Designing ESP	1 wk	FT	£340	Jun, Dec	Degree or equiv + 2-3 yrs exp	Adrian Pilbeam	First Part LCCI	12
University of Manchester	English Level 5	3 wks	FT	£240	Sep, Jan	FCE/CAE or equiv	Fran Beaton	FEFC funding Due	20
	Preliminary English Workshop	1 yr	PT	£150	Sep, Jan		Fran Beaton	FEFC funding Due	20
Milner Intl Coll, Perth	Short Course	on appl	FT PT	varied	on appl	on appl	Warren Milner	Tailored to clients	
Newnham Language Centre	Overseas Teachers of English	3 wks 2 wks	FT	£548 £365	Jan Jul	Qualified overseas teachers	Mr Michael Short		14
Oxford Academy	Refresher	3 wks	FT	£210	Jan, Jun, Aug	Non-native Teachers	Anthea Bazin	Accomm avail	
Polyglot Lang Services, London	Teaching ESP	1 wk	FT	£245	Feb, Jun, Sep, Dec	1 yr exp	Secretary		8
Portsmouth University	Refresher	2 wks	FT	£395	July	Teaching exp	Mrs Bailey	eligible for LINGUA funding	15
Reading University	English through Theatre	3 wks	FT	£880	July	Theatre & language studies	Course administrat		15
	British Studies	2 wks	FT	£635	July	Practising Teachers	Course administrat	Incl accomm	15
Richard Lang College, Bournmouth	Teacher Development	varies	FT	On appl	as required	Previous EFL exp	D P Vann		-
	Refresher	1 wk	FT	N/A	as required	Previous EFL exp	D P Vann		12

Short Courses

College	Course Title	Course length	FT/PT	Fees	Start dates	Entry requirements	Contact	Comment	Max. no. of student
St Giles, Highgate	Refresher	2 wks 4 wks	FT	£295 £580	Aug, Jul, Jan	Practising EFL Teachers	Patricia Samuels		12
St Giles, San Francisco	Foreign Teachers of English	2 wks	FT	$595	Feb, Jun, Dec	Cambridge Profiency level	Claudia Schuster		12
Scarborough International School	Teachers Course	2 wks	FT	TBA £977	Jun, Jul	Qualified Teacher	Mrs R Glyde		-
Saxoncourt Teachers Training, London	TEFL for Younger Learners	1 wk	FT	£140	Aug, Oct, Nov	Tefl qualification	Russell Yates		12
Skola Teacher Training, London	DTFLA Refresh Exam Prep Method Theory	4 days 4 wks	FT	£200 £400	April; Throughout yr	Exp non-native speaker teachers	Lyndel Sayle	Observation incl	2
Study Space, Thessaloniki	Refresher	10 wks	PT	£90	Feb- Oct	Teaching 2 yrs exp	Chrissie Taylor		8
Study Space, Thessaloniki	Dir of Studies Course	10 wks	PT	£145	Feb, Oct	4 yrs EFL exp	Chrissie Taylor		8
Sussex University Language Centre	Ovseas Teacher Refresher	8 days	FT	£260	Mar	CPE + Teachers exp	Margaret Khidhayir	Non-native teachers	12
Swan School, Oxford	Mature Students	2 wks	FT	£410-£520	Throughout year	25 yrs+ Intermediate level	Mrs H A Swan		8
Swan School, Oxford	Overseas Teachers	2-4 wks	FT	£490-£820	Throughout year	Overseas English teachers	Mrs H A Swan		12
Swan School, Oxford	General English	2-4 wks	FT	£420 -£792	Throughout year	Intermediate level	Mrs H A Swan		12
University of Edinburgh	English for TFL & Appl. Ling.	4 wks	FT	£794	Sep	Practising Eng teachers	Secretary IALS		12
University of Edinburgh	Adv. English Studies for Teachers	4 wks	FT	on appl	Throughout year		Secretary IALS		12
University of Edinburgh	Drama for TEFL	3 wks	FT	£697	Aug		Secretary IALS		12
University of Edinburgh	Teaching Literature in EFL	3 wks	FT	£657	July		Secretary IALS		12
University of Edinburgh	Grammar, Communicative Teaching of English	3 wks	FT	£657	Aug	2 yrs experience	Secretary IALS		12
University of Edinburgh	Teaching English for Medicine	2 wks	FT	£434	July	2 yrs experience	Secretary IALS		12
University of Edinburgh	Teaching ESP	3 wks	FT	£657	July	2 yrs experience	Secretary IALS		12
University of Edinburgh	Teaching Young Learners	3 wks	FT	£657	July	1 yr experience	Secretary IALS		12
University of Edinburgh	Teaching & Learning English	3 wks	FT	£657	Jul, Aug	1 yr experience	Secretary IALS		12
University of Glamorgan	TEFL Meth for Overs Students	2-3-4 wks	FT	on appl	Throughout year	Practising Eng teachers	Centre Lang Studies		12
UTS Oxford Centre	ESP Teacher Training	2 wks	FT	£450	Jul, Aug	FCE or better	Mark Bartram		14
University of Waikato, New Zealand	Overseas Teachers of English	as req	FT PT	on appl	Throughout year	Group of 10 from one country	Academic Adv		12
Words Language Services	Refresher for TEFL Teachers	2 wks	FT	IR£200	April, July, Aug	Practising Eng teachers	Mary Butler	All teachers	10

CEELT Courses

College	Course length	FT PT	Fees	Start dates	Entry requirements	Contact	Comments	Max no of students
Aberdeen College	65 hrs	PT	£80	Oct	Min FCE C pass	Ann Bain		12
Associacion Bahiense de Cultura Inglesa	1 yr	PT		Mar	FCE, CPE	Sara Stewart de de Lasa		12
Basil Paterson College, Edinburgh	2 wks	FT	on appl	Jul, Aug	Practising overseas EFL teachers	Mary Beresford-Peir		14
BEET Lang Centre, Bournemouth	3 wks	FT	£590	Jul	Practising/trainee EFL teachers	Lindsay Ross		14
Bell Language School, Norwich	3 wks	FT	£995	Jul	Teachers of English	Steve Terry		14
Bell Iskolak Kft Budapest	14 wks	PT	£200	Sep, Feb	Practising/trainee EFL teachers			12
Brasshouse Centre, Birmingham	1 month	FT	£200	Jul, Aug	FCE/ CPE level	Deborah Cobbett	Also poss 1:1	12
British Council, Lisbon	varied	PT	TBA	Oct, Jan, Apr	Teaching exp & Eng competence	Julie Tice		10
British Council Barcelona	150 hrs	PT	N/A	Oct	FCE level 1	Angela Hennelly		12
British Council Madrid	35 hrs	PT	30,000 PTS	March, Nov	Min first level cert	Masia Trivino		20
British Council, Rome	20 wks	PT	N/A	Oct		Nancy Rossy		14
British Council, Thessaloniki	135 hrs	FT PT	N/A	Oct, Jun	CPE	Camilla Ralls		16
British Institute of Florence	1 yr	PT	990000 ITL	Oct	FCE level 1 or CPE level 2 pref	Sarah Ellis		12
Cambridge Exams, Finland	8 mths	PT	FM 380-420	Sep	Finnish Matric.	Bernard A. Jones		25
Canterbury Christ Church College	2 wks	FT	£337	July	2 yrs teaching experience	Ms Hammersley	Help with accomm	15
Chichester School of English	2 wks	FT	£330	July		Dir of Studs	Also tailor made courses	20
Chichester Inst Bognor Regis	3 weeks	FT	£670	Jul, Aug	Practising overseas teachers	Gilly Lloyd	Formely West Sussex Institute	15
City of Bath College	3 wks	FT	£372	Aug	Non-native speaker teachers	EFL Section		12
City of Liverpool Comm College	3 wks	FT	£420	July	Upper Intermediate English	Diane Lane		10
Clarendon College, Nottingham	3 wks	FT	TBA	Jun	Good FCE pass	Linda Taylor		15
Devon School of English	2 wks	FT	£500	July, Aug	Practising overseas teachers	John Hawthorne		12
Eastbourne School of English	2 wks	FT	£360	July	FCE or equiv	Dorothy Rippon	Accomm avail	12
Eastern Med. Uni, Turkey	6 mths	PT	N/A	Sep	Degree + 1 yrs exp	Edward Casassa	In-house only	20
GLOSCAT, Cheltenham	2 wks	FT	On appl	Jul, Aug	Good level of English	Mrs B M Grant		£14
Hendon College, London	6 mths	PT	£360	Sep, Jan	As per UCLES	Dina Brook		15

CEELT Courses

College	Course length	FT/PT	Fees	Start dates	Entry requirements	Contact	Comments	Max no of students
Hilderstone College Broadstairs	2 wks	FT	£544 + exam fee	July, Aug	Teachers of English Second or Higher Ed	Int Student Office	Accom incl	£12
International Centre, Bilbao	1 yr	PT	£115 term + exam fee	Oct	FCE or equiv	Director of studies		10
Intl. Language Academy	3 wks	FT	£525 + exam fee	July	Teachers of English	Nick Kenny		15
International House, London	4 wks	FT	£605	Jul, Aug	Own language test	TT Dept		
Instituto Chileno-Britanico Chile	8 mnths	FT	£500	Mar	Teachers of English	Anthony Adams		20
Kingsway College	10 wks	PT	£195	Jan, Mar	Interview	David Roswarne		18
Richmond Adult & Comm College	13 wks 19 wks	PT	£200 £280	Sep Jan	Min A/B pass at FCE	Hugh Burney	Apply early	12 20
Stevenson College Edinburgh	4 weeks		£400	Aug, Sep		Sarah Woolard		12
St Giles, Eastbourne	3 wks	FT	£490	July	Upper Intermediate English	Reynold Elder		12
SBCI, Brazil	1 yr	PT	$1000	Feb	Cambridge First Cert	Linda Ruas		15
International House, Goiania, Brazil	10 mnths	PT	TBA	Mar	Post SCE/ Post CAL	Maria Brown	On demand	14
Saxoncourt Teachers Training, London	2 wks	FT	£140	Apr, Jul, Aug	Upper int level English, practising teacher	Russell Yates		12
Skola Teacher Training, London	3 wks	FT	£465	Jul,	Teaching exp & English prof	Lyndel Sayle		15
South Thames College, London	12 wks	PT	£200	Jan, Sep	UCLES, FCE or equiv	Sarah Ovans		12
Stanton School of English, London	3-4 wks	FT	238	Throu year		David Garrett		12
Study Space, Thessaloniki	3 mnths	PT DL	£125 + exam fee	Feb, Oct	EFL teaching or attending Meth. Course	Chrissie Taylor	Once a week	8
University College Cork, Ireland	4 wks	FT		Aug	Practising or trainee teacher	Goodith White	Accomm avail	12
University of Essex	10 wks	FT	£1385	Jan, March	Non-native teachers of English	Dilly Meyer	Post-grad and CEELT	5-10
Stevenson College Edinburgh	TBA	FT PT	£400 + exam fee £85	Aug, Sep	Non-native teachers of English, Good educ	David Gibson		12
Waltham Forest College, London	varied	FT PT	on appl	on appl	FCE/ CPE; Degree/ rel exp	CEELT Course Tutor	CEELT I & II	10
University of Edinburgh	3 wks	FT	£657	Aug	FCE or equiv	Secretary IALS		12
University of Waikato, NZ	12 wks	FT	NZ$4,420 + exam fee	Mar, Sep		Enrolment Officer		15
Westminster College, London	12 wks	PT	£154	Jan, Apr, Sep		Georgie Raman		-

Teaching Business English

If you are looking for a new challenge why not consider teaching Business English? There are lots of opportunities worldwide for teachers with the right qualities.

Qualified and experienced teachers can enter this lucrative area of the profession without a business background. But all teachers should think carefully about the move and consider studying for a specific business English teaching course. See grid on facing page.

The teacher has to be able to strike up a rapport with everyone from the managing director to the telephonists.

Working with business people demands special skills, knowledge and interests. The business English teacher has to maintain a consistent professional image, be logical, well-organised, an excellent time-manager and communicator, and most importantly, be interested in and have a good understanding of business.

There are two very different kinds of business English teaching: firstly, teaching students of business, perhaps on business studies, economics or MBA courses in colleges and universities, and, secondly, teaching working business people, usually sent on courses paid for by their companies. We will mainly concentrate here on the second kind of teaching.

Business people have particular needs, both as employees and individuals, which the teacher has to be sensitive to and flexible enough to respond to. In addition, every client has different learning needs so the teacher has to be able to quickly design, write or adapt course materials.

Many courses are given in-house, and the teacher has to be able to strike up a rapport with everyone from the managing director to the telephonists. One business English teacher recruiter says he looks for a near-journalistic curiosity in teachers since this drives them to come to an understanding of somebody else's business.

Companies are making a large investment in training and students are usually highly self-motivated.

Although a business background is desirable, it is not essential. The teacher must have business skills knowledge, but need not necessarily be an expert on the professions of his or her students. It is more a question of being interested in the way that business works and being widely read.

It is useful to read the business pages in the newspapers, business magazines and textbooks to keep up with new developments, especially if you are teaching abroad. Some teachers may even wish to take a formal business qualification such as an MBA or diploma in management studies. However, the ability to come to an understanding of the students' needs and concerns is more important.

Experienced general English teachers must modify their approach when teaching business English learners. Business people often want to learn everything in a minimum amount of time, so classes have to be very practical and pragmatic.

You cannot hope to teach the depth or the refinements of the English language which perhaps you would do in other kinds of English teaching. It is much more a question of giving people hands-on skills geared to specific tasks such as telephoning or giving presentations. There is a big emphasis on performance rather than knowledge of the language.

There can be particular difficulties when a business person is put into the role of learner. Executives, for example, may be quite powerful and very competent in their jobs, and may have difficulty accepting that as learners, they might struggle. In a group, they may not relax and can be reluctant to contribute. This requires sensitivity and diplomacy on the part of the teacher.

Compared to general English classes, the presentation of classes and use of materials is quite different for business English. More so than with general English students, business people may have to be 'sold' an exercise by being clearly shown its purpose and benefits. This may involve adapting the language you use in the classroom. One teacher says: "After a while your language becomes corporate if you are good. When you have worked with business people, you mirror and model good business behaviour because you learn what they respond well to."

Teaching business English can be rewarding, but it is also very demanding. Companies are making a large investment in training, and students are usually highly self-motivated. Teachers must integrate the pedagogical elements of the course with students' business needs. Courses are often intensive and demand total commitment from the teacher, who can sometimes feel overburdened.

Opportunities for business English teachers are bright in eastern and central Europe, Japan, and the Pacific Rim. If you decide on business English teaching, you may like to join the IATEFL business English special interest group.

Teaching English for Business

College	Course length	FT/ PT	Fees	Start dates	Entry requirements	Contact	Comments	Max no of students
AngloLang, Scarborough	2 wks	FT	£580	Jun, Jul, Aug	Teaching Qual; Eng prof	Jenny Clark	Fee incl accom	15
British Council, Hong Kong	30 hrs	FT PT	HK$ 1500	TBA		Tim Gore		
University of Edinburgh	2 wks	FT	£434	Aug	2 yrs exp	Secretary IALS		12
Inlingua, Cheltenham	3 days	FT	£100	Mar, Dec	CTEFLA + 1 yr exp	Dagmar Lewis	Intro to Teaching Bus Eng	10
International House, Budapest	1 wk 2 wks	FT	£150 £250	on appl	CTEFLA or equiv	Head of TT		12
International House Hastings	5 dys 2 wks	FT	£228 £432	Jan Aug	On appl.	Adrian Underhill	Accom avail	12
International House, Lisbon	1 wk	FT	£80	Sep	CTEFLA + 1 yr exp	Kathryn Gordon	TE to Professionals	15
International House, London	2 wks 8 wks	FT PT	£635 £715	Aug, Nov	Degree + CTEFLA + 2 yrs exp	TT Dept	Accomm service	15
London Guildhall University, Lang Servs Centre	2 wks	FT	£385	Mar, July, Jan	Tefl Qual + 1 yr exp			LCCI Cert TEB	15
	As required	FT	on appl	As req	Locally set	The Secretary, Language Services Centre	Seminars arranged in UK & overseas	-
	2x3 wks	FT	£1,435	July	Tefl Qual + 1 yr exp teaching EfB		LCCI Awarded Dip TEB	15
LTS Training & Consulting, Bath	2 wks	FT	£560	Jun, Jul, Dec	Degree + Teaching Qual + 2-3 yr exp	Adrian Pilbeam	LCCI Awarded Dip TEB	12
Lydbury English Centre, Shropshire	1-3 wks	FT	£430 pw	Every wk	Experienced teachers only	Duncan Baker	For non-native teachers	1
UTS Oxford Centre	1 wk min	FT	On appl.	Every wk		Mark Bartram	Closed grps only	-

If you are interested in teaching English for Business, see Section Five for in-depth information.

UNIVERSITY OF essex

The *Department of Language and Linguistics* offers MA and PhD programmes in:

Applied Linguistics
Descriptive & Applied Linguistics
English Language Teaching
English Language and Linguistics
Language Acquisition

MA courses are either 9 months or 12 months full-time and PhD programmes are 3 years full-time (all courses are also available part-time)

The Department is a centre of excellence of training and research, receiving a top-rated score of 5 in each of the last three reviews of research in UK universities, and by the award of a category A by the Economic and Social Research Council. It has a staff of over 40, and 150 graduate students, and offers a wide range of special areas of study.

For MA/PhD programme information contact:
Caroline White (GE)
Department of Language and Linguistics
University of Essex, Wivenhoe Park
Colchester, Essex CO4 3SQ
Tel: 01206 872083 Fax: 01206 872198

The *EFL Unit* offers:

DIPLOMA in Teaching English as a Foreign Language [D.T.E.F.L.] A modular nine-month course for experienced graduate teachers, a chance of combining CTEFL and CTESP, or CTEFL with a dissertation, and having additional courses of its own.

CERTIFICATE in English for Teaching English [C.E.T.E.] An English course for Classroom management, communicative activities, teaching techniques and materials, plus the Cambridge Examination in English for Language Teachers. (Spring Term)

CERTIFICATE in Teaching English as a Foreign Language [C.T.E.F.L.] A ten-week course for experienced teachers wishing to improve their knowledge of basic disciplines. (Autumn Term)

CERTIFICATE in Teaching English for Specific Purposes [C.T.E.S.P.] An intensive ten-week course (Summer Term) for experienced graduate EFL teachers concerned with ESP teaching.

For further information, write to: D Meyer, A 25, Department of Language and Linguistics, University of Essex, Wivenhoe Park, COLCHESTER, Essex CO4 3SQ England. Tel: 01206 872217 Fax: 01206 837107

The University of Reading

MA in TEFL

The Centre for Applied Language Studies offers experienced EFL teachers a course of continuous or discontinuous study leading to an MA in the Teaching of English as a Foreign Language. The course can be completed in a minimum of 12 months.

Module one is available on the following dates:

1995
July 10th to September 17th
October 9th to December 15th

1996
January 15th to March 22nd
July 8th to September 13th
October 7th to December 13th

For more information, please contact:

The Course Administrator (EFG), Centre for Applied Language Studies,
The University of Reading, Whiteknights, PO Box 218,
Reading RG6 2AA
Tel: (01734) 318511/2
Fax: (01734) 756506

Diploma in ELT

A three-term course for qualified teachers of English as a foreign language, or teachers with at least three years' experience. Other applicants with relevant backgrounds can also be considered.

Module One
October 9th to December 15th 1995

Module Two
January 15th to March 22nd 1996

Module Three
29th April to 5th July 1996

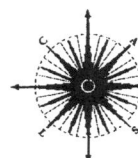

Centre for
Applied Language Studies

THE UNIVERSITY of LIVERPOOL

Applied English Language Studies Unit
MA in Language Teaching and Learning

Choose your own programme of study from the range of modules on offer.
The modules are designed to allow you to move from the analysis of language (discourse analysis, functional grammar, etc) to language teaching methodology (communicative teaching and testing methods, materials design, etc).

To apply, or for more details, write to:
Professor Michael Hoey,
Applied English Language Studies Unit,
Department of English Language and Literature,
University of Liverpool,
PO Box 147, L69 3BX UK
Tel: 0151-794 2771; Fax 0151-794 2739
Please quote ref: EFLG/MA

RSA/Cambridge DTEFLA Distance Training Programme

International House's 8-month Distance Training Course leading to the RSA/Cambridge DTEFLA is for experienced EFL teachers who are working a minimum of 12 hours per week with adult classes either overseas or in the UK.

Applications should be made by early April for courses starting the following July.

For information and application forms contact:
Susan Bagley
Distance Training Programme Secretary

ih
International House

Argentina
Australia
Austria
Brazil
Cyprus
Czech Republic
Egypt
England
Estonia
Finland
France
Georgia
Germany
Hungary
Italy
Lithuania
Poland
Portugal
Romania
Singapore
Spain
Ukraine
USA

International House
106 Piccadilly London WIV 9FL
Tel: 0171 491 2598 Fax: 0171 499 0174
Telex: 299811 ENGINT G

ih

CENTRE for ENGLISH LANGUAGE TEACHING
University of Stirling

Situated on a beautiful campus in central Scotland with excellent sports facilities, shopping and arts centre, the University offers the following:

- MSc/PgDIP in TESOL (1 year)
- MSc in CALL & TESOL (1 year)
- MEd in TESOL (1 year)
- BEd STUDIES (TESOL) (1 year)
- PRE-SESSIONAL COURSES in ENGLISH (from April to Sept)
- BA in ENGLISH as a FOREIGN LANGUAGE (3 years)
- BA in ENGLISH LANGUAGE TEACHING (3 years)
- YEAR-ROUND ENGLISH LANGUAGE COURSES

For brochure and further information please contact:

The Associate Director CELT,
University of Stirling
Stirling FK9 4LA,
Scotland, UK
(01786) 467934 Fax (01786) 463398

UNIVERSITY OF YORK
DEPARTMENT OF LANGUAGE & LINGUISTICS SCIENCE

MA in Linguistics and English Language Teaching. A one year course for experience teachers. Assessed by course work and dissertation.
Diploma in Linguistics and English Language Teaching. A nine month course assessed by course work and project.
MA in Linguistics. A one year course assessed by essays and dissertation.
MA in Linguistics (by research). A one year course assessed by dissertation only.

For further details please contact:
The Departmental Secretary,
The Department of Language and Linguistics Science,
University of York,
York Y01 5DD
Telephone 01904 432652

THE UNIVERSITY OF OXFORD
DELEGACY OF LOCAL EXAMINATIONS

THE OXFORD-ARELS EXAMINATIONS IN ENGLISH AS A FOREIGN LANGUAGE

The effective way to test learners' practical abilities in reading, writing, speaking, and understanding English, offered at intermediate and advanced levels.

The **Preliminary Level** (with **Junior Counterpart** for the 12-17 age group) is a test of basic 'survival' skills in communication. The **Higher Level** is aimed at those wanting to work or study in an English-speaking environment. Both the written and the spoken examinations are available at least three times a year at Centres all over the world. Oral examinations are available on demand.

At Higher Level these examinations are a recognised English language qualification for entry into a number of British and American universities.

OXFORD INTERNATIONAL BUSINESS ENGLISH CERTIFICATE

The Oxford International Business English Examinations offer a complete, 4-skills package at two levels, assessing the use of English in authentic business and commercial situations. These examinations are held three times a year.

The examination at Executive Level is accepted by universities in the UK as a qualification in English for non-native speakers wishing to enroll on a degree course. All candidates receive a Mark Profile showing their results: successful candidates receive an Oxford certificate.

For further details contact:
Elizabeth Lowen or Don Malpass
University of Oxford Delegacy of Local Examinations
Tel: (++44) (0)1865 54291 or 514272 Fax: (++44) (0)1865 510085
Ewert House, Ewert Place, Summertown, Oxford OX2 7BZ, UK

The University is an Equal Opportunity Employer.
The University has charity status and exists to provide education and research facilities.

English in Business

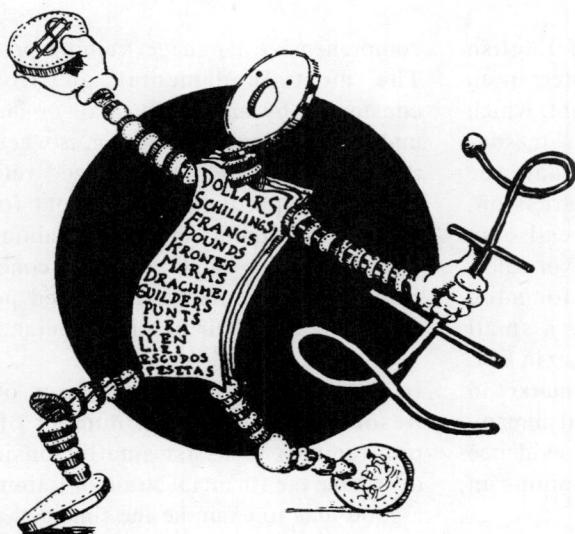

For training/personnel managers, consultants, school managers or business English teachers, this section assesses the trends in the market, shows you how to determine the language needs of your staff, how to decide which is the most cost-efficient training option for your needs and how to assess the proficiency of English speaking employees. The section ends with two case studies: one from a German multinational and one from a specialist language school, after which we explain how, with some help from the experts, your computer system can provide translation and language support.

Business Introduction: Why Buy Now?

Business English training is now within the reach of smaller companies. As professional opportunities grow, English language training is attracting more and better qualified instructors.

While individuals see English as a means of career progression, organisations invest in training to realise a financial advantage.

By its very nature, the business of English language training tends to be presented in an academic rather than a commercial light, which detracts from the majority of consumers' reasons for learning English. While individuals see English as a means of career progression, organisations invest in training to realise an advantage, be it in terms of efficiency or sales. There are those who learn English for more ethereal reasons, but they are only a small minority. Teachers embarking on a career in EFL must consider the development of the market in which they intend to work. There are also many potential consumers who require hard evidence of the benefit of English language training in order to justify the expenditure.

In order to profile consumers within the language training market, the general employment and training market must be examined. The world recession has taken its toll on the employment market, but this does not necessarily reflect on the training market. Traditionally, this market stands up well during recession, because individuals turn to training in order to increase their chances of employment. Demand for teacher training courses in EFL has been huge during the economic recession of the early 1990s. The result of this is that there is a larger pool of better specialist teachers, which, in turn, has led to more specific and cost effective training - in fact, a better deal for the purchaser.

So for those who have opted for such a career, who will they be teaching over the next few years? Over the last ten years, there has been a recognition within Europe that employment growth will be generated by small to medium sized enterprises (SMEs, firms with less than 500 employees), rather than through the expansion of larger multinational firms. This theory is based upon the experience of the US market and reflects developments within Europe.

That is not to say that the traditional large-scale consumers of training, the multinationals, are no longer an important market, but personnel or training managers within smaller companies are being encouraged to learn from the example set by firms with the resources to implement comprehensive language training programmes. The most fundamental question to be considered by any firm, small or large, when undertaking language training, is whether or not the cost justifies the perceived return. This question is particularly pertinent for smaller companies without substantial training budgets operating under harsh economic conditions, so many governments have adopted policies to assist SMEs in their training programmes.

In Europe, the EU's Task Force on Human Resources has set up a number of funding programmes to assist smaller businesses to overcome the financial strain of training, so it is a good idea to examine the financial assistance available before finalising a training policy (see p168). Some schemes have rigorous qualification criteria, which make it difficult to adapt a programme for eligibility once it is in place.

One example of national commitment is that of the French government which has made it a legal requirement that all companies spend 1.4% of their gross profits on training. Many companies use these funds for English language training. The globalisation of commerce is a development resulting largely from improved communications, which has been accelerated by the signing of international cooperation agreements, such as NAFTA (the North American Free Trade Area), EEA (the European Economic Area, incorporating EFTA, the European Free Trade Area and the EU) and ASEAN (the Association of South-East Asian Nations). Its effect on most businesses is that international trade is the route to expansion, so language training is no longer just a perk for multinational executives, but an integral part of corporate staff training.

English has become a practical necessity for employees at different levels of seniority in companies of all sizes.

English has become a practical necessity for employees at different levels of seniority in companies of all sizes. Through a balance between different training methods and by capitalising on assistance available, most companies can now benefit from having staff capable of communicating with expanding markets without an enormous budget. This is good news for teachers of EFL, who are entering an evolving but exciting career.

Assessing the Language Needs of Your Company

Which members of your staff need to improve their English? What kind of training best suits their needs and how will they maintain new skills?

Companies are experts on their own products and markets and usually have quite a clear idea of the kind and level of English they need at what level. But what are the precise needs of each type of employee? Who should you train, and how? Is your company making the most effective use of the English-speaking staff which it already has? And how can you choose from among the plethora of courses and methods of learning which are now available? The best way to answer these questions is to carry out a language audit with a professional auditor from outside the company.

The language auditor

A good business language auditor has language expertise and understands commercial needs. The auditor will want to get to know your company in order to assess existing language competence and discover your company's present and future requirements. He or she will conduct research into which specific tasks and in which specific situations English is needed.

The auditor will assess whether employees must speak, write, read or listen to English, and decide on the level of fluency and accuracy they require. He or she will then recommend training to close the gap between the existing skills and abilities of employees and their goals.

The auditor should suggest various training options and methods within your budget and other constraints such as working conditions and availability of employees. The auditor will also suggest options such as translation and interpreting, where appropriate.

There are a growing number of independent specialist language consultancies who carry out audits. Some of the private language schools with branches, affiliates, or franchisees in many countries, can also offer this service.

The British Council may be able to help you find a language auditor and in some locations will undertake the task itself for a fee. Two British Councils, in Quito, Ecuador and Dhaka, Bangladesh, carry out regular language audits, and those in Singapore and Hong Kong have strong links with industry.

The precise methods which each auditing company employs are often guarded as 'secret'. Most audits will generally follow the principles outlined here, which draw on the model developed by the London-based Centre for Information on Language Teaching and Research (CILT).

You are more likely to benefit from an auditor's services if you do some preliminary research on your company's needs, have a clear idea of what you want to achieve, and have begun to develop a language policy which fits into your company policy as a whole.

Language training can be viewed in two ways. Firstly, you might see it as a way of satisfying short-term and operational requirements, with limited objectives, such as the need for telephonists and receptionists to handle calls in English and welcome English-speaking visitors. Secondly, you can look at it in terms of your company's medium to long-term strategy. This is appropriate when you expect to be in a market long-term or are planning to enter a new market.

You should concentrate on who needs to use English. To help decide this you should consider all the tasks and roles which involve using the language, such as:
- meetings: formal, informal and social, both with customers and colleagues
- sales: presentations, describing the product, telemarketing
- telephone calls, answering enquiries
- negotiating
- seminars, conferences, exhibitions
- video-conferencing
- travelling
- technical support
- training operators/personnel abroad
- product development
- customer feedback

Even before an audit takes place, you can promote English in your company by giving status to language skills and making them prominent in recruitment. Ideally, you should adopt a long-term policy towards language training to cover the updating of existing skills, new training, the recruitment of English-speaking staff, and the forecasting of future requirements.

A good business language auditor has language expertise and understands commercial needs.

You are more likely to benefit from an auditor's services if you do some preliminary research on your comapny's needs.

In devising a corporate language policy, you should consider the following issues:

(1) Do you want to foster an international outlook in the company or just satisfy specific requirements?

(2) On what basis will trainees be selected? the needs of the company? the motivation of the employee? the employee's previous language experience?

(3) What priority will language learning have in your company's budget?

(4) What incentives will you give employees?

(5) Will training be in-house or at a school?

(6) Will the training take place in the employees' own time, the company's time, or both?

(7) How will you encourage employees to use foreign languages?

(8) How will language skills be maintained?

The decisions you make on these issues will affect the training required. For example, if you wish to foster an international outlook you might want to encourage all employees who come into contact with English-speakers to learn the language. If this is not your intention, you may choose to select a small number of employees within any one occupation to handle English-speakers, so that, for example, one telephonist deals with calls in English, and certain sales clerks specialise in business with English-speaking countries.

The language audit

A language audit is usually carried out in cooperation with the company's training or personnel manager, and as it progresses, will help you clarify some of the policy issues above. This, in turn, will have an effect on the auditor's recommendations. An audit has four main stages: a survey of existing skills; the identification of training needs; the selection of training and other solutions; and the drawing up of a programme to maintain the skills acquired.

Survey of existing skills

The auditor may be able to advise you on the format and content of a preliminary in-house questionnaire. This will help you take stock of the usable language skills among your workforce, discover the extent to which employees are able or willing to use these skills, and what they think about training to improve their ability. The audit will often discover that employees have skills which you are unaware of. It will also signal to employees that your company is serious about promoting language learning and training.

On a first visit to the company, the auditor may define the audit's objectives and agree terms of reference. When the results of the questionnaire are available the auditor will proceed to review your company's current provision of training, and will draw up a timetable for the audit.

Identifying training needs

Different groups or individuals within the company will require different kinds of training. Sales and marketing employees may require a very high degree of fluency, while receptionists and switchboard operators will need to be trained in the specific type of language used on the telephone. Some staff may require cultural training which is a vital complement to language training. It may provide essential information on business etiquette in English-speaking countries, introduce them to local customs and laws, and show them how to use an interpreter.

The auditor may need to have in-depth conversations with staff at all levels to establish exactly what their job involves and determine precisely how and when improved English language ability could help them. Employees are likely to be more motivated if they can see clear benefits stemming from better language skills. Taking into account your company's training policy and future needs, the auditor will report on the skills required by specific groups and individuals.

Selecting training

Once needs have been identified, the auditor will help your company examine and evaluate affordable training solutions. Language learning is essentially a long-term project and the programme devised should take account of the need to absorb and practise new skills. Various types of training provider and approaches to learning may be recommended. Training may be intensive or non-intensive; it may be in-company, at a local language school, or at a language school in an English-speaking country; classes may be one-to-one or on a group basis.

Maintaining language skills

If employees do not use their language skills over a long period of time they very quickly become 'rusty'. They need to remain confident so a programme to keep skills fresh is essential. The auditor may suggest in-house refresher courses with a home study element.

The auditor's role

Once training solutions have been chosen, you should give the auditor an on-going role to monitor and assess the training programme. Changes in your company's markets may lead to a change in its language needs and training programmes may have to be adapted or modified. It is a good idea to keep an updated record of the language ability of all employees.

The language audit will often discover that employees have skills which you are unaware of

Various types of training provider and approaches to learning may be recommended.

Training Solutions

You have decided to invest in language training for your staff. What factors should you consider when choosing from the many training options available?

SELECTING TRAINEES

When choosing employees for language training you must assess a number of interrelated factors such as company needs, employees' roles, each individual's aptitude for learning a language, and his or her willingness to do so.

Company needs and employees' roles can be assessed during a language audit. Aptitude may be measured either by an auditor or a training provider. Experts say that aptitude tests are not entirely reliable, but the following factors are generally recognised as affecting the rate at which individuals can learn a language:
-the level of existing knowledge of a language or languages
-motivation to learn the language
-interest in the country or people where the language is spoken
-a genuine interest in learning
-ability to learn new strategies
-ability to overcome fear of making mistakes in public
-the personal relationship between tutor and student
-the student's perception of the relevance of the course
-incentives
-family support

Grouping trainees

If you choose group training, you should consider the size and make-up of the groups very carefully. While for non-language training it may be most cost-effective to train as many employees as possible in one class, this is rarely the case for language training. It is most effective to group students according to needs and level, and this will not always coincide with your company's hierarchy. You may have to make compromises when a potential group with the same needs does not have the same language level and vice-versa. Some schools with a high level of organisation may be able to group all those students with the same level together for some lessons and bring all those with the same needs together for others. If a student misses a lesson, he or she may fall behind and lose motivation. If this happens with many different students over a number of weeks, the group is likely to break down.

TRAINING OPTIONS

Face-to-face. Classroom or workplace learning with a tutor, "one-to-one" or in small groups. This is usually regarded as essential. Students get the chance to practise their English with a teacher.

Distance learning open or self-study. Students work on their own with self-study materials, including books, cassettes, videos, computer programmes or even multimedia CD-ROMs. Colleges, universities or libraries may be able to offer this facility in some countries, or the company may decide to invest in materials and/or computer hardware. On its own, this is usually not sufficient for effective learning, and students can lose motivation without the support of a teacher. It can be an excellent supplement to face-to-face learning and good for students who want to maintain or refresh their language skills and knowledge.

A combination of face-to-face learning and distance learning, open or self-study may be the most comprehensive and effective package. If employees take up self-study opportunities, perhaps in their own time, the company will derive maximum return from its investment in language training, particularly if the two forms of study are integrated.

One-to-one tuition. Individual or "one-to-one" tuition is usually the fastest way to learn. The trainer is able to take full account of the student's needs, language level, and objectives. But the student has no contact with other students and it may be difficult to carry out role plays which need three or more participants, such as seminars or negotiations. The cost per student is usually much higher than for group classes.

What kind of course?

Intensive: up to 30 hours a week, six hours each day (including self-study time) over 2-3 weeks. Such courses can be extended but a one-week break is recommended. This is good for employees who are imminently going abroad, as a kick-start for non-intensive courses, or as a refresher.

Non-intensive: usually 1-2 hours per session, twice a week. The problem with such courses is that motivation can be difficult to maintain (progress may be slow for beginners who may feel they are getting nowhere), but they are ideal for an on-site programme at the end of the working day with a group of 5-8 employees. Maximum benefit can be derived if time on the course is matched by time on self-study.

You should consider the size and make-up of the groups very carefully.

Individual or "one to one" tuition is usually the fastest way to learn.

CHOOSING A TRAINING PROVIDER
An in-house teacher

Getting a teacher to come to your premises saves the time and cost of travelling to a language school, which can detract from students' ability to learn, especially after a tiring day at work. Whether you choose a teacher from the local language school or a freelance trainer, you should ask to see a list of his or her former clients and check his or her qualifications, experience and business background. You should ask for a sample lesson or request a teacher with specialist knowledge if this is what you require.

If the trainer is freelance, check that he or she can provide continuity should you decide to renew the training contract. Will he or she disappear once the contract ends? The British Council in many countries can offer appropriately qualified and experienced in-company trainers.

The disadvantages of in-company courses compared to those at language schools include the risk of interruptions to classes, when, for example, students have to take urgent telephone calls or are summoned by a superior. You also need to ensure that you have an appropriate room available and the necessary equipment - at least a blackboard or whiteboard, but perhaps also an overhead projector, tape recorders and a video player.

Recruitment agencies may be able to help you find a suitable trainer. Check that the agency has experience in your field of business, and compare their rates with local schools. An agency's commission might seem high, but using one can save a lot of time and expense. English for Specific Purposes (ESP) consultancies may also be able to help. To find one, ask reputable recruitment agencies (see page 53).

Language schools

Some employees may feel that, compared to the workplace, the atmosphere of a school is 'unnatural'. Those whose compulsory education ended many years ago may react badly to being 'back in school'. But others may find they can study better in a place dedicated to learning. A school may have equipment, such as a language laboratory, which it would be expensive to install at a company.

Make sure that a prospective school can do the following: give a demonstration lesson; test the aptitude of students to learn languages; group students by level/ability; map a training plan against learning goals; adapt your company's materials into the proposed language course; select a method in line with individuals' learning style; provide self-study facilities; allow your company to discuss selection of tutors; monitor quality of training; offer public tests or exams; and provide end-of-course test and reports.

Local schools can be convenient and costs are relative to the local economy. Check that the school has a history of teaching business English, that teachers the teachers are qualified, preferably in business English, and that they have business experience, preferably with knowledge of the business culture of the English-speaking country you work with. Ask about class sizes and request references from former clients.

Local schools are likely to have classes of students who all speak the same native language, which means they are not forced to communicate with each other in English and may feel uncomfortable doing so. There is no opportunity to learn about the culture of an English-speaking country first-hand.

Schools in an English-speaking country

There are schools specialising in business English in the UK, the USA, Canada, Australia, New Zealand and Malta. Their main advantages over local schools are experience and expertise in running business English courses, the chance to learn about a country's culture first-hand, and opportunities to practise and learn English outside the classroom, perhaps with a host family. Students in groups may be of several different nationalities and work for different companies, which creates a natural need and desire to communicate in English.

Good schools will send students a needs analysis in the form of a questionnaire to fill in before they arrive. Check that schools are members of the recognition system operating in their country. In Europe, they may also be members of Europe-wide organisations which ensure high quality (see page 179). Some schools also offer courses combining English tuition with a special interest, such as golf.

Homestay in an English-speaking country

This offers a learning environment that can be intensive but relaxing. Students live in the trainer's home and so benefit from his or her hospitality, speaking English in non-teaching situations as well as during lessons. There is an opportunity to "live" the language, not just study it.

Cultural training

All good schools should have a component of this in their courses, even if it is not explicit. But for some employees, additional cultural training may be desirable. Farnham Castle Centre for International Briefing, Farnham, Surrey, is the UK's leading centre in this field. Language Training Services in Bath also run a systematic course. In the USA, The Society of International English Cultural Training and Research (SIETAR) runs teaching courses in crosscultural training. The Society can also provide advice and recommendations on other training organisations which may be more suitable for you. Contact: SIETAR, 733 15th Street NW, Suite 900, Washington DC, 20005 USA.

Check that the agency has experience in your field.

Homestay offers a learning environment that can be intensive but relaxing.

Technological Solutions

Multimedia applications promise to transform language learning strategies, but to what extent should they replace traditional methods?

With foreign language learning becoming an urgent management priority for many companies, firms are increasingly looking towards technology to meet their training needs. Multimedia is the buzz word of the moment and features strongly at educational trade fairs. But how useful is technology in language learning? Do new computer applications packages satisfy your training needs, and what issues should you address before investing in expensive hardware?

Educational consultants have noted two common scenarios to avoid when choosing training technology. Perhaps an enthusiastic training manager is given a free hand to choose whichever training media he or she prefers. He or she has stores full of expensive, unused equipment and runs out of money or company support before an efficient training programme can be set up. Or a company decides to plump for one training technology throughout the company using the latest hi-tech systems even if this is not the most appropriate or cost-effective solution.

Managers should be wary of wanting to use technology for technology's sake when traditional methods may be more suitable. As is often pointed out, the humble book is a random-access, highly portable piece of technology. Audio cassettes too, have advantages over other media: they can be used by trainees in their cars. Dr A.W. Bates, professor of educational media research at the UK's Open University, warns in a paper dealing with the issue: "In educational and cost terms, there is no 'super-medium'; different media have different strengths and weaknesses. This means that a combination of media is usually the most appropriate decision."

For language learning, most trainers advise that technology should be used as a backup or supplement to face-to-face training. It can be used before residential courses abroad, and by employees wishing to maintain or refresh their language skills. Perhaps most effectively of all, it can be used concurrently with language school or in-company courses. The advantages for companies are plain: expensive face-to-face training is extended and reinforced by employees who may be motivated to use technology at self-access learning facilities in their own time.

So which technology and which platforms is it best to employ? A recent Keynote market review predicted that analogue video and LaserDisc systems will still remain significant within the training industry due to the considerable investment which some companies have already made. But it is likely that cheaper computer-based digital video systems, and CD-ROM drives, whether stand-alone CD-I or as part of a PC or network, will become the dominant training platform of the future.

It is claimed that multimedia has certain benefits over traditional methods of learning. It responds quickly to students, giving them further information and correcting them more quickly than a teacher. This is vital since it allows each learner to learn at his or her own pace. In addition, it can instantly replay sounds (unlike a tape which has to be rewound), which is useful for pronunciation practice, and it can be highly involving and motivating. Language teachers, however, warn that no computer programme - however sophisticated - can replace the unpredictable interaction which takes place in a student group and the exposition and problem-solving skills of a human teacher.

Full-motion video and voice recognition are the keys to the future of language learning hi-technology. It may be a long time before the latter becomes widely available, but full-motion video is already here. Low-cost platforms such as CD-ROM and Philips CD-I are capable of replaying video (in combination with Indeo, MPEG or other compression technology), although it takes up a large amount of memory. LaserDisc has the greatest capabilities in this area, but has not gained widespread currency as a language training medium.

As yet voice-recognition technology is not refined enough to meet learner's pronunciation training needs. Most CD-ROMS are only capable of a 'parrot' function which allows the student to listen to a recording of a native speaker (the model), then record his or her own effort to copy the model, and finally compare the two. However, one company has now developed a programme which compares the student's pronunciation efforts on a scale of 1 to 10 with an electronically-stored model.

As long as it is part of a well thought-out language policy, hi-technology can be an efficient training solution for your learners and your company. Take time to analyse its costs and benefits compared to lowtech and non-technical solutions and it may become an important element in your company's training strategy.

Managers should be wary of using technology for technolgy's sake when traditional methods may be more suitable.

Full-motion video and voice recognition are the keys to the future.

Recruiting English Speakers

The staff you hire will show you their language qualifications, but do you know what they mean?

Having established that your organisation would benefit from an improved level of English, you may decide to recruit staff with language skills. However, in addition to the standard difficulties recruitment presents to most organisations, assessment of language capability must also be taken into account. Depending on your budget and the importance of the position, you may choose to engage a specialist agency with the capability to determine candidates' language level, or trust in your own selection procedure. In either case, there are a number of key questions which will influence your recruitment decision.

The position

The level and type of language ability required are dependent upon the role that the prospective employee will play in your organisation. Although this may seem obvious, it is essential to keep this in mind throughout the recruitment process. A receptionist must be able to answer telephone queries in another language, but it is of little significance to you if he or she can translate Shakespeare. Should you wish to test candidate's language skills, devise a practical scenario which reflects what the position will involve on a daily basis. Remember that linguistic ability is a tool with which someone can improve the way in which they do a job; it is no substitute for the ability to do the job in the first place.

Qualifications

Unless your own English is impeccable, the most reliable way of judging a candidate's skills is by their qualifications and matching those qualifications to your needs. A Master's degree in English Literature may look very impressive on paper, but it is no proof of its owner's ability to sell your latest product to a Swedish chain-store.

There is now a selection of internationally recognised English qualifications (and so many confusing acronyms) that some sort of a guide to what the qualifications actually mean is essential. The following table gives a brief summary of the main examinations, but the amount of information is naturally restricted. It is worth noting that new specialist qualifications, such as LCCI's English for Tourism and Cambridge's CBET, are always being developed, so you can be quite specific in your demands.

For fuller details of all examinations, see The Longman Guide to English Language Examinations (Longman 1989).

Key To Coverage	Key to Level		Notes
W = Writing **R** = Reading **L** = Listening **S** = Speaking	**1**= Beginner **2** = Elementary **3** = Pre-intermediate **4** = Lower-intermediate (Waystage)	**5** = Intermediate (Threshold) **6** = Upper-intermediate **7** = Post-intermediate Proficiency **8** = Advanced **9** = Bilingual	These indicate aims and status. For more details, see English Language Entrance Requirements in British Educational Institutions (HMSO 1991).

NB. This table is not intended to be a comprehensive list of EFL examinations available.

Board	Examination	Coverage	LEVEL: on scale (1-9)	Notes
ARELS	Diploma	general LS	pass = 8	Spoken English exams conducted in a language lab or with radio equipment. Oral counterparts of the Oxford EFL exams.
	Higher Certificate		pass = 6	
	Preliminary Certificate		pass = 4	
Educational Testing Service	TOEFL	general LR	550 = 5/6	TOEFL 550 accepted by most US universities. UK institutions may demand evidence of writing and speaking. EuroCert = TOEFL + TSE + TWE.
	TSE	general S		
	TWE	general W		
	TOEIC	business LR	level 5 = 5	Widely used in commerce/industry
International Baccalaureate	English as a Second Language	general RWS	not available	Higher: college entrance exam for English majors. Subsidiary: for non-English majors.
International Certificate Conference	Language Certificate System - English	general+ ESP R (W) L S	not available	German-based exams available in Europe. Business, Hotel & Catering, Technical English exams also available.

Board	Examination	Coverage	LEVEL on scale (1-9)	Notes
London Chamber of Commerce	English for Commerce	business RWS	1st = 3 2nd = 5 3rd = 7.	Traditional business English exam.
	English for Business	business RWS		More recent business English exam.
	SEFIC	business LS	Threshold = 5 Intermediate = 6 Advanced = 7	= Spoken English for Industry & Commerce. Available in combination with EfB and EfC (above).
	English for Tourism	tourism LS	1st = 3 2nd = 5	Language exam for tourism industry.
Michigan	MELAB	general R W L (S)	75 = 5/6	Accepted by most US universities.
NEAB (JMB)	University Entrance Testing ESOL	academic R W L S	pass = 6.	Widely accepted by UK universities.
Pitman	ESOL & spoken ESOL	general L R W & L S	Intermediate = 5 Higher Intermediate = 6 Advanced = 7.	Five-stage exams available on demand. Higher Intermediate accepted by some UK universities.
	English for Business Communication	business L R W	Elementary = 5 Intermediate = 6 Advanced = 7.	Three-stage business exams available on demand.
Trinity College London	Spoken English Grades	general L S + R W at higher levels	Initial (1-3) = 1/2 Elementary (4-6) = 3/4. Intermediate (7-9) = 4/5 Advanced (10-12) = 6/8.	A series of 12 graded tests in spoken English with examiners from the UK.
University of Cambridge (UCLES)	Proficiency (CPE)	general R W L S	pass = 7	Established exam accepted by most UK universities.
	Cert in Advanced English (CAE)	general R W L S	pass = 6	Newer exam accepted by most UK universities.
	1st Certificate (FCE)	general R W L S	pass = 5	Established exam widely accepted by employers.
	Preliminary English Test (PET)	general R W L S	pass = 4	Elementary test to encourage further learning.
	Key English Test (KET)	general R W L S	pass = 3	Lower-level exam introduced in 1994.
	Cert in Communicative Skills in English (CCSE)	general R W L S	1 = 4, II = 5, III = 6, IV = 7	Formerly RSA CUEFL
	IELTS	academic R W L S	Bands 1-9 = bands 1-9 on scale	Bands 6/7 accepted by UK universities.
	CEIBT	business R W L S	pass =7	Cert in English for International Business & Trade.
University of London (ULEAC)	GCE O Level (Syllabus B)	general R W	pass = 6	Grade C accepted by most UK universities.
	Certificates of Attainment	general R W L (S)	1 = 3, 2 = 4, 3 = 5, 4 = 6, 5 = 7, 6 = 8	Six-stage graded tests with optional speaking tests.
University of Oxford (UODLE)	EFL Certificates	general R W	Higher = 6 Preliminary = 3	Higher (credit) + ARELS Higher accepted by some universities.
	International Business English Certificate	business R W L S	First = 4/5 Executive = 6/7	Business and Tourism exams based on authentic situations.
	Tourism English Proficiency	business R W L S	First = 4/5	

Business Case Study:
The Medium-sized Enterprise

How do other companies assess their language training needs and decide on the right programmes? L'Electrofil, France, outline their training solutions.

L'Electrofil, a medium-sized manufacturing company in Lyon, France, has carefully considered the range of language training solutions to find those which suit it and its employees best.

Language training has become essential in order to ensure the company's steady growth.

Founded nearly 60 years ago, *L'Electrofil* is a privately-owned company with a turnover of around 350 million French francs and a workforce of around 500. It is the leader in the supply of high tension ignition wire sets to the European motor industry, holding around 10% of the world market. Language training has become essential in order to ensure the company's steady growth over recent years. Increased exports to countries including Sweden, UK, Germany, Spain, Poland, Mexico, South Africa, India and Japan now account for over 50% of turnover.

The company is constantly searching for improvements in all its activities including management skills and personnel development. Every year the company spends 5 to 7% of its total salary bill on training, much more than the 1.5% required by French law. This has been rewarded by a series of quality awards, the company being rated a grade A supplier by most of its major customers and recently gaining the coveted ISO9001 certification.

Until 1992 language training was carried out throughout the company but without a formal needs analysis. After 1992, Jonathan Foley, Training Manager and Quality Director, dealt with needs assessment, strategy, and selection of schools. Any person in the company could ask for training on condition that the request was countersigned by his superior. In this way Foley could ensure that requests were centralised, in order to organise groups. On the same document the trainee would note his assessment of the quality of the training relevant to his own or the company's needs. This information was also used for the annual assessment interview.

Student motivation is higher if group members have similar levels of language ability.

There has been a definite shift in emphasis towards the business needs of the company away from the personal priorities of the individual. Every department submits a training plan including language training, the emphasis being on people who need to speak to the company's cus-

tomers or otherwise use English for technical documents. Every participant on an English course is a volunteer and courses usually take place outside working hours.

The company established that its employees needed to work on the following: general English, technical English, and commercial English. Foley then asked selected schools to determine the level of each individual (in France they use a scale from 1 to 5) enabling him to organise the different categories. Since 1994 a new Human Resource Director has taken over responsibility for training but the same system is used.

Training Solutions

A. Group training in-house by an outside school for two hours per week is used for technicians, clerks, internal sales people and engineers. There are usually six students in a group and although the company has managed to create fairly homogenous groups in terms of level the priority was technical or commercial need. Foley admits that this strategy has not been totally successful. He discovered that student motivation is higher if group members have similar levels of language ability. In future the company will form groups according to this principle.

B. Individual tuition at a specialised school in Lyon has been chosen for some senior managers (2 or 3 a year). This intensive programme is very expensive and is only used because managers can be flexible with the programme and cancel at short notice. Results from this programme have not always been good as the managers frequently miss classes because of work pressures, sometimes leading to big gaps in their learning programme. It is also extremely demanding on the individuals. After a stressful day's work they have to drive 30 minutes into the city of Lyon to the school, and find it difficult to concentrate on their English class.

C. Telephone courses have been implemented for secretaries who use English when dealing with customers, managers, senior managers and directors. The course consists of a series of 30-minute classes conducted by telephone.

L'Electrofil uses a French company near Lyon which specialises in this method. This technique encourages the student to talk about his or her professional life, and can include work tailored to a student's particular needs, such as practising specific vocabulary or perfecting telephone manner. At the end of the session the student receives a fax correcting the language used and suggesting further improvements.

Although this method does not help with written English, the company has found it to be successful for several reasons: most of all it increases confidence; it encourages the students to speak on the telephone, usually considered a hurdle; it is very flexible, with no travel involved and no classrooms to reserve; being one-to-one it is intensive and rapid progress is made; it meets the company's need for its employees to sharpen their spoken English abilities. However, it does not improve presentation or negotiating skills, enhance salesmanship, or work on any of the other important requisites for successful face to face business contact. It is a programme less suited for use with executives.

D. Total immersion courses are used for managers/directors and project leaders. L'Electrofil uses a school at Folkestone for the 2-week Keyman executive course consisting of intensive training in Business English and skills as well as an Anglo-Saxon cultural 'conversion course'. The students are lodged with non-French speaking families, adding considerably to the amount of practice they have. L'Electrofil appreciates the presentation and business confidence skills which the course gives to students, not least because they are in contact with other foreign high-profile managers throughout the course.

L'Electrofil reports that everyone who has been on this course has returned highly satisfied with their progress, though extremely tired. The company finds it very cost-effective although it is totally inflexible - managers are away from work for two weeks on a pre-booked course. This is a major disincentive for choosing this training option more often.

Cultural training
L'Electrofil meets its cultural training requirements through residential courses. Most of the company's customers are non-native English speakers originating from many different countries and cultures, so training in only English culture proved to be of little help. The company found that specialised individual cultural training was a cost effective way to meet their needs. Four employees specialising in full-time

contracts with foreign customers are now wholly familiar with the cultural background of those customers.

For L'Electrofil's needs, Foley rates the effectiveness of the various training solutions in the order CDAB.

Telephone courses include work tailored to a student's specific needs.

Summary
The company has identified several problems in the provision of language training which other companies may encounter, and outline solutions to some of these. Some senior staff cannot afford the time to attend courses, and the company has adopted telephone training as a training solution. Employees lack sufficient opportunity to practise their newly-acquired English, so the company has bought a CD-ROM interactive work station which is available on a self-access basis - but it is too early to judge its effectiveness. The problem of non-homogenous group levels, however, is proving difficult to solve.

Foley warns other companies looking into language training that there are a lot of schools in the market place, and they vary greatly in quality. He suggests that companies should ensure that the school employs native English speakers, and that the school is willing to work hard for the company. Schools should carry out a needs analysis, an initial level assessment, present a formal work programme and provide an individual report at the end of the course. Having chosen a good school, companies should persevere - as the school gets to know the company it will be able to improve the services it offers.

L'Electrofil is now happy with most of its language training provision. The success of a language training programme depends largely on the attitude of the workforce towards gaining new skills. Foley stresses that the company's employees were motivated and eager to speak English at the outset, and is sure that this has contributed a lot to the company's success.

The success of a language training programme depends largely on the attitude of the workforce towards gaining new skills.

European Grants

As language training becomes a greater priority within the European Union, you may find that your company qualifies for public funding.

Language training for company staff is part of continuing vocational training (CVT), administered by many different bodies in the various EU countries, with varying training patterns and funding arrangements.

In **Italy,** companies are responsible for the (CVT) of their workers. The Regions finance training activities with subsidies provided by the State through a special fund, while the European Social Fund (ESF) usually co-finances state expenditure (50%). Trade Unions have developed autonomous training programmes. English is the language most often taught to businesses.

In **Luxembourg,** CVT is organised by the Ministry of National Education, professional chambers, communes and recognized private organisations.

In Spain all training programmes include a foreign language element.

In **Denmark,** public authorities partly finance certain CVT activities through a training fund co-managed by management and unions, the 'social partners'. Employees can take language courses run by The Adult Continuing Education sector. A Training Advisory Council, consisting of the social partners advises the Ministry on general matters concerning CVT.

In **Germany,** CVT is regulated by the Federal government and the Länder governments. The Chambers of Commerce and Industry are not as enthusiastic as they might be about language training, especially in the new Länder, where there are other priorities. The job specifications within the German training system are being revised to include foreign language learning needs.

The job specifications within the German training system are being revised to include foreign language learning needs.

In **The Netherlands,** companies finance the CVT of their employees through funds created by collective agreements. The State may partly subsidize certain training activities organized in this context. The responsibility for training is with the Education Ministry.

In **Spain,** the Ministry of Education has joint programmes with the Ministry of Social Affairs which form part of a National Plan for Professional Training. CVT is publicly part-financed by the National Employment Institute (INEM). A significant part of training is co-financed (50%) by the ESF. A transfer of powers to the Autonomous Communities is in progress. These already contribute 10% to public financing of training. Language training is very important and all training programmes include a foreign language element. A dialogue between the Ministry of Education and institutions responsible for the Chambers of Commerce and Small and medium-sized enterprises (SMEs) has yet to take place.

In **Belgium,** the three Regions, Flanders, Wallonia and Brussels are responsible for continuing training for independent professions and for managers of SMEs, through bodies such as the Institut de Formation Permanente pour les Classes Moyennes et les PMEs, in the French Community. In the Dutch-speaking community, industry and the SMEs have themselves set up courses. Foreign language courses enjoy great success, with much use of new technology, and industry support by means of study leave.

In **Portugal,** enterprises finance their employees' CVT. The state may co-finance training in enterprises in difficulty and the ESF provides financing to companies, either directly or through the Institute of Employment and Vocational Training (IEFP). Adults have access in the evenings to each of the education cycles.

In **France,** state financing of CVT depends on framework agreements with the professional sectors concerned. The state also contributes to the financing of individual training leave. Regional councils organise annual programmes of continuing training, in consultation with the regional economic and social committee and the Regional Vocational Training Committee. The Association Française des Chambres de Commerce et d'Industrie (AFCI) has established a language training network - Centres d'Etudes des Langues (CEL) throughout the country. More than 12,000 SMEs have used them.

In **Greece,** the OAED (Manpower Employment Organisation) and EOT (Greek Organisation for Tourism) run CVT along with public and private companies. The Association of Greek Industries (SEV) with the General Confederation of Greek Workers (GSEE) is responsible for institutes which train managers and executives. The Ministry of Labour has largely decentralised responsibility for the use of EU funds in training to Regional Councils. For training activities receiving EU financing, the employers, the ESF and the OAED share the costs equally.

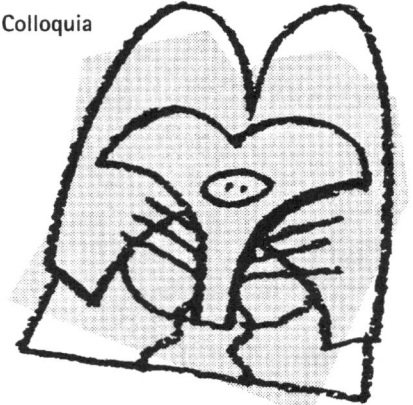

Appendix

not only

but also

This section serves as a quick reference for acronyms, recognition bodies, book suppliers, associations, publications, major events and useful addresses throughout the world.

Terminology

As with most specialist business or academic sectors, the English Language Training industry has a number of standard acronyms, which are often interchangeable, but have specific meanings as outlined below. In order to avoid repetition and confusion, the term EFL has been used throughout this book as the general term for English for non-native speakers of the language.

EFL
English as a Foreign Language
-the general UK term, although in the US and Australia it is used to refer to teaching abroad only.

ELT
English Language Teaching or Training
-a general international term used widely by publishers.

ESL
English as a Second Language
-the general US term for any English language teaching within the country, but in the UK and Australia it refers to teaching English for immigrants.

ESOL
English for Speakers of Other Languages
-another general US term.

TEFL
TESL
TESOL
-the prefix (T) simply stands for **Teaching.**

ELICOS
English Language Intensive Courses to Overseas Students
-the general Australian term.

EAP
English for Academic Purposes
-preparation for university education using English.

ESP
English for Specific Purposes
-for example, English for Aviation or English for Computing. Often includes Business English, although this has now become a specialisation in its own right.

Recognition Schemes

A quick guide to the major recognition bodies and related associations.

When choosing a language school, remember that there are various organisations which have been set up to monitor the standards of teaching and student welfare throughout the world. Some schemes also guarantee deposits on course fees. Unfortunately the recognition schemes can be confusing - Britain has several. Non-membership of an organisation does not mean the school is necessarily inadequate. However, the major recognition organisations in Anglophone countries are worth contacting if you want to research a school or college.

Australia
The ELICOS (English Language Intensive Courses for Overseas Students) Association represents English language colleges. It established the National ELICOS Accreditation Scheme (NEAS). This approves schools and colleges which meet its required standards.

Canada
English teaching is largely confined to the state sector. The University and College Intensive English Programs aim to advance standards in intensive English courses at Canadian universities and colleges.

Ireland
In Ireland, standards in private language schools are maintained by the Advisory Council for English Language Schools (ACELS) under the aegis of the Department of Education. ACELS has representation from The Recognised English Language Schools Association (RELSA) and NATEFLI (National Association of TEFL in Ireland). The Association for Teacher training in TEFL (ATT) has been set up to ensure Irish TEFL qualifications are of a similar standard to international qualifications.

New Zealand
FIELSNZ (the Federation of Independent English Language Schools) and CRELS (Combined Registered English Language Schools) represent the interests of private language schools, and member schools have been approved by the New Zealand Qualifications Authority (NZQA). NZEIL (New Zealand Education International Limited) is a cooperative venture between the New Zealand Government's Trade Development Board and the education institutes, and aims to support private schools and state colleges in providing educational services to international students.

United Kingdom
The situation is complicated. The British Council run an accreditation scheme for private language schools. The seven categories that are checked for recognition of these schools are : management and administration, premises, resources, professional qualifications, academic management, teaching and welfare. However, some schools are not eligible for accreditation - schools that have been running for less than two years, for example. Eighty percent of the British Council accredited schools also join ARELS, which is the trade organisation for recognised private language schools and has 195 members. However, smaller schools may not be able to afford to join ARELS.

Another group of language schools decided to set up their own association, FIRST, the membership of which now stands at 24 institutions and it is not expected to rise above 50. Standards are upheld by a system of Initial and Mutual Audit - FIRST's members are audited by fellow member institutions.

The situation is further complicated by the British Council's validation scheme for state colleges and polytechnics - which requires colleges to be members of BASELT (the British Association of State English Language Teaching). The British Council operate their own internal monitoring programme for their courses in English for Academic Purposes. Fortunately in the future there may be a European accreditation scheme.

United States
There is no accreditation agency specifically for English as a Second Language (ESL) programs, although some states run courses which must meet particular state requirements. In Florida, private schools are accredited by ACCET (Accreditation Council for Continuing Education and Training). The American Association of Intensive English Programs (AAIEP) is open to organisations offering intensive courses, and aims to promote professional standards and the awareness of opportunities for English language study in the USA.

TESOL has developed a program of self study for adult training courses which are based on a 'Statement of Core Standards for Language and Professional Training Programs'. The TESOL statement is generally accepted as the standard by the profession.

Somes schemes also guarantee deposits on course fees.

Non-membership of an organisation does not mean the school is necessarily inadequate.

An insider's guide: Technology

All teachers are having to come to terms with the technological revolution brought about by the use of computers, telecommunications and videos in education. This is what you need to know to get you by.

Since we teach communication, video is an excellent source of effective lessons.

The recent rapid advance of technology, together with dramatically falling prices, means that a wider range of technological resources is becoming available to teachers. More resources means more opportunity to experiment, more ideas for what to do with your class, and the excitement and enthusiasm of learning something new that you can share with your students.

Discovering new ways of teaching, experimenting and finding out what works with your students' styles of learning, and your own styles of teaching, are an essential part of the success of English language teaching. On training and refresher courses teachers are often very keen to find out more about using computers and video in the classroom. Recently there has been a lot more interest in multimedia - what it is and how you can use it in both classroom and self-access centre. As video, computers and multimedia do not often feature in general teacher training courses, yet could change your whole pattern of working, it is worth spending some time examining the options.

Video

Television is one of the most powerful and persuasive mediums of communication. Since we teach communication, video is an excellent source of effective lessons. There are two basic sorts of video you can use in the classroom, off-air (recorded by yourself or another teacher, or the videos of TV programmes you can hire from your local video store), and published courses.

Students are highly motivated knowing the language is entirely authentic and up to date.

Off-air video is often the most useful, but you must ensure that you receive permission from the programme's producers before you re-broadcast it, or you could face legal action. For educational purposes, permission is often granted - contact the production company credited at the end of the programme. Students are highly motivated knowing the language is entirely authentic and up to date, and it is easier to find something that matches the interests of the whole class. 'The News' is a favourite, partly because everyone is interested in some item, and partly because there are so many ways of using it. You can, for example, ask students to watch the news one evening, use the video in class

the next day, then follow it up by using newspapers in the next day's classes. Some teachers have even prepared a standard set of exercises, structured in the format of a particular news programme, so that it works whatever the content of the news that day.

Obviously you can do more with off-air videos in higher level classes, but the range of exercises suitable for lower levels is surprising: advertisements are popular - short memorable presentations that serve as excellent mnemonic structures; limited in language and often funny.

ELT publishers are producing an increasing number of video titles. Some are courses in themselves, others, especially the more recent titles, accompany coursebooks, adding another dimension to presentation phases and providing further practice and consolidation. There are published videos for all types of student; younger learners, general English, and business English for experienced business people, as well as students thinking of a business career. Many published videos feature a variety of story lines that continue from unit to unit throughout the course. Others feature short sketches or independent units that can be easily integrated into your scheme of work for this week - these are probably the best place to start experimenting with published videos.

As video has been around for quite a long time now there are several excellent resource books for teachers, full of lesson plans and ideas that cover all aspects, from making your own videos to work with small and large classes, to further ideas for exploiting coursebook videos.

Computers

As prices gradually continue to fall, private sector language schools are catching up with the state sector in the use of computing power, which in language learning is usually referred to as CALL (Computer Assisted Language Learning). CALL falls into three main areas; traditional CALL, the facilities available in office type applications, such as word-processors, and the increasingly influential CD-ROM-based Multimedia packages.

The traditional CALL packages put standard EFL-type exercises, such as gap-fills, matching and multiple-choice onto computer screens. Many of these packages are Authoring Programs; the teacher/author enters the content (text, question content, etc.) into a standard program/exercise structure. It is very easy to understand and operate these programs as there are simple commands on each screen in use. The best traditional programs came out four or five years ago, with the notable exception of concordancing programs.

A concordance is a list of all the instances of a particular word, part-word or phrase in a body of text, together with the line references. When you specify the word you are interested in, the concordancer highlights every instance of that word with as much context as you want on either side. This makes it especially suitable for experiential learning: your students can arrive at an understanding based on comparing different examples of the word's actual usage. In addition to vocabulary study, concordancers are a great help with grammar words; students can make and/or check hypotheses about how the language operates in a general or specific context. There are books full of ideas for using concordancing programs and manuals full of teaching suggestions. Although it is possible to input the text(s) of your choice, this can take a lot of time. If you have the choice, pick a concordancing package that comes with plenty of texts, covering a range of subjects, so there is always something to interest every student and ample instances of the teaching point you want to make.

Computers with office-type applications, such as word-processing, spread-sheets and presentation programs, are becoming increasingly available in classrooms and self-access centres. Many adult learners use office-type applications at work. Learning to write formal or business letters on a computer and printing it out, rather than writing by hand, is far more motivating for these students. Even if your students are not familiar with word-processing or the particular package available to you, teaching them the basics is a subject for a lesson that the students are usually delighted to learn.

Word-processing is probably the most useful program, not least because there are endless ways of exploiting it in class. As well as the standard editing facilities, modern programs have built-in spelling-checkers, thesauruses, grammar and style checkers. They are also ideal for teachers to prepare, develop and store lessons, and so are probably the best place to start with CALL.

Multimedia

Multimedia is the continuing convergence of television, computers and the telephone. In ELT at the moment, multimedia is the integration of written text, sound, graphics, still photos, animation and full-motion video. A multimedia compatible computer can run any one or any combination of these at a time.

There is a wide range of exercise types; dictionary work, basic phrases, games, exercises - based on fairy stories for children and lessons based on dialogues animated by a video sequence or pictures of the speakers. These dialogues are a good illustration of multimedia; the learner can watch and listen to the whole scene or selected parts and phrases. Accompanying subtitles can be switched between different languages, turned off altogether or, like the sound, limited to one side of the dialogue. The learner can play either role, recording their voice, and then listening back.

Although there are a number of formats that can store different media together, CD-ROM is emerging as the most popular. CD-ROM is the same as a music CD, except that it reproduces words and pictures as well as sound.

As with video, some multimedia packages are courses in their own right, sometimes with accompanying workbooks. Others provide practice and consolidation through digital recordings of texts and listening exercises in coursebooks. Longman recently launched the first interactive CD-ROM dictionary that allows learners to reference words by seeing and hearing, as well as reading, through a database taken from a complete range of dictionaries, including pronunciation, grammar and typical mistake dictionaries.

The current range of commercially available titles covers language learning for children, for general purposes and for business. Most publications so far cater for the lower levels; beginners to mid-intermediate. At these levels where learners tend to rely on translating, the translation facilities are particularly useful and can save a lot of time.

The format of CD-ROM packages is self-explanatory and extremely simple to use. Multimedia in language learning provides a rich immersion environment that reduces the workload of the teacher in class and allows faster students to cover more. It encourages autonomous learning at home or in self-access use. Of all the technologies in language learning we can reasonably expect to hear and see a lot more of multimedia in the coming year.

Pick a concordancing package that comes with plenty of texts.

Word-processing is probably the most useful program.

An insider's guide: Methodology

Like all professions, EFL has its own history, phrases and terminology for its working methods. Here is a quick reference to the major developments, so you will have an idea of what people are talking about.

The rigid practice of structural patterns has fallen out of favour, as to some extent has the use of language laboratories.

Grammar and translation

In the beginning there was grammar and translation. Language learners studied a text and learned the grammar with analysis of parts of speech, and then translated it. The classroom language was overwhelmingly the mother tongue, not the language being learned, and the aim was the imparting of content (knowledge of the language) rather than teaching a skill (ability to use the language). In the cyclical way of things, grammar is back with a bang, but translation has never quite recovered its hold on the classroom.

Louis Alexander, the distinguished coursebook author, once said that a coursebook had three lives. First, its life in the methodologically advanced, affluent native speaker teacher-oriented metropolitan schools of the UK, the USA, and Western Europe, Latin America, and parts of the Far East. Then its life in schools in less affluent markets. And thirdly came its life in new markets coming on stream but non-existent at the time the course was originally launched. In this way, said Louis Alexander, a coursebook might have a life of up to 15-20 years and different methods used by different generations of coursebooks might co-exist at different locations in the world.

As with coursebooks, so with methodology. Grammar and translation is alive and well and living in a large number of classrooms, but is not a recommended approach for new teachers.

Audio-lingual/ Direct Method

In the Fifties and Sixties the audio-lingual method was adopted by language schools in the UK and US, influenced by behavioural psychology. This method was characterised by a shift from teaching about language to teaching a language skill. Stress was placed on students speaking rather than listening to the teacher and on language practice rather than on translation. The use of the mother tongue became frowned upon in the classroom, as emphasis was firmly placed on breaking down the language into small structural units easily presented in simple English or through drawings and actions.

The Direct Method, as the application of the audio-lingual method was called, was highly

At the end of the sixties, a major shift occurred in the way teachers understood language.

structural. Students were taken up the verbal ladder from present continuous to present simple to present perfect. Highly ingenious, but very rigid, drills were developed to practise the new patterns learned in the classroom. Often the practice took place through language laboratories, with students sitting in booths listening to recordings, repeating and altering pattern sentences according to instructions.

This method has left its mark on teaching today with its insistence on structured progression; in systematic lesson progression from presentation to practice to free expression; in the demand that teachers talk less and learners talk more; and in the use of English wherever possible. The rigid practice of structural patterns has fallen out of favour, as to some extent has the use of language laboratories.

Situational teaching

The rigid structural progression and learning of language patterns was tempered somewhat by the incorporation of new patterns in situations - meeting a friend, losing and finding things and so on. Expressed through the work of Louis Alexander, situational teaching bridged the gap between the structural approach and the functional approach that followed.

The functional/notional approach

At the end of the sixties, a major shift occurred in the way teachers understood language, influenced by the research of Professor Noam Chomsky into language learning and the existence of a Language Learning Device (LLD), which is the ability of the brain to automatically make sense of the language it absorbs. In the mid seventies David Wilkins at Reading University formulated the functional and notional approach to language description, which categorised language not into a structural framework, but into how it was used. This meant that instead of teaching tenses, teachers focused first on functions, such as how to greet, how to apologise. They then taught the appropriate structures in relation to the function being presented. The aim was to get learners using the language in a meaningful way as soon as possible. This format was enshrined in the

Council of Europe Threshold Level Specification for English in 1974. Functional approaches to languages then caused a shift in emphasis from presentation of new structures in situations to the development of communication skills among learners. The functional approach is still central to the way we look at language analysis today.

The communicative approach

The communicative approach describes a way of applying a functional analysis of language to the classroom. Functionalism stresses the teaching of language as it is used in real life, so the stress is on the development of communicative skills - listening, speaking, reading and writing. Skills work in the classroom is not new, but the development of functional analysis meant that language could be taught in a different way. Take listening and reading, for example - a listening comprehension once had a text with a series of questions (mainly multiple choice). With a communicative approach stress was placed on problem solving - listening for gist, retrieving specific information, identifying locations and characters and even identifying the likely source and type of communication - an answerphone message, a radio broadcast or a lecture. In other words the aim became to make the learner conscious of the automatic processes that go on in them as native speakers.

Alongside this approach came the greater introduction of authentic materials - the use of materials not especially developed for learning English - in the classroom. Bus tickets and train timetables as well as newspaper ads became the raw materials of reading and listening. At the same time, in developing speaking and writing skills, learners were asked to carry out roleplays and simulations, write specimen letters to newspapers, write film reviews and answer job advertisements.

Communicative teaching is enormously influential today. It has given learners a greater sense of relevance in the language they are learning and teachers have gained greater opportunities for creativity both in the classroom and in the development of their own materials.

But there has been a downside. With a clear eye on structural progression and informed teaching of lexis, communicative teachers have had great success. But the approach has inevitably favoured native or near-native speakers of English over the non-native speaker (most English teachers) and, in unprofessional hands, could lead to an unstructured, 'phrase book' type of instruction in which little systematic knowledge of the grammatical framework or the pronunciation system was imparted.

Where are we now?

Firstly, the pendulum has swung back, with the recognition of the importance of the grammatical framework, but teachers and writers have adopted a 'multi-syllabus' approach, in which a teaching programme includes not just a grammatical and lexical syllabus, but also pronunciation, study skills and cross-cultural awareness.

Secondly, there's a growing focus on autonomous and independent learning to support the classroom teacher. This is reflected in the growth of self-access learning centres in schools as a supplement to their classwork. What makes learning centres different from libraries is that these materials are accompanied by graded worksheets and monitored by a qualified teacher so that students can read authentic and graded materials appropriate to their level.

The name of the teaching game now is 'eclecticism'. This doesn't mean, 'Do what you like', but rather 'develop your own teaching style using the principles of good teaching and good classroom management that have been developed in EFL over the last 30-40 years'.

Alternatives

A couple of fringe developments have been and are now very influential in language teaching and learning.

Professor Stephen Krashen of the University of Southern California developed, in the seventies and eighties, 'the natural approach' to learning language. Instead of strictly graded texts at a presupposed level, Krashen proposed the idea of 'Comprehensible Input' - comprehension material that was just slightly above the level of the student. Although controversial on their introduction, many of Krashen's ideas have been quietly absorbed into language teaching materials and methods.

Research into how the brain learns and in particular the understanding of 'Whole brain learning' - recognising the particular characteristics of the right side of the brain - have led to an important, but lesser known, subgroup of methods and materials, which we can categorise as humanistic disciplines. These are a mutually exclusive group of approaches usually developed by a charismatic psychologist or teacher. Foremost among these are 'Suggestopaedia' developed by Dr Georgi Lozanov in Bulgaria, 'The Silent Way' by Dr Caleb Gattegno in the US, 'Counselling Learning' by Father Charles Curran, 'Total Physical Response' (TPR) developed by Professor James Asher.

Bus tickets and train timetables as well as newspaper ads became the raw materials of reading and listening.

Recognising the particular characteristics of the right side of the brain has led to an important, but lesser known, subgroup of methods.

International ELT Book Suppliers

ARGENTINA
Libreria Rodriguez, Sarmiento 835, Buenos Aires.

AUSTRALIA
AEE, PO Box 455, Cammeray, NSW 2062
The Bridge Bookshop, 10 Grafton Street, Chippendale NSW 2008
Language Book Centre, 555 Beaufort Street, Mount Lawley, Western Australia 6050.
The Language People, 207 Boundary Street, West End, Queensland, 4101.

BRAZIL
Sodilvro, Rua Sa Freire 40, CP 3655, 20930 Rio De Janeiro RJ.
Livraria Nobel SA, Rua de Balsa 559, 02910 Sao Paulo SP.

CANADA
Dominie Press, 1316 Huntingwood Drive, Unit 7, Agincourt, Ontario, M1S 3JI.

CYPRUS
Bridgehouse Bookshop, PO Box, 4527 Bridgehouse Building, Nicosia.

DENMARK
Atheneum International, Booksellers, 6 Norregade, 1165 Kobenhavn.

ECUADOR
The English Book Centre, Acacias 613, y Avenida Las Monjas, Guayaquil.

EGYPT
International Language Bookshop, Mahmoud Asmy ST, PO Box 13, Embaba, Cairo.

FINLAND
Akateeminin Kirjakauppa, Keskuskatu 1 SF-00100 Helsinki.

FRANCE
Keltic Paris, 22 Passage Dauphine, 75006 Paris.
Bradleys Bookshop, 32 Pl Gambetta, 3300 Bordeaux.
Just Books, 1 Rue de la Paix, Grenoble.
Decitre, 29 Pl Bellecour, 69002 Lyon.
English Books, 8 Rue Doree, 30000 Nimes.
Librairie des Facultes, 2 Rue de Rome, Strasbourg.

GREECE
The Bookstall, Harilou Trikoupi 6-10, 106 79 Athens.
Efstathiadis Group, Olympou 34, 546 30 Thessaloniki.

HONGKONG
Commercial Press, 9-15 Yee Wo Street, Causeway Bay, Hong Kong.

ICELAND
Bokabud Malsog Menningar, Laugavegi 18, 101 Reykjavik.

INDONESIA
Triad Book Centre, Jl Purnawarman 76, Bandung, 40116.

IRELAND
International Books, 18 South Frederick Street, Dublin
Modern Languages Ltd., 39 Westland Row, Dublin 2

ISRAEL
Eric Cohen Books, 5 Hanakin St, Ra'anana 43 464.

JAPAN
Biblos, Fl Bldg 1-26-5 Takadanobaba, Shinjuku-ku, Tokyo 160.

JORDAN
Jordan Book Centre, PO Box 301, (Al Jubeiha) Amman.

KENYA
Book Distributors Limited, PO Box 47610, Weruga Lane, Nairobi.

KUWAIT
Kuwait Bookshops, Thunayan Al Ghanem Bldg, PO Box 2942, Safat.

MALAYSIA
STP Distributors, SDN BHD 31 Green Hall, 10200 Penang.

MEXICO
Libreria Britannica SA, Serapio Rendon 125, Col San Rafael, 06470 DF.

MOROCCO
Librairie Nationale, 2 Avenue Mers Sultan, Casablanca
American Bookstore, 4 Zankat Tanja, Rabat.

NEWZEALAND
University Bookshop, 34 Princes Street, Auckland.

NORWAY
Olaf Norlis Bokhandel, Universitetsgt 18-24, 0162 Oslo.
Norsk Bokirnport, Postboks 784 S Ovre Vollgate 15, 0106 Oslo 1.

SPAIN
Turner, C/ Génova 3 y 5, 28004 Madrid.

SWEDEN
The English Book Centre, Surbrunnsgatan 51,102 34 Stockholm.

SWITZERLAND
Librairie Francke, Neuengasse 43\Von Werdt Passage, 3001 Bem.

Elm Video and Books, 5 rue Versonnes, 1207 Geneva.

TAIWAN
Caves Books, 103 Chung Shan N Road, Sec 2 Taipei.

TURKEY
ABC Kitabevi, 461 Istiklal Cad, Istanbul.
Baris Kitabevi, Koca M Pasa Cad, No5914, Cerrahoasa, Istanbul.

UNITEDKINGDOM
BEBC London, 106 Piccadilly, London W1
European Bookshop, 4 Regent Place, London W1R 6BH
KELTIC, 25 Chepstow Comer, Chepstow Place, London W2 4TT.
LCL Benedict Ltd, 104 Judd Road, London WC1.
Skola Books, 27 Delaney Street, London NW1 7RX.
Bournemouth English Book Centre, 15 Albion Close, Parkstone, Poole, Dorset BH12 3LL.
The English Language Bookshop, 31 George Street, Brighton, East Sussex, BN2.
Cambridge International Book Centre, 42 Hills Road, Cambridge, CB2 1LA
Cactus Bookshop, 104 College Road, Stoke on Trent ST4.
Albion Bookshop, 13 Mercery Lane, Canterbury, Kent.
James Thin Ltd, Buccleuch Street, Edinburgh.
John Smith & Son Ltd, 578 St Vincent Street, Glasgow.
International Bookshop, Palace Chambers, White Rock, Hastings.
Haigh and Hockland Ltd, The Precinct Centre, Oxford Road, Manchester.
Hudsons Bookshop, 116 New Street, Birmingham, B2 4JJ.
Blackwells, 50 Broad Street, Oxford OXI 2BQ.
The English Book Centre, 24 Middleway, Oxford OX2 7LG.
Sherrat and Hughes, 94 Above Bar, Southampton SO9.
Thornes Bookshop, Grand Hotel Percy Street, Newcastle Upon Tyne, NE1 7RS.
Thomas C Godfrey Limited, 32 Stonegate, York, North Yorkshire Y01.

USA
Alta Book Center, 14 Adrian Court, Burlingame CA 94010.
Athelstan, Inc, PO Box 8025 -N, La Jolla CA 92038.
Delta Systems Co, 1400 Miller Pkwy, McHenry IL 60050.
Lado Institute Bookstore, 2233 Wiscon sin Avenue, Washington DC 20007.
Literacy/Curriculum Connections, 159 Thorndike Street, Cambridge MA 02141.

Keeping in touch

How newspapers, magazines, associations, conferences and the radio can keep you company no matter where in the world you are.

Stuck in a classroom on 25 or more teaching hours a week? Feeling lonely and uninvolved? Wondering how all those intellectual vistas you marvelled at when you entered the profession have shrunk? Experienced in the widening of horizons that comes from a year at a prestigious university and then wondering where it all went when you got back to the chalkface? Read on.

A monthly trade newspaper landing on your doorstep is simply the best way of keeping up to date.

Professionally and personally teachers need contact as well as new, fresh ideas. EFL is by and large an enthusiast's profession and it is well-serviced with ways in which the classroom teacher can keep in touch with the profession at large. This article suggests a range of ways in which you can keep your professional awareness and personal motivation alive.

EFL Gazette

Yes, it is produced by the sister organisation of the *EFL Guide*, but a monthly trade newspaper landing on your doorstep with news of the profession, recruitment, topical teaching material, surveys of academic fields and different countries, as well as pedagogical articles, conference reports and materials reviews is simply the best way of keeping up to date. If you are looking for a job or want to further your career, you will need to read it. Specimen copies are usually available at major conferences or from 10 Wright's Lane, London W8 6TA, UK. The *EFL Gazette* is available from specialist bookshops and on subscription and costs £22.50 (UK), £26 (Europe) and £30 or $65 (rest of the world) in 1994. (Visa/Mastercard telephone orders on +44 171 938 1818, Fax: +44 171 937 7534). Distributed with the Gazette is ENGLISH, which periodically reviews areas of interest to teachers and ELT professionals. Some issues are in-depth reviews of geographical, such as the Pacific Rim or the USA, whilst others concentrate on a specific subject, such as Cultural Studies or New Technology. These reviews are excellent reference guides.

If you are working in a third world country, it is worth finding out if there is a Peace Corps or a VSO office in the capital.

Language Journals

There are a number of specialist journals which keep you up to date with developments in thinking about the English Language. One of the most popular and easily approachable is *English Today*, a quarterly review published by Cambridge University Press, The Edinburgh Building, Shaftesbury Road, Cambridge CB2 2RU, UK. For word buffs, *Verbatim* is the answer. A monthly magazine produced by Lawrence Urdang, former editor in chief of the Random House dictionaries. There is also *Applied Linguistics* published by the International Applied Linguistics Association.

Pedagogic Journals

ELTJ (the English Language Teaching Journal) is the EFL profession's journal of record. It appears four times a year and is published by Oxford University Press, Walton Street, Oxford OX2 6DP, UK. It contains articles on methodology and linguistics and also reviews courses and teachers' books.

TESOL Matters and *Tesol Quarterly* are the journals of the TESOL association (See overpage under Associations and Conferences). They are provided as part of your membership of TESOL and reflect on developments in research and methodology.

The British Council and USIA

A very important source of information once you are in a particular country is the British Council or the American Cultural Centers. Both organisations have libraries including ELT materials and run seminars. They are useful for advice on local associations and resources. The relevant contact in the British Council is the ELO (English Language Officer). The relevant USIA contact will be the Director of the American Cultural Center. The headquarters of the British Council is Medlock Street, Manchester M15 4AA, UK and the US Information Agency headquarters is 301 4th Street West, Washington DC 20547, USA.

If you are working in a third world country, it is worth finding out if there is a Peace Corps or a VSO office in the capital. These can also be a source of support.

Associations and Conferences

Ask your colleagues about local EFL organisations whose meetings you can attend. There are two major international organisations that you should know about, one British-based and one US-based.

IATEFL (The International Association of

Teachers of English as a Foreign Language) is a major international organisation which has its headquarters in the UK. It publishes its own newsletter four times a year and holds its conference once a year (usually in April) attended by about 1000 delegates from all sectors of ELT. All individual members automatically receive free membership to one special interest group (SIG) of which there are thirteen. These hold their own seminars at various points of the year and publish their own newsletters. Annual membership of IATEFL costs £23.00 for individuals and £60.00 for institutions. Details are available from Jill Stajduhar, Executive Officer, IATEFL, 3 Kingsdown Chambers, Whitstable, Kent. IATEFL also has 34 branches and 24 affiliates, which help maintain international networking in ELT.

TESOL (Teachers of English to Speakers of Other Languages) is the largest association, with over 20,000 members and national affiliates running their own local organisations in a number of countries. Like IATEFL, TESOL has a network of special interest groups. It publishes reference books and two magazines, *TESOL News* and *TESOL Matters* and holds an annual international conference usually in March at a major North American city and attended by up to 10,000 teachers. Details of membership from TESOL, 1600 Cameron Street, Suite 300, Alexandria, Virginia, USA 22314.

Other regional conferences that attract an international group of teachers are the JALT (The Japan Association of Language Teachers, Central Office, Shamboru dai-2, Kaweseki 305, 1-3-17 Kaizuka, Kawasaki-ku, Karagawa 210, Japan) conference held in Japan every October or November, LABCI (Latin American British Cultural Institutes) biannual conference held in Latin America, the British Council Convenio for teachers of English in Italy. (NB. If you want to get really involved and present a conference paper at one of these conferences remember that the deadline for offering a presentation may be issued up to ten months ahead of the conference.)

An association for people interested in alternative approaches to language teaching is SEAL (the Society for Effective Affective Learning). SEAL attracts teachers with a special interest in Suggestopaedia, Neuro Linguistic programming and similar disciplines and has a newsletter and biannual international conference. Details from Emma Grant, SEAL, The Language Centre, University of Brighton, Falmer, Sussex BN1 9PH, UK. The US equivalent is SALT (Society for Alternative Learning and Teaching).

For teachers in Australia, a very good source of information is NCELTR (National Centre for English Language Teaching Research), School of English and Linguistics, Macquarie University, Sydney, NSW 2109.

Broadcasting and Publishing

The BBC World Service's English by Radio Department offers regular programmes for teachers such as its *Speaking of English* magazine programme, offering interviews and reviews for teachers. Schedules and details of programmes can be obtained from *BBC Worldwide* magazine, PO Box 76, Bush House, London WC2B 4PH, UK. The US equivalent is Voice of America. Pick up schedules and details from your local US embassy.

This is what is available to keep you in touch at the international level. At the national and local level there is so much more. So don't get locked in. Go out and find it!

IATEFL also has a number of national affiliated organisations, mainly in central and eastern Europe.

TESOL is the largest association, with over 20,000 members.

Conference calendar

The major international language fairs of 1995-6.

28 March -   *Tesol '95*
1 April   Long Beach,
California

      Contact: TESOL Conventions Dept.
1600 Cameron Street,
Alexandria
Virginia,
22314-2751 USA

9 - 12 April   *IATEFL, Twenty-Ninth*
International Conference
University of York,
York,
UK.

      Contact: IATEFL
3 Kingsdown Chambers
Kingsdown Road
Tankerton
Whitstable
Kent CT5 2DJ
UK

25-27 April   *Moscow Student Fair*,
Moscow, Russia

      Contact: ICEF,
Tel: + 49 228 22 30 86.
Fax: + 49 228 22 26 43.

26 - 30 April   *Mondolingua*,
Palexpo,
Geneva,
Switzerland

      Contact: Mondolingua,
chemin du Pont-du-Centenaire
109,
CP 930-1212 Grand-Lancy 1,
Geneva,
Switzerland

8 May -   **NAFSA 47th Annual Conference**
2 June   New Orleans
USA

      Contact: Berit Boegli
Registration Coordinator
NAFSA, USA
Tel: + 1 202 939 3102 ext. 3026
Fax: + 1 202 939 3115

29-31 August   *ARELS Workshop,*
Metropole Hotel,
Brighton, UK

      Contact: ARELS
2 Pontypool Place,
Valentine Place,
London SE1, UK.

October   *Japan Association of Language*
Teachers
Japan

      Contact: Jalt '95
Jalt Central Office,
2-32-10 Nishinippori,
Arakawaku, Tokyo 116,
Japan

26-30 March   *TESOL '96 Annual Conference*
1996   'The Art of TESOL'
Chicago,
Illinois,
USA

      Contact: TESOL Conventions Dept.
1600 Cameron Street,
Alexandria
Virginia,
22314-2751 USA

UNITED KINGDOM

Aberdeen College of Further Education
Dept of English & Communication
Holburn Street, Aberdeen AB9 2YT

Aberdeen College
Gallowgate Centre, Gallowgate
Aberdeen AB9 IDN

Abbey College, The
Wells Road, Malvern
Worcs. WR14 4JF

Abon Language School
25 St. Johns Road, Clifton, Bristol BS8 2HD

Albion Bookshop
13 Mercury Lane, Canterbury, Kent

Anglia Polytechnic University
East Road, Cambridge CB1 1PT

Anglo School
146 Church Road, London SE19 2NT

Anglo-Continental School of English
33 Wimbourne Road, Bournemouth BH2 6NA

Anglo European Study Tours
8 Colesbridge Mews, Porchester Road, London W2 6EU

Anglo Lang
20 Avenue Road, Scarborough, North Yorkshire YO12 5JX

Anglo-World, Cambridge
75 Barton Road, Cambridge CB3 9LJ

Anglo-World Oxford
108 Banbury Road, Oxford OX2 6JU

A R A
26 Hay's Mews, London W1X 7RL

ARELS (Association of Recognised English Language Schools)
2 Pontypool Place, Valentine Place, London SE1 8QF

BALEAP (British Association of Lecturers in English for Academic Purposes)
English Language Unit, Huw Owen Building, OCW, Penglais, Aberyswyth, Dyfed, Wales

BASELT (Association of UK State Colleges)
Cheltenham and Gloucester College of Higher Education,
Francis Close Hall, Swindon Road, Cheltenham, Glos GL50 4AZ

Basil Paterson College
22-23 Abercromby Place
Edinburgh EH3 6QE

Bedford College of Higher Education
School of Humanities Mander Buildings, Cauldwell Street, Bedford MK42 9AH

Bedford College Access Group
13 The Crescent, Bedford MK40 2RT

Bedford Study Centre
94-96 Midland Road,
Bedford MK40 1QE

Beet Language Centre
Nortoft Road, Charminster,
Bournemouth BH8 8PY

Bell Language School, Bath
Henley Lodge, Western Road,
Bath BA1 2XT

Bell Language School, Norwich
Bowthorpe Hall, Norwich NR5 9AA

Bell Language School, Cambridge
Red Cross Lane
Cambridge CB2 2QX

Bell Language School, London
34 Fitzroy Square
London W1P 6BP

Bell Language School, The Old House, Norwich
Church Lane, Eaton,
Norwich NR4 6NW

Bell Language School, Saffron Walden
South Road, Saffron Walden
Essex CB1 3DP

Berlitz Publishing Co Ltd
Berlitz House, Peterley Road
Oxford OX4 2TX

Berlitz School of Languages Ltd
Wells House, 79 Wells Street
London W1

Blackpool and The Flyde College
Ashfield Road, Bispham, Blackpool SY2 0HB

Bournemouth & Poole College of Further Education
Landsdowne Centre, Bournemouth BH1 3JJ

Bone & Company (International Ltd)
Les Brehauts St Peter, Guernsey CI

B E B C
9 Albion Close, Parkstone, Poole, Dorset, BH12 3LL

BEBC London
International House, 106 Piccadilly, London W1V

Birmingham UCF
Faculty of Education, Westbourne Road, Birmingham

Bradford and Ilkley Community College
English Language Centre
Great Horton Road, Bradford
West Yorkshire

Brasshouse Centre
City of Birmingham Education Dept,
Brasshouse Passage, Birmingham B1 2HR

Brighton University
The Language Centre
University of Brighton
Falmer, Brighton BN 9PH

Bristol University
School of Education
35 Berkeley Square, Bristol BS8 ITA

British Council
10 Spring Gardens, London SW1A 2BN

British Council
Medlock Street, Manchester
M15 4AA

Brooklands Technical College,
Heather Road, Weybridge, Surrey KT138TT

Brudenell School of English
Larnerton House, 27 High Street
London W5 5DF

Cambridge Centre for Languages
Sawston Hall, Cambridge CB2 4JR

Central Bureau for Exchange
Seymour Mews House,
Seymour Mews, London W1H 9TE

Central Manchester College
St Johns Centre
Lower Hardman Street
Manchester

CfBT Education Services
Quality House, Gyosei Campus,
London Road, Reading RW1 5AQ

Cheltenham International Language Centre
Fulwood Park, Suffolk Square,
Cheltenham, Glos Gl60 2 EB

Chichester College of Technology
General Studies Westgate Fields
Chichester, W Sussex PO19 1SB

Chichester School of English
Tutorial College, 45 East Street
Chichester, W Sussex PO19 1HX

Chichester Institute of Higher Education
CIEM
The Dome, Upper Bognor Road
West Sussex PO21 1HR

Chippenham Technical College
Commercial & Media Studies
Cocklebury Road
Chippenham SN15 3QD

Christ Church College
Language Studies,
North Hulmes Road, Canterbury CT11QU

Christians Abroad
1 Stockwell Green, London SW9 9HP

Cicero Languages International
42 Upper Grosvenor Road
Tunbridge Wells, Kent TN1 2ET

Clarendon College of Further Education
The Berridge Centre, Stanley Road
Fimest Fields, Nottingham NG7 6HW

Colchester Institute
Dept of Humanities, Sheepen Road
Colchester, Essex CO3 3IL

Colchester English Study Centre
19 Lexden Road, Colchester, Essex

College of Ripon and York St John
College Road, Ripon HG4 2QX

Concorde International
Radnor Chambers, Cheriton Place
Folkestone, Kent CT20 2BB

College of St Mark & St John
International Education Centre
Derriford Road, Plymouth
PL6 8BH

College of St Paul & St Mary
TEFL Unit, Francis Close Hall
Swindon Road, Cheltenham
GL50 4AZ

Coombe Cliff Centre
Coombe Road, Croydon CRO 5SP

Coventry Technical College
Meridian, Tesol Centre, Butts
Coventry CV1 3GD

Croydon College of Continuing Education
Fairfield, College Road, Croydon
CR9 1DX

Davies School of English
56 Ecclestone Place
London SW1V 1PO

Devon School of English
The Old Vicarage
1 Lower Polsham Road
Paignton, Devon TQ3 3HF

DSS (Overseas Branch)
Newcastle upon Tyne NE 98 1YX.

East Berkshire College
Station Road, Langley, Slough
SL3 8BY

Eastbourne School of English
8 Trinity Trees, Eastbourne BN21 3LD

Eastbourne College of Art and Technology
St Annes Road,
Eastbourne BN21 2HS

East European Partnership
15 Princeton Court
53-55 Felsham Road
London SW16 1AZ

Eaton Hall International
Retford, Nottinghamshire
DN22 OPT2

Edinburgh Tutorial College
29 Chester Street, Edinburgh EH3 76N

Edinburgh Language Foundation
Dugdale-McAdam House
22-23 Abercromby Place
Edinburgh

The Education Policy Information Centre
The Mere, Upton Park, Slough, Berks
SL1 2DQ

EF International
1/2 Sussex Square, Brighton BN2 1FJ

EF Schools
74-80 Warrior Square
St Leonards-on-Sea, Hastings

EFL Gazette
10 Wright's Lane, London, W8 6TA

ELC Norwich
46 Unthank Road, Norwich NR2 2RB

Elmbridge Institute of Adult Education
The Day Centre, 19 The Green,
Esher, Surrey

ELT Banbury
20 Horsefair Road, Oxon, OX16 9AH

English and Spanish Studies
London House
High Street Kensington
London W8

English Language Centre Bournemouth
163-169 Old Christchurch Road,
Bournemouth BH1 1JU

English Language Teaching Division
Dept of Morden Languages
Livington Tower
24 Richmond Street, Glasgow Gi 1XH

English Teaching Information Centre
The British Council, 10 Spring
Gardens, London SW1A 2BN

English Worldwide
17 Concordia Wharf, Mill Street,
London SE1 2BB

Eurocentre, Bournemouth
26 Dean Pk Road,
Bournemouth BH1 1H2

Eurocentre, Lee Green
21 Meadowcourt Road, London SE3 8EU

European Council of International Schools
21b Lavant Street
Petersfield
Hampshire GU32 3EL

European Training & Communications
83-85 Ferensway, Hull
North Humberside HU2 8LD

Executive Training Centre
8 St. Peter's Grove, York YO3 6AQ

Farnborough College of Technology
Manor Park Centre, Manor Walk,
Aldershot, Hampshire GN12 4JN

Filton Technical College
EFL Dept, Filton Avenue,
Bristol BS12 7AT

Frances King School of English
3 Queensberry Place
South Kensington, London SW7 2DL

GEOS
55-61 Portland Road, Hove,
Sussex BN3 5DQ

Globe English Centre
71 Holloway Street, Exeter, Devon
EX2 4JD

Gloscat
Dept of Management & Business,
The Park Campus, 73 The Park,
Cheltenham Glos GL50 2RR

Godmer House
90 Banbury Road, Oxford OX2 6JT

Goldsmith's College
Lewisham Way, London SE14

Greenhill College
Lowlands, Harrow, Middx HA1 3AQ

Grove House Language Centre
Carlton Avenue, Horns Cross
Dartford Kent DA9 9DR

Hammersmith & West London College
Dept of English Studies, Gliddon
Road, Barons Court, London W14 9BL

Harrogate Language Academy
8a Royal Parade, Harrogate,
N Yorks H61 2SZ

Harrow House International College
Harrow Drive, Swanage,
Dorset BH19 1LE

Hart Villages Centre (Basingstoke)
Robert Mays School, West Street,
Oldham, Basingstoke RG25 1NA

Hendon College of FE
Montague Road Centre, Hendon
London NW4 3ES

Hilderstone College
English Study Centre, St Peters Road
Broadstairs, Kent CT10 2AQ

Hopwood Hall College
St Mary's Gate, Rochdale OL12 6RY

House of English
24 Portland Place
Brighton BN21DG

Huddersfield Technical College
New North Road, Huddersfield
HD1 5NN

Hull College
Queen's Gardens, Hull HU1 3DG

IATEFL (International Association of Teachers of English as a Foreign Language)
3 Kingsdown Chambers, Tankerton,
Whitstable, Kent CT5 2DJ

ICELS,
Oxford Brookes University
Headington, Oxford OX3 6BP

ILC Recruitment
1 Riding House Street, London
W1A 3AS

inlingua School of Languages
55-61 Portland Road
Hove, Sussex BN3 5QD

inlingua Teacher Training & Recruitment
Rodney Lodge, Rodney Road
Cheltenham Gl50 1JF

inlingua Teacher Service
Essex House, Temple Street,
Birmingham B2 5D8

Institute of Education
University of London, TESOL Dept.,
20 Bedford Way, London WC1 0AL

International Language Academy
12-13 Regent Terrace, Cambridge
CB2 1AA

International Language Academy
Hinton Chambers, Hinton Road,
Bournemouth BH1 2EN

International Language Academy
4 Russell Gardens, London W14 8EY

International Language Academy
7 Norham Gardens, Oxford OX2 6PS

International Language Academy
Castle Circus, Union Street, Torquay
TQ1 3DE

International House, Hastings
ITTI, Whiterock, Hastings,
E Sussex TN34 1JY

International House, London
106 Piccadilly, London W1V 9FL

International House
14-18 Stowell Street
Newcastle upon Tyne NE1 4XQ

ILC (International Language Centre)
24 Polworth Gardens, Edinburgh EH11

International Language Institute
County House, Vicar Lane,
Leeds LS1 7JH

International Language Services
36 Fowlers Road
Salisbury Wilts SP1 2QU

International Teacher Training Centre
674 Wimbourne Road, Bournemouth
BH9 2EG

International Training Network
28 Howard Road, Bournemouth
Dorset BH8 9EA

ITS English School, Hastings
43-46 Cambridge Gardens,
Hastings, E. Sussex TN34 1EN

Intuition Languages
109 Shepperton Road, London N1 3DF

James Thin Ltd
Buccleuch Street, Edinburgh

Japan Information and Cultural Centre
Embassy of Japan, 104 Piccadilly,
London W1V 9FN

JET Programme Officer
Japan Information Centre,
Embassy of Japan, 9 Grosvenor
Square, London W1H 9LB

KELTIC Bookshop
25 Chepstow Corner,
Chepstow Place, London W2 4TT

Kings College London
The English Language Unit,
Kensington Campus, Camden Hill
Road, London W8 7AH

Kingsway College
EFL Unit, Vernon Square Centre,
Penton Rise, London WC1X 9El

Kirkby College of F.E.
Faculty Gen Education, Oman Road,
Linthorpe, Middlesborough,
Cleveland TS5 5PJ

Language Matters
4 Blenheim Road, Moseley,
Birmingham B13 9TY

Language Project, The
78-80 Colston Street
Bristol BS1 5BB

Language Training Services
5 Belevedere, Lansdowne Road,
Bath, BA1 5ED

LCCI
Marlow House, Station Road,
Sidcup, Kent, DA15 7BJ

LCL Benedict Ltd
104 Judd Road, London WC1

Linguarama Ltd
53 Pall Mall,
London SW1Y 5JH/

Oceanic House,
89 High Street,
Alton, Hants GU34 1LG

Liverpool Community College
Bankfield Road, Liverpool L13 OBQ

Living Language Centre
Highcliffe House, Clifton Gardens,
Folkstone, Kent CT20 2EF

London Guildhall University
Old Castle Street, London E1 7NT

London Study Centre
Munster House, 676 Fulham Road,
London SW6 5SA

Luton College of HE
Park Square, Luton
Bedfordshire LU1 3JU

LTS Training & Consulting
5 Belvedere, Landsown Road
Bath, Avon BA1 SED

Lydbury English Centre
The Old Vicarage, Lydbury North
Shropshire SY8 8AV

Mancatz
Lower Hardman Street
Manchester M3 3ER

Manchester Business School
Language Centre, Booth Street West,
Manchester M15 6PB

Manchester Central College
Lower Hardman Street,
Manchester M3 3FP

Manchester City College
Fielden Centre, Barlow Moor
Didsbury, Manchester M20 2PQ

Manchester Metropolitan University
Faculty of Community Studies,
799 Wilmslow Road
Manchester M20 8RR

Marble Arch Teacher Training
21 Star Street, London W2 1QB

Mid-Cheshire College FE
Management Dept, Chester Road,
Hertford Campus, Northwich CW8 1LJ

Millbrook College
TEFL, Bankfield Site, Bankfield Road,
Liverpool, Lancs L13 0BR

Moray House College of Education
Holyrood Road, Edinburgh EH8 8AQ

Multilingua
St Michaels House, 53 Woolbridge
Road, Guildford GU1 4RF

NATFHE (National Association of Teachers in Further and Higher Education)
27 Britannia Street, London
WC1X 9JP

National Extension College
18 Brooklands Avenue
Cambridge CB2 2HN

NEATEFL
Newcastle College
Rye Hill
Newcastle on Tyne

Newnham Language Centre
8 Grange Road
Cambridge CB3 9DV

Nord Anglia International Ltd
10 Eden Place, Cheadle
Stockport, Cheshire SK8 1AT

North East Surrey College of Technology
Reigate Road, Ewell,
Fosom, Surrey KT17 3DS

North Trafford College
Talbot Road, Stretford,
Manchester M32 0XH

NUT (National Union of Teachers)
Hamilton House, Mabledon Place,
London WC1

OCTAB (The Overseas Contract Teachers and Advisors Branch of the IPS)
The Secretary, 24 Ashford Road,
Manchester M20 4EH

Oxford Brookes University
Gypsy Lane Campus, Headington,
Oxford OX3 0BP

Oxford College
Oxpens Road, Oxford OX1 1SA

Oxford House College
28 Market Place, London W1N 7AL

Park Lane College
Park Lane, Leeds LS3 1AA

Pilgrims Language Courses
8 Vernon Place, Canterbury ,
Kent CT1 3NG

Pitman School of English
154 Southampton Row,
London WC1B 5AX

Polyglot Language Services
Bennet Court, 1 Bellevue Road
London SW17 7EG

Practical TEFL Training
PO Box 191, London SW1Z

Primary House
300 Gloucester Road, Bristol BS7
8PD

Regency School of English
Royal Crescent, Ramsgate, Kent

Regent Capital Centre
4 Percy Street, London W1 PF

Regent Schools
5 Percy Street, London W1P NFA

Regent School of English
Teacher Training, 4 Percy Street,
London W1P 9FA

Returned Volunteer Action
1 Amwell Street, London EC1R 1UL

Richard Language College
43-45 Wimborne Road
Bournemouth, Dorset

**Richmond Adult Community
College**
Clifden Road, Twickenham TW1 4LT

**Royal Holloway & Bedford
New College**
English Dept, Egham Hill,
Egham, Surrey TW20 0EX

Salisbury School of English
36 Fowlers Road,
Salisbury, Wiltshire SP1 2QU

Sandwell College
Pound Road, Oldbury,
W. Midland B68 8HA

Saxoncourt (UK) Ltd
59 South Molton Street,
London W1Y 1HH

**Scarborough International
School**
Cheswold Hall, 37 Stepney Road,
Scarborough, W Yorks YO12 5BN

Scot-Ed
1-3 St Colme Street, Edingburgh EH3
6AA

SOAS
University of London
Thorhaugh Street, Russell Square
London WC1H OXG

Severnvale
Central Language Academy
Shrewsbury SY1 1ES

Sheffield College, The
Stradbroke Centre
Spinkhill Drive, Sheffield S1B 8FD

Sheffield Hallam University
The TESOL Centre, Totley Hall Lane
Sheffield S17 4AB

Skill Share Africa
3 Belvoir, Leicester LE1 6SL

SLS York
Cromwell House, 13 Ogleforth
York YO1 2JG

Skola Teacher Training
21 Star Street, London W2 1QB

Stevenson College
Bankhead Avenue
Edinburgh EH11 4DE

**South Devon College of Arts
& Technology**
Newton Road, Torquay,
Devon TQ2 5BY

South London College
Knights Hill, West Norwood,
London SE27 0TX

South Thames College
50-52 Putney Hill, London SW15 6QX

**Southampton Institute of
Higher Education**
East Park Terrace,
Southampton, Hants SO9 4WW

Southend College of Technology
Dept of Gen Education & Science
Carnarvon Road, Southend-on-Sea
Essex SS2 6LS

Southwark College
209-215 Blackfriars Road,
London SE1 8NL

St Brelade's College
Mont Lex Vaux, St Brelade, Jersey
JE3 8AF

St Giles, Brighton
69 Marine Parade,
Brighton, E Sussex BN2 1AD

St Giles' College, London
51 Shepherds Hill,
Highgate, London N6 5QP

St George's School of English
37 Manchester St, London W1M 5PE

St Mary's University College
Strawberry Hill
Waldegrave Road
Twickenham TW1 45X

Stanton School of English
167 Queensway, London N2 4SB

Stevenson College
Bankhead Avenue
Sighthill, Edinburgh EH11 4DE

Studio School of English
6 Salisbury Villas, Station Road,
Cambridge CB1 2JF

Stoke on Trent College
Stoke on Trent S14 2DG

The Sudan Embassy
The Recruiting Officer, Cultural
Section, 31 Rutland Gate, London
W7 1PG

**Surrey Youth and Adult
Continuing Education Centre**
Danesfield Centre, Grange Road
Woking, Surrey GU21 4DA

**Surrey Youth and Adult
Education Area**
Henriatta Parker Centre, Ray Road
West Molesley, Surrey KT8 2LG

Surrey Language Centres
Sandford House, 39 West Street
Farnham, Surrey GU9 7DR

Sutton College of Liberal Arts
St Nicholas Way, Sutton, Surrey
SM1 1EA

Swan School of English
11 Guild Street, Stratford-upon-Avon
CV37 6RE

**Swan School of English
(Oxford)**
11 Banbury Road, Oxford OX2 6JX

Trebinshun Group
Brecon, Powys, Wales LD3 7PX

Thames Valley University
St. Mary's Road, Ealing, London
W5 3RE

Thomas C Godfrey
32 Stonegate, York, North Yorkshire
YO1

Thurrock Technical College
Woodview, Grays, Essex ILM16 4YR

Trinity College, London
11-13 Mandeville Place,
London W1M 6AQ

UCLES
1 Hills Road, Cambridge CB1 2EU

UNIPAL
12 Helen Road, Oxford OX2 0DE

United Nations Association
UNA International Service,
3 Whitehall Court, London SW1A 2EL

UTS Oxford Centre
Wolsey Hall, 66 Banbury Road,
Oxford
OX2 6PR

United Nations Volunteers
c/o VSO,
317 Putney Bridge Road
London SW15 2PN

Universal Language Training
The Old Forge, Ockland Lane,
Ockham, Surrey GU23 6NP

**University College Of Wales,
Bangor**
Dept of Education, Deinol Road,
Bangor LL57 2UW

**University College of Wales,
Cardiff**
P.O. Box 78, Cardiff CF1 1XL

**University College of Wales,
Aberyswyth**
Dept of Education,
Old College, King Street,
Aberystwyth, Dyfed S723 2AX

University of Aberdeen
Dept of English, Aberdeen AB9 1FX

University of Aston
Language Studies Unit
Aston Triangle, Birmingham B4 7ET

University of Birmingham
Dept of English, P.O. Box 363
Birmingham B15 2TT

University of Brighton
Language Centre, Falmer, Brighton,
Sussex BN1 9PH

University of Bristol
School of Education, 35 Berkley
Square, Bristol BS8 1JA

University of Cambridge
Dept of TEFL, 1 Hills Road,
Cambridge CB1 2EU

University of Central England
Perry Bar, Edgebaston,
Birmingham B42 2SU

University of Durham
Elvet Riverside, 11 New Elvet,
Durham DH1 3JT

University of East Anglia
School of Modern Languages,
Norwich

University of Edinburgh
Applied Ling & Lang Studies
21 Hill Place, Edinburgh EH8 9DP

University of Essex
Wivenhoe Park, Colchester CO4 3SQ

University of Exeter
School of Education, St Lukes,
Heavitree Road, Exeter EX1 2LV

University of Glasgow
English Lang Dept, Glasgow
G12 8QQ

University of Hertfordshire
Watford Campus, Aldenham, Watford
Herts WD2 8AT

University of Hull
Language Centre, Cottingham Road
Hull HU6 7RX

University of Kent
Inst. Lang & Ling, Cornwallis Building,
Canterbury, Kent CT2 7NF

University of Lancaster
Dept of Lings & Mod Eng Lang
Lancaster LA1 L7T

University of Leeds
Overseas Education Unit
School of Education, Leeds LS2 9JT

Leeds Metropolitan University
The Language Centre, Beckett Park
Campus , Leeds LS6 3QS

University of Leicester
School of Education, 21 University
Road, Leicester LE1 7RF

University of Liverpool
E L Unit, Mod Langs Building
P.O. Box 147, Liverpool L69 3BX

**University of London, Birbeck
College**
Applied Linguistics, 20 Bedford Way,
London WC1H 0AL

**University of London, Birbeck
College**
Malet St, London WC1E 7HX

University of Luton
Faculty of Humanities, 75 Castle St
Luton, Beds LUI 3AJ

University of Manchester
CELSE, School of Education, Oxford
Road, Manchester M13 9PL

**University of Newcastle-upon-
Tyne**
St Thomas Street, Newcastle-upon-
Tyne NE1 7RU

**University of Northumbria
at Newcastle**
Lipman Building,
Newcastle-upon-Tyne NE1 8ST

University of Nottingham
Dept of English Studies
University Park, Nottingham NG7 2RD

**University of Oxford Delegacy
of Local Examinations**
Ewert House, Summertown,
Oxford OX2 7BZ

University of Portsmouth
Wiltshire Building, Hampshire
Terrace, Portsmouth PO1 2BU

University of Reading
Centre for applied Lang Studies
Whitenights, PO Box218 Reading ,
Berks RG6 2AD

University of Sheffield
ELT Centre, Arts Tower,
Sheffield S10 2TN

University of Salford
Special Studies Unit,
Salford, Lancs, M5 4WT

University of Southampton
Dept of Education, Southampton
SP9 5NH

University of Stirling
Centre for Eng Lang Teaching
Stirling FK9 4LA

University of Strathclyde
Livingstone Tower, Richmond Street,
Glasgow G1 1XH

University of Surrey
English Language Institute
Guilford, Surrey

University of Sussex
Language Centre, Arts A,
Falmer, Brighton BN1 9QN

University College Swansea
Centre for Applied Lang Studies
Swansea SA2 8PP UK

University of Ulster at Coleraine
Education Faculty
Cromore Road, Coleraine
Co. Londonderry NI BT52 1SA

University of Wales
Education Dept, Old College,
King Street, Aberyswyth SY23 2AX

University of Warwick
Centre for English Lang Teaching
Westwood, Coventry CV4 7AL

University of Woverhampton
Stafford St, Wolverhampton WV1 1 SB

University of Westminster
School of Languages, Peter Street,
London W1V 4HS

University of York
Dept of Linguistic Science & Lang
Teaching Centre, Heslington, York
YO1 5OD

Voluntary Services Overseas
317 Putney Bridge Road
London SW15 2PN

Waltham Forest College
Gen. Ed. Dept, Forest Road,
Walthamstow, London E17 4JB

Waverley Adult Ed. Institute
Bridge Road, Godalming,
Surrey GU7 3DU

Western Language Centre Ltd
Forge House, Kemble, Glos GL7 6AD

Wigston College of F.E.
Station Road, Wigston Magna,
Leicester LE8 2DW

Woking & Chertsey Adult Ed. Institute
Danesfield Centre, Grange Road
Woking, Surrey GU21 4DA

Women in TEFL
42 Northolme Road, London N5 2UX

AUSTRALIA

ATESOL
P O Box 296, Rozelle, NSW 2039

Australian Centre for Languages
Teacher Education Institute
420 Liverpool Road, South Stratfield
NSW 2136

Australian College of English (C/D)
P O Box 82, Bondi Junction, NSW 2022

Australian TESOL training Centre
PO Box 82, Bondi Junction, NSW
2022, Australia

Bond University English language Institute
Gold Coast, Queensland 4229

Canberra College of Advanced Education
P O Box 1, Canberra 2616

ELICOS Association
3 Union Street, Ayrmont, NSW 2009

Institute of Technical and Adult Teacher Education (D)
62 Kameruka Road, Northbridge, 2063

International College of English
230 Flinders Lane, Melbourne
Victoria 3000

International TESOL Training Centre
185 Spring Street,
Melbourne 3000

La Trobe University
Kingsbury Drive,
Bundoora 3083,
Victoria

Macquarie University
N.S.W. 2109

Milner International College of English
1st Floor, 195 Adelaide Terrace
Perth WA 6004

National Curriculum Resource Centre
5th Floor, 197 Rundal Mall
Adelaide 5000

Overseas Service Bureau
P O Box 350, 71 Argyle Street
Fitroy, 3065 Victoria

RMIT, Technisearch Centre for English Language Learning
480 Elizabeth Street, Melbourne ,
Victoria 3000

South Australian College of English
254 North Terrace, Adelaide, S.
Australia 5080

Sydney College of Advanced Education
Office of the Principal, Secretary &
Admin, 53-57 Renwick Street,
Redfern 2016, P O Box 375, Waterloo,
New South Wales

University of New South Wales
P O Box 1, Kensington, NSW 2033

University of Melbourne
Perkville, Victoria 3052

University of South Australia
CALLSA
GPO Box 2471, Adelaide
South Australia

University of Sydney
NSW 2006

University of Woolongong
Northfield Av,
Keiraville, NSW 2522

University of Canberra
Tesol Centre, PO box 1
Bellonen ACT

Western Australian College of Advanced Education
Rensen Street, Churchlands 6018
P O Box 217, Western Australia 6018

AUSTRIA

International House
Schwedenplatz 2/6/55, Alolo, Vienna

BRAZIL

Britannia Association for Teacher Education
Rua Nascimento Silva 154, Ipanema
Rio De Janeiro

British Association for Teacher Education Brasil (Bate)
Rua Vinicius De Moraes 179
Ipanema 22411, Rio De Janeiro

Braztesol
Rua Julia da Costa 1500, 80430
Curitba PR

International House
Rua 4, No 80, Setor Oeste, Goiana-Go

LAURELS (Latin American Association of Registered English Language Schools)
c/o Liberty English Centre, Rua Aminta
de Barros 1, 05980 Curitiba Paran

Sociedad Cultura Brasiliera da Cultura Inglese
Av Graca Aranha, 327-7CP
Caixa Postal 821 Rio de Janeiro

CANADA

Canadian Council of Second Languages
151 Slater Street, Ottawa, Ontario T1P 5NI

Canadian University Services Overseas
135 Rideau Street, Ottawa

Columbia college
6037 Marlborough Ave
Vancouver V6A3J3, British Columbia

University of Calgary
2500 University Drive NW
Calgary AB, T2N 1N4

University of Alberta
Edmonton AB, T6G 2G5

McGill University
3700 McTavish Street, Montreal QC
H3A 1Y2

University of Victoria
PO Box 170, Victoria BC, V8W 2YS

Simon Fraser University
Burnaby BC, V5A 1S6

University of British Columbia
2125 Main Mall, Vancouver V6T 125

Ontario Institute for Studies in Education
252 Bloor St. West, Toronto M5S 1V6

Concordia University
1455 de Maisonneuve Blvd
Montreal QC, H3G 1M8

CHILE

Instituto Chileno- Britanico de Cultura
Casilla 3900, Santiago

COLOMBIA

Association Colombiana de Profesores de Lenguas
Centro Oxford, Apartado Aereo
102420, Unicentro, Bogota

CYPRUS

Bridge House Bookshop
PO Box 4527, Bridgehouse Bldg,
Nicosia

The English Institute
c/o The English School, Nicosia

CZECH REPUBLIC

The Bell School
Nedvezska 29, 100 00 Praha 10

DENMARK

Association of English Teachers in Adult Education
EETAE, Toftegardsvej
24 DK 3500 Vaerlose

ECUADOR

Ecuadorian English Teachers Society
PO Box 10935, Guayaquil.

EGYPT

American University of Cairo
Centre for Adult and Continuing
Education, English Studies Division
Room 407, PO Box 2511, Cairo

British Council
192 Sharia El Nil, Agouza, Cairo

International Language Institute
American University
El Sahafeyeen, PO Box 13, Embaba
Cairo

International Language Institute
2 Mohamed Bayoumi Street,
Heliopolis, Cairo

FINLAND

Association of Teachers of English in Finland
Rautatielaisenkatu 6A 00520, Helsinki

FRANCE

ESIEE
Cite Descartes, 2Bd Blaise Pascal -
BP99, 93162 Noisy-le-Grand Cedex

International Language Centre
20 Passage Dauphine, 75006 Paris

The British Institute
11 Rue de Constantine, 75007 Paris

TESOL France
71 rue St. Denis, 75002 Paris

University Lyon 11-Formation
86 Rue Pasteur, 69007 Lyon

GERMANY

Munich English Language Teachers Association
Maistrasse 21, 8000 Muenchen 2.

GREECE

British Council
Plateia Philikis Etairias 17, Kolonaki
Square, PO Box 3488, Athens 10216

British Council
9 Ethnikis Amynis, P O Box 10289
541013 Thessaloniki

Efstathiadis Group
Olympu 34, 546 30 Thessaloniki

TESOL Greece
87 Academis Street, Athens

HONG KONG

The British Council
English Language Institute
Easey Commercial Building
255 Hennessy Road

HUNGARY

International House
PO Box 95, Budapest 1364

BELL Iskolak Kft
Tulipan u. 8. 1022 Budapest II

Kecskemet Association for Teachers of English
Akademia Korut , 20.1.31 Kecsemet 6000.

Bell Iskolak Kft
Tulipan u.8 H-1022, Budapest

INDONESIA

The British Institute
Setiabudi Building 2, Jalan HR Rasuna Said, Jakarta 12920

The British Institute
Jalan RE Martadinata 63
40115 Bandung

IRELAND

NATEFLI National Association of Teachers of English as a Foreign Language in Ireland
PO Box 1917, Dublin 2

Academy of Education
44 Lower Leeson Street, Dublin 2

Alpha College of English
4 North Great George St,
Dublin 1

Centre of English Studies
31 Dame Street, Dublin 2

Cork Language Centre International
Wellington House, St Patrick's Place,
Wellington Road, Cork

Dublin School of English
11 West Moreland Street, Dublin 2

Emerald Cultural Institute
10 Palmerston Park
Rathgar, Dublin 6

English Language Education Institute
30 The Mall, Tralee, Co. Kerry

English Language Studies Institute
99 St. Stephen's Green, Dublin 2

Galway Language Centre
The Bridge Mills, Galway

Grafton Tuition
Grafton Buildings, 34 Grafton Street,
Dublin 2

International Study Centre
67 Harcourt Street, Dublin 2

Irish College of English
2 Ross Terrace, New Street, Malahide
Dublin

Irish Tourist Board
Baggot Street Bridge, Dublin 2

Langtrain International
Torquay Road, Foxrock, Dublin 18

Language Centre of Ireland
9-11 Grafton Street, Dublin 2

Trinity College
Centre for Language and
Communication Studies, Dublin 2

University College of Dublin
Belfield, Dublin 4

Words Language sevices
109 Lower Baggot Street, Dublin 2

Westlingua Language School
Cathedral Blds, Middle Steet, Galway

ITALY

Academia Brittanica
International House, Viale Manzoni
57, 00185 Rome

AISLI
British Institute, via Quattro Fontane
109, Rome

British Council
Via Manzoni 38
20121 Milano

British Council Naples
Via Dei Mille 48, Palazzo D'Avalos
80121 Naples

British Institute of Florence
Via Tornabuoni 2, 50123 Firenze

British School of Friuli-Venezia Giulia
Via Torrebianca 18
34-132 Trieste

British School of Milan
Via Monte napoleone5, Milan 210121

British Institute
Via S Stefano 11, 40125 Bologna

British Schools
Viale Liegi 14, Rome

CLM-Bell
Via Pozzo 30,
38100 Trento

CLM-Bell
Vialle Venezia/Venedigstrabe 3
Bolzano/Bozen

CLM-Bell
Via Canella 14
38066 Riva del Garda

BMC-Bell School of English
Viale dei Mille, 2, 42100 Reggio Emilia

Cambridge School
Via S Rocchetto 3, 37100 Verona

International House
Viale Manzoni 22, 00185 Rome

Regent School of Rome
Via Monterone 4, 00185 Rome

The British School
Via Montenapoleone 5, 20121 Milan

The Milan Training Centre
Via Fabio Filzi 27, 20131 Milano

JAPAN

The British Council
2 Kagurazaka 1, Chome Shinjuku-Ku,
Tokyo 164

International Education Service
Shin Taiso Building, 2-10-7
Dogensaka
Shibuya-ku, Tokyo 150

International Language Centre
Iwanami Building 9F, 2-1 Jimbo-Cho
Kanda, Chiyoda-Ku, Tokyo 101

International Language Centre
Shirakabe Building 7F, Shibata 114-7
Kita-Ku, Osaka

JALT (The Japan Association of Language Teachers)
Lions Mansion Kawaramachi 111
Kawaramachi Matsubara-Agaru
Shimogyo-ku, Kyoto 600

Language Resources Ltd
Tayo Bldg 6F, 1-2 Kitanagasa-Dori, 5-Chome, Chuo-Ku, Kobe-Shi, F650

Stanton School of English
Ikebukuro School (Academic Division)
5F West Building, Higashi Ikebukoro
Toshima-Ku, Tokyo 170

KOREA

TESOL Korea
Kangnung University San-1,
Chi byon-dong, Kangnung,
Kang-won-do 210-702

KUWAIT

The British Council
P O Box 345, Safat

International Language Centre
Military Language Institute
P O Box 3310, Salmiya 22034

LUXEMBOURG

Association Luxembourgeoise des Enseignants d'Anglais
BP 346, L-2013 Luxembourg

English Language Centre
65 Avenue Gaston Diderich,
Luxembourg 1420

MALAYSIA

British Council Language Centre
P O Box 595, 10770 Penang

British Council Language Centre
3rd Floor, Wisma Hangsam
Box20, 1 Jalan Hang Lekir 5000 K.L.

MEXICO

Anglo Mexican Cultural Institutes
Antonio Caso 127, Mexico 4, D.F.

Institute Anglo-Mexicano de Cultura AC
Felipe Villanueva No 52, Colonia
Guadalupe Inn, 01020 DF

Institute Anglo-Mexicano de Cultura AC
APDO 12755, Guadalajara, Jalisco

Institute Anglo-Mexicano de Cultura
Plaza Crystal 9-12A
Blvd Valsequilo y Cir. Int., Puebla
Pve, CP 72440

NEW ZEALAND

Auckland Language Centre
1-11 Short Street, PO Box 1652,
Auckland

Auckland Institute of Technology
School of Languages
450 Queen Street
Private Bag 92006
Auckland

Capital Language Academy
PO box 1100, Wellington

FIELSNZ
PO Box 2577, Auckland

International Language Academy
PO Box 25-170, Christchurch

Languages International
21 Princes Street Auckland
Po Box 5293, Wellesley St, Auckland

Massey University
Dept of Linguistics and Second
Language Teaching
Palmerston North

NZEIL
PO Box 10500, Wellington

University of Waikato language Institute
Private Bag 3105
Hamilton

NORWAY

LMS Modern Language Association of Norway
Jonas Liesvei, 1B 1412 Sofiemyr.

OMAN

The British Council
P O Box 73, MedinaQaboos 115

PAKISTAN

SPELT
F 25 D, Block 9, Clifton, Karachi
75600

PARAGUAY

Centro Anglo Paraguay
Artigas 356, Asuncion

PERU

Newton College
Apartado 18-0873, Miraflores, Lima 18

POLAND

The British Council
AL. Jerocolimskie 59
00-697, Warsaw

Gama-Bell School of English
ul Smolensk 29, 31-112
Krakow

PORTUGAL

APPI
Associaco Portuguese de
Professores de Ingles
Apartado 2885, 1122 Lisbon

Cambridge School
Avenida da Libertade, 173
1200 Lisbon

Institute Britanico Em Portugal
Rua Cecilio de Sousa 65
1294 Lisbon Codex

International House
Rua Marques Sa Da Bandiera 16
1000 Lisbon

QATAR

British Council
PO Box 2992, Doha, SINGAPORE

Art Language Centre
7th & 8th Floors, Tanglin Shopping
Centre, Tanglin, 1024

SOUTH AFRICA

English Language Educational Trust
74 Aliwal Street, Durban 40

SPAIN

Academia de Idiomas Lacunza
Urbieta 14-1, San Sebastian 20006

APAC Associaco de Professors
D'Angles de Catalunya
Apartado 2287, 08080 Barcelona

Association de Professors de Ingles de Galicia
Apartado de Correo 1078
Santiago de Compostela

British Council
Calle Almagro 5, 28010 Madrid

British Council
Teacher Development Unit
General Martinez Campos 31, 28010
Madrid

British Language Centre
Bravo Murillo 377/2, 28020 Madrid

International House
Zurbano 8, 28010 Madrid

International House
Trafalgar 14 Entlo, Barcelona 08010

International House
Escuela Industrial 12, 08201 Sabadell,
Barcelona

International House
Pascual y Genis 16, 46002 Valencia

International House
Paseo de Mallorca 36,
Palma de Mallorca 07012

Stanton School of English
Montera 24 2 Piso, 28013 Madrid

TESOL Spain
Universidad de Cordoba,
Departmento de Ingles, Cordoba 10678

York House Language Centre
Mutaner 479, 08021 Barcelona

SRI LANKA

Colombo International School
28 Gregory's Road, Colombo 7

SWEDEN

Kursverksamheten Vid
Lunds Universitet
Regementsgatan 4, 21142 Malmo

Kursverksamheten Vid
Stockholms Universitet
P O Box 7845, 10398 Stockholm

LMS Lars Ake Kall
Wallingaten 12, S 111 60 Stockholm

SWITZERLAND

Benedict - Schools
P O Box 300, CH1000 Lausanne 9

Ecole Lemania
3 Chemin de Preville, 1001 Lausanne

ELCRA Bell
12 Chemin des Colombettes
1202 Geneva

ETAS (English Teachers' Association Switzerland)
Bolsternstrasse 22, 8483 Kollbrun

Inlingua
Weisenhuasplatz 28, 3011 Berne

The Bell School
Genferstrabe 23, 8002 Zurich

Klubschule Migros
Oberer Graben 35, 9000 St Gallen

Volkshochschule Zurich
Limmatquai 62, CH 8001 Zurich

TURKEY

Bilkent University School of English Language
PO Box 40, 06660 Kucukesat Ankara

British Council
9 Kirlangic Sokak, Gaziosmanpasa
06700 Ankara

British Council
Ors Turistik Is Merkezi Istiklal
Caddesi 251-253, Kat 2,3,5, Beyoglu
Istanbul 80060

Istanbul Turco-British Association
Suleyman Nazif Sokak 10
Nisantasi, 80220 Istanbul

METU, DBE
Dept of basic English, Ankara 06531

School of Languages
Bogazici University
PK2 Bebek, Istanbul

THAILAND

St John's-Bell Language Centre
St John's College, Ladprao
Bangkok 10900

Assumption Thonburi-Bell Language Centre
Bangphai, Pasicharoen, Bangkok 10160

UNITED ARAB EMIRATES

The British Council
P O Box 6523, Abu Dhabi

ECS Ltd
PO Box 25018, Abu Dhabi

UNITED STATES OF AMERICA

American Language Academy
2105 Grove Street, Berkeley
California 94704

Berlitz International Inc
Research Park,
2923 Wall Street
Princeton NJ 08540

ELS
5761-6 Buckingham Parkway
Culver City CA 90230

English International
655 Sutter Street (Suite 500)
San Francisco Ca 94102

ERIC
Centre for Applied Linguistics
118 22nd Street NL, Washington DC

Eastern Mennonite University
1200 Park Road, Harrisonburg
VA 22801

Eurocentres
101 North Union Street, Suite 3000
Alexandria, Virginia VA 22314

Goshen College
1700 S-Main St, Goshen IN 46526

International Language Institute
1601 Connecticut Avenue NW
Washington DC 20009

International Educator (The)
International Educators Institute
PO Box 103
West Bridgewater
MA 02379

Inlingua School of Languages
551 Fifth Avenue, New York NY 10176

International School of Languages
P O Box 6188
958 W Pico Boulevard
90212 Beverley Hills, CA

Monterey Institute of International Studies
425 Van Buren Street, Monterey
California 93940

Old Dominion University,
Dept. of English
Norfolk, VA 23529-0078

Peace Corps
1990 K St NW, Washington DC 20526

St Giles College Educational Trust
2280 Powell Street
94133 San Francisco CA

School For International Training
Brattleboro, Vermont 05301

School of Teaching EFL
2601 NW 56th St, Seatle WA 98107

TESOL
1600 Cameron Street, Suite 300
Alexandria, Virginia 22314-2705

Adelphi University
Harvey Hall, Room 130, Garden City
New York 11530

University of Alabama
Department of English, Morgan Hall
PO Box 870244, Tuscaloosa
Alabama 35487-0244

The American University
Asbury Building, Room 326
4400 Massachusetts Avenue NW
Washington DC 20016-8045

University of Arizona
Department of English
Modern Languages Room 458
Tucson, Arizona 85721

Arizona State University
Language and Literature Building
Room B504, Tempe
Arizona 85287-0302

Azusa Pacific University
901 East Alosta Avenue, Azusa
California 91702-7000

Ball State University
Department of English
Muncie, Indiana 47306

Biola University
Marshburn Hall, 13800 Biola Avenue
La Mirada, California 90639-0001

Boston University
TESOL Program, School of Education
605 Commonwealth Avenue
Boston , Mass 02215

University of California at Davis
Titus Hall, Room 130, Davis
California 95616

University of California at Los Angeles
Dept of TESL and Applied Linguistics
3300 Rolfe Hall,
405 Hilgard Avenue
Los Angeles, California 90024

California State University, Dominguez Hills
Carson, California 90747

California State University, Fresno
Leon S Peters Building Room 383
5245 North Backer Avenue
Fresno, California 93740-0092

California State University, Fullerton
Humanities Building Room 835C
Fullerton, California 92634

California State University, Long Beach
1250 Bellflower Boulevard
Long Beach, California
90840-2403

California State University, Northridge
Sierra North 318, Northridge
California 91330

California State University, Sacramento
6000 J Street, Sacramento
California 95819-2694

University of Colorado
Admissions Committee Chair
Linguistics-Box 295,
Boulder, Colorado 80309-0295

University of Delaware
Department of Educational Studies
206 Willard Hall,
Newark, Delaware 19716

East Carolina University
GCB 2201 Greenville
North Carolina 27858-4353

Eastern Michigan University
Foreign Languages and Bilingual
Studies
219 Alexander
Ypsilanti
Michigan 48197

University of Florida
112 Anderson Hall
Gainesville
Florida 32611

Florida International University
School of Education DM 291
Tamiami Trail
Miami
Florida 33199

Fordham University at Lincoln Center
Room 1025
113 West 60th Street
New York NY 10023

George Mason University
Department of English
Fairfax
Virginia 22030

Georgetown University
School of Languages and Linguistics
Washington DC 20057

University of Georgia
Aderhold 125
Athens
Georgia 30602

Georgia State University
Atlanta
Georgia 30302-4018

Harvard University
54 Dunster Street
Cambridge
Mass 02138

University of Hawaii at Manoa
Moore Hall 570
1890 East-West Road
Honolulu
Hawaii 96822

Hofstra University
236 Gallon Wing
Mason Hall
Hempstead
New York 11550

University of Houston
University Park
Department of English
Houston
Texas 77004

Hunter College of the CUNY
Department of Curriculum and
Teaching
West Building Room 1025
695 Park Avenue Box 568
New York 10021

University of Idaho
Dept of English
Moscow
Idaho 83843

**University of Illinois at
Chicago**
Department of Linguistics Box 4348
Chicago
Illinois 60680

Illinois State University
Normal
Illinois 61761

Indiana University
Department of Linguistics
Lindley Hall 401
Bloomington
Indiana 47405

**Inter American University of
Puerto Rico, San German
Campus**
Call Box 5100
San German
Puerto Rico 00683

**Inter American University of
Puerto Rico, Metropolitan
Campus**
PO Box 1293
San Juan
Puerto Rico 00919-1293

University of Iowa
Iowa City
Iowa 52242

Iowa State University
Department of English
203 Ross Hall
Ames
Iowa 50011

University of Kansas
427 Blake Hall
Lawrence
Kansas 66045-2140

University of Miami
222 Merrick Building
PO Box 248065
Coral Gables
Florida 33124

Michigan State University
Center for International Programs
East Lansing
Michigan 48824-1035

University of Minnesota
1425 University Avenue Southeast
Minneapolis
Minnesota 55455

University of Mississippi
School of Education
Room 152b
University
Mississippi 38677

**Monterey Institute of
International Studies**
425 Van Buren Street
Monterey
California 93940

Nazareth College
4245 East Avenue
Rochester, New York 14618

University of Nevada, Reno
Reno, Nevada 89557-0031

University of New Mexico
Mesa Visa Hall 3090, Albuquerque
New Mexico 87131

College of New Rochelle
Chidwick 103
Castle Place
New Rochelle
New York 10805-2308

New York University
TESOL
829 Shrimkin Hall
50 West 4th Street
New York NY 10003

**State University of New York
at Albany**
TESOL Program
Albany
New York 12222

**State University of New York
at Buffalo**
Dept of Learning & Instruction
593 Christopher Baldy Hall
Buffalo
New York 14260

**State University of New York
at Stony Brook**
Dept of Linguistics
Stony Brook
New York 11794-4376

Northern Arizona University
Box 6032
Flagstaff, Arizona 86011-6032

University of Northern Iowa
Baker Hall 155
Cedar Falls, Iowa 50614-0502

Notre Dame College
2321 Elm Street
Manchester
New Hampshire 03104

Nova University
3301 College Avenue
Fort Lauderdale
Florida 33314

Old Dominion University
Norfolk
Virginia 23529-0078

University of the Pacific
School of Education
3601 Pacific Avenue
Stockton
California 95211

Pennsylvania State University
305 Sparks Building
University Park
Pennsylvania 16802

Portland State University
PO Box 751
Portland
Oregon 97207-0751

University of Puerto Rico
Rio Pedras
Puerto Rico 00931

Rhode Island College
Mann 043
600 Mount Pleasant Avenue
Providence, Rhode Island 02908

Saint Michael's College
Center for International Programs
Winooski Park
Colchester
Vermont 05439

University of San Francisco
School of Education
2130 Fulton
San Francisco
California 94117

San Francisco State University
Department of English
1600 Holloway Avenue
San Francisco
California 94132

San Jose State University
San Jose
California 95192

Seton Hall University
400 South Orange Avenue
South Orange
New Jersey 07079

University of South Carolina
Linguistics Program
Tampa
Florida 33620

**Southeast Missouri State
University**
Grauel Language Arts Building
Room 208B
Cape Girardeau
Missouri 63701

**University of Southern
California**
Dept of Linguistics
Los Angeles
California 90089-1693

**Southern Illinois University at
Carbondale**
Faner 3236
Carbondale
Illinois 62901

University of Southern Maine
400 Bailey Hall
Gorham
Maine 04038

**University of Southern
Mississippi**
George Hurst Building
Room 110
Southern Station Box 5038
Hattiesburg
Mississippi 39406

Syracuse University
316 HB Crouse
Syracuse NY 13244-9489

**Teachers College of Columbia
University**
525 West 120 Street
New York NY 10027

Temple University
Ritter Hall
Broad and Montgomery
Philadelphia
Pennsylvania 19122

**University of Texas at
Arlington**
Box 19559
Arlington
Texas 76019

University of Texas at Austin
Education Building 528
Austin
Texas 78712

**University of Texas at San
Antonio**
6900 North Loop 1604W
San Antonio
Texas 78259

**University of Texas Pan
American**
Edinburg
Texas 78539

University of Toledo
University Hall 5040
Toledo
Ohio 43606-3390

**United States International
University**
Daley Hall of Science
Room 307
10455 Pomerado Road
Poway
California 92131

University of Utah
OSH 341
Salt Lake City
Utah 84112

University of Washington
English Graduate Office GN-30
Seattle
Washington 98195

Washington State University
Pullman
Washington 99164-5020

West Chester University
Main Hall 550
West Chester
Pennsylvania 19383

Western Kentucky University
Bowling Green
Kentucky 42101

**University of Wisconsin-
Madison**
Department of English
5134 Helen C White Hall
600 North Park Street
Madison, Wisconsin 5370

**University of Wisconsin-
Milwaukee**
Enderis Hall
Room 355
PO Box 413
Milwaukee
Wisconsin 53201

USIA Information Agency
English Language Teaching Division
301 4th Street South West
Washington DC 20547

Worldteach
Phillips Brooks House
Harvard University
Cambridge
Mass 02138

Wright State University
438 Millet Hall
Colonel Glenn Highway
Dayton
Ohio 45435

Index of Advertisers

* Inside Front Cover

Index